Why do most children acquire speech easily yet bog down when it comes to learning to read? This important question is the starting point for the twenty-two contributions to *Language by Ear and by Eye.* Based on a research conference on "The Relationships between Speech and Learning to Read," which was sponsored by the Growth and Development Branch of the National Institute of Child Health and Human Development, National Institutes of Health, the book brings together contributions by distinguished specialists in linguistics speech perception, psycholinguistics, information processing, and reading research. These summarize what is currently known about the similarities and differences between processing language by eye and processing it by ear.

Three aspects of the comparison between speech perception and reading provide a structural framework for the book. Part I, Speech and Writing as Vehicles of Language, considers the possibility that the terminal signals of spoken and written language (the sound of speech, the visible characters of writing) might relate to the concept of language in significantly different ways. Chapters in Part II, Speech Perception and Reading as Converging Processes, take up the problem of how and where the child's newly acquired reading skill converges on the spoken language he has already mastered. Finally, contributions to Part III, Problems Peculiar to Learning to Read, focus on the child's acquisition of reading skills and on those facts and theories pertinent to the comparison with his performance in speech.

James F. Kavanagh is Health Scientist Administrator for Learning and Human Communication Research with the Growth and Development Branch of the National Institute of Child Health and Human Development, National Institutes of Health; Ignatius G. Mattingly is Professor of Linguistics at the University of Connecticut, Storrs, and a Research Associate at the Haskins Laboratories, New Haven.

Language by Ear and by Eye

The Relationships between Speech and Reading

Proceedings of a conference on "The Relationships between Speech and Learning to Read" in a series entitled "Communicating by Language," sponsored by the National Institute of Child Health and Human Development, National Institutes of Health

The MIT Press   Cambridge, Massachusetts, and London, England

Language by Ear and by Eye

The Relationships between Speech and Reading

EDITED BY JAMES F. KAVANAGH AND
IGNATIUS G. MATTINGLY

This book was designed by The MIT Press Design Department.
It was set in Linotype Baskerville
by The Maple Press Company
printed on Mohawk Neotext Offset
by The Maple Press Company
and bound in Interlaken AV1-570 Matte
by The Maple Press Company
in the United States of America.

Library of Congress Cataloging in Publication Data
Main entry under title:

Language by ear and by eye.

   "Proceedings of a conference on 'the relationships between speech and learning to read' in a series entitled Communicating by language, sponsored by the National Institute of Child Health and Human Development, National Institutes of Health [held May 16–19, 1971, at Belmont, Elkridge, Md.]"
   1. Reading. 2. Speech. 3. Children—Language. I. Kavanagh, James F., ed. II. Mattingly, Ignatius G., ed. III. United States. National Institute of Child Health and Human Development.
LB1050.L35   372.6   72-3392
ISBN 0-262-11044-X
ISBN 0-262-61015-9 (pbk)

CONTENTS

This volume is the edited proceedings of a research conference which explored "The Relationships between Speech and Learning to Read," sponsored by the Growth and Development Branch of the National Institute of Child Health and Human Development and held May 16 through 19, 1971, at Belmont, the Smithsonian Institution's conference center at Elkridge, Maryland. The conference was organized by Drs. James F. Kavanagh of the Growth and Development Branch and the Cochairmen, Alvin M. Liberman and James J. Jenkins; Franklin S. Cooper and Ignatius G. Mattingly also participated in the early planning sessions.

The National Institute of Child Health and Human Development (NICHD) is one of the ten mission-oriented National Institutes of Health (NIH), the research arm of the Public Health Service in the Department of Health, Education, and Welfare. Since it was established in 1963, the NICHD has vigorously stimulated, developed, and supported basic biomedical and behavioral research that has extended our knowledge of child health and human development. The Institute has been concerned with both normal and certain pathological processes and with the whole individual as well as with specific systems. From such knowledge and understanding gained through relevant research have come rational guides for optimizing normal human growth and development as well as establishing appropriate diagnostic, treatment, and ameliorating procedures.

As a significant part of this research effort, the NICHD has supported basic investigations that are leading to a better understanding of the processes whereby individuals acquire and develop the ability to communicate, particularly with language, and the role of communication in human growth and development.

The conference series, "Communicating by Language," has been an integral part of this important research program. The first meeting in the series, which was held at Princeton, New Jersey in 1964, was an interdisciplinary exchange between scientists who were actively engaged in studying the Speech Process. (The edited transcript is now out of print.) The second conference, which was convened at Old Point Comfort, Virginia in 1965, examined Language Development in Children from a psycholinguistic point of view. (The proceedings were later published by The M.I.T. Press as *The Genesis of Language*.) The third conference in the series, held in New Orleans in 1968, was an informal, interdisciplinary meeting of experts who were concentrating their research efforts on the Reading Process. (The proceedings were published by the Government Printing Office as *Communicating by Language:*

The Reading Process.) By means of each of the four meetings and the resultant publications, the Institute has attempted to determine existing and potential directions for research in particular aspects of human communication, and to identify the roles which various disciplines can and do play in expanding that knowledge, both independently and jointly.

The point of departure for this, the fourth conference was the contrast between the ease with which most children acquire speech and the difficulty they generally have with reading. By comparing the processes that underlie these forms of linguistic communication, and by studying the relationships between them, we hope it will be possible to understand better why so many children who can listen and speak so well should find it so very difficult to read and write. Our aim is to reveal what is now known about this comparison, and by framing the important questions, to stimulate appropriate and useful research.

The conference participants were

William F. Brewer
Department of Psychology
University of Illinois
Urbana, Illinois

John B. Carroll
Educational Testing Service
Princeton, New Jersey

R. Conrad
Medical Research Council
Applied Psychology Unit
Cambridge, England

Franklin S. Cooper
Haskins Laboratories
New Haven, Connecticut

Robert Crowder
Department of Psychology
Yale University
New Haven, Connecticut

Eleanor J. Gibson
Department of Psychology
Cornell University
Ithaca, New York

Philip B. Gough
Department of Psychology
University of Texas
Austin, Texas

Morris Halle
Department of Foreign Literatures and Linguistics
Massachusetts Institute of Technology
Cambridge, Massachusetts

James Jenkins
Center for Research in Human Learning
University of Minnesota
Minneapolis, Minnesota

James F. Kavanagh
Growth and Development Branch
National Institute of Child Health and
Human Development
Bethesda, Maryland

Edward S. Klima
Department of Linguistics
University of California at San Diego
La Jolla, California

Paul A. Kolers
Department of Psychology
University of Toronto
Toronto, Canada

David LaBerge
Department of Psychology
University of Minnesota
Minneapolis, Minnesota

Alvin M. Liberman
Haskins Laboratories
New Haven, Connecticut

Lyle L. Lloyd
Mental Retardation Branch
National Institute of Child Health and
Human Development
Bethesda, Maryland

John Lotz
Center for Applied Linguistics
Washington, D.C.

Samuel E. Martin
Department of Linguistics
Yale University
New Haven, Connecticut

Ignatius G. Mattingly
Department of Linguistics
University of Connecticut
Storrs, Connecticut

George A. Miller
The Rockefeller University
New York, New York

Donald A. Norman
Department of Psychology
University of California at San Diego
La Jolla, California

Wayne O'Neil
Departments of Humanities and Linguistics
Massachusetts Institute of Technology
Cambridge, Massachusetts

Monte Penney
National Center for Educational Research
and Development
U.S. Office of Education
Washington, D.C.

Michael I. Posner
Department of Psychology
University of Oregon
Eugene, Oregon

Merrill S. Read
Growth and Development Branch
National Institute of Child Health and
Human Development
Bethesda, Maryland

Harris B. Savin
Department of Psychology
University of Pennsylvania
Philadelphia, Pennsylvania

Donald Shankweiler
Department of Psychology
University of Connecticut
Storrs, Connecticut

Kenneth N. Stevens
Department of Electrical Engineering and
Research Laboratory of Electronics
Massachusetts Institute of Technology
Cambridge, Massachusetts

Due to a sudden illness, Dr. Martin was unable to attend the conference, but his paper included in these proceedings was orally summarized by Dr. John Lotz and then discussed by the conferees.

Some of the data reported in Dr. Crowder's paper were collected with the support of grant GB 15157 from the National Science Foundation. Dr. Crowder would also like to thank the Academic Press, Inc. for its permission to reprint Figure 3 from R. G. Crowder. The role of one's own voice in immediate memory, *Cognitive Psychology*, 1970, 1:157–158; and Figures 1 and 2 from R. G. Crowder. The sound of consonants and vowels in immediate memory, *Journal of Verbal Learning and Verbal Behavior*, 1971, 10:587–596.

Dr. Gibson's work was supported in part by a grant (USOE OEG–2–9–420446–1071–010) from the U.S. Office of Education. Dr. O'Neil received support through grant MH–13390–04 from the National Institute of Mental Health.

Dr. Halle acknowledges assistance received from the National Institute of Child Health and Human Development (5T01 HD 00111) and from the National Institute of Mental Health (MH–13390). Dr. Halle also wishes to express his appreciation to Professor Willard Walker for permission to use portions of an unpublished paper entitled "An Experiment in Programmed Cross-Cultural Education."

Dr. Posner's research was supported in part by the National Science Foundation under grant GB–21020, and by the Air Force Offices of Scientific Research under contract F–44620–67–0099. Dr. Posner and his coauthors also wish to thank Dr. H. K. Beller and Dr. B. Schaeffer for permission to use their unpublished data, which appears in Figure 1 of the Posner paper.

Some of Dr. Kolers's remarks were first developed at Project Zero, Harvard Graduate School of Education. Their preparation was aided by a grant from the National Research Council of Canada. Dr. Kolers also acknowledges the permission given him by the American Psychological Association to reproduce the material which appears in Table 1 of his paper.

Dr. Mattingly wishes to acknowledge support from the National Institute of Child Health and Human Development (NIH), Office of Naval Research, Veterans Administration, and the Provost and Fellows of King's College, Cambridge. He also wishes to acknowledge permission from Holt, Rinehart and Winston, Inc. to quote a passage from *Linguistics and Reading* by C. C. Fries.

Preparation of Dr. Gough's paper, and some of the research reported therein, was supported by NSF–USDP Grant GU–1598 and NSF Grant

GU–3285 to the University of Texas at Austin. Dr. Gough also wishes to express his gratitude to Jack Lumbley for his assistance in combing the literature on reading acquisition, and to Dennis McFadden for valuable hours of discussion of the "second of reading" under consideration.

Preparation of Dr. Klima's paper was supported in part by the National Science Foundation under Grant GS–2982. Dr. Savin is especially indebted to his colleague Paul Rozin both for useful discussions about a dozen children they worked with together and for his further observations of other children. The work reported by Dr. Shankweiler was supported in part by a grant to the University of Connecticut from the U.S. Office of Education (principal investigator, I. Y. Liberman) and in part by a grant to Haskins Laboratories from the National Institute of Child Health and Human Development. Many of the ideas expressed in the Shankweiler presentation were contributed by colleagues at Haskins Laboratories in the course of many discussions. A. M. Liberman and L. Lisker read a draft of the paper and made many valuable comments. Their help is gratefully acknowledged.

The research reported by Drs. Cooper and A. Liberman was made possible in part by support from the following sources: Information Systems Branch, Office of Naval Research Contract 0014–67–A–0129–0001 Req. NR–048–225; National Institute of Dental Research Grant DE–01774; National Institute of Child Health and Human Development Grant HD–01994; Research and Development Division of the Prosthetic and Sensory Aids Service, Veterans Administration Contract V–1005M–1253; National Institutes of Health General Research Support Grant FR–5596; and Connecticut Research Commission Grant Award RSA–70–9.

Finally, the editors would like to thank Miss Betty Barton and Mrs. Meryom Lebowitz for their help in planning and arranging the conference, Mrs. Mary Ellen Elwell for her careful typing of parts of the manuscript of this volume, Mrs. Christine Donnelly and Mr. Gary Kuhn for technical assistance in editing the manuscript, and above all, Mrs. Marian Young for her invaluable help in the preparation both for the conference and for this book.

James F. Kavanagh
Ignatius G. Mattingly

Language by Ear and by Eye

The Relationships between Speech and Reading

JAMES J. JENKINS AND ALVIN M. LIBERMAN

Background to the Conference

The starting point for our conference is the striking contrast in difficulty between reading and speech perception. An enormous amount of time is ordinarily devoted to formal instruction in reading, yet many children fail to acquire this important skill. Perception of the spoken language presents no such problem. Except in cases of deafness and other special impairments, the perception of speech comes easily and without tuition; the child's ability to understand what is said to him is limited primarily by the size of his vocabulary, or by his general level of cognitive development. At all events, the "reading problem" as we know it would not exist if, in dealing with language, all children could do as well by eye as they do by ear.

One might think that speech perception is easier than reading for reasons that are obvious or trivial; in that case, there would be no point to our conference. One might suppose, for example, that the ear is a better channel than the eye—surely we cannot expect to communicate language efficiently through so poor a channel as the nose—or that the sounds of speech are better signals than the printed characters. But when we make the proper comparisons, as was done in one session of an earlier conference in this NICHD series [Kavanagh 1968, pp. 121–124], we find reasons for supposing that print, not speech, should be the easier to perceive. Surely the eye is superior to the ear by almost any general standard we can apply. Less obvious but no less relevant is the fact that printed characters are much clearer signals than the sounds of speech and bear a much simpler relation to the linguistic message they convey. Such paradoxes suggest not only that the important differences between speech and reading are not so apparent as we might have thought, but also that they are likely, on further consideration, to prove revealing. On that basis some of the people who were at the earlier conference in this series decided that a further comparison of speech perception and reading might be useful. Accordingly, they determined to organize a conference, and they asked us to be cochairmen.

In selecting participants for this conference, and in suggesting to each what we hoped he would contribute, we and our colleagues had in mind three aspects of the comparison between speech perception and reading. We thought it appropriate, first, to consider that the terminal signals of spoken and written language—the sounds of speech in the one case and the visible characters in the other—might relate to the language in significantly different ways. This aspect of our concern appears in this book as Part I: Speech and Writing as Vehicles of Language. The second aspect of the comparison derives from the fact that the child normally learns to read after he has acquired the spoken language. It seemed to us important, therefore, to consider how and where this newly acquired skill converges on the old. The papers that are, in one way or another, relevant to this aspect of our design appear as Part II: Speech Perception and Reading as Converging Processes. Finally, we wanted to deal more explicitly with the fact that speech perception is a more natural, hence easier, task for the child, and to ask in that connection what reading requires of the child beyond his already developed ability to speak and listen. For that purpose we suggested to some participants that they look at the acquisition of reading by the child, with particular attention to those facts and theories that bear on the comparison with his performance in speech. These contributions appear in Part III: Problems Peculiar to Learning to Read.

The selection of participants was complicated by the fact that no one's work deals directly with the kind of comparison between reading and speech perception that is the subject of our conference. To find people whose interests are nevertheless relevant to our aim, we had to draw from several different areas. One consequence is that some of the people we invited have not been concerned in their research with the problems of reading; others have not dealt intensively with speech. Another consequence is that all had to bend their knowledge and interests to fit the structure of the conference; moreover, since they come from different disciplines, they had to make a special effort to communicate with each other. We think our participants managed these accommodations remarkably well. On that account, and on many others, we are immensely grateful to them.

References

Kavanagh, J. F. (ed.), 1968. *Communicating by Language: The Reading Process.* Bethesda, Md.: U.S. Department of Health, Education, and Welfare, National Institutes of Health, Government Printing Office.

ELEANOR J. GIBSON

Reading for Some Purpose

Keynote Address

"Reading maketh a full man, conference a ready man, and writing
an exact man." So said Francis Bacon; and now, 350 years later, we
have come together to confer and to write about reading. This is by
no means the first time for many of us, and one may wonder that we
still have a problem to solve in understanding how a child learns to
read, or in constructing a model of the reading process in an educated
adult. Would it suffice to draw up a model that specifies, in some detail,
how written symbols are decoded to the spoken language? I think we
would agree that this enterprise, even well done, would be far from
sufficient. If you will permit me another quotation, we are instructed
by the Book of Common Prayer to "Read, mark, learn, and inwardly
digest." There's the trouble. It's no good just to decode some ciphers,
one must digest them. One must mark what is important and get some
meaning from it. You are thinking, no doubt, that a phrase like "reading
for meaning" is so trite that I won't dare utter it. But I shall, because
it is that aspect of language—both spoken and written—that we have
as psychologists and linguists so dismally failed to handle. I hope this
conference will focus a large share of its concentrated wisdom on the
problem of meaning.

Why is it that journals, especially educational ones, flood us with
literature on the reading process that seems ever staler, more faddish,
or more oriented toward administrative problems, like getting a machine
to do it? I think it is because we do not have a good psychological
theory of reading. The best I can do then is to tell you briefly the
kind of theory I have been trying to formulate, and suggest an outline
of the problems we have to solve.

To begin with, I will state boldly and baldly an assumption that
I take for granted. Reading is a cognitive process. No S-R theory is
going to help us. It starts with perception, it requires perceptual learning
of many things, and it ends up as a conceptual process, a tool for thinking
and learning that can take the place of first-hand experience. Just one
more quotation (from Shakespeare, to round out the sources): "Me,

poor man, my library / Was dukedom large enough." (Prospero, Duke of Milan in *The Tempest*). But for that, one must get knowledge and experience from reading, second-hand experience that is just as good as first-hand.

I admit to one more basic assumption, about language in general this time. The psychological basis of language is *abstraction*. It is not just emitting sounds in a given sequence, but a conceptual ability of one or many kinds that makes language possible. A parrot or a mynah bird can emit speechlike sounds, but they must be copied. Chimpanzees can use signs like tokens or gestures as instructions to act, or perhaps even with a "naming" kind of reference. But it is doubtful that the sequences of manual signs of Washoe, for instance, have anything resembling human syntax, and it is even more doubtful that any of these strings are predications. Looking through Washoe's repertory [Gardner and Gardner 1969], I am struck by the absence of "comment," that is, statements relating to events that are not demands or instructions to act. Finding the covariation between an event, such as someone going out of a room, and a verbal statement about it, is a very high-order achievement. The meaning of the event and the symbolic semantic referent must converge, their redundancy be noticed, and the usefulness of this redundancy appreciated. A human child does just this, however, when he is about 20 months old, and says "Kitty all-gone" as the cat flees his embrace.

If all this is true of spoken language, it would seem to apply even more to reading. (No one has even tried to teach a chimpanzee to read.) People who do research on reading have spent a great amount of time looking for correspondence rules between phonological features of language and graphological features of writing; and some time on syntax, chiefly showing that knowledge of grammar seems to induce some expectations in the adult reader. But we lack a learning theory that tells us how order and superordinate structure are picked up, and how already learned invariants and meanings in speech are transferred (if they are) or in some way activated in reading.

A Theory of Perceptual Learning

I think we must begin with a theory of perceptual learning, and then try to apply it to the reading process. This is what I have been attempting to do, with more or less success, for eight or ten years now [Gibson 1969]. Let me review briefly my theory of perceptual learning and then remind you of what is learned in speech and in reading—what we have to explain before we can state principles for instruction. I divide my theory into three questions: What is learned? What learning processes are involved? And what is the motivation and reinforcement for the learning?

What is learned in perceptual learning are, first, distinctive features of things, like faces and apples and trees and voices, and then of representations of things, especially symbolic ones like letters and printed words. As an example, my students and I have been trying for a long time to work out a satisfactory set of distinctive features for letters—the Roman capitals. In a recent experiment, we had subjects make same-different judgments for pairs of letters and recorded both errors and decision time. Using these data we constructed confusion matrices, which we analyzed by Johnson's hierarchical cluster analysis [Johnson 1967]. When the analysis is represented in tree form, the nodes should tell us what contrastive features are operating at each branching. We have come up consistently with such feature contrasts as straight vs. curve, horizontal or vertical vs. diagonality, open vs. closed, etc. There are distinctive features of written symbols at higher levels than that of the letter, of course, and I will come to that.

Second, what is learned in perceptual learning are invariants of *events*. This is a long-neglected problem in psychology, but the necessity of studying it becomes apparent when we consider predication and meaning in either spoken or written language. We talk or write *about* something. Somebody performs an action on something, for instance, and that is an event. Let me give a simple example. Size constancy, for the young child, is revealed by way of an event—the approach or receding of an object from the child, or his approach to or retreat from it. Only in this active process can the rule that describes the invariant for constant size of a thing be discovered. Shape constancy is a similar case. To discover that an object has a permanent, rigid shape a child must rotate an object through many angles, or locomote around it. The importance of such an event for language shows up later when a child makes a distinction between the count noun and the mass noun, between a detachable object and a substance. Discovery of object permanence by observation of progressive, partial occlusion and disocclusion is another important event in the perceptual learning of invariants, and one that is reflected very early in the child's predications. This is easily checked in looking at the content of children's early utterances, as Bloom [1970] has pointed out.

Finally, what is learned is structure of many orders. Distinctive features have a relational structure, and so do events, but this structure may be of many levels of complexity, and discovery of structural complexity may proceed in two directions—toward superordination or subordination, and progression in picking up both levels of the hierarchy seems to be learned during development. Restle [1970] has shown that "(a) some patterns are easily learned, (b) other sequences of events hardly form a pattern at all, and (c) the pattern is a property inherent in the sequence of events." [p. 481] Restle worked first with simple sequences of musical runs and trills, but he has carried his analysis further to the complex tree structure of an entire composition (a Bach invention). Linguists have known for a long time that such a structural analysis can be made for language, but we have made little progress in discovering how it is picked up. Written words have structural relations that are surely very important for reading—palindromes, for instance, like *saw* and *was*, that may cause confusions, and spelling patterns over sets of words that can facilitate the reading process enormously once they have been discovered. More important, it seems obvious that meaning in speech and written language is related to perceiving the correspondence of the phrases, sentences, and so on to event structures of different orders of complexity.

So much for *what is learned* in perceptual learning. Let us turn to the pick-up process. How do we do it? I am less confident about this than about what is learned, but I have found it necessary to hypothesize three processes that play a role. Not one of them is the process of association. One can present a child with flash cards and attempt to teach him to read by a paired associates method, as Itard did with the wild boy of Aveyron, but I do not believe that he is likely to do more than memorize a word (painfully and hating the procedure) this way. I think the essential process is what we have referred to always as *abstraction* in the cognitive processes that are further removed from the stimulus display. Abstraction, I think, occurs at a perceptual level as well. Realizing that I am on dangerous ground in this company of experts, I give you the example of the infant listening to his parents' speech and gradually (so I have always supposed) learning to segment it and to extract from it phonemes, or rather, a system of phonemic contrasts. It must be a process of abstraction, since the phoneme [Liberman, Cooper et al. 1967] has no invariance over a speech segment smaller than a syllable, and furthermore must be recognized over different voices, pitched high or low, whispering or shouting, sweet or harsh.

Abstraction has its importance in learning rule systems for much larger language patterns as well, I think, such as the spelling patterns of the English language, which are not reducible to mere probability of one letter following another but form a real, generalizable system that includes morphemic information. Syntax would seem to me to be a clear case of abstraction of rules, but I had better leave this vexing and hotly debated question to the experts who are to follow me.

I think abstraction is accompanied in perceptual learning by a kind of opposite process of *filtering*. The invariant relations are abstracted and enhanced, as neurologists have suggested for auditory acuity [von Békésy 1967] by an inhibitory process of filtering out what is irrelevant. William James spoke of abstraction as a process of "dissociation by varying concomitants." This is presumably what happens to the varying concomitants. There is the familiar evidence from the dichotic listening experiments. There is also evidence now [Schapiro 1970] that inhibitory filtering actually occurs, with suitable experience, with graphic material. Schapiro used a search task, but I think the process will be found to be important in the perceptual learning involved in reading. There is the fact, for instance, that reading a subsequent letter or word as the eye moves rapidly over the page does not mask the perception of the previous one. Blurring that should occur, according to knowledge of the perceptual process gained from tachistoscopic experiments, simply does not occur in reading.

My third process is an obvious one, and here, at least, I anticipate little argument. Perceptual learning involves active exploration, orienting, tuning if you like, of the sense organs [J. J. Gibson 1966]. We do not just see, we look; we do not just hear, we listen. Furthermore, we develop, as we grow from infancy, progressively better strategies of focusing on and monitoring auditory and visual information in stimulation. These strategies are integral with the abstraction and the filtering processes. Examples are hardly necessary, but the scanning strategies of an expert reader will occur to you. There have been numerous studies, especially by Soviet psychologists, of the evolution during development of active strategies of information pick-up in tactual and visual identification. One can describe the stages, but I hope no one will ask me just what neurological processes account for this progressive change in attentive strategies because I do not know, and neither does anyone else.

Now let me turn to my third question: What is the motivation and reinforcement for perceptual learning? My students often tell me that I should forget this question, that it is an anachronism, a hang-over from my dark past as a Hullian psychologist. But I still worry that there has to be something to account for what is selected to be learned— the distinctive feature, or the good search strategy. My answer is that reinforcement for cognitive learning is not externally given but is, instead, reduction of uncertainty. What is learned is the distinctive feature, the feature that is invariant over transformations, and the structure that chunks the most information into one rule or ordering. The abstraction and filtering processes are geared to do this, and insofar as learning occurs (sometimes it doesn't, unhappily) it is because the learner finds the economical strategy or the order that encompasses many cases and reduces a number of bits to one superordinate unit.

I could give innumerable examples of the operation of this principle and it is especially applicable to language perception. Here is one example, an experiment I happened to read the morning I wrote these lines [Baddeley 1971]. It is well known that a subject who has read or who is shown a sequence of letters, and who is asked to give them back at once tends to code them in an auditory or articulatory form [Conrad 1964]. The evidence for this is that letters whose names rhyme are confused. But Baddeley found that this interference (and thus presumably coding to the letter's name) drops out as the string of letters more and more approximates English spelling and finally forms a word. The subject chunks what he hears; if the string begins with "B-E-D," he picks up "BED," not "B-E-D," and with discovery and practice of this strategy he will do this even better and of course remember more.

The potential features of a word that have most utility for a given task, like finding a telephone number, or remembering it for 30 seconds, or making sense out of something one is reading, *vary with the task,* and the skilled human reader learns to assign priority to features to suit the task and is able to shift his processing strategies—a wonderful example of economy of information pick-up that we surely want to encourage and develop in the young reader.

What Is Learned in Speech and Reading?

Now let me talk for a few minutes about just what is learned in spoken and written language and what might be some possible relations between the two systems. There is little here that will be new to any of you, but it will serve to remind us of the problems that must be tackled, if they have not been already.

A book called *The Psychology and Pedagogy of Reading* was published 63 years ago by a pyschologist named Edmund Burke Huey. It is amazing to read this book in 1971 and find out how little we have discovered about reading since that time. Huey knew about the eye-voice span, he knew about right-left laterality on the retina, he knew that a five-letter word can be read with as short an exposure as a single letter. He said that "consciousness is not a picture-gallery, or a magic lantern exhibition with slide displacing slide in rapid succession."[p. 160] He thought con-

sciousness (and reading) were a search for meaning. He knew a surprising amount about eye movements in reading—as much, it seems to me,
as we know today, despite the fact that we have sophisticated electronic
equipment instead of mechanical drop-shuttered tachistoscopes and levers
connecting a cup on the eye to a smoked drum.

What Huey didn't know about was psycholinguistics, since of course
no such discipline had been born. Many psychologists have felt, since
its advent, that all our worries about reading would soon be over, because
reading is language, just as speech is, and anything we find out about
speech can simply be transferred to our understanding of the reading
process. We read words, as well as hear them; written language has
grammar and syntax, as well as spoken language. So what is the problem?
Isn't it enough to point to the parallels?

Let me show you a rather simplified chart of what is learned in hearing-speaking and in reading-writing. (I deliberately emphasize the productive as well as the perceptive aspects of both, since there is surely
feedback from one to the other, especially during early stages of
learning.)

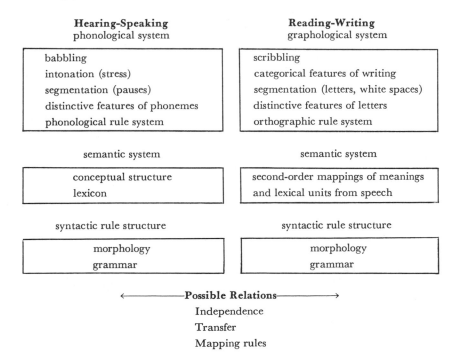

Figure 1. Some parallels between what is learned in speech and in reading.

Consider first hearing-speaking. What is learned (or develops in some way) can be usefully divided into the three aspects that we have come to call the phonological system, the semantic system, and the syntactic system. These systems are distinguished in three boxes of the diagram and some further distinctions are made within the boxes. One could write a book about each of them, but a few obvious summary statements about what is learned in each case (subject to correction by the experts present) must suffice.

Learning the *phonological* system begins, many have thought, with an infant's babbling activity. The babbling, over several months of time, "drifts" toward a reduced set of sounds that appear to be more and more constrained by the language the infant is hearing. There is disagreement about the role of babbling in the emergence of real words and phonemic distinctions [Jakobson 1968; Kaplan and Kaplan 1970], but feedback from the infant's own vocal production is certainly going on and apparently assisting phonetic development. Intonation or stress patterns also develop early, before real speech, and may provide the primary features that categorize speech sounds as speech and distinguish them from all the other sounds of the infant's world—the cat meowing, the radiator gurgling, the telephone ringing. That discrimination of different intonations develops sometime between 3 and 8 months has been demonstrated experimentally [Kaplan 1969].

If perception of stress patterns develops early, must the infant learn to segment this pattern into subordinate units; to analyze it into component words and phrases, for instance? It would seem so, and there is reason to think that this learning is not complete until the child is 5 or 6 years old. Pauses do not always exist where we hear them in a train of speech, but we discover eventually that a sentence is made up of lexical elements that can be recombined (and that we must differentiate if we are to learn to read). We discover further that there are smaller phonological units than words, component sounds that constitute them, and even these phonetic units can be analyzed into bundles of features that characterize them. How early does an infant distinguish one phonetic unit from another perceptually? We do not know, but there is evidence [Eimas, Siqueland et al. 1971] that a phonetic distinction between two consonants, [b] and [p], is possible by 6 months or even earlier. Hearing a phoneme as *invariant* over different words and speakers involves further learning [Liberman, Cooper et al. 1967], and also involves extraction of information from context. We do not yet understand the developmental process for this achievement; I have said that I think it involves abstraction, but we know only that there is development. Accurate phonemic production, with proper use of all distinctive features, is not fully learned until a child is 4 or 5, though he may perhaps hear the distinctions earlier.

One thing should be said about the phonological system, even in this abbreviated account. What the child learns is not a mere collection of items of information about sounds at different levels of structure. He learns, rather, a phonological rule system. In his native language, whatever it is, certain sounds may precede and follow others. Some combinations, on the other hand, are not permissible. There are typical consonant clusters that can begin a word, and typical ones that can end it. A 4-year-old [Morehead 1971] has internalized much of the phonological rule system of his native language.

Although acquisition of the phonological system is as yet poorly under-stood, acquisition of the *semantic* properties of language is a still greater mystery and a matter for psychological dispute. Let us hazard a few reasonable statements just the same. The child as he observes and acts in the world around him discovers distinctive features of objects and invariant properties of events, leading him to develop first perceptions, and then a conceptual scheme of the permanent properties of his world. This conceptual structure, in turn, he learns to encode in symbols; the conceptual structure is mapped to speech. The organization of this sym-bolic conceptual structure is a semantic system, a system of meanings. Psychologists have made little progress in the study of meaning. But we know that every child acquires a lexicon—a vocabulary of the words of his language. The words or, rather, words in proper combinations, are a kind of code for real events and things and ideas. Words have meaning, and this meaning I consider to be based on perceptual knowledge.

The third aspect of speech is its *syntactic* rule structure. Words from the lexicon are not strung together hit or miss, but in an agreed-upon order. The function of syntactic rules is often said to be that of linking conceptual structures with the phonological representation of them [Langacker 1967]. In any case, the syntactical rule structure is a complex one, specifying the sequential arrangement of units, types of units, and their hierarchical arrangement. It is characterized by superordinate and subordinate parts, embedded units. Units at many levels are formed by the syntactic rules. How these rules are learned is again a matter for heated debate, but it is generally supposed that they are induced by the child from the samples of speech that he is exposed to. He learns by induction the rules of grammar and morphology. A child's grasp of the rules for morphological transformation is reflected in a tendency, during early stages of learning, to overgeneralize the rule. He shows that he has learned the rule about forming a past tense, for instance, by applying the regular inflection to an irregular verb (e.g., "the fly bited me").

Now let us turn to reading-writing and consider what is learned in this form of language. It is again convenient to differentiate three aspects. Parallel to the phonological system in speech is the *graphological* system in writing. Productive speech begins with babbling. Graphic production begins with scribbling. Given the materials, the average child of 18 months will scribble spontaneously [Cattell 1960]. His scribbling is not mere muscular exercise but is closely linked to its visual feedback. The child wants to see what he scribbles, and his production even by 2 years will vary appropriately with size of the paper, and so on. Like babbling, the feedback provides an opportunity for learning by self-regulation. The categorical features of writing—a set of distinctive features, recombination of elements, and repetitive regularity, for instance—are learned quite early as shown by the child's ability to distinguish samples of writing from other marks on paper [L. Lavine, 1972]. The distinctive features that render each individual letter unique must also be learned, like distinctive features of phonemes in speech. Is the learning process similar in the two cases? We do not know, but we can point to more parallels in what is learned. Invariant features of graphemes must be extracted from samples of different handwritings, for instance, just as the hearer must extract invariant features of phonemes over many voices. That there are differences is certain, however. Liberman, Cooper et al. [1967] have made the point very strongly that the speech code is not an alphabetic one. Insofar as this is true, the learning processes would be expected to vary.

Just as hearing-speaking has a phonological rule system, so has reading-writing an orthographic rule system. Certain consonant clusters can begin the spelling of a word (e.g., *qu, str, fl*) but cannot end it; whereas others (e.g., *pt, ng, rt*) can end but not begin it. Environment determines orthography, as it does phonology. Now comes an important question. Is there a specifiable relationship between phonology and orthography, between the phonological and orthographic rule systems? Can we find mapping rules defining correspondences between the two? Such a relation has always been presumed to exist (i.e., a letter is an instruction to utter a particular sound). Writing is a code for speech. But the mapping rule is not simply one letter for one phoneme. It would not even be particularly useful if this were true, if a phoneme is heard as invariant only over a speech segment no smaller than a syllable, at best [Liberman,

Cooper et al. 1967]. Learning to read must surely benefit from the correspondence rules with speech, since any rule system reduces enormously the amount that has to be learned. But it is important not to oversimplify the nature of the relationship. Coding, combination rules, and underlying invariant properties must all be considered. Work by Venezky [1970], by Carol Chomsky [1970], and by Chomsky and Halle [1968] suggests that the correspondence rules are morphophonemic and abstract, not simply the mapping of a letter to a sound.

In earlier experiments, investigations were made of the usefulness of grapheme-phoneme correspondences in facilitating reading [Gibson, Pick et al. 1962; Gibson, Osser et al. 1963]. Two sets of unfamiliar pseudo-words were invented that were "pronounceable" by rules of English phonology in one set but not in the other. They were composed, in the first case, of a consonant cluster which could permissibly begin a word and one that could end a word (e.g., *blong*). In the second case, the consonant clusters were transposed to make the word unpronounceable (e.g., *ngobl*). These words were presented to the subjects tachistoscopically. The "pronounceable" words were very consistently read with fewer errors. They made better units. Was this because phonological and orthographic rules corresponded, so that transfer could take place from one rule system to the other? Perhaps so, but the same experiments with deaf subjects yielded similar results [Gibson, Shurcliff et al. 1970), so the orthographic rule system *can,* at least, operate on its own to create larger units for reading. How it is learned, in either case?

What about the *semantic* aspect of reading? Here the relationship, for the mature reader, might seem to be one of direct transfer. If the reader can decode a written word to its phonological representation, he hears it and presumably might discover its meaning at once without further learning. The mapping of meanings to written symbols in that case would be a second-order one. Spoken words are symbols for things, events, and ideas, and written words are symbols for spoken ones. Since the lexical units of speech have direct counterparts in writing, why should a hearing-speaking child have to relearn the conceptual-symbol system? But everyone knows that "reading for meaning" does not come easily in the early stages of learning to read. The difficulty of reading (especially when the meaning is "hard") without any subvocal activity [Hardyck and Petrinovich 1970] may be relevant to the means by which the semantic properties of written language are derived.

Evidence suggests that getting meaning directly from a written word, even when its spoken counterpart is well known, is not immediate and automatic as soon as the child is able to decode the written symbols to speech. He progresses gradually toward immediacy in grasping meaning from the spoken word. For the adult reader a written word specifies its meaning, and the meaning is *in* the word. It is so immediate that it interferes with his performance in the Stroop test of naming colors, for instance. But there is developmental progress toward this immanent semantic property of the written word [Gibson, 1971]. It is not enough, then, to speak of simple transfer of meanings from spoken to written messages—even if we knew how the meaning got into the spoken ones.

The syntactic aspect of reading looks superficially a little easier. The rules of grammar are identical for spoken and written language. Perhaps the child has only to learn the formalities of punctuation to get a complete transfer. But how are the rules activated for reading and writing? Is the order—the subordinate and superordinate structure—immediately obvious? Reading is sequential, as is hearing, but the sequence is controlled by the reader and no prosodic cues are given him. Syntactical structure must be picked up to process units that communicate something but it is not at all obvious how one does this in reading.

Weber [1967, 1970] studied the errors of children reading aloud to each other at the end of first grade. Few of these errors comprised grammatical mistakes. When a mistake occurred it was followed by an ungrammatical conclusion only 29 percent of the time. The good readers, in particular, tended not to violate grammaticality, or they corrected the error if they did. These findings show that grammatical rules are in general available to children at this age. But the important question is whether the child can *use* this knowledge to select economical units for reading.

This question has been the subject of a number of experiments by H. Levin and his students [Levin and Kaplan 1970]. At what age does a child stop reading word by word and begin making use of textual redundancies, such as syntactical constraints in sentences? The technique employed was the "eye-voice span." In one experiment, Levin and Turner [1968] studied eye-voice span for simple active sentences with subjects at six grade levels. There were active sentences made up of two-word phrases, active sentences of three-word phrases, and active sentences of four-word phrases. Unstructured word lists were also included. The mean length of the span was significantly longer for the sentences than for the unstructured word lists, and there was a tendency for the span to be longest on the three-word-phrase sentences. Older subjects had longer spans than younger ones, and faster readers had longer spans that slower readers. The eye-voice span tended to extend to a phrase boundary, except in the youngest (second grade) sample.

Other experiments have demonstrated further the role of syntactic constraints in creating units for reading. It has been shown that the latter half of passive sentences is more highly constrained than the corresponding part of active sentences. It was predicted, therefore, that the eye-voice span should become longer toward the middle of the passive form, but not for the active form. Levin and Kaplan [1968] demonstrated that with college students this is indeed the case; the eye-voice span was longer for passive sentences at that point where the active and passive forms began to be differentially constrained.

Another type of constraint, the difference between left-embedded and right-embedded sentences, was explored by Levin, Grossman et al. [1972]. Using a modified Cloze procedure, it was ascertained that right-branching sentences are more highly constrained than left-branching ones. Eye-voice spans were then determined for these sentences, with college students as subjects. The spans were longer for the more highly constrained right-embedded sentences. So the skilled reader actively searches for and uses regularities in language structure. His knowledge of the rules tells him where and how far to look, and thus assists him to chunk the material in higher-order units.

How early is this admirable cognitive economy available to young readers? The Levin and Turner study suggested that even by the end of second grade, there is a difference in eye-voice span between random strings of words and sentences, although there was progress after that in using intrasentence constraints such as phrase boundaries. Perhaps it is the meaning in the sentences, rather than grammatical structure, that is responsible for the difference observed in the second graders. We need to explore farther the developmental progress in pick-up of constraints and redundancies of both kinds. We do not know how this learning occurs. Are habits of doing this already internalized for spoken language, and simply transferred to reading? I do not think the answer is this easy; I think there are clues to syntax on the printed page that are comparable, perhaps, but by no means identical with those in heard speech.

An analysis of the progressive use of finer clues to syntactical units was undertaken by Gibson and Guinet [1971], who studied pick-up of morphological transformations (verb inflections) in third-grade and fifth-grade children and college sophomores. Words were flashed one at a time on a screen, with a brief exposure. There were three types of stem words (actual words, pronounceable pseudowords, and unpronounceable pseudowords). The words varied in length from 4 to 7 letters. There were four versions of each one; the stem word, the third person singular (*s* added), the past tense (*ed* added), and the progressive (*ing* added). The questions were whether the verb ending functioned as a unit, resisting errors and permitting a longer word to be read, and whether such a tendency, if present, was learned by third grade or only later.

As in earlier experiments, the real words were read with fewest errors and the pronounceable pseudowords with next fewest. A stem word lengthened by an inflectional suffix was *not* read more correctly than a word of equivalent length that did not contain a suffix. But the inflectional endings were read with fewer errors than noninflectional endings on pseudowords of equivalent length. Furthermore, if an error was made on the inflected ending, there was a tendency to substitute one of the other inflections (for example, *ing* for *ed*). Both these latter tendencies increased from third to fifth grade. Thus, inflectional endings do come to be processed as unitary word features, and this is done increasingly as reading skill develops. They can therefore serve as clues to the structure of a phrase or a sentence.

Is there redundant information beyond the sentence that can improve the economy of reading? Intuitively, we certainly suppose so, but much more research is needed on the problem of how we learn to read in units beyond the word. Skilled adult readers do use morphological, grammatical, and semantic structure. But we know very little about how this skill develops. How the structural information is incorporated in our reading habits is as much a mystery as the same question is for speech. It is not something that is explicitly taught, for the good reason that perceptual learning is involved, so reinforcement must be internal and self-regulated.

Conclusion

For about ten years now a fair number of people have been concerned with what might be called theory-based research on reading. The work of this group has been mainly devoted to a few questions. One of them has been how the perceptual differentiation of visual symbols develops. Another has been the attempt to describe the correspondence rules between phonological and graphological features, the rules that are relevant to the decoding process. Another has been research on processing times in various word recognition tasks. There has also been a good deal of work on the role of grammar in reading. On the whole, this latter research has been with the view of showing that knowledge of syntax induces some kind of expectation in the reader, that grammar actually functions in the reading process. We have been making an unjustified assumption, I am afraid, that there is a direct application; that the person who brings a knowledge of grammar with him to reading is able to transfer this knowledge automatically, once he can decode the graphic items to speech and has some knowledge of punctuation.

I am aware of three glaring deficiencies as I contemplate this research to date. Even though I call it theory-based research it seems to me clear that we have done far too little by way of developing a good theory. One of the deficiencies is how the correspondences between spoken and written language make contact with one another. Finding the superordinate structure in written language is a crucial problem for the reader. How does this happen? The answer must include knowledge of how already learned rule structures in speech are put to use or activated in reading.

The second deficiency, and I need not dwell on it, is our failure to come to grips with the problem of meaning in reading. How is meaning picked up from the written word? I hope someone at this conference is going to tell me how and show that I am wrong in thinking we have made little progress in this area.

Finally, I return emphatically to the title of this paper, "Reading for Some Purpose." Reading has many purposes and written words as well as spoken ones contain many kinds of information. Words have many features—graphological, phonological, syntactic, and semantic. The reader, depending on his task, may adopt many different strategies in picking up these features. He may want only to scan down a page looking for a telephone number or a word in the dictionary that he has forgotten how to spell. He may be whiling away the time in a dreary airport with a detective story. His purpose in reading it is not to remember the story a few hours later but only to engage his mind and escape from boredom. He may be reading a poem, slowly savoring its rhythm, rhyme, and metaphor. He may be studying a lesson, reading difficult material and doing his best to comprehend it. He may be reading as an editor, not so much concerned with the semantic aspects of the information before him, but chiefly with punctuation, spelling, and style. All of these tasks and all the other tasks that a reader may perform require the assignment of different priorities to the information contained in the words. An adult reader has become very skilled in actively assigning priorities to the features that have the greatest utility for his present task. A model or theory of reading that fails to take into account the shift in these priorities, depending on the task the reader has set himself, will be an unsatisfactory and incomplete model; and we must ask, as well, how the young reader learns to assign priorities as the task changes.

Indeed, the problem of assigning economical priorities for picking up information is one of the deepest in cognitive psychology which, of course, includes reading. I finish then with the question that seems to me most important. How is it that we are able to read to some purpose?

References

Baddeley, A. D., 1971. Language habits, acoustic confusability, and immediate memory for redundant letter sequences. *Psychonomic Sci.* 22:120–121.

Békésy, G. von, 1967. *Sensory Inhibition.* Princeton: Princeton University Press.

Bloom, L., 1970. *Language Development: Form and Function in Emerging Grammars.* Cambridge, Mass.: MIT Press.

Cattell, P., 1960. *The Measurement of Intelligence of Infants and Young Children* (rev. ed.). New York: Psychological Corporation.

Chomsky, C., 1970. Reading, writing, and phonology. *Harvard Ed. Rev.* 40:287–309.

Chomsky, N. A., and M. Halle, 1968. *The Sound Pattern of English.* New York: Harper and Row.

Conrad, R., 1964. Acoustic confusions in immediate memory. *Brit. J. Psycho.* 55:75–84.

Eimas, P. D., E. R. Siqueland, P. Jusczyk, and J. Vigorito, 1971. Speech perception in infants. *Science* 171:303–306.

Gardner, R. A., and B. T. Gardner, 1969. Teaching sign language to a chimpanzee. *Science* 165:664–672.

Gibson, E. J., 1969. *Principles of Perceptual Learning and Development.* New York: Appleton-Century-Crofts.

———, 1971. Perceptual learning and the theory of word perception. *J. Cog. Psych.* 2:351–368.

Gibson, E. J., and L. Guinet, 1971. The perception of inflections in brief visual presentations of words. *J. Verbal Learning and Verbal Behavior* 10:182–189.

Gibson, E. J., H. Osser, and A. Pick, 1963. A study in the development of grapheme-phoneme correspondences. *J. Verbal Learning and Verbal Behavior* 2:142–146.

Gibson, E. J., A. Pick, H. Osser, and M. Hammond, 1962. The role of grapheme-phoneme correspondence in the perception of words. *Amer. J. Psych.* 75:554–570.

Gibson, E. J., A. Shurcliff, and A. Yonas, 1970. Utilization of spelling patterns by deaf and hearing subjects. In *Basic Studies on Reading,* H. Levin and J. P. Williams (eds.), New York: Basic Books.

Gibson, J. J., 1966. *The Senses Considered as Perceptual Systems.* Boston: Houghton Mifflin.

Hardyck, D. C., and L. F. Petrinovich, 1970. Subvocal speech and comprehension level as a function of the difficulty level of reading material. *J. Verbal Learning and Verbal Behavior* 9:647–652.

Huey, E. B., 1908. *The Psychology and Pedagogy of Reading.* New York: Macmillan. Reprinted Cambridge, Mass.: MIT Press, 1968.

Jakobson, R., 1968. *Child Language, Aphasia and Phonological Universals.* A. R. Keiler (tr.) The Hague: Mouton.

Johnson, S. C., 1967. Hierarchical clustering schemes. *Psychometrika* 32:241–254.

Kaplan, E. L., 1969. The role of intonation in the acquisition of language. Unpublished doctoral dissertation, Cornell University.

Kaplan, E. L., and G. A. Kaplan, 1970. The prelinguistic child. In *Human Development and Cognitive Processes,* J. Eliot (ed.), New York: Holt, Rinehart and Winston, pp. 358–381.

Langacker, R. W., 1967. *Language and Its Structure.* New York: Harcourt, Brace and World.

Lavine, L. O., 1972. The development of perception of writing in pre-reading children: A cross-cultural study. Unpublished doctoral dissertation, Cornell University.

Levin, H., J. Grossman, E. Kaplan, and R. Yang, 1972, in press. Constraints and the eye-voice span in right- and left-embedded sentences. *Language and Speech.*

Levin, H., and E. Kaplan, 1968. Eye-voice span within active and passive sentences. *Language and Speech,* 2:251–258.

Levin, H., and E. Kaplan, 1970. Grammatical structure and reading. In *Basic Studies on Reading,* H. Levin and J. P. Williams (eds.), New York: Basic Books.

Levin, H., and A. Turner, 1968. Sentence structure and the eye-voice span. In *The Analysis of Reading Skill: A Program of Basic and Applied Research,* final report, Project 5–1213, Cornell University and U.S. Office of Education, pp. 196–220.

Liberman, A. M., F. S. Cooper, D. P. Shankweiler, and M. Studdert-Kennedy, 1967. Perception of the speech code. *Psych. Rev.* 74:431–461.

Morehead, D. M., 1971. Processing of phonological sequences by young children and adults. *Child Development,* 42:279–289.

Restle, F., 1970. Theory of serial pattern learning: Structural trees. *Psych. Rev.* 77:481–495.

Schapiro, F., 1970. Information extraction and filtering during perceptual learning in visual search. Unpublished doctoral disseration, Cornell University.

Venezky, R. L., 1970. *The Structure of English Orthography.* The Hague: Mouton.

Weber, R. M., 1967. Grammaticality and the self-correction of reading errors. *Project Literacy Reports,* July, no. 8, 53–59.

————, 1970. First graders' use of grammatical context in reading. In *Basic Studies on Reading,* H. Levin and J. P. Williams (eds.), New York: Basic Books.

General Discussion of Keynote Address by Gibson

The discussion centered on Gibson's analogy between scribbling and babbling. Liberman pointed out that, at a very early age, children babble certain phonetic segments spontaneously and accurately, in a fairly uniform developmental sequence. He asked whether her 2-year-old children, while scribbling, produce letter shapes, or at least distinctive features of letters, and whether a developmental sequence can be observed.

Gibson said that the Figure 1, showing the analogies between acquisition of spoken language and written language, should not be taken too literally. It can be interpreted in three different ways: (1) the acquisition of written language is parallel to but independent from the acquisition of spoken language; (2) transfer of learning takes place at some point; (3) though written and spoken language are independent, the child discovers that there are useful relationships between the two. As for babbling and scribbling, her children produce curved lines, straight lines, and intersections (the components of letters) if not actual letters; and they can distinguish between pictures and writing—even Hebrew and Arabic writing—long before they can name letters. She agreed, however, that the analogy was perhaps a superficial one that should not be pushed too far. In fact, her reading of Jakobson [1968], McNeill [1970] and others had convinced her that babbling has no role in the development of speech. She did not believe that a child babbles phonemes randomly and is reinforced by his parents when he happens to utter a phoneme of their language.

Liberman said that babbling plays a role in the development of language even though there is no differential reinforcement. He cited a study by Preston, Yeni-Komshian et al. [1967] which reported that one-year-old children babble voiceless unaspirated stops. These stops are universal; they occur in all or almost all languages and are considered to be linguistically "unmarked." Only after the children begin to speak (15–17 months old) do they produce the "marked" voiceless aspirated stops which contrast with the voiceless unaspirated stops in English.

Jenkins asked whether scribbling is important for reading and writing because it gives the child an opportunity to see the results of his motor activity. Cooper pointed out that a similar function has been attributed to babbling: the child gets an insight into the relationship between what he tells his muscles to do and what he hears himself say. This might suggest (though Cooper was reluctant to push the notion this far) that cursive writing might be as easy or easier to read than ordinary print.

Jenkins added that Swiss schools for the deaf start the training of children in language with cursive writing. Gibson agreed that the visual feedback from motor activity is extremely important.

Gibson said that the ability of her subjects to perform tasks related to reading and writing stops rather suddenly when they begin to attend school. She wondered whether their teaching fails to capitalize on the experience the children already have.

Carroll suggested an alternative explanation, that the transfer from spoken to written language may be easier when the experience of acquiring the spoken language is still recent. By school age this experience has been forgotten. Children studied by Moore and by Durkin [1966] read as early as 2½ years. Gibson and others were skeptical about generalizing from these studies, because the subjects were unrepresentative of the general population in I.Q. or cultural background.

References

Durkin, D., 1966. *Children Who Read Early: Two Longitudinal Studies.* New York: Teachers College Press.

Jakobson, R., 1968. *Child Language, Aphasia and Phonological Universals.* A. R. Keiler (tr.) The Hague: Mouton.

McNeill, David, 1970. *The Acquisition of Language.* New York: Harper and Row.

Preston, M. S., G. Yeni-Komshian, and R. E. Stark, 1967. Voicing in initial stop-consonants produced by children in the pre-linguistic period from different language communities. *Annual Report,* Baltimore: Neurocommunications Laboratory, Johns Hopkins University School of Medicine.

PART I

Speech and Writing as Vehicles of Language

FRANKLIN S. COOPER

How Is Language Conveyed by Speech?

In a conference on the relationships between speech and learning to read, it is surely appropriate to start with reviews of what we now know about speech and writing as separate modes of communication. Hence the question now before us: How is language conveyed by speech? The next two presentations will ask similar questions about writing systems, both alphabetic and nonalphabetic. The similarities and differences implied by these questions need to be considered not only at performance levels, where speaking and listening are in obvious contrast with writing and reading, but also at the competence levels of spoken and written language. Here the differences are less obvious, yet they may be important for reading and its successful attainment by the young child.

In attempting a brief account of speech as the vehicle for spoken language, it may be useful first to give the general point of view from which speech and language are here being considered. It is essentially a process approach, motivated by the desire to use experimental findings about speech better to understand the nature of language. So viewed, language is a communicative process of a special—and especially remarkable—kind. Clearly, the total process of communicating information from one person to another involves at least the three main operations of production, transmission, and reception. Collectively, these processes have some remarkable properties: open-endedness, efficiency, speed, and richness of expression. Other characteristics that are descriptive of language processes per se, at least when transmission is by speech, include the existence of semantically "empty" elements and a hierarchical organization built upon them; furthermore, as we shall see, the progression from level to level involves restructuring operations of such complexity that they truly qualify as encodings rather than encipherings. The encoded nature of the speech signal is a topic to which we shall give particular attention since it may well be central to the relationship between speech and learning to read.

The Encoded Nature of Speech
It is not intuitively obvious that speech really is an encoded signal or, indeed, that it has special properties. Perhaps speech seems so simple because it is so common: everyone uses it and has done so since early

childhood. In fact, the universality of spoken language and its casual acquisition by the young child—even the dullard—are among its most remarkable, and least understood, properties. They set it sharply apart from written language: reading and writing are far from universal, they are acquired only later by formal instruction, and even special instruction often proves ineffective with an otherwise normal child. Especially revealing are the problems of children who lack one of the sensory capacities— vision or hearing—for dealing with language. One finds that blindness is no bar to the effective use of spoken language, whereas deafness severely impedes the mastery of written language, though vision is still intact. Here is further and dramatic evidence that spoken language has a special status not shared by written language. Perhaps, like walking, it comes naturally, whereas skiing does not but can be learned. The nature of the underlying differences between spoken and written language, as well as of the similarities, must surely be relevant to our concern with learning to read. Let us note then that spoken language and written language differ, in addition to the obvious ways, in their relationship to the human being—in the degree to which they may be innate, or at least compatible with his mental machinery.

Is this compatibility evident in other ways, perhaps in special properties of the speech signal itself? Acoustically, speech is complex and would not qualify by engineering criteria as a clean, definitive signal. Nevertheless, we find that human beings can understand it at rates (measured in bits per second) that are five to ten times as great as for the best engineered sounds. We know that this is so from fifty years of experience in trying to build machines that will read for the blind by converting letter shapes to distinctive sound shapes [Coffey 1963; Cooper 1950; Studdert-Kennedy and Cooper 1966]; we know it also—and we know that practice is not the explanation—from the even longer history of telegraphy. Likewise, for speech production, we might have guessed from everyday office experience that speech uses special tricks to go so fast. Thus, even slow dictation will leave an expert typist far behind; the secretary, too, must resort to tricks such as shorthand if she is to keep pace.

Comparisons of listening and speaking with reading and writing are more difficult, though surely relevant to our present concern with what is learned when one learns to read. We know that, just as listening can outstrip speaking, so reading can go faster than writing. The limit on listening to speech appears to be about 400 words per minute [Orr, Friedman et al. 1965], though it is not yet clear whether this is a human limit on reception (or comprehension) or a machine limit beyond which the process used for time compression has seriously distorted the speech signal. Limits on reading speed are even harder to determine and to interpret, in part because reading lends itself to scanning as listening does not. Then, too, reading has its star performers who can go several times as fast as most of us. But, aside from these exceptional cases, the good reader and the average listener have limiting rates that are roughly comparable. Is the reader, too, using a trick? Perhaps the same trick in reading as in listening?

For speech, we are beginning to understand how the trick is done. The answers are not complete, nor have they come easily. But language has proved to be vulnerable to experimental attack at the level of speech, and the insights gained there are useful guides in probing higher and less accessible processes. Much of the intensive research on speech that was sparked by the emergence of sound spectrograms just after World War II was, in a sense, seduced by the apparent simplicities of acoustic analysis and phonemic representation. The goal seemed obvious: it was to find acoustic invariants in speech that matched the phonemes in the message. Although much was learned about the acoustic events of speech, and which of them were essential cues for speech perception, the supposed invariants remained elusive, just as did such promised marvels as the phonetic typewriter. The reason is obvious, now that it is understood: the speech signal was assumed to be an acoustic cipher, whereas it is, in fact, a code.

The distinction is important here as it is in cryptography from which the terms are borrowed: "cipher" implies a one-to-one correspondence between the minimal units of the original and final messages; thus, in Poe's story, "The Goldbug," the individual symbols of the mysterious message stood for the separate letters of the instructions for finding the treasure. In like manner, speech was supposed—erroneously—to comprise a succession of acoustic invariants that stand for the phonemes of the spoken message. The term "code" implies a different and more complex relationship between original and final message. The one-to-one relationship between minimal units has disappeared, since it is the essence of encoding that the original message is restructured (and usually shortened) in ways that are prescribed by an encoding algorithm or mechanism. In commercial codes, for example, the "words" of the final message may all be six-letter groups, regardless of what they stand for. Corresponding units of the original message might be a long corporate name, a commonly used phrase, or a single word or symbol. The restructuring, in this case, is done by substitution, using a code book. There are other methods of encoding—more nearly like speech—which restruc-

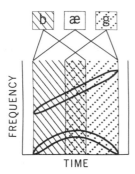

Figure 1. Parallel transmission of phonetic segments after encoding (by the rules of speech) to the level of sound (Liberman, 1970, p. 309).

ture the message in a more or less continuous manner, hence, with less variability in the size of unit on which the encoder operates. It may then be possible to find rough correspondences between input and output elements, although the latter will be quite variable and dependent on context. Further, a shortening of the message may be achieved by collapsing it so that there is temporal overlap of the original units; this constitutes parallel transmission in the sense that there is, at every instant of time, information in the output about several units of the input. A property of such codes is that the output is no longer segmentable, that is, it cannot be divided into pieces that match units of the input. In this sense also the one-to-one relationship has been lost in the encoding process.

The restructuring of spoken language has been described at length by Liberman, Cooper et al. [1967]. An illustration of the encoded nature of the speech can be seen in Figure 1, from a recent article [Liberman 1970]. It shows a schematic spectrogram that will, if turned back into sound by a speech synthesizer, say *bag* quite clearly. This is a simpler display of frequency, time, and intensity than one would find in a spectrogram of the word as spoken by a human being, but it captures the essential pattern. The figure shows that the influence of the initial and final consonants extend so far into the vowel that they overlap even with each other, and that the vowel influence extends throughout the syllable. The meaning of "influence" becomes clear when one examines comparable patterns for syllables with other consonants or another vowel: thus, the pattern for *gag* has a U-shaped second formant, higher at its center than the midpoint of the second-formant shown for *bag*; likewise, changing the vowel, as in *bog,* lowers the frequency of the second formant not only at the middle of the syllable but at the beginning and end as well.

Clearly, the speech represented by these spectographic patterns is not an acoustic cipher, that is, the physical signal is not a succession of sounds that stand for phonemes. There is no place to cut the syllable *bag* that will isolate separate portions for [b] and [æ] and [g]. The syllable is carrying information about all of them at the same time (parallel transmission), and each is affected by its neighbors (context dependence). In short, the phonetic string has been restructured, or encoded, into a new element at the acoustic level of the speech signal.

But is speech the only part of language that is encoded? Liberman's article, from which the illustration was drawn, asserts that comparable processes operate throughout language; that the encoding of speech and the transformations of syntactic and phonological structures are broadly similar and equally a part of the grammar. Thus, Figure 2 from the same article shows diagramatically the kind of restructuring and temporal compression that occurs in the syntactic conversion between deep and surface structure. Conventional orthography is used to represent the three deep-structure sentences and the single composite sentence at the surface. Again, there are overlapping domains, and compactness has been bought at the price of substantial changes in structure.

Encoding and Decoding

We see then, in all of spoken language, a very substantial degree of encoding. Why should this be so? Does it serve a purpose, or is it merely an unavoidable consequence of man's biological nature, or both? We have seen, in speech, that there is a temporal telescoping of the phonetic string into syllables and that this speeds communication; also, at the level of syntax, that there is a comparable collapsing of the deep structures into surface structures, with further gains in speed. Moreover,

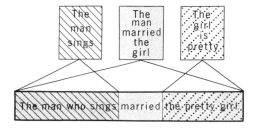

Figure 2. Parallel transmission of deep structure segments after encoding (by the rules of syntax) to the level of surface structure (Liberman, 1970, p. 310).

there are cognitive advantages that may be even more important, and that may explain why the encoding seems to have been done in stages, resulting in a hierarchical structure for language. George Miller [1956] has given us an account of how the magic of encoding lets us deal with substantial quantities of information in spite of limited memory capacity.

These are impressive advantages, but the price seems very high. We would suppose, from the foregoing, that the task of the person who listens to speech is staggeringly difficult: he must somehow deal with a signal that is an encoding of an encoding of an encoding. . . . Indeed, the difficulties *are* very real, as many people have discovered in trying to build speech recognizers or automatic parsing programs. But the human being does it so easily that we can only suppose he has access to full knowledge (even if implicit) of the coding relationships. These relationships, or a model of the process by which the encoding is done, could fully rationalize for him the involved relation of speech signal to underlying message and so provide the working basis for his personal speech decoder [Liberman 1970].

Our primary interest is, of course, in how speech is perceived, since this is where we would expect to find relationships with reading and its acquisition. It is not obvious that a person's implicit knowledge of how his own speech is produced might help to explain how another's speech can be perceived. Actually, we think that it does, although, even without such a premise, one would need to know how the encoding is done since that is what the decoder must undo. So before we turn to a discussion of how speech is perceived, let us first consider how it is produced.

The Making of Spoken Language

Our aim is to trace in a general way the events that befall a message from its inception as an idea to its expression as speech. Much will be tentative, or even wrong, at the start, but can be more definite in the final stages of speech production. There, where our interest is keenest, the experimental evidence is well handled by the kinds of models often used by communications engineers. This, together with the view that speech is an integral part of language, suggests that we might find it useful to extrapolate a communications model to all stages of language production.

The conventional block diagram in Figure 3 can serve as a way of indicating that a message (carried on the connecting lines) undergoes sequential transformations as it travels through a succession of processors. The figure shows a simple, linear arrangement of the principal processors

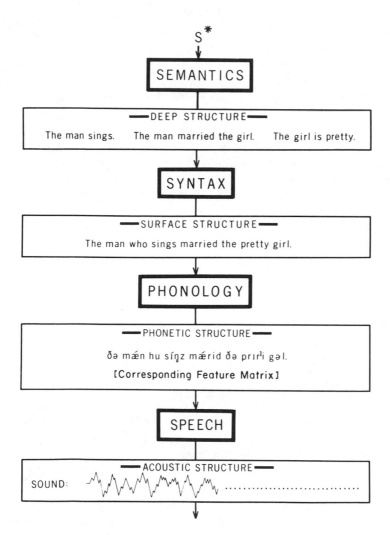

Figure 3. A process model for the production of spoken language. The intended message flows down through a series of processors (the blocks with heavy outlines). Descriptions are given (in the blocks with light outlines) of the changing form of the message as it moves from processor to processor. (Adapted from Liberman, 1970, p. 305.)

(the blocks with heavy outlines) that are needed to produce spoken language and gives descriptions (in the blocks with light outlines) of the changing form of the message as it moves from processor to processor on its way to the outside world. The diagram is adapted from Liberman [1970] and is based (in its central portions) on the general view of language structure proposed by Chomsky and his colleagues [Chomsky 1957, 1965; Chomsky and Miller, 1963]. We can guess that a simple, linear process of this kind will serve only as a first approximation; in particular, it lacks the feedback and feedforward paths that we would expect to find in a real-life process.

We know quite well how to represent the final (acoustic) form of a message—assumed, for convenience, to be a sentence—but not how to describe its initial form. S*, then, symbolizes both the nascent sentence and our ignorance about its prelinguistic form. The operation of the semantic processor is likewise uncertain, but its output should provide the deep structure—corresponding to the three simple sentences shown for illustration—on which syntactic operations will later be performed. Presumably, then, the semantic processor will somehow select and rearrange both lexical and relational information that is implicit in S*, perhaps in the form of semantic feature matrices.

The intermediate and end results of the next two operations, labeled Syntax and Phonology, have been much discussed by generative grammarians. For present purposes, it is enough to note that the first of them, syntactic processing, is usually viewed as a two-stage operation, yielding first a phrase structure representation in which related items have been grouped and labeled, and second a surface structure representation which has been shaped by various transformations into an encoded string of the kind indicated in the figure (again, by its plain English counterpart). Some consequences of the restructuring of the message by the syntactic processor are that (1) a linear sequence has been constructed from the unordered cluster of units in the deep structure and (2) there has been the telescoping of the structure, hence encoding, that we saw in Figure 2 and discussed in the previous section.

Further restructuring of the message occurs in the phonological processor. It converts (encodes) the more or less abstract units of its input into a time-ordered array of feature states, that is, a matrix showing the state of each feature for each phonetic event in its turn. An alternate representation would be a phonetic string that is capable of emerging at last into the external world as a written phonetic transcription.

This is about where contemporary grammar stops, on the basis that the conversion into speech from either the internal or external phonetic representation—although it requires human intervention—is straightforward and essentially trivial. But we have seen, with *bag* of Figure 1 as an example, that the acoustic form of a message is a heavily encoded version of its phonetic form. This implies processing that is far from trivial—just how far is suggested by Figure 4, which shows the major conversions required to transform an internal phonetic representation into the external acoustic waveforms of speech. We see that the speech processor, represented by a single block in Figure 3, comprises several subprocessors, each with its own function: first, the abstract feature matrices of the phonetic structure must be given physiological substance as neural signals (commands) if they are to guide and control the production of speech; these neural commands then bring about a pattern of muscle contractions; these, in turn, cause the articulators to move and the vocal tract to assume a succession of shapes; finally, the vocal tract shape (and the acoustic excitation due to air flow through the glottis or other constrictions) determines the spoken sound.

Where, in this sequence of operations, does the encoding occur? If we trace the message upstream—processor by processor, starting from the acoustic outflow—we find that the relationships between speech waveform and vocal tract shape are essentially one-to-one at every moment and can be computed, though the computations are complex [Fant 1960; Flanagan 1965]. However, at the next higher step—the conversion of muscle contractions into vocal tract shapes—there is substantial encoding: each new set of contractions starts from whatever configuration and state of motion already exist as the result of preceding contractions, and it typically occurs before the last set is ended, with the result that the shape and motion of the tract at any instant represent the merged effects of past and present events. This alone could account for the kind of encoding we saw in Figure 1, but whether it accounts for all of it, or only a part, remains to be seen.

We would not expect much encoding in the next higher conversion— from neural command to muscle contraction—at least in terms of the identities of the muscles and the temporal order of their activation. However, the contractions may be variable in amount due to preplanning at the next higher level or to local adjustment, via gamma-efferent feedback, to produce only so much contraction as is needed to achieve a target length.

At the next higher conversion—from features to neural commands—we encounter two disparate problems: one involves functional, physiological relationships very much like the ones we have just been considering, except that their location in the nervous system puts them well beyond

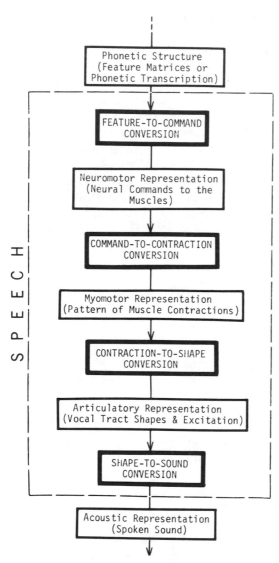

Figure 4. Internal structure of the speech processor. Again, the message flows from top to bottom through successive processors (the blocks with heavy outlines), with intermediate descriptions given (in the blocks with light outlines).

the reach of present experimental methods. The other problem has to do with the boundary between two kinds of description. A characteristic of this boundary is that the feature matrix (or the phonetic transcription) provided by the phonological processor is still quite abstract as compared with the physiological type of feature that is needed as an input to the feature-to-command conversion. The simple case—and perhaps the correct one—would be that the two sets of features are fully congruent, that is, that the features at the output of the phonology will map directly onto the distinctive components of the articulatory gestures. Failing some such simple relationship, translation or restructuring would be required in greater or lesser degree to arrive at a set of features which are "real" in a physiological sense. The requirement is for features rather than segmental (phonetic) units, since the output of the conversion we are considering is a set of neural commands that go *in parallel* to the muscles of several, essentially independent articulators. Indeed, it is only because the features—and the articulators—operate in this parallel manner that speech can be fast even though the articulators are slow.

The simplistic hypothesis noted above, that there may be a direct relationship between the phonological features and characteristic parts of the gesture, has the obvious advantage that it would avoid a substantial amount of encoding in the total feature-to-command conversion. Even so, two complications would remain. In actual articulation, the gestures must be coordinated into a smoothly flowing pattern of motion which will need the cooperative activity of various muscles (in addition to those principally involved) in ways that depend on the current state of the gesture, that is, in ways that are context dependent. Thus, the *total* neuromotor representation will show some degree of restructuring even on a moment-to-moment basis. There is a further and more important sense in which encoding is to be expected: if speech is to flow smoothly, a substantial amount of preplanning must occur, in addition to moment-by-moment coordination. We know, indeed, that this happens for the segmental components over units at least as large as the syllable and for the suprasegmentals over units at least as large as the phrase. Most of these coordinations will not be marked in the phonetic structure and so must be supplied by the feature-to-command conversion. What we see at this level, then, is true encoding over a longer span of the utterance than the span affected by lower level conversions and perhaps some further restructuring even within the shorter span.

There is ample evidence of encoding over still longer stretches than those affected by the speech processor. The sentence of Figure 2 provides an example—one which implies processor and conversion operations that lie higher in the hierarchical structure of language than does speech. There is no reason to deny these processors the kind of neural machinery that was assumed for the feature-to-command conversion; however, we have very little experimental access to the mechanisms at these levels, and we can infer the structure and operation only from behavioral studies and from observations of normal speech.

In the foregoing account of speech production, the emphasis has been on processes and on models for the various conversions. The same account can also be labeled a grammar in the sense that it specifies relationships between representations of the message at successive stages. It will be important, in the conference discussions on the relationship of speaking to reading, that we bear in mind the difference between the kind of description used thus far—a process grammar—and the descriptions given, for example, by a generative transformational grammar. In the latter case, one is dealing with formal rules that relate successive representations of the message, but there is now no basis for assuming that these rules mirror actual processes. Indeed, proponents of generative grammar are careful to point out that such an implication is not intended; unfortunately, their terminology is rich in words that seem to imply active operations and cause-and-effect relationships. This can lead to confusion in discussions about the *processes* that are involved in listening and reading and how they make contact with each other. Hence, we shall need to use the descriptions of rule-based grammars with some care in dealing with experimental data and model mechanisms that reflect, however crudely, the real-life processes of language behavior.

Perception of Speech

We come back to an earlier point, slightly rephrased: how can perceptual mechanisms possibly cope with speech signals that are as fast and complex as the production process has made them? The central theme of most current efforts to answer that question is that perception somehow borrows the machinery of production. The explanations differ in various ways, but the similarities substantially outweigh the differences.

There was a time, though, when acoustic processing per se was thought to account for speech perception. It was tempting to suppose that the patterns seen in spectrograms could be recognized *as patterns* in audition just as in vision [Cooper, Liberman et al. 1951]. On a more analytic level, the distinctive features described by Jakobson, Fant, and Halle [1963] seemed to offer a basis for direct auditory analysis, leading to recovery of the phoneme string. Also at the analytic level, spectrographic patterns were used extensively in a search for the acoustic cues for speech perception [Liberman 1957; Liberman, Cooper et al. 1967; Stevens and House, 1972]. All of these approaches reflected, in one way or another, the early faith we have already mentioned in the existence of acoustic invariants in speech and in their usefulness for speech recognition by man or machine.

Experimental work on speech did not support this faith. Although the search for the acoustic cues was successful, the cues that were found could be more easily described in articulatory than in acoustic terms. Even the "locus," as a derived invariant, had a simple articulatory correlate [Delattre, Liberman et al. 1955]. Although the choice of articulation over acoustic pattern as a basis for speech perception was not easy to justify since there was almost always a one-to-one correspondence between the two, there were occasional exceptions to this concurrence that pointed to an articulatory basis, and these were used to support a motor theory of speech perception. Older theories of this kind had invoked actual motor activity (though perhaps minimal in amount) in tracking incoming speech, followed by feedback of sensory information from the periphery to let the listener know what both he and the speaker were articulating. The revised formulation that Liberman [1957, p. 122] gave of a motor theory to account for the data about acoustic cues was quite general, but it explicitly excluded any reference to the periphery as a necessary element: "All of this [information about exceptional cases] strongly suggests . . . that speech is perceived by reference to articulation—that is, that the articulatory movements and their sensory effects mediate between the acoustic stimulus and the event we call perception. In its extreme and old-fashioned form, this view says that we overtly mimic the incoming speech sounds and then respond to the appropriate receptive and tactile stimuli that are produced by our own articulatory movements. For a variety of reasons such an extreme position is wholly untenable, and if we are to deal with perception in the adult, we must assume that the process is somehow short-circuited—that is, that the reference to articulatory movements and their sensory consequences must somehow occur in the brain without getting out into the periphery."

A further hypothesis about how the mediation might be accomplished [Liberman, Cooper et al. 1968] supposes that there is a spread of neural activity within and among sensory and motor networks so that some of the same, interlocking nets are active whether one is speaking (and listening to his own speech) or merely listening to speech from someone else. Hence, the neural activity initiated by listening, as it spreads to the motor networks, could cause the whole process of production to be started up just as it would be in speaking (but with spoken output suppressed); further, there would be the appropriate interaction with those same neural mechanisms—whatever they are—by which one is ordinarily aware of what he is saying when he himself is the speaker. This is equivalent, insofar as awareness of another's speech is concerned, to running the production machinery backward, assuming that the interaction between sensory and motor networks lies at about the linguistic level of the features (represented neurally, of course) but that the linkage to awareness is at some higher level and in less primitive terms. Whether or not such a hypothesis about the role of neural mechanisms in speaking and listening can survive does not really affect the main point of a more general motor theory, but it can serve here as an example of the kind of machinery that is implied by a motor theory and as a basis for comparison with the mechanisms that serve other theoretical formulations.

The model for speech perception proposed by Stevens and Halle [1967; Halle and Stevens 1964] also depends heavily on mechanisms of production. The analysis-by-synthesis procedure was formulated initially in computer terms, though functional parallels with biological mechanisms were also considered. The computer-like description makes it easier to be specific about the kinds of mechanisms that are proposed but somewhat harder to project the model into a human skull.

It is unnecessary to trace in detail the operation of the analysis-by-synthesis model but Figure 5, from Stevens' [1960] paper on the subject, can serve as a reminder of much that is already familiar. The processing within the first loop (inside the dashed box) compares spectral information received from the speech input and held in a temporary store with spectral information generated by a model of the articulatory mechanism (Model I). This model receives its instructions from a control unit that generates articulatory states and uses heuristic processes to select a likely one on the basis of past history and the degree of mismatch that is reported to it by a comparator. The articulatory description that is used by Model I (and passed on to the next loop) might have any one of several representations: *acoustical,* in terms of the normal modes of vibration of the vocal tract; or *anatomical,* descriptive of actual vocal tract configurations; or *neurophysiological,* specifying control signals that would cause the vocal tract to change shape. Most of Stevens' discussion deals with vocal tract configuration (and excitation); hence, he treats comparisons in the second loop as between input configurations (from the preceding loop) and those generated by an articulatory control (Model II) that could also be used to drive a vocal-tract-analog synthesizer external to the analysis-by-synthesis system. There is a second

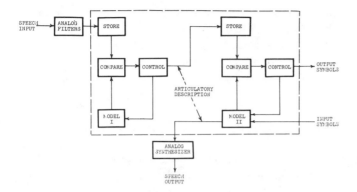

Figure 5. Analysis-by-synthesis model of speech recognition. The acoustic signal enters at upper left and is "recognized" in the form of a string of phonetic symbols that leave at center right. Model I stores the rules that relate articulatory descriptions to speech spectra, and model II stores the rules that relate phonetic symbols to articulatory descriptions. Model II can serve also to generate a speech output from an input of phonetic symbols (Stevens, 1960, p. 52).

controller, again with dual functions: it generates a string of phonetic elements that serve as the input to Model II, and it applies heuristics to select, from among the possible phonetic strings, one that will maintain an articulatory match at the comparator.

A virtue of the analysis-by-synthesis model is that its components have explicit functions, even though some of these component units are bound to be rather complicated devices. The comparator, explicit here, is implicit in a neural network model in the sense that some neural nets will be aroused—and others will not—on the basis of degree of similarity between the firing patterns of the selected nets and the incoming pattern of neural excitation. Comparisons and decisions of this kind may control the spread of excitation throughout all levels of the neural mechanism, just as a sophisticated guessing game is used by the analysis-by-synthesis model to work its way, stage by stage, to a phonetic representation—and presumably on upstream to consciousness. In short, the two models differ substantially in the kinds of machinery they invoke and the degree of explicitness that this allows in setting forth the underlying philosophy: they differ very little in the reliance they put on the mechanisms of production to do most of the work of perception.

The general point of view of analysis-by-synthesis is incorporated in the constructivist view of cognitive processes in general, with speech perception as an interesting special case. Thus, Neisser [1967, p. 10] in the introduction to *Cognitive Psychology,* says, "The central assertion is that seeing, hearing, and remembering are all acts of construction, which may make more or less use of stimulus information depending on circumstances. The constructive processes are assumed to have two stages, of which the first is fast, crude, wholistic, and parallel while the second is deliberate, attentive, detailed, and sequential."

It seems difficult to come to grips with the specific mechanisms (and their functions) that the constructivists would use in dealing with spoken language to make the total perceptual process operate. A significant feature, though, is the assumption of a two-stage process, with the constructive act initiated on the basis of rather crude information. In this, it differs from both of the models that we have thus far considered. Either model can, if need be, tolerate input data that are somewhat rough and noisy, but both are designed to work best with "clean" data, since they operate first on the detailed structure of the input and then proceed stepwise toward a more global form of the message.

Stevens and House (1972) have proposed a model for speech perception that is, however, much closer to the constructivist view of the process than was the early analysis-by-synthesis model of Figure 5. It assumes that spoken language has evolved in such a way as to use auditory distinctions and attributes that are well matched to optimal performances of the speech generating mechanism; also, that the adult listener has command of a catalog of correspondences between the auditory attributes and the articulatory gestures (of approximately syllabic length) that give rise to them when he is a speaker. Hence, the listener can, by consulting his catalog, infer the speaker's gestures. However. some further analysis is needed to arrive at the phonological features, although their correspondence with articulatory events will often be quite close. In any case, this further analysis allows the "construction" (by a control unit) of a tentative hypothesis about the sequence of linguistic units and the constituent structure of the utterance. The hypothesis, plus the generative rules possessed by every speaker of the language, can then yield an articulatory version of the utterance. In perception, actual articulation is suppressed but the information about it goes to a comparator, where it is matched against the articulation inferred from the incoming speech. If both versions match, the hypothesized utterance is confirmed; if not, the resulting error signal guides the control unit in modifying the hypothesis. Clearly, this model employs analysis-by-synthesis principles. It differs from earlier models mainly in the degree of autonomy that the control unit has in constructing hypothesis and in the linguistic level and length of utterance that are involved.

The approach to speech perception taken by Chomsky and Halle [1968] also invokes analysis-by-synthesis, with even more autonomy in the construction of hypotheses; thus, "We might suppose . . . that a correct description of perceptual processes would be something like this. The hearer makes use of certain cues and certain expectations to determine the syntactic structure and semantic content of an utterance. Given a hypothesis as to its syntactic structure—in particular its surface structure—he uses the phonological principles that he controls to determine a phonetic shape. The hypothesis will then be accepted if it is not too radically at variance with the acoustic material, where the range of permitted discrepancy may vary widely with conditions and many individual factors. Given acceptance of such a hypothesis, what the hearer 'hears' is what is internally generated by the rules. That is, he will 'hear' the phonetic shape determined by the postulated syntactic structure and the internalized rules." This carries the idea of analysis-by-synthesis in constructivist form almost to the point of saying that only the grosser cues and expectations are needed for *perfect* reception of the message (as the listener would have said it), unless there is a gross mismatch with the input information, which is otherwise largely ignored. This extension is made explicit with respect to the perception of stress. Mechanisms are not provided, but they would not be expected in a rule-oriented account.

In all the above approaches, the complexities inherent in the acoustic signal are dealt with indirectly rather than by postulating a second mechanism (at least as complex as the production machinery) to perform a straight-forward auditory analysis of the spoken message. Nevertheless, *some* analysis is needed to provide neural signals from the auditory system for use in generating hypotheses and in error comparisons at an appropriate stage of the production process. Obviously, the need for analysis will be least if the comparisons are made as far down in the production process as possible. It may be, though, that direct auditory analysis plays a larger role. Stevens [1971] has postulated that the analysis is done (by auditory property detectors) in terms of acoustic features that qualify as distinctive features of the language, since they are both inherently distinctive and directly related to stable articulatory states. Such an auditory analysis might not yield complete information about the phonological features of running speech, but enough, nevertheless, to activate analysis-by-synthesis operations. Comparisons could then guide the listener to self-generation of the correct message. Perhaps Stevens will give us an expanded account of this view of speech perception in his discussion of the present paper.

All these models for perception, despite their differences, have in common a listener who actively participates in producing speech as well as in listening to it in order that he may compare his internal utterances with the incoming one. It may be that the comparators are the functional component of central interest in using any of these models to understand how reading is done by adults and how it is learned by children. The level (or levels) at which comparisons are made—hence, the size and kind of unit compared—determines how far the analysis of auditory (and visual) information has to be carried, what must be held in short-term memory, and what units of the child's spoken language he is aware of—or can be taught to be aware of—in relating them to visual entities.

Can we guess what these units might be, or at least what upper and lower bounds would be consistent with the above models of the speech process? It is the production side of the total process to which attention would turn most naturally, given the primacy ascribed to it in all that has been said thus far. We have noted that the final representation of the message, before it leaves the central nervous system on its way to the muscles, is an array of features and a corresponding (or derived) pattern of neural commands to the articulators. Thus, the features would appear to be the smallest units of production that are readily available for comparison with units derived from auditory analysis. But we noted also that smoothly flowing articulation requires a restructuring of *groups* of features into syllable-size or word-size units, hence, these might serve instead as the units for comparison. In either case, the lower bound on duration would approximate that of a syllable.

The upper bound may well be set by auditory rather than productive processes. Not only would more sophisticated auditory analysis be required to match higher levels—and longer strings—of the message as represented in production, but also the demands on short-term memory capacity would increase. The latter alone could be decisive, since the information rate that is needed to specify the acoustic signal is very high—indeed, so high that some kind of auditory processing must be done to allow the storage of even word-length stretches. Thus, we would guess that the capacity of short-term memory for purely auditory forms of the speech signal would set an upper bound on duration hardly greater than that of words or short phrases. The limits, *after conversion to linguistic form,* are however substantially longer, as they would have to be for effective communication.

Intuitively, these minimal units seem about right: words, syllables, or short phrases seem to be what we say, and hear ourselves saying, when we talk. Moreover, awareness of these as minimal units is consistent with the reference-to-production models we have been considering, since all of production that lies below the first comparator has been turned over to bone-and-muscle mechanisms (aided, perhaps, by gamma-efferent feedback) and so is inaccessible in any direct way to the neural mechanisms responsible for awareness. As adults, we know how to "analyze" speech into still smaller (phonetic) segments, but this is an acquired skill and not one to be expected of the young child.

Can it be that the child's level of awareness of minimal units in speech is part of his problem in learning to read? Words should pose no serious problem so long as the total inventory remains small and the visual symbols are sufficiently dissimilar. But phonic methods, to help him deal with a larger vocabulary, may be assuming an awareness that he does not have of the phonetic segments of speech, especially his own speech. If so, perhaps learning to read comes second to learning to speak and listen *with awareness.* This is a view that Mattingly will, I believe, develop in depth. It can serve here as an example of the potential utility of models of the speech process in providing insights into relationships between speech and learning to read.

In Conclusion

The emphasis here has been on the processes of speaking and listening as integral parts of the total process of communicating by spoken language. This concentration on speech reflects both its role as a counterpart to reading and its accessibility via experimentation. The latter point has not been exploited in the present account, but it is nonetheless important as a reason for focusing on this aspect of language. Most of the unit processors that were attributed to speech in the models we have been discussing can, indeed, be probed experimentally: thus, with respect to the production of speech, electromyography and cinefluorography have much to say about how the articulators are moved into the observed configurations, and sound spectrograms give highly detailed accounts of the dynamics of articulation and acoustic excitation; examples with respect to speech perception include the use of synthetic speech in discovering the acoustic cues inherent in speech, and of dichotic methods for evading peripheral effects in order to overload the central processor and so to study its operation. Several of the papers to follow will deal with comparable methods for studying visual information processing. Perhaps the emphasis given here to processes and to the interdependence of perception and production will provide a useful basis for considering the linkages between reading and speech.

References

Chomsky, N., 1957. *Syntactic Structures*. The Hague: Mouton.

———, 1965. *Aspects of the Theory of Syntax*. Cambridge, Mass.: M.I.T. Press.

Chomsky, N., and M. Halle, 1968. *The Sound Pattern of English*. New York: Harper and Row.

Chomsky, N., and G. A. Miller, 1963. Introduction to the formal analysis of natural languages. In *Handbook of Mathematical Psychology*, R. D. Luce, R. R. Bush, and E. Galanter (eds.), New York: Wiley.

Coffey, J. L., 1963. The development and evaluation of the Battelle Aural Reading Device. In *Proceedings of the International Congress on Technology and Blindness*, New York: American Foundation for the Blind.

Cooper, F. S., 1950. Research on reading machines for the blind. In *Blindness: Modern Approaches to the Unseen Environment*, P. A. Zahl (ed.), Princeton: Princeton University Press.

Cooper, F. S., A. M. Liberman, and J. M. Borst, 1951. The interconversion of audible and visible patterns as a basis for research in the perception of speech. *Proc. Nat. Acad. Sci.* 37:318–328.

Delattre, P. C., A. M. Liberman, and F. S. Cooper, 1955. Acoustic loci and transitional cues for consonants. *J. Acoust. Soc. Amer.* 27:769–773.

Fant, C. G. M., 1960. *Acoustic Theory of Speech Production*. The Hague: Mouton.

Flanagan, J. L., 1965. *Speech Analysis Synthesis and Perception*. New York: Academic Press.

Halle, M., and K. N. Stevens, 1964. Speech recognition: A model and a program for research. *IRE Trans. Info. Theory*, 1962, *IT-8*, 155–59. Also in *The Structure of Language*, J. A. Fodor and J. J. Katz (eds.), Englewood Cliffs, N.J.: Prentice-Hall.

Jakobson, R., C. G. M. Fant, and M. Halle, 1963. *Preliminaries to Speech Analysis*. Cambridge, Mass.: M.I.T. Press.

Liberman, A. M., 1957. Some results of research on speech perception. *J. Acoust. Soc. Amer.* 29:117–123.

———, 1970. The grammars of speech and language. *Cogn. Psych.* 1:301–323.

Liberman, A. M., F. S. Cooper, D. P. Shankweiler, and M. Studdert-Kennedy, 1967. Perception of the speech code. *Psych. Rev.* 74:431–461.

Liberman, A. M., F. S. Cooper, M. Studdert-Kennedy, K. S. Harris, and D. P. Shankweiler, 1968. On the efficiency of speech sounds. *Z. Phonetik, Sprachwissenschaft u. Kommunikationsforschung* 21:21–32.

Miller, G. A., 1956. The magical number seven, plus or minus two, or, some limits on our capacity for processing information. *Psych. Rev.* 63:81–96.

Neisser, U., 1967. *Cognitive Psychology.* New York: Appleton-Century-Crofts.

Orr, D. B., H. L. Friedman, and J. C. C. Williams, 1965. Trainability of listening comprehension of speeded discourse. *J. Ed. Psych.* 56:148–156.

Stevens, K. N., 1960. Toward a model for speech recognition. *J. Acoust. Soc. Amer.* 32:47–55.

————, 1971. Perception of phonetic segments: Evidence from phonology, acoustics, and psychoacoustics. In *Perception of Language,* D. L. Horton and J. J. Jenkins (eds.), Columbus, Ohio: Merrill.

Stevens, K. N., and M. Halle, 1967. Remarks on analysis by synthesis and distinctive features. In *Models for the Perception of Speech and Visual Form,* W. Wathen-Dunn (ed.), Cambridge, Mass.: M.I.T. Press.

Stevens, K. N., and A. S. House, 1972. Speech perception. In *Foundations of Modern Auditory Theory,* Vol. 2, J. Tobias (ed.), New York: Academic Press.

Studdert-Kennedy, M., and F. S. Cooper, 1966. High-performance reading machines for the blind: Psychological problems, technological problems, and status. In *Proceedings of the International Conference on Sensory Devices for the Blind,* R. Dufton (ed.), London: St. Dunstan's.

KENNETH N. STEVENS

Segments, Features, and Analysis by Synthesis

A Discussion of Cooper's Paper

Cooper has made quite clear the special nature of the speech production and perception processes, and has indicated the form that models of these processes must take. He has touched on the important attributes of speech, both in its underlying form and its manifestation in the acoustic signal. I shall try to expand on certain ideas that he has presented, perhaps approaching them from a slightly different point of view.

I

Let me first explore further the manner in which phonetic segments are coded in the acoustic signal. Cooper has given a graphic example of the fact that the acoustic manifestations of a given phoneme may be spread out in time, sometimes overlapping the cues for an adjacent phoneme. In order to understand the reasons for these characteristics of speech, we need to look in detail at the articulatory activities that give rise to the speech sound output.

The production of speech can be regarded as a sequence of movements from one articulatory target to another. A phonetic segment can be defined in terms of such a target, which specifies the positions or shapes that are to be achieved by the various articulatory structures (although, of course, not all structures are necessarily involved in actualizing a particular segment). During rapid speech, the structures may not always reach their target positions, since their motions may be sluggish, and an instruction to move toward a new target may be initiated before the previous target is reached.

There are three ways in which the information in the sound wave can provide cues for the identification of a phonetic segment or for some features of that segment.

(a) For some phonetic segments, the sound radiated from the mouth at the time the articulatory structures are close to their targets and are in more or less fixed positions gives relatively complete information about the features that characterize the segment. Examples of such segments are nondiphthongized vowels and strident fricative consonants like [s] and [š].

(b) In the case of some classes of segments, the characteristics of the radiated sound when the articulators are in their target positions are not sufficient to identify all the features of the segment. For example, when there is a complete closure at some point along the length of the vocal tract, as in the case of a stop consonant, no sound emerges from the mouth. Acoustic attributes that identify place of articulation for a stop consonant reside in the time interval when the articulators are moving either toward or away from the constricted configuration. Thus for a stop consonant like [d] occurring before a vowel, information about the place of articulation is carried in the 40-odd msec following release of the closure, that is, after the tongue blade has shifted away from the target position for [d] and is moving toward a position appropriate for the following vowel. These acoustic cues reside in a relatively brief, transient time interval. All phonetic segments with the feature [+consonantal] [Chomsky and Halle 1968] seem to have this attribute that at least some acoustic cues for the segment reside in the rapid transitions toward or away from the articulatory target and are, in a sense, nonsynchronous with the target.

(c) There are certain acoustic properties that specify the durations of events or that indicate slow changes in the spectral characteristics of the signal. Some of these properties may provide cues for the identification of segmental features that characterize the lexical items. Others help to identify features that are related to the syntactic bracketing of the utterance, or provide cues for word boundaries. For example, information about voicing of a final stop consonant following a stressed vowel is contained in the duration of the vowel (e.g., [bæt] versus [bæːd]). The stressed vowel in a polysyllabic word is indicated by some kind of change in fundamental frequency, the change extending over perhaps several hundred msec in the vicinity of the vowel. The decoding of acoustic cues of this type requires that the acoustic data be stored in some form for several hundred msec, in order to measure the duration of one event in relation to another, or to interpret the characteristics of the signal at one point in time in the context of or with reference to those at another.

II

Cooper's Figure 4 is a block diagram representing the speech production process as a series of operations on a string of discrete phonetic segments, yielding a sound output in which acoustic evidence for the segments and features has been greatly smoothed out and distorted. It may be misleading, however, to view the process as a linear sequence of operations ending with an acoustic representation that is maximally remote from the discrete phonetic input. The features and segments in fact owe their existence to the special properties of the peripheral speech-generating mechanism and the sound-processing capabilities of the auditory system. When the articulatory structures assume a certain set of positions, the sound output that results from these articulatory maneuvers has a set of distinctive characteristics that can be discriminated in the auditory system from other acoustic outputs. This combination of articulatory and acoustic events defines a feature.

Thus, for example, there is a feature [+continuant] for which the distinctive acoustic output is the lack of an abrupt increase or decrease in sound amplitude. Complete closure at some point along the midline of the vocal tract is necessary in order to achieve this kind of acoustic output when the closure is released.

Or, there is a feature [+coronal] which specifies that the blade of the tongue is to be raised and brought close to or in contact with some point along the hard palate. This articulatory gesture (or the act of releasing the tongue blade to form a following vowel) gives rise again to a well-defined property of the sound that distinguishes it clearly from the sound resulting from other gestures. The distinctive acoustic property may depend on the degree of closure formed in the vocal tract by the tongue blade, and on what is happening in other parts of the vocal tract. Thus the consonants [n s t] all have the feature [+coronal], although the acoustic attributes that indicate this fact are somewhat different.

A way of viewing the "phonetic representation" that forms the output of the phonological component of the grammar at the top of Cooper's Figure 4, therefore, is as a sequence of goals or targets that are to be actualized by the articulatory mechanism. The commands to the muscles to achieve a particular goal depend on the previous position of the articulatory structures. In this view, therefore, the invariance lies not in the neural commands to the muscles but in the target shapes and positions that are to be achieved by the structures. It would suggest that greater invariance is likely to be found in an X-ray picture of the vocal apparatus than in the neural activities underlying the movements. The underlying neural representation of a feature, whatever form it might take, may require some processing or reorganization (depending on the context) before commands are transmitted to the muscles.

III

Cooper has argued that direct auditory analysis which scans for acoustic attributes or cues cannot easily accomplish the decoding of speech, since the acoustic cues for many of the features are strongly context-dependent. He notes that some proposed models of speech perception attempt to circumvent this difficulty by making reference to the generative process. Analysis by synthesis is one such model. Our views about analysis by synthesis have evolved somewhat since we proposed the model referred to in Cooper's presentation, and it may be worth reviewing the analysis-by-synthesis framework as we now see it.

A block diagram of a current analysis-by-synthesis model, at the level where reference is made to the acoustic signal, is shown in Figure 1. The sound first undergoes some kind of peripheral analysis and is then placed in temporary store, as in the early stages of the model reproduced as Figure 5 in Cooper's paper. The peripheral analysis is presumably somewhat more complex than a simple analog filtering, and may involve some kinds of property detectors, as well as representing the signal in the form of running spectra or the equivalent. We attach particular importance to a component labeled "preliminary analysis" (not shown in the version in Cooper's paper). The role of this component is to derive from the signal certain phonetic features that are not strongly context-dependent and can be identified by direct operations on the acoustic attributes that are accessible at the output of the peripheral

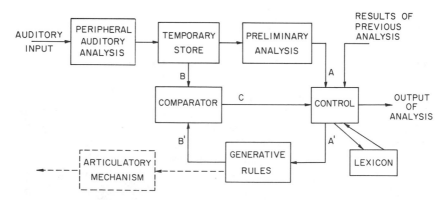

Figure 1. Analysis-by-synthesis model. See description in text.

analysis. The output of the preliminary analysis is a partial specification of the feature matrix of the utterance.

The heart of the model is the control component, which directs the operation of the system. This component has access to (1) the results of the preliminary analysis as a partial feature specification of the utterance; (2) the results of analysis of earlier parts of the utterance, including lexical items and their syntactic and semantic features; (3) the lexicon; and (4) the output of the comparator (to be described below). On the basis of these kinds of information, the control component makes a hypothesis concerning the representation of the utterance in terms of phonetic segments and features. This hypothesized representation forms the input to a set of generative rules, which determine certain relevant attributes that the signal would possess if it had this phonetic representation. These attributes are compared (in the comparator) with the attributes of the analyzed signal residing in temporary store, and the comparator provides to the control component an indication of the degree of match. As indicated at the lower left of the figure, the output of the generative rules can also take a form appropriate for controlling the articulatory mechanism, to produce an acoustic output.

Close scrutiny of this model reveals several inadequacies and unanswered questions. The representation at points B and B′ in Figure 1 is presumably in prelinguistic or precategorical form. But what is the precise nature of the temporary memory in which this representation is stored? The output C of the comparator is also presumably in prelinguistic form, but what kinds of comparisons are made between B and B′ to yield the "error" C? A phonetic representation in terms of segments and features (at some level of abstraction) appears at points A and A′. But how does the control component sift all the information that is available to it to yield an hypothesized phonetic string A′? The control component would assume a still larger burden if we were to add to this model an input from the visual system during reading, since this processed input would presumably enter the control component directly. Here it would have access to the lexicon and to the results of previous analysis, stored in some kind of short-term memory.

In contrast with some earlier versions of analysis-by-synthesis, the model of Figure 1 provides for both a direct analysis of the signal and an internal generative process. The relative importance of these two types of processing would presumably depend on the degree to which context must be utilized in decoding the input. While in earlier discussions we stressed the active, generative aspects of the model, we would now assign increased importance to the direct analysis. Our experience with acoustic analysis of speech convinces us that many attributes of the signal for certain features do indeed often remain invariant with context, if one permits the inventory of attributes to include certain kinds of time-varying spectral changes as well as simple quasistatic spectral patterns.

Reference
Chomsky, N., and M. Halle, 1968. *Sound Pattern of English*. New York: Harper and Row.

General Discussion of Papers by Cooper and Stevens

Miller asked, in view of the parallels between speech and reading presented earlier by Gibson, whether Cooper or Stevens thought that analysis-by-synthesis is an appropriate model for both processes. Stevens thought not, since there is nothing in reading corresponding to the lack of invariance between the speech signal and the underlying phonetic segments that makes synthesis necessary. At higher linguistic levels, however, analysis-by-synthesis may play a role in both reading and writing. Cooper agreed. He pointed out that while learning to understand speech involves hearing oneself talk, learning to read need not involve seeing oneself write.

Kolers asked what units—phonemes, words, or syntactic sequences—are hypothesized in an analysis-by-synthesis model. Stevens replied that at the lowest level, articulatory features of some kind are hypothesized, though he was not happy with the articulatory description implied by the features, and wanted "better kinds of units."

Cooper said that a hypothesis in terms of articulatory features is the most likely. Conrad [1964], Studdert-Kennedy and Shankweiler [1970], and Miller and Nicely [1955] have done experiments that confirm the naturalness of articulatory categories, such as place and manner, in speech perception. Furthermore, since the production mechanism drastically restructures the message, this mechanism must somehow be taken account of in perception. Analysis-by-synthesis is needed, at the very least, to recover the form of message at the point where the motor nerves contact the muscles: "You make use of the analysis-by-synthesis loop primarily to account for the strange things that the nervous system can't do, that it must delegate to those very inferior workmen at the muscular and bone and cartilage levels."

Kolers suggested that the listener must therefore be doing at least as much decoding as the speaker. Cooper agreed, but Stevens thought that the listener needs to check his hypotheses only sporadically to ensure that they are being consistently fulfilled. This would require much less computation. Cooper pointed to a difficulty with this idea. The message up to the point at which it was checked would have to be stored in unanalyzed form for later comparison, which seemed to him unlikely. He suggested as an alternative, that analysis-by-synthesis goes on continuously, so as to keep down the amount of unanalyzed material to be stored, but that the listener may well fail to pay attention continuously.

Norman observed that the two storage systems in Cooper's Figure

5 do not account for semantic synthesis. What other types of storage would be required? Cooper replied that the processes of production and perception must operate in stages, because of limits on memory if for no other reason, and this implies a series of representations, each part of an analysis-by-synthesis loop. This assumes that one has to go "all the way to the top" in order to follow what had been said. But his introspections about his consciousness of silent speech suggest that this consciousness is at a low neural level, close to the output.

Norman commented that neither of the two memories in Cooper's Figure 5—one a "tape recorder" memory and the other a phonetic memory—seem to correspond to what has usually been called short-term memory by psychologists.

Gibson asked whether Stevens and Cooper thought that speech perception is unrelated to meaning. Cooper said that this is true in a sense: speech perception can go on without reference to meaning. Thus, subjects can "shadow" speech but are unable to report what they shadow. Kolers said that the same observation can be made about conference translators, yet they obviously must deal with the meaning of what is translated. Kavanagh said that the stenotypist for the present conference had told him that "she does follow the context, but if she starts to think about it, she breaks up the stream."

Halle set forth the boundary conditions which he thought any reasonable theory of speech perception must meet. It must explain the speaker-hearer's ability to repeat a sentence he has just heard, to paraphrase the sentence meaningfully, to answer questions, and to correct unconsciously minor phonetic details in what the speaker has actually said. These abilities are part of one's knowledge of a language, and a good theory of speech perception must explain how this knowledge is used. Unfortunately, no theory has yet been proposed that meets these boundary conditions.

Brewer referred to the observations of early introspective psychologists about reading. These psychologists suggested that the reading process involves both an auditory imagery component and a kinesthetic imagery component. A reader does not need both, since he can keep the kinesthetic component occupied by whistling or talking, and still go on reading. Brewer said that his own introspections supported these conclusions. Can they be reconciled with the motor theory of speech perception? Cooper said that Brewer was talking about conscious, peripheral processes. The motor theory does not imply that a conscious or peripheral process with sensory feedback is necessary for perception, or that the listener must produce a sensory message with his articulators. The analysis in terms of motor commands is carried out by neural machinery well below the level of awareness. In the same way, subjects in short-term memory experiments make errors that show that phonetic similarity is a source of confusion, but they are not consciously aware of such a pattern in their errors.

Jenkins said that an appeal to the neural level does not really answer the question, since motor commands are needed to control talking or whistling. If the neuromotor system is at the same time engaged in analyzing speech coming into the ear, some sort of "time-sharing" would be necessary.

Brewer referred to an experiment of his in which the subject is required to recite "13, 14, 15" repeatedly as fast as he can while reading. The additional task did not seem to impair the subject's reading performance. Conrad said that the literature is in conflict on this matter; there is also evidence that comprehension *is* impaired in experiments like Brewer's. The difficulty is that the subject controls the timing, and since he need not read every word, he can say the numbers at times that do not conflict with the processing of what he reads. Crowder said that when the timing of the vocal task is irregular and controlled by the subject rather than the experimenter, reading performance is very poor. Crowder also pointed out that it was very easy to bring short-term memory confusions to consciousness. Asked to memorize eight letters whose names rhyme, a subject quickly realizes why this task is difficult. Conrad said that lip-readers who get stuck on a word try to get information about the word by consciously mouthing it.

References

Conrad, R., 1964. Acoustic confusions in immediate memory. *Brit. J. Psych.* 55:75–84.

Miller, G., and P. Nicely, 1955. Analysis of perceptual confusions among some English consonants. *J. Acoust. Soc. Amer.* 27:338–352.

Studdert-Kennedy, M., and D. Shankweiler, 1970. Hemispheric specialization for speech perception. *J. Acoust. Soc. Amer.* 48:579–594.

EDWARD S. KLIMA

How Alphabets Might Reflect Language

They spell it Vinci and pronounce it Vinchy;
foreigners always spell better than they pronounce.

Mark Twain

For a long time English orthography was considered an utter abomination. More recently, however, the tide of scholarly opinion has changed. The title of an article by Weir and Venezky, English Orthography—More Reason than Rhyme [1968], is indicative of the new wave. In discussing the spelling of *paradigm, damn,* and *bomb,* they write: "In a pure and direct spelling-to-sound analysis, one is forced to the conclusion that the *g* in *paradigm,* the *n* in *damn* and the final *b* in *bomb* are functionless graphemes. When viewed, though, from a morphophonemic standpoint, the pairs *paradigm* : *paradigmatic, damn* : *damnation, bomb* : *bombard* reveal a regular morphophonemic alternation that is preserved in the orthography. . . . Without the retention of the full consonant cluster in final position, the identity of the common morphemic element in such pairs would be obscured on the graphemic level." [p. 192] In their monumental study on the generative phonology of English, Chomsky and Halle [1968] are even more eloquent in their praise of English orthography for its clarity in reflecting the linguistically well-motivated deep structure of English words. The general rules that Chomsky and Halle [1968, p. 49] discovered for English phonology suggest an underlying phonological form for *giraffe* with abstract feature segments corresponding approximately to /giræffe/ with a double /ff/ and a final /e/.[1] The English word *courageous,* they argue, has an underlying lexical form /koræge-ɔs/, with an /e/ like the orthographic

[1] The notational conventions I have adopted here are as follows: slashes / / enclose the segments of underlying lexical representations and underlying phonemes (roman type); and of spellings according to various orthographic conventions (*italic* type). Brackets [ ] enclose phonetic representations. An underlined symbol is to be understood in its phonetic value. In both the surface and underlying representations of segments, I use ordinary English spelling when the argument does not rest on the particular phonetic or phonological value of the segments represented. To indicate tense (or diphthongal) vowels, I have adopted the convention of writing a line above the vowel, as is done in Webster's New International Dictionary. The double cross # represents a word boundary; the plus + represents a formative boundary. The arrow → is read "is rewritten as."

representation. They conclude as follows: "Once again, a quite abstract underlying form, very similar to conventional orthography, accounts for the variant forms by rules of great generality and wide applicability. There is, incidentally, nothing particularly surprising about the fact that conventional orthography is, as these examples suggest, *a near optimal system* for the lexical representation of English words. The fundamental principle of orthography is that phonetic variation is not indicated where it is predictable by general rule. . . . Orthography is *a system designed for readers* who know the language, who understand sentences and therefore know the surface structure of sentences. . . . It is noteworthy that English orthography, despite its often cited inconsistencies, comes remarkably close to being an optimal system for English." (The italics are mine.) French orthography, which once vied with our English system as the nadir in consistency, is now also extolled by Schane [1968, p. 16] in his generative analysis of French.

Let us interpret orthography in this context to mean a general principle by which units of the language (words, utterances) are represented by orthographic units, such that the reader can reconstruct the linguistic units from their orthographic representation. Without specifically formulating the principle that seems to be operative in general in the English writing system, Chomsky and Halle [1968] observe that it is in the direction of representing abstract underlying forms. The general principle, of course, can be considered independently of the particular graphemic conventions themselves (e.g., that certain orthographic units may be realized as two letters as in *th;* that there is a convention for doubling letters in certain contexts, e.g., *get : getting*). The Chomsky-Halle claim, I assume, is only that the *general principle* of English orthography is felicitous and not necessarily that the particular realizations in the form of letters are as clear or as consistent as they could be.

Moreover, the cogency of the Chomsky-Halle claim does not at all rest on spellings like *giraffe* and *courageous* or the spelling of *bomb* reflected in the phonetic form of *bombard, paradigm* in *paradigmatic, nation* in *native; satiate* in *satiety, suspicion* in *suspect,* where the underlined spellings seem at first glance phonetically arbitrary or inconsistent. These are of interest at all only in that independently motivated regularities of great generality suggest, but do not necessitate, underlying forms which would be reflected by these nonphonetic or otherwise arbitrary spellings. But for the moment let us assume the extreme, and possibly unreasonable, position that these morphological relationships and others like them actually exist in the language structure and that the grammar expresses, by equivalence in underlying representation, all the morphologically related forms whose ultimate phonetic differences can be accounted for by well-motivated phonological rules. The ideal "language-knower" would know, that is, would have internalized, all the phonological rules of English and would have stored, in some analyzed form, the vocabulary in such a way that the phonological rules would have optimal applicability.

The Accessibility of Linguistic Structure

Even with the ideal language-knower, however, we can pose some interesting hypothetical questions about optimal orthographies if we allow that the various levels of language structure may, by their very nature, not be equally accessible to him in his capacity as language-user with respect to the orthography.

Let me illustrate the notion of levels of linguistic structure in the following way. Take, for example the word *rediscover*. At one and the same time, such a form is many different things. At one level of linguistic structure, *rediscover* is a complex phonetic continuum; at the same time, it is a string of distinct sound segments; at the same time, but at yet another level, it is a composite of the recurring morphological units *re-*, *dis-*, and *cover;* at the same time, it is the prefix *re* and the verbal stem *discover;* and finally, at another level of structure it is itself a verb meaning 'to obtain knowledge of, once again.' It is at one and the same time all this and more. Which of these levels is most immediate to us when we read or write? Consider once again the case of the ideal language-knower. English orthography might well be a manageable one for him as reader, but it might be less than optimal for him as learner and, more strikingly, as writer.

Of course, there is no reason to assume that any actual language-user has the degree of integration postulated for the ideal language-knower. In fact, there is no reason, a priori, to preclude variation in underlying lexical representations even among speakers of the same dialect who have the same vocabulary. Let us consider for example the triplet: *acknowledge, knowledge, know* in some dialect of English whose speakers have not learned English orthography (just to minimize the extent to which the orthography itself may contribute to learning the language in the direction of the knowledge of the ideal speaker-hearer). Of any two speakers of this dialect each might differ in his underlying lexical representation of these vocabulary items (i.e., in whatever actual correlate there is to the theoretical construct we refer to as an underlying lexical representation). One speaker might have the three most highly integrated with underlying lexical representations corresponding to:

ac-know-ledge, know-ledge, know, another might well relate the three
as sharing *now,* that is, *ack-now-ledge, now-ledge, now.* Their language,
in the ordinary sense of the word, is the same nonetheless. Similarly,
for many speakers of English, *crux* may well not be systematically related
to *crucial, satiated* to *sated,* or *ingratiate* to *ingratitude,* in such a way
as to motivate a common underlying representation including /crūc/,
/sāt/, and /ingrāt/.

While there are no systematic studies of the accessibility or of the
reality of such morphological relations, the well-known difficulties in
English spelling suggest that certain of these relationships exist, if at
all, only at a very inaccessible level. But these, after all, are only individual, more or less isolated sets of examples, not very interesting in
themselves with respect to general principles of orthography for the real
language of real language-users. Much more relevant, however, are pairs
like *delude : delusion, deride : derision, invade : invasion, erode : erosion,*
etc., where a verb ending in the [d]-sound has a corresponding nominalization in [žon].[2] The more or less highly integrated system will treat
the phonetic variation between [d] and [ž] as predictable from very general phonological rules like those that predict the phonetic variation
between [s] and [z] in the final sound segments of *laps* and *labs,* quite
differently, that is, from the more purely morphological, rather than
phonological, relationship between, for example, *was* and *were.*

Weir and Venezky [1968] suggest that one of the advantages of English
orthography is that it preserves the identity of common morphemic elements (that would otherwise be obscured) by not requiring a uniform
direct correspondence between the letter and the sound—as indeed
English does not require in the first two orthographic *a*'s in *Canadian,*
as opposed to the corresponding two in *Canada,* or in the second *t*
in *rotate,* as opposed to the corresponding *t* in *rotation.*

This indeed is the case, but it is not obvious that the identity need
be preserved within the orthography since that identity, where it is real,
is already represented in the language. Again the question really involves
what we do when we read: do we reconstruct the underlying form
from the orthography and then assign it a phonetic form, or do we
assign a phonetic form to the orthographic representation and then from
that reconstruct the underlying form? The extent to which we utilize
either or both of these strategies is, of course, an empirical question.
The remarks by Chomsky and Halle [1968] are consistent with the letter-

[2] The vowels of the affixes -*(i)on,* -*(i)an,* and -*er* will be represented by their
English orthographic forms since their true phonetic or phonological nature is
not essential to this discussion.

to-underlying-form hypothesis. And their remarks suggest a very strong claim about optimality in orthography: an optimal orthography is one in which *no* phonetic variation is indicated orthographically where it is predictable by general phonological rule—regardless of the degree of abstractness of the ensuing orthographic representation. "Abstractness," in this context, would mean remoteness from individual letter-to-sound correspondence in the word. The tendency to preserve morphological identity mentioned by Weir and Venezky [1968] would automatically follow from this general principle.

The notion of optimal orthography suggested by Chomsky and Halle [1968] follows a general principle of economy with respect to predictability in the linguistic structure. The optimality claimed by them, however, is optimality only for the reader who already knows the orthographic system and, of course, the language. But, it should be emphasized again, the question becomes more complicated when we consider the problem of learning to read. And perhaps writing presents so many problems of its own that it should be viewed apart. In the following section, nonetheless, we shall consider certain relevant characteristics of writing systems that may suggest some directions toward a more inclusive notion of optimal orthography.

Aspects of an Optimal Orthography

It seems to me that some interesting results with respect to an optimal orthography will be obtained if we consider writing systems from the following four points of view: (1) the degree of arbitrariness in the relationship between the orthographic units and the corresponding linguistic units: the less arbitrary the orthography the easier it will be to learn; (2) the degree of redundancy in the orthographic representation vis-à-vis the linguistic form: the greater the parsimony of the orthography the better (I disregard entirely here differences in discriminability of particular letter *forms*); (3) the degree of ambiguity in the orthographic representation with respect to the linguistic form represented: the orthography must be suitably expressive; (4) standardization: one and the same word should not have several spellings, that is, a difference in spelling should represent a difference in linguistic structure. The optimal orthography for a language would be expected to reach the proper balance in minimizing arbitrariness, minimizing redundancy, and maximizing expressiveness while still maintaining a standardized spelling. In referring to a writing system in relation to the language it represents, we shall always presuppose that the learner and user of that orthography already knows the language. We shall presuppose, that is, that he has some sort of internal representation of the inventory of underlying distinctive sound segments (the underlying, or systematic, phonemes) out of which are constituted the underlying lexical representations. He has also internalized the phonological (and other grammatical rules of the language. And he has a representative vocabulary. We assume, however, that not all levels of linguistic structure are necessarily of equal accessibility. Nothing will be said here about a very important consideration in evaluating orthographies in general: the degree to which they accommodate dialectal, as well as ideolectal, variation.

ARBITRARINESS

Of course, all writing systems are arbitrary to some extent, but the arbitrariness is minimal if orthographic units are correlated with the elements of the linguistic structure—linguistic elements that the language user already knows just by the fact that he knows the language. Thus to assign to all the words of English one or more random letters, in much the way that pure logographic systems do, like *lb.*, for *pound, Mr.* for *mister, Mrs.* for *missis,* without regard for the relationship between the letters and the internal sound structure of these words would represent a high degree of arbitrariness. Having learned the sound forms of the *words* of the language—which are themselves in essence arbitrary with respect to their meaning—he would then have to associate with these as many arbitrary sequences of letters. Such a system of writing does not capitalize on a structural characteristic of every human language, namely, that the sound forms of the thousands of words in each are all made up of a limited number of distinctive sounds. Thus there is a reduction of arbitrariness when letters, while themselves arbitrary, have a fixed relationship to the form of the word. Thus *pound* differs from *round* in the language by its first segment and in the orthography by its first letter. In a writing system that consistently follows this principle of correspondence between sound and unit, learning the writing system can take a very short time, whereas a grapheme-to-morpheme system like Chinese characters take years to learn. In fact, the history of writing shows a clear development to less and less arbitrariness: from the character to the syllabary to the alphabet.[3] Viewed exclusively from the point of view of minimizing arbitrariness the end of this development would logically be a system where characteristics of the form of the

---

[3] This is not to say that the syllabary is less appropriate than the alphabet for languages with a particular type of structure.

letters would be related in a systematic way to distinctive phonetic features of the individual sound segments.

Our own cursive (or italic) letters (*c, i, a, j, q, l, d*) have as formative
elements the open arc *c*, the normal vertical line ı, the upward extended
vertical line ᛁ, and the downward extended vertical line ॱ. The composition of the individual letters in terms of these formatives is, of course,
arbitrary from the point of view of their value in the sound system.
But of course each formation could correspond to some feature of the
sound of the composite letter.

Although orthographies devised for orthographic reforms, like the
Shaw alphabet designed by Read, Barrett, Magrath, and Pugmire [Shaw
1962], reflect features of the sound by the form of the letter, orthographies in current use that are more or less consistently based on phonological features are rare. (The Korean orthography is generally considered an exception to the rule.) Many languages do, however, incorporate
selected aspects of feature representation, especially when one culture
adopts the writing system of another whose language lacks certain sounds.
The letters that occur with and without the hachek in Czech represents
at least related phonological characteristics (c:$\check{c}$; s:$\check{s}$) and in English
the similarity in the phonological feature involved in the place of articulation in pairs like /t/ : /θ/, /p/ : /f/ is preserved by the digraphs with
h,–t : th, p : ph.[4]

If orthography provides a visual representation of an utterance (words,
expressions, phrases), then an orthography is not sufficiently expressive
if two words, which have different inherent sound forms, do not differ
in their orthographic representation. We shall assume that an optimal
orthography would not tolerate a situation like that in English where
read (present tense) and *read* (past tense) or *lead* (meaning 'to con-
duct') and *lead* (the metal) have a different sound-form but have the
same orthographic representation. Our consideration of the expressive
power of a writing system need not necessarily be restricted to the sound
form of the word, to the exclusion of other levels of language. Consider,
for example, the general phenomenon of homophony—when two different lexical items have the same sound forms: *bill* 'a demand for payment'
versus *bill* 'the beak of a bird'; *meat* 'flesh of an animal' versus *meet*
'a gathering.' The orthography is more expressive of the language if

---

[4] The fact that English uses *h* not only as part of a digraph but also as an
independent letter can lead to segmentally ambiguous strings: *disheveled*
(*di / sheveled* or *dis / heveled*). This, of course, is undesirable in an orthography.

it distinguishes these forms which, while identical at the sound-level, are distinct at the lexical level. With such a distinction the orthography would be more expressive than the language is at the sound level. Suppose that some writing system differentiated homonyms consistently (as English does sporadically) by a difference in spelling. While this would constitute an advance in expressiveness, it would also increase arbitrariness in that for every pair of such words an arbitrary choice would have to be made (and learned) as to the assignment of the two spellings. The case is different, on the other hand, when a language distinguishes homophones according to a general grammatical or semantic category, such as the convention in English orthography of capitalizing all proper names. While the particular representation is arbitrary, the distinction is then systematically applicable to a wide range of cases, since the distinction between proper and common nouns is already represented in the grammar, that is, in what the speaker knows when he knows the language. Again in this case, the orthographic representation would be more expressive than the sound-form of the language. In this discussion, we will be concerned only with adequate expressiveness.

ECONOMY

While an orthography should be expressive, it should also be economical. For an orthography to reach the minimum requirements of economy we shall assume that no variations in the sound form which is *everywhere* determined by its environment will be indicated by the orthography. Let me take as an example certain well-known facts about the sound-system of American English. In *cop,* the /k/ is backed; in *coop,* the /k/ is medial, and in *keep,* the /k/ is fronted. In terms of expressiveness alone, one might expect an optimal writing system to have three different letters to express these variations in sound form. Close examination of the possible occurrence of these three sound forms in English, on the other hand, shows that the variation is predictable in all instances from the immediate phonological context of the segment. The velar /k/ occurs only and always before back vowels; the palatal /k/ occurs only and always before front vowels; and the medial /k/ occurs elsewhere. In no case are there two forms in English that differ only in one having a fronted /k/ and the other a backed /k/. The phonology of English contains a rule (i.e., expresses the generalization) that the velar stop is backed before back vowels and fronted before front vowels. As the linguistic system itself imposes this completely determined variation on the sound form, the writing system would not be adequately economical if it duplicated it. The language then has, as an inherent characteristic, a regularity that could be captured by a phonological rule something like the following:

[K] → [K, FRONT]/—[VOWEL, FRONT][5]

Let us consider a slightly more complicated phonetic variation. In English the vowel-sound in *ride* is consistently longer than that in *write* (rīːd] : [rīt]).[6] Let us assume, for simplicity of discussion, that the final consonants remain distinct, as in "careful speech." Let us imagine a language otherwise identical to English except that between vocalic segments as in *rider* and *writer,* a flap [ř] occurs but [t] and [d] never occur and that the flap occurs only between vowels. That is, we are imagining a language in which the "loose" pronunciation as [rīːřer] : rīřer] is the only pronunciation. Given the distribution of vowel length, the restricted occurrence of the flap in just those intervocal positions in which the dental stops do not occur, and the morphological regularity of verb-stem followed by *-er,* the language would be assumed to have the following *ordered* rules expressing the fact that both the flap and the difference in vowel length are predictable.

Rule I.   Vowel-lengthening[7]

   [V] → [V:]/—[C, VOICED]

Rule II.   Flap

   [DENTAL, STOP] → [DENTAL, FLAP]/[V, STRESS]—[V]

The derivation would look something like:

rider	writer	
# r ī d e r #	# r ī t e r #	Underlying Form
I. # r īː d e r #		([ī] → [īː])
II. # r īː ř e r #	# r ī ř e r #	([t] and [d] → [ř])

The writing system for such a language would not be adequately economical, with respect to the language, if vowel length and the dental flap [r], which are everywhere predictable by the surrounding sound

[5] Read as follows: The segment abbreviated here as K has the phonological feature abbreviated here as FRONT when it occurs before a segment which is vocalic and front.
[6] Vowel length as indicated by : and [i:] is to be interpreted as a long tense (diphthongal) vowel.
[7] V is a cover symbol for any vowel, C is a cover symbol for any consonant.

segments, are symbolized by *additional* orthographic symbols to indicate the weakly articulated dental and the long vowel. Why use five orthographic symbols (*t, d, ř, ī,* and *ī:*) when three (*t, d,* and *ī*) will suffice with equal expressiveness, given, of course, the structure of the language.

The reader will recall that in their remarks about an optimal orthography, Chomsky and Halle similarly argued in terms of the phonological rules of the language. But rather than eliminating from orthographic symbolization only those phonetic variations that are everywhere determined by phonological rule, they proposed, for optimality in orthography, the elimination of all phonetic variation that is anywhere determined by phonological rule. Let us consider the Chomsky-Halle position as maximizing the structural economy of the orthography (i.e., maximizing economy with respect to what is predictable by phonological rule). Let us consider another possible notion of optimal orthography, an orthography which minimizes the total number of orthographic symbols required and also the number required for representing individual words. Let us refer to this as representational economy of an orthography to contrast with structural economy. In the case of *coop : keep* and *rider : writer,* the two principles will not make a difference. But of course, the principles will make a difference for a language like English in cases like *rotation* (*ration, nation*) and *delusion* both in the number of orthographic symbols used to represent the word and in the particular symbols that represent the same segment of the word. In the phonological structure of English there are regular phonological rules of great generality which derive [rōtāšon] from an underlying lexical representation something like /rōtāt+ion/ after the initial assignment of stress. Similar rules derive [dēlūžon] from an underlying /dēlūd+ion/.

	rotation	delusion	
	rōtā t + i o n	dēlū d + i o n	Underlying Form
I.	rōtā t + y o n	dēlū d + y o n	([ion] → [yon], as in *rebellion*)
II.	rōtā s + y o n	dēlū z + y o n	([t], [d] → [s], [z], as in *resident: residence*)
III.	rōtā š + y o n	dēlū ž + y o n	([s], [z] → [š], [ž], as in *regress: regression*)
IV.	rōtā š + - o n	dēlū ž + - o n	([y] → non-segment)
V.		dēlū: ž + - o n	([ū] → [ū:])

Chomsky and Halle suggest that if it maximizes structural economy the optimal orthography could spell these something like /rōtātion/ and /dēlūdion/. An orthographic principle optimalizing representational adequacy—that is, staying close to the surface—would spell these rather like /rōtāšon/ and /dēlūžon/ (but not, of course, as /dēlū:žon/ since vowel length is everywhere predictable).

With respect to economy, the choice of the correct notion of "optimal orthography for a particular language" leads us back to that basic question, about which I, as a linguist, have only my own private prejudices: which levels of linguistic structure (all of which are, of course, in some sense or other "known" by the native speaker) are then *most readily accessible* in the process of reading and writing? For which levels do we have the strongest linguistic intuitions? When we fix our visual attention on the written word or set about to write it, are we dealing *most directly* with something like /dēlūd+ion/ or /dēlūžon/? Both of the positions suggested above already assume that phonetic variation—for example, the length of the vowel in *rider*—is somehow less readily accessible.

Some Principles of Orthographic Representation[8]

We can, I think, profitably examine the relationship between orthographic representation and language (or types of language) by considering how certain general principles of orthographic assignment would represent a language from the point of view of economy, expressiveness, and arbitrariness. Let me emphasize that in every case, it must be assumed that the orthography is an orthography for the speaker-hearer who already knows the language. That is, he knows the inventory of basic sound segments out of which the underlying lexical representations are constituted; he knows the vocabulary (or a representative vocabulary); he knows the phonological rules that describe the relationship between the underlying lexical representation of the items of this vocabulary and their phonetic form. He knows everything else there is to know that is meant by knowing a language. He knows that *stronger* is related by regular phonological rules to *strong* (even though the final *g* is not sounded) in much the same way as *bigger* is related to *big*, that *delusion* is related to *delude* in much the same way as *rebellion* to *rebel*. He knows, let us assume, that [jɨræf] *giraffe* has an underlying representation with, in some abstract sense, a double continuant and a final vocalic segment; he knows that the sound form of *residence* has in its underlying representation a final vocalic segment preceded

[8] Other approaches along somewhat similar lines can be found in Palmer [1930] and Halle [1969].

by a segment which in other contexts is realized as a [t] (*resident*) or a [š] (*residential*). He knows all this, without, of course, necessarily being able to touch on all of such relationships with the same ease in the performance of derivative activities like reading and writing.

I. AN ORTHOGRAPHY PRESUPPOSING THE DOMINANCE
OF SURFACE PHONEMES

Consider once again the more surface-oriented notion of representational economy, where only those variations that are everywhere predictable by the phonological rules are not represented in the orthography. We shall assume that a Phoneme Letter is associated with each underlying phoneme (systematic phoneme). Let us further assume, as has been argued by some generative grammarians, that English does not contain /ŋ/ among its underlying phonemes. Let us consider now a rule for the assignment of letters to surface words, where a surface word is considered to consist of a horizontal row of sound segments and also silent segments (boundary symbols and deleted underlying segments): Letter Assignment Convention I ignores boundaries and deleted segments and operates on surface sound segments in the following way. The vertical columns representing the sound segments in the phonological derivation of a word is scanned upward. At the first occurrence, in the column, of a feature specification that is equivalent to a feature specification of an underlying phoneme, the phoneme letter of the latter is assigned to the surface segment. For the sound segments of *rider, writer,* the rule will operate in the following way (the encircled segment specifications, abbreviated with a phonetic symbol, are those which are equivalent to an underlying base phoneme).

rider	writer	
# r ⓘ d e r #	# r ī ⓣ e r #	Underlying Form
I. # r ī: ⓓ e r #		[V] → [V:]
II. # ⓡ ī: ř ⓔ ⓡ #	# ⓡ ⓘ ř ⓔ ⓡ #	[t,d] → [ř]
/rīder/	/rīter/	Orthographic Form

By this convention, *rotation* would be spelled something like /rōtäšon/ and *delusion*, /dēlüžon/ (disregarding the correct letter assignment for the last syllable in each word).

Such a letter assignment convention would however not be adequately expressive without further modification in that it would falsely assign to the [ŋ]-segment in *king* the letter *n,* thus not differentiating *king* from *kin*. The problem is caused by the loss of the segment [g] after the latter has caused the phonetic variation in [n].

king
_____

	#	k	i	ⓝ	g	#	Underlying Form
I.	#	k	i	ŋ	g	#	[ng] → [ŋg]
II.	#	ⓚ	ⓘ	ŋ	-	#	[ŋg] → [ŋ]
	kin						Orthographic Form

Therefore an Adjustment Rule would have to assign the segment [ŋ] an arbitrary letter (let's say /ŋ/).

Let me emphasize that the letter assignment conventions are not to be thought of as spelling rules for the individual speaker-hearer. They are, rather, abstract schemata which characterize orthographic systems in terms of various possible hypotheses about the relative accessibility of linguistic structures for the speaker-hearer/reader-writer.

While Letter Assignment Convention I is representationally economical and (with the addition of Adjustment Rules) adequate in terms of expressiveness, each adjustment rule adds to its arbitrariness and thus makes the convention less adequate in providing an optimal orthographic system. The adjustment rules are, of course, just a cover-up for the loss of elements of predictability that are clearly present in the language structure. It is interesting, nonetheless, that to a very great extent the Shaw orthography [Shaw 1962] is described by Convention I and its adjustments. The real question is to what extent the limitations on the depth of the linguistic level represented by the writing system violate the linguistic intuitions of speakers of at least certain types of languages. Why should we not consider that a more optimal system will lean more heavily on the predictability inherent in the language structure by assigning its letter representation to more abstract levels of derivation than permitted by Convention I?

II. AN ORTHOGRAPHY PRESUPPOSING THE OPACITY OF SURFACE PHONEMES

Let us consider then a less restricted letter assignment convention—less restricted in that it assigns letters not only to surface segments but to any segment which is a sound segment in the underlying lexical representation (but not to the purely abstract boundaries in the underlying representation). Letter Assignment Convention II, will, however, refrain from abstractness by associating letter assignment with the lowest segment specification that is equivalent to a systematic phoneme. The arbitrariness of the adjustment rules will be circumvented, as is seen below, and this principle for an optimal grammar will have the minimum expressiveness that is required of any writing system. We shall assume, just for fun, that the underlying representation of *fashion* includes /fac-/.

king

	#	k	i	(n)	g	#	Underlying Form
I.	#	k	i	ŋ	(g)	#	[ng → ŋg]
II.	#	(k)	(i)	ŋ	-	#	[ŋg → ŋ]
	/king/						Orthographic Form

fashion

	#	f	a	c	+	i	o	n	#	Underlying Form
I.	#	f	a	s	+	i	o	n	#	[c] → [s]
II.	#	f	a	s	+	y	o	n	#	[ion] → [yon]
III.	#	f	a	š	+	(y)	o	n	#	[s] → [š]
IV.	#	(f)	(a)	(š)	+	-	(o)	(n)	#	[y] → nonsegment
	/fašyon/									Orthographic Form

Rotation and *delusion* would be spelled /rōtāšyon/ and /dēlūžyon/. Our English spelling of *fashion*, given the digraphic convention for representing [š] as *sh*, would come fairly close to the result of our second convention.

Let us turn now to the sorts of phonological phenomena that are predictable by phonological rule but that would nonetheless not be indicated by an orthographic system assigning letters according to the two surface-oriented letter assignment conventions discussed above. Consider, for example, the regular morphological formation in English of past tense/past participle, and of verb third person singular/noun plurals as shown at top of page 71.

It is very clear that the phonetic variation [d]:[əd]:[t] and [z]:[əz]:[s] of these morphemes is very regular: [əd] is the realization of the past tense/past participle in words ending in an alveolar stop; [t] its realization in words ending in a voiceless consonant; and [d] its realization elsewhere. In much the same way [əz] is the realization of the third singular present as well as that of the plural noun in words ending in a sibilant ([s], [z],

	verb past	verb third singular/noun plural
pay	pay[d]	pay[z]
tab	tab[d]	tab[z]
fizz	fizz[d]	fizz[əz]
judge	judge[d]	judg[əz]
bathe	bathe[d]	bathe[z]
seed	seed[əd]	seed[z]
seat	seat[əd]	seat[s]
tap	tap[t]	tap[s]
mess	mess[t]	mess[əz]
lunch	lunch[t]	lunch[əz]

[š], [ž], [č], [ǰ]) ; [s] is their realization after words ending in a voiceless stop; and [z], their realization elsewhere.

Let us assume that *tabbed, tapped,* and *patted* have derivations, something like the following:

tabbed	tapped	patted

	#tab#d	#tap#d	#pat#d	Underlying Form
I.			#pat#əd	[t#d] → [t#əd]
II.		#tap#t		[p#d] → [p#t]
	tabd	*tapt*	*patəd*	Orthographic Form

Both Letter Assignment Conventions I and II would differentiate, in their spelling, these predictable variations of the same underlying past morpheme /d/ as: /tabd/, /tapt/, /patəd/. Both conventions do, it must be emphasized, maintain the minimal expressiveness that we require of an orthographic system: to differentiate words which represent different soundforms. And the . . . *apt* sequence in *tapt* is the same as that of the word *apt.* The linguistic side of the phenomenon is quite straightforward. There is neutralization in the final sequences; sound segments [d] and [t], [z] and [s], which elsewhere do contrast, do not occur contrastively after stops; rather only phonetic [t] and [s] occur after voiceless stops and only phonetic [d] and [z] occur after voiced stops.

In the case of the past tense, English orthographically reflects the unity of the morpheme economically by *ed* where by conversion conventions the *e* represents a sounded segment or not, and the *d* a voiced segment or not, depending on the final consonant segment. The genitive *s* similarly leaves the completely predictable variations to the language rather than expressing them in the orthography. Thus *Joe's* [z], *Bob's* [z], *Pat's* [s], *Keith's* [s], *Jess's* [əz], *Liz's* [əz], *Butch's* [əz]. The *s:es* of noun-plural and third person singular only tends toward unnecessary phonetic detail in expressing in the orthography the difference between the syllabic and nonsyllabic form of the morpheme. At first glance one might conclude that in terms of differences in sound form alone, English orthography might well rid itself of the orthographic distinction between the possessive [z] on one hand and the third singular/noun plural [z] on the other. But here English is, in fact, superbly expressive on the phonetic level, thus distinguishing the genitive [housəz] as in *a house's roof* from the plural [houzəz] as in *two houses*.

In many languages, the neutralization of a contrast described in the inflectional affixes *-ed* and *-es* of English is found in word-final position of stems. In Russian, for example, the stems *lyod* 'ice' and *lyot* 'flight' contrast when there are inflectional endings following the /d/ and /t/ segments. But when /d/ and /t/ are at the end of a phonological word, they do not contrast, but rather are phonetically [t]; the other voiced versus voiceless consonant pairs in Russian behave similarly. In German, the situation is similar; with the stem /bunt-/ 'colorful' there is [bunte] spelled *bunte* and [bunt] spelled *bunt,* whereas with the stem /bund-/ 'association' there is [bunde] spelled *Bunde* but then [bunt] spelled non-phonetically *Bund*.[9]

There is no need to multiply the number of examples that indicate that some real orthographies do often—or, even in some constructions, do as a rule—reflect more nearly the underlying lexical representation of a word than its sound form when the two diverge. More important for this informal study is the fact that the letter assignment conventions informally described above would preclude an abstractness of representation that is indeed common in many real orthographies and that, as in the English *s* and *ed* inflectional endings and the German and Russian stem endings, reflect some of the most basic, native aspects of the structure of the language.

IIIa. AN ORTHOGRAPHY PRESUPPOSING THE DOMINANCE OF UNDERLYING SOUND SEGMENTS

Let us focus our attention once more on the notion of an optimal orthography to see what sort of general orthographic principle (i.e., what sort

---

[9] With respect to neutralization of voiced-voiceless contrasts in word-final position, both Russian and German consistently reflect the more abstract structure rather than the phonetic form.

of Letter Assignment Convention) would provide for the sort of *structural* economy suggested by this deep-structure orientation of certain aspects of English orthography, and would at the same time maintain its expressiveness vis-à-vis at least the sound-form of utterances without becoming overly arbitrary. Let us entertain first the strongest claim—that the optimal orthography will manifest full structural economy, that is, that the orthography itself will not represent any phonological variation that is determined by a phonological rule. This is the position suggested by Chomsky and Halle. Let us consider Letter Assignment Convention III as one realization of such a notion of optimality: The feature specification of a segment as it appears in the underlying lexical representation of a word (or the highest feature specification that coincides with that of a base phoneme) determines directly the phoneme letter by which the vertical column is represented; internal boundaries are not represented. An orthography based on this convention would be structurally economical with respect to the neutralizations in German and Russian that involve stem-final consonants occurring in word-final position (*Bund* : *bunt*). Convention III would assign the letters *d* and *t* respectively to these phonetically identical occurrences of the stops. Letter Assignment Convention III would be similarly effective in representing the phonetically predictable variations in the English inflectional endings [d], [t], [əd] and [z], [s], [əz], choosing a single orthographic representation in each case (/d/ and /z/, if /d/ and /z/ are the underlying representations of these inflectional morphemes). To the extent that the segments of an underlying lexical representation undergo phonological rules that mention only other sound segments and the final word boundary, Letter Assignment Convention III will be maximally economical from the point of the language structure, while at the same time maintaining adequate expressiveness.[10] In a language like English, however, it is readily seen that the phonetic variation of the segments occurring in the underlying

---

[10] It is important to note how crucial the representation of the word boundary is (i.e., how crucial the space between words is) for the economy of the orthographic system if it is to maintain adequate expressiveness. Consider for example the spellings of similar parts of two utterances *as to pin it* and *a stop in it*. The rules of the language tell us that the /p/ of /pin/ is aspirated because it is word initial, and that the /p/ of /spin/ is not aspirated because it follows an /s/ of the same word. The indication of the phonological word by a space in the orthography keeps the orthography adequately expressive without indicating totally predictable phonetic variation. Consider now what the situation would be if English indicated only sound segments and not word boundaries. Both of the sequences would have the form /astopinit/ and the orthography, given the lack of a significant space, would have to specify predictable phonetic variation: /aztʰopʰinit/ versus /astopinit/. The writing systems of some languages in fact do not represent word boundaries. Sanskrit is an example.

lexical representations are not, in fact, dependent only on other sound segments and the final word boundary.

Internal word boundaries are involved in an interesting class of exceptions to this restriction, presupposed by Convention III, on the nature of the phonological rules operative in the language. The exceptions are significant in a language like English, where they abound, in that they are a measure of the added arbitrary orthographic devices that would have to be added to Letter Assignment Convention III in order to preserve adequate expressiveness. Leaving aside now the whole question of compound nouns, let us consider the following facts about English structure from the point of view of Convention III.[11] Convention III would assign to the words *finger, linger, anger, hunger, single* (phonetically [. . . ŋg . . .] but with an underlying representation /. . . ng . . ./) a spelling like that of English spelling; and likewise to *sing* (phonetically [siŋ] but with an underlying representation ending in /. . . ng/). The phonological rules, which specify that /n/ becomes [ŋ] before velars and that subsequently /g/ is deleted when it occurs between the nasal and the end of the word, predict the phonetic variation. In the case of orthographic *sing* there is no problem for Convention III, but in English there is not only *finger* but *singer, singing, longish,* and there is even a pair [loŋger] : [loŋer] ('having greater length' versus 'one who longs'). In terms of the phoneme segments of these underlying representations, all of these forms have the same characteristic form: an /. . . ng . . ./ internal to the word. Convention III would assign these the same orthographic representation, as English orthography does. This would, of course, result in a system that is inadequate in expressive power on the sound level, for the underlying segments of the members of each pair: *linger : singer, anger : banger;* the *longer* of 'length' and the *longer* of 'one who longs' are the same or equivalent. Accordingly, they do not themselves determine the regular phonetic difference of [ŋg] in the first member of each pair, as opposed to the [ŋ] alone in the second member. To be expressively adequate the orthography pre-

---

[11] While the compound words (*bedroom, milkman, living room, garbage man*), like the uncompounded word (*carpenter*), are single units at one level of grammatical structure (i.e., *carpenter, milkman,* and *garbage man* are all nouns), the basic stem elements of the compound word behave with respect to some phonological phenomena quite differently from the elements of a simple word—(i.e., in terms of some phonological rules the stem elements maintain a word boundary between them). The writing system must, then, to be adequately expressive in its representation of words, represent this difference orthographically, as English does with the space (which is the orthographic representation elsewhere of the word boundary) or by a hyphen. A more optimal orthographic system would be consistent.

scribed by Convention III would have to be fortified by the addition of arbitrary letter variation (capitalizing the *g* of all verbs ending in a /g/ or assigning it some arbitrary diacritic). In terms of the linguistic structure, however, the principle involved is relatively clear: the /g/ drops at the end of a word (as in *sing*) and in *singing* and *singer* the /ng/ is still, in a relevant sense, at the end of the word *sing*. In *anger, hunger, finger,* on the other hand, /ng/ is in no sense at the end of a word.[12] The underlying lexical representation does, in fact express this, but by an internal word boundary rather than by a segment.

IIIb: THE SAME ORTHOGRAPHY REFLECTING INTERNAL AS WELL AS EXTERNAL WORD BOUNDARIES

In the light of the regularities mentioned above, we could extend Letter Assignment Convention III so as to represent not only the external word boundary (represented by a space) but also the internal word boundary. Let us arbitrarily represent the latter by an apostrophe rather than a space. Just as the base phonemes are associated with phoneme letters, the base word boundaries have a space and an apostrophe associated with them. The underlying representations of *finger* and *singer* would be approximately /finger/ and /sing#er/ and our revised convention would assign them a spelling /*finger*/ and /*sing'er*/. Consistency would dictate that the /'/ would occur wherever there was an internal word boundary and not, of course, just where the orthographic symbol is needed to disambiguate one from another. The internal word boundary also occurs in English after the very productive, free prefixation with *de* and *re*: *sign* and *re-sign* 'to sign again,' *seat* and *de-seat*. The underlying lexical representations are something like /rē#sign/ and /dē#sēt/. In both cases the underlying /s/ is phonetically [s]. By the enriched Convention these words would be represented orthographically as /*rē'sign*/ and /*dē'sēt*/. There are other occurrences of these prefixes, however, in which they are simple morphological formatives of a word, as in *resign* 'to renounce' and *design* 'to draw.' The morpheme -*sign* in these is the same as in *consign* and *assign*, but the /s/ is realized phonetically as [z], having undergone a regular phonological rule that voices /s/ between vowels. The rule does not apply to an [s] after a word boundary and thus /rē#sign/ : /rē+sign/, phonetically [rēsīn] : [rēzīn], would be distinguished as /*rē'sign*/ and /*rēsign*/ by the letter assignment convention. The verb /*re-sign*/ is, in a very relevant sense, the verb *sign* modified by the prefix *re-*; whereas the verb *resign* 'to renounce' is in no sense the verb *sign* modified by

[12] The adjectives ending in . . . *ng* are all exceptions to this regularity; *longer* and *stronger* preserve the phonetic [g], but *wronger* would still be /wrong#er/.

re. The verb *resign* is the verb *resign* pure and simple, although it has the formative elements *re-* and *-sign.* It would seem to be reasonable to assume that the formative boundary between the components of verbs like *resign* and *design* is of quite a different nature from the word boundary that occurs between the elements of *re-sign.* That is, one might well postulate that the internal word boundary is, in a sense relevant to reading and writing, more accessible than the formative boundary. This, of course, is an empirical question.

IV. AN ORTHOGRAPHY PRESUPPOSING THE OPACITY OF MORPHOPHONEMIC
PROCESSES NOT INVOLVING LEXICAL CATEGORIES

The question of the difference between forms of the same word and words consisting of frequently recurring forms brings us back to the distinction, suggested in the introduction of this discussion, between *rotation, delusion, possession,* on the one hand, and *nation, ration, passion, fashion,* on the other. Let us assume, as the structure of the language indicates, that *nation* (as in *native*) and *rotation* (as in *rotate*) have in their underlying segmental representation respectively /nāt/ followed by /ion/ and /rōtāt/ followed by /ion/. Similarly, let us assume that *passion* has an underlying lexical representation as approximately /pat/ (as in *compatible*) followed by /ion/. The realization of /. . . tion/ as [šon] in *nation* and *passion* on the one hand and in *rotation* on the other, involves formative boundaries in at least two crucial levels of their derivation:[13]

Rule I

$$
\left\{
\begin{matrix}
t \\
d \\
\left\{ \begin{matrix} s \\ c \end{matrix} \right\}
\end{matrix}
\right\}
+ i \, V \rightarrow
\left\{
\begin{matrix}
t \\
d \\
s
\end{matrix}
\right\}
+ y \, V
$$

(i.e., [i] → [y,] but in this context only after a formant boundary: thus in *dutiable,* /i/ does not become [y] because the /i/ is part of the stem /duti+able/ and therefore the phonetic realization is not [dušable]; similarly, *ratio* is pronounced [rašo], since its underlying form is /rat+io/, whereas *patio* is pronounced [patio] since it has no formant boundary.)

[13] The phonological rules are roughly equivalent to those given by Chomsky and Halle [1968, pp. 223–245].

Rule II

$$\left\{\begin{matrix} t \\ d \end{matrix}\right\} + y \rightarrow \left\{\begin{matrix} s \\ z \end{matrix}\right\} + y$$

(i.e., [t], [d] become [s], [z], respectively, in this context only when followed by a formant boundary.)

Rule III

$$\left\{\begin{matrix} s \\ z \end{matrix}\right\} \rightarrow \left\{\begin{matrix} š \\ ž \end{matrix}\right\} /\text{—y V}$$

Rule IV

y → nonsegment

The segments that condition the change are underlined:

	nation		Underlying Form
	nā*t* + ion	rōtā*t* + ion	Underlying Form
I.	nāt + *y*on	rōtāt + *y*on	
II.	nās + *y*on	rōtās + *y*on	
III.	nāš + *y*on	rōtās + *y*on	
IV.	nāṣ̌ + on	rōtāṣ̌ + on	

Similarly for underlying forms /rāt+ion/, /pat+ion/, /fac+ion/, /dēlūd+ion/, /suppress+ion/.

There is, however, an interesting difference between *rotation* (*delusion, suppression, confusion*) and *nation* (*ration, passion, fashion*)—a difference similar to that between *re-sign* and *resign*. While the noun *rotation* is, in fact, the nominalization of the verb *rotate,* the noun *nation,* is not the nominalization of any verb, though its stem is still, of course, analyzable as /nat+ion/. This suggests that *rotation* differs from *nation* in having an internal word boundary (thus /rōtāt#ion/ but /nāt +ion/). By a rule of phonological structure # becomes + in certain environments.

Let us consider another letter assignment convention, a more constrained version of the previous one. Letter Assignment Convention IV states that the segments and the word boundaries of the underlying lexical representation are represented directly by their underlying phoneme symbols and word boundary symbol; if, however, in the course of its derivation, a segment undergoes a feature change conditioned by a formative boundary, i.e., +) that segment will be represented by the phoneme letter corresponding to the new feature specification, unless the formative boundary represents a word boundary in the underlying lexical representation. According to this convention, *rotation* would be represented as /rōtāt'ion/ and *delusion* as /dēlūd'ion/, whereas *nation* would be represented as /nāsyon/, *fashion* as /fasyon/ and *passion* as /pasyon/ (less arbitrary, perhaps, from the point of view of the writer than current English spelling).

Letter Assignment Convention IV presupposes a very special interpretation of the significance of boundary symbols, especially with respect to the internal word boundary and the formative boundary. The word boundaries of *rotate*, it will be recalled, are preserved in the underlying representation of its morphologically regular nominalization /rotat#ion/ and are, according to the convention, represented in the orthography as /rotat'ion/. In the course of its phonological derivation, however, the segments [t] [ion] show the phonetic variations characteristic of the sequence [. . . t+ion]: i.e., at one level of linguistic structure the sequence is [. . . t#ion], while at the same time, but at another level, it is [. . . t+ion]. The same is characteristic of denominal adjectives like *Egyptian* (phonetically, *Egyp*[šən]) from Egypt, *Lilliputian* from Lilliput. *Egyptian* would, of course, be spelled /Ēgypt'ian/. However, in languages in which there is variation in the treatment of the internal word boundary with respect to the same derivational affix (e.g., *-ion* and *-ian* in English), that is, where, at one level of derivation, the word boundary in some cases retains its full force and in others represents only a formative boundary, an orthography represented by Letter Assignment Convention IV would not maintain expressive adequacy. Such is in fact the case in the following pairs in English: *Egyptian* [. . . šan] but *Kant* : *Kantian* [. . . tian]. Letter Assignment Convention IV would assign, to phonetically distinct sequences (with respect to the segmental sequence /t/ /iən/), the same orthographic representation: *Ēgypt'ian* and *Kant'ian*. To that extent the orthography would not be adequate in expressive power. The problem involves the fact that two linguistic units (the internal word boundary, on the one hand, and the formative boundary, on the other hand) are equivalent in terms of form: neither is itself realized as a sound segment, but manifests itself, rather, only in its effect on the surrounding segments. And yet in this case the two have different effects.

V. AN ORTHOGRAPHY PRESUPPOSING THE TRANSPARENCY OF ONLY REGULAR PHONOLOGICAL RULES

Let us consider one final letter assignment convention that will weed out the source of the problem posed by the differing effects of the two boundaries by excluding from orthographic representation only those phonetic effects that are ascribable to surrounding sound segments (at whatever level of abstraction) and the word boundary (internal or external). Such a convention would presuppose that rules with this limited phonetic effect are in some sense more regular (i.e., more accessible) than those that involve formative boundaries at any level of structure. Letter Assignment Convention V states that each segment of the underlying lexical representation is represented directly by the appropriate phoneme letters, unless in the course of derivation the segment undergoes a phonological change conditioned by a formative boundary, in which case that segment will be represented by the phoneme letter corresponding to the new feature specification; only those word boundaries that are not altered in the course of a derivation will be represented in the spelling.

Letter Assignment Convention V would assign spellings somewhat like the following: /Kant'ian/ and /dē'sēt/ but /Ēgypsyan/, /rōtāt/ but /rōtāsyon/, /dēlūd/ but /dēlūzyon/, and, of course /nāsyon/ (nation), and /crūsyal/ (crucial), /rāsyo/ but /patio/, /oblivion/ but /rebelyon/.

There is no need here to describe other letter assignment conventions, though certainly no claim is made that those presented would be adequate for English or any other language. The objective of this very informal inquiry has been to consider a few very different positions one might take regarding the relative accessibility of various levels of linguistic structure and to see in what direction those positions might lead us if we take our current conclusions about the structure of the language seriously and at the same time make certain basic assumptions about adequacy in orthography from the point of view of expressiveness, and arbitrariness.

References
Chomsky, Noam and Morris Halle, 1968. *The Sound Pattern of English*. New York: Harper and Row.

Halle, Morris, 1969. Some Thoughts on Spelling. In *Psycholinguistics and the Teaching of Reading,* Kenneth S. Goodman and James T. Fleming (eds.), Newark, Del.: International Reading Association.

Palmer, H., 1930. *Principles of Romanization.* Tokyo: Maruzen.

Schane, Sanford A., 1968. *French Phonology and Morphology.* Cambridge, Mass.; MIT Press.

Shaw, Bernard, 1962. *Androcles and the Lion (with a Parallel Text in Shaw's Alphabet).* Baltimore: Penguin Books.

Weir, Ruth and Richard Venezky, 1968. English Orthography—More Reason than Rhyme. In *The Psycholinguistic Nature of the Reading Process,* Kenneth S. Goodman (ed.), Detroit: Wayne State University Press.

SAMUEL E. MARTIN

Nonalphabetic Writing Systems: Some Observations

Most major languages in the world today are written with symbol systems of symbols that are similar in spirit to our own alphabet. The native writer makes use of a relatively small inventory of symbols to represent phonological elements—typically syllables or phonemes, but in some cases morphophonemic and even componental elements. For various reasons, every writing system is in some way defective even when first instituted, and the institutionalization itself prevents the continuous revision that would keep the conventions of writing as well matched to the continuously changing spoken language as they may have been in the beginning. As a result, literate people tend to create formal written languages characterized by older forms, phonological and grammatical, which persist with very little change for long periods of time, until some sort of revolution demands a new written language that will correspond more closely to the living tongue.

The language spoken by more people than any other, Chinese, is usually written with a nonalphabetic system, a relatively large stock of characters that primarily represent words or parts of words. At the time the writing system developed, the overwhelming majority of Chinese words were single morphemes and the morpheme itself was in virtually all instances a single "syllable"—traditionally defined as an initial plus an ending, the latter consisting of a vocalic nucleus with a tone and an optional coda. Accordingly, the writing has variously been called logographic or morphemic or monosyllabic, and there is no need to worry unduly about the slight inaccuracies implied by any of these terms. (The term "logographic" was popularized by Bloomfield and Kennedy, who seem to have taken it from Du Ponceau [1838:110]: "I would not call the Chinese characters a syllabic, but a logographic system of writing." Du Ponceau also uses the term "lexigraphic.")

Chinese characters, and the principles behind them, have spread beyond the traditional borders of China. The Vietnamese, for example, not only imported characters (called chữ Nho 'Confucian-scholar characters' or chữ Hán 'Han characters') to write borrowed Chinese words and occasionally even native Vietnamese words of similar pronunciation (as when nhật 'sun' was written for nhặt 'strict'), but also invented new characters along the same lines to write native words, which have a very similar structure in that most consist of one syllable and one morpheme; for example, the character for nam 'south' was put to the left of the character for 'five' to write the native numeral năm. The Vietnam-created characters were called chu nôm 'demotic script,' and went out of use with the introduction of Roman letters several centuries ago.

In Korea, on the other hand, the characters were largely restricted to the writing of classical Chinese, the official language of records. The fifteenth-century invention of the native Korean script, now called Hankul (or Han-gŭl [haŋgɨl]) 'Han (= Korean) writing' and earlier known as Enmun (or Ŏn-mun [ë:mmun]) 'vernacular script,' made it possible to write the pronunciation both of native Korean words and of the many Chinese loanwords, but until quite recently it has been customary to use the Chinese characters for most of the known Chinese loanwords.

In passing, it should be noted that the Korean script is remarkable both for its internal structure and for its graphic origins. Since the latter have been known since the discovery of an old text in 1941, made readily accessible in Lee [1957], it is unfortunate that so many erroneous notions are still current [e.g., Alleton 1970, p. 110n]; perhaps this is a good place to summarize the correct information. The basic Hankul symbols were intended to depict, in the first instance—and well before John Wilkins' "Organic Alphabet" (1668) and Alexander Melville Bell's "Visible Speech" (1867)—the actual articulations of the consonants; those considered to be secondary consonants were derived by adding an extra stroke as a diacritic, so that the heavily aspirated /kh/ was written by inserting a stroke in the symbol for /k/, which pictures the tongue touching the palate. The phonetic notions were derived from traditional Chinese phonologists, who had sometimes chosen a symbolic term that demonstrated the consonant in its own initial, much as we now use 'sibilant' and 'shibilant' and once used the word 'guttural' to mean (among other things) 'velar.' That is what accounts for the inverted-V symbol chosen as a picture of a tooth to represent sibilants and affricates; the palatal series in Chinese were called "tooth" sounds by virtue of the fact that the word for tooth began with a palatal initial, retracted to retroflex in the modern Peking chǐ. (The actual function of the teeth in effecting a sibilant sound was probably not known.) To represent the vowels, three basic symbols were chosen to depict HEAVEN (a round dot), EARTH (a flat line), and MAN (an upright line); the choice was based on obscure metaphysical notions that may have been introduced in the hope they would give the writing system some higher authority to offset reactions to its drastic simplicity. The ways these three vowels (respectively representing the articulations back low, back high unrounded, and high front unrounded) were combined to represent other vowels seems somewhat arbitrary but not unmotivated. It is possible to use the Hankul symbols as a linear alphabet, but traditionally they are combined into equidimensional blocks like Chinese characters, with various calligraphic adjustments comparable to western ligatures or the two kinds of sigma in Greek; these blocks are used to represent syllables, either phonemic or morphophonemic. Thus the modern Korean orthography incorporates representation of phoneme components, phonemes, morphophonemes, syllables, and—to the extent that certain morphophonemic syllables (such as kkoch 'flower') are unique shapes—morphemes. In addition, as we have remarked, the Chinese characters are often used as direct logographic or morphemic symbols to represent borrowed elements in a Korean text.

What are these Chinese characters, and how many of them are there? The K'anghsi (Kāngxī) dictionary of 1716 lists 40,545 different characters; Morohashi's recent dictionary carries nearly fifty thousand. Yet among the 9,312 characters assigned arbitrary numbers in the Telegraphic Code there are about 55 that are not found in these dictionaries, nor in any other that has come to my attention [Dougherty et al. 1963, l.xvi]. If we were to take all the characters that have ever existed, it is said, the total number would reach eighty thousand [Du Ponceau 1838, p. 7n; Alleton 1970, p. 47]. Of course, there is no one who knows or uses more than a small part of this staggering number. If you have a dictionary with eight thousand characters in it, you will but rarely feel at a loss; Mathews' Chinese-English dictionary numbers only 7,773 characters. Today it is estimated that a thousand common characters will account for 90 percent of the text occurrences in popular publications on the mainland [Alleton 1970, p. 47]. Various limited lists have been proposed and officially adopted in the several political states that use Chinese characters; see, for example, the remarks below about Japan.

How are the Chinese characters structured? By tradition the graphs are divided into six categories, according to their origins; but the sixth category ("derivative characters") is so small and controversial that it is best ignored. The five other categories are as follows:

(1) *Pictographs* are direct iconic representations, such as those that depict the sun, the moon, a tree, a mouth, a mountain, a well, a bow, a stream, a gate, a shell, etc. Most characters have become highly stylized with the passage of time so that the original picture is not always obvious at first glance.

(2) *Simple ideographs* depict a logical idea: three horizontal lines to represent the number three, a pointer above or below the line to signal the words for up and down, etc.

(3) *Compound ideographs* represent an abstract idea by combining two simple graphs, as when MOON is put to the right of SUN to represent the word for 'bright.' Two TREEs are put together to represent the word for 'grove'; three are combined to represent the word for 'forest.'

(4) *Phonetic loans* borrow a graph to represent a different word with the same or some similar sound, as when the character depicting a dust-pan was borrowed to write the similar-sounding qí 'its,' or the character depicting a kind of wheat was borrowed to write lái 'come.'

(5) *Phonetic compounds* contain an element that hints at the meaning, usually called the *radical,* and an element called the *phonetic* that hints at the sound. The radicals, a kind of semantic classification system, were reduced in number from the 540 of the first-century dictionary Shuō Wén to the 214 found in the eighteenth-century K'anghsi (Kāngxī) dictionary. The present list of 214 was actually first used by Ming Ting Tso in the dictionary Zìhǎi of 1615 [Chao 1948, p. 63n]. The modern classificatory system is an expensive one, for more than half of all charac-ters belong to one of the twenty most frequent radicals [Chao 1948, p. 64]. And it is confusing, since the same element may be a phonetic in one character but a radical in another: dāo 'knife' is a radical in about 80 characters, a phonetic in about 12 [Alleton 1970, p. 38]. The phonetic can appear anywhere in a character, though certain modern lexicographers have arbitrarily reclassified the characters so as to favor certain positions, notably the left and the top. Instead of classifying characters by traditional or redefined radicals, you can order them by the total number of strokes; that is the way, for example, that family names are listed in drawing up an "unordered" list of people [Alleton 1970, p. 28]. And philologists sometimes list the characters by phonetic groups, of which Karlgren found some 1260 [Alleton 1970, p. 36]; a more practical list of under 900 can be studied in Soothill [1942].

It is said that 90 percent of all characters are phonetic compounds, with about 5 percent simple pictographs or ideographs and the remaining 5 percent compound ideographs or phonetic loans [Alleton 1970, p. 33). But in the modern shapes, both those created in China and those created in Japan, the phonetic and/or the radical sometimes disappears in the process of simplification. And we would expect the proportion of simple pictographs and ideographs to rise slightly as the number is restricted to the more frequent characters.

The shapes of the characters reflect a two-thousand-year history of brushwork calligraphy, of which one of the most important features is equidimensionality. Each character occupies an imaginary space of identical size, so that the same element must be given a smaller shape as it enters into more complex characters. A component at the left or on the top is underproportioned, usually no more than a third the size of the remainder; thus there is a radical meaning 'village' on the left that is slender by comparison with another radical meaning 'town,' of different origin but with the same configuration, that appears on the right. Not all obvious configurations are themselves radicals or phonetics; it is often possible to break larger elements down into recurrent graphic components that contain more than one stroke. Alleton [1970, p. 49] refers to a Czech attempt to explain the characters in terms of a "double articulation" of stroke-to-element then element-to-character; others have toyed with similar ideas. Wang [1971] perceptively notes that the average number of strokes in a character, reduced from six or seven to four or five in the new simplified shapes, is now about the same as the average number of letters in an English word, so that there is an obvious "parallelism in information content between the stroke and the letter." Traditionally, there are eight basic kinds of stroke, but some authorities list as many as 64 [Alleton 1970, p. 26]. An important aspect of the characters is often overlooked: each shape has a kind of internal constituency based on the rhythms with which it is normally written. In some cases the "junctures" of the character are obvious to the reader, whether he has mastered the art of brushmanship or not, but in other cases they are quite subtle, yet contribute to the recognition and identification of the character. The esthetic of the brushwork traditions is carried over into the writing of the kana syllabaries in Japan and the Hankul symbols in Korea, as well. Alleton [1970, p. 95] tells us that a simple character has its main axes and a center of gravity; for the complex character you must consider the size of each of the component elements, the center of gravity of each, and the center of gravity of the ensemble; and the radical is usually smaller than the phonetic.

For reasons apparently unknown, texts in East Asia have traditionally been written in vertical lines arrayed from right to left. But modern nonfiction publications have made increasing use of horizontal left-to-right printing, since that makes it easier to incorporate the foreign words and symbols so necessary in scientific works. Chang [1942, p. 55] after tests on Chinese readers in New York and in China came to the conclusion that "The results of both performances suggest that the horizontal arrangement is peculiarly adapted to reading purposes"; he says there is an optical illusion that makes vertical lines seem longer than horizontal lines and feels that the resulting overestimate of line length would require a greater expenditure of energy.

The problem of decoding Chinese texts is much the opposite of that of decoding texts in European languages. In the latter the word divisions are given and the problem is to make a correct morphemic analysis; for example, you must recognize that the word *bedraggled* is to be treated like *bedazzled* rather than like *bedridden* or you will come up with the nonexistent if evocative word *bed-raggled*. We have all known experiences, I believe, such as I had the other day when in a learnèd context I ran across the adjective "unchic" and assumed some arcane Greek source ˣunkhikos until the context forced me to consider the correct hypothesis that a well-known French loanword had acquired a Germanic negative prefix. In Chinese the problem is to group the clearly given morphemes into appropriate larger words; these may be compound lexemes or they may be opaque lexical primitives, since modern Chinese prefers its content words to be dissyllabic.

Although Chinese writing is essentially logographic or morphemic, the characters are also used phonetically to transliterate foreign names; these, however, are often abbreviated to the first syllable, especially when well known and when cited with a title. (Monosyllabic surnames are bound in Chinese so that they are normally accompanied by the given name or by a title: "Mao Tse-tung" or "Chairman Mao.") Although the characters are not being used in their original senses, an attempt is made to choose characters that have a pleasant or neutral connotation, unless referring to a political personality, when the writer is free to vent his feelings by picking characters with abusive meanings. Hence to represent the name of a western statesman the newspapers in Peking may choose characters quite different from those in use in Taiwan or Hongkong. The transliterative use of characters—an extension of the "phonetic loan"—is quite old, as shown by the many early loanwords from India and Central Asia. It is from such traditions that the Japanese took the inspiration for their syllabaries; and these in turn inspired the Chinese in 1918 to create a set of phonetic symbols—representing initial, medial, and final (plus tone)—called zhùyīn zìmǔ that have been used primarily as a notation to teach the standard pronunciation of the characters, now often done on the mainland by the Romanization system known as pīnyīn.

In like manner, though western writing is essentially alphabetic, non-alphabetic symbols are also used [cf. Edgerton 1941]. The sentence "$2 + 2 = 4$" contains symbols for the words *plus* and *equals,* the latter perhaps containing two morphemes; the writing is logographic, not ideographic, since the sentence is not properly read as its paraphrases 'two and two are/is/make(s) four' but only as 'two and two equals four' with an implied ellipsis '(the sum of) two and two' to account for the fact that the verb is marked as singular. The symbols for the numerals, on the other hand, are more complex, since they represent different elements in, say, "24" and "42d," to say nothing of "½." Arithmetical systems, like formal logic, would appear to be technological inventions thrust upon natural languages, and thus we do not expect them to be amenable to descriptions of the sort linguists feel relevant. But there are other logographic elements in western writing. The ampersand, if we put aside its use in "&c" = "etc.," is normally read only 'and,' never 'plus.' In some instances, inversion is required: "$20" is read 'twenty dollars'—losing its plural marker in "$20 bill." The musical symbols for 'sharp' and 'flat' are logographic, as is the symbol for 'percent.' Other symbols may have a conventional reading but are intended as direct representations of meaning: the magic arrows in transformational grammars can be read 'yields,' 'transforms into,' 'converts into' as well as 'is (to be) rewritten as,' but often they are interpreted more directly, as are ideographic traffic signs, some of which are highly iconic.

When Chinese characters reached Japan they were eagerly embraced by an inquisitive people who admired discipline, respected learning, and showed an extraordinary taste for variety. Unfortunately they also had tin ears. The phonetic simplicity of their native language, with well under a hundred original syllables, made it a tortuous task to assimilate the more elaborate syllables of classical Chinese. Because of the richer syllable structure, Korean versions of Chinese words sound like Cantonese without tones; Japanese versions have a flavor all their own. The characters were repeatedly imported on different occasions and by different contacts with the mainland; as a result, the Japanese ended up with more than one "Chinese" reading for many of the characters. Now, in Chinese itself a number of characters have more than one traditional reading, the result of ancient derivational processes or of dialect mixture. Among those commonly used in Sino-Korean words, I have found about 82 characters with two (and in some cases three) different readings, for the most part corresponding to differences within Chinese. But in Japanese the several strains of borrowings led to different Sino-Japanese readings for many characters that have only a single reading in Chinese or Korean. The main strain, called the (Kan (=Hàn) readings, were and are highly productive in creating new words within Japanese; the Go (=Wú) readings came in with Buddhist terminology but spread into other domains, as well; and the so-called Sō (=Sòng)

and Tō (= Táng) readings arrived later in words that usually represented a technological borrowing of some sort, such as isu 'chair.' To
some extent we can devise rules—or, better, discover principles—to predict particular readings, so that an intelligent guess can be made whether
to read jin or nin for the character 'man' in a word one has never
seen before. But for the most part the distribution of readings in particular words must be left for the lexicographer to catalog.

When the Japanese borrowed Chinese characters they made an innovation that was to have far-reaching consequences. The characters represented Chinese morphemes, which the Japanese dutifully borrowed as
words and as bound elements; but the morphemes themselves represented
meanings, and the Japanese already had ways to express many of these
meanings in their own, vastly different, language. So the Japanese started
to associate a given character not only with the Chinese morpheme
or morphemes imported with it but also with native words that were
translational equivalents, calling these the "Kun" (explanatory) readings
as contrasted with the "On" (phonetic) readings. Needless to say, the
match between Chinese meanings was not always a happy one, for classical Chinese enjoyed a much larger vocabulary than early Japanese. In
a modern dictionary of medium size there are twenty characters that
have a traditional Kun reading mí(ru) 'see,' of which ten are in the
restricted list of 1850 known as Tōyō-Kánji; while only one in the list
(KEN) is sanctioned to be given that particular Kun reading, you will
sometimes run across others so used in modern prose, for example, the
characters KAN and SATSU that together form the word kansatsu 'observation.' In Morohashi's massive dictionary, there are 217 characters with
the reading mí(ru) 'see' [Ōkubo in Ōno 1962, pp. 145–146]. In the
further curtailed list of 881 characters known as the Kyōiku-Kánji 'educational characters' there are four that are sanctioned to be read as
haká(ru) 'measure' and also four that are read osamé(ru) 'obtain; master; rule.' On the other hand, Japanese sometimes has two different
Kun readings for a single Chinese character, as when one—already
burdened with three On readings of KŌ, GYŌ, and AN—is read both
i(ku) 'go,' or its variant yu(ku), and okona(u) 'do, act.'

With over fifteen hundred years to build up such associations, the
resulting state of the language today presents a tangled web that is
far from easy to describe in terms of linguistic structure. The relationship
between two different On readings and between either or both of these
and a Kun reading may be any of the following.

(1) They may contrast as free words, with somewhat different meanings: séi 'sex' or 'nature' is written with the same character as shó

'nature, disposition; quality' and as jō 'sentiment, passion'; they are different On readings of the same character, which has the Kun reading nasaké. (The first two are also used as suffixes -sei and -jō, with secondary voicing of 'disposition.')

(2) They may contrast as morphemes in different words: TAI and DAI both mean 'great,' and in most combinations only one or the other is appropriate; but when followed by the character meaning 'event' (JI/ kotó) we find that táiji is a noun that means 'matter of moment' or 'great deed' and daijí means (as a noun—sometimes with a different accent) 'great undertaking' or 'grave affair' and also (as an adjectival noun) 'important.'

(3) Two On readings may be in complementary distribution with each other, yet one of them as a free word will contrast with a Kun reading: kane is a noun meaning 'metal' or 'money'; the On reading KIN is used as a noun kín 'gold,' yet is lexically noncontrastive with the other On reading KON and its secondary variant -GON, which are always bound and mean either 'metal' or, specifically, 'gold.'

(4) The On and the Kun readings may be in complementary distribution, with the Kun occurring as a free noun or in compounds with other free elements, and the On limited to combinations with other bound Chinese elements: chi is a noun meaning 'blood' and its Kun reading KETSU is always bound, as in ketsuatsu 'blood pressure'; tsukí 'moon, month' is a free noun and its Kun readings GETSU and GATSU are bound and lexically noncontrastive.

While no painstaking study has been made of the associations (see Martin [1952] for some preliminary attempts), we get the feeling that the latter case is the ideal; we are tempted to say that chi and KETSU on the one hand and tsukí, GETSU, and GATSU on the other are, respectively, allomorphs of single morphemes. But the Japanese often make up new words out of Chinese elements—or abbreviate longer words; and they sometimes attach the Chinese elements to morphemes of other origins, so that a latent contrast in distribution must be recognized even for those cases that seem to show complementary distribution in the current vocabulary. The problem of the morphemic analysis can be felt, to some extent, if we ask ourselves the question how many morphemes are shared by the two English synonyms "inevitable" and "unavoidable." I will return to the problem of morpheme associations below.

But first let us note that the Japanese early took up the Chinese use of characters to transliterate foreign (in this case, Japanese) names and other words that were not easily translatable into Chinese. Out of this usage, sometimes called Man'yō-gana—from the use of full characters for a syllabary as exemplified in the poems of the Man'yō-shū—there gradually developed abbreviated characters used only for phonetic purposes, and these eventually were consolidated into two uniform systems: the katakana were created by taking bits and pieces from the printed-style forms and the hiragana were stylized from the shorthand or "grass-hand" styles of rapid brushwork.[1] Using either of these syllabaries it is possible to write any Japanese sentence, but today the usual orthography is a mixture of Chinese characters (called Kanji), used to write the Sino-Japanese morphemes and also many common content words of native origin, the squarish katakana (used for foreignisms, mimetic words, and other exotic elements), and hiragana used for everything else (grammatical elements, words of native or obscure origin, etc.). This sort of mixed script, called kana-mājiri, was described by Chamberlain [1899, p. 5] as a "backbone of Chinese characters with *kana* ligaments." Since the exact mixture of the three scripts depends upon an individual's education, knowledge, and whim, it is not surprising to find widespread anarchy in orthographic practices up until the educational reforms that followed Japan's defeat in World War II; these reforms have attempted to bring some semblance of standardization to the orthography, as well as a general simplification. Miller [1967, p. 133] tells us, "In 1927 the major Tokyo newspapers kept in stock printing type for between 7,500 and 8,000 different Chinese characters, and it was estimated at the time that an 'educated reader' would be 'familiar' with about 5,000 of these." Isemonger [1929, p. 94] says, "The maximum number . . . kept in stock by newspaper and printing offices . . . is about 9,500 of which some 3,000 are admittedly uncommon, so that 6,500 represents the approximate number kept in all the usual variety of sizes." Thirty years earlier Chamberlain [1899, p. 6] had written that "scholars carry over 4,000 characters in their heads, the general public about 3,000."

The postwar reforms aimed at reducing the number of characters and limiting the sanctioned readings to those deemed essential. Writers were asked to restrict. themselves to a list of 1850 characters "for the time being," called Tōyō-Kánji, and to use these only according to the prescribed orthographic standards; of these a reduced list of 881 essential characters was required to be taught during the six years of elementary education. It is interesting to note that Morohashi's dictionary has 1766 characters listed under the "water" radical alone, almost as many as the

[1] Most of the kana symbols are based on Chinese readings of the characters from which they are reductions. Exceptionally, both systems use Kun readings for the symbols TSU, TO, and ME; and the katakana system uses the Kun for E, CHI, MI, and WI as well.

number of characters in the entire Tōyō-Kánji list [Ōkubo in Ōno 1962, p. 142].

The results of these limitations on the number of sanctioned characters can be seen in studies of actual usage; I will cite the results reported by the National Language Research Institute (Kokuritsu Kokugo Kenkyū-jo), most readily accessible in the English summaries contained in KKK [1966]. Report 19 (1960) gives the following figures on the use of written forms in Japanese cultural reviews:

Sample Frequency	Different Characters	Running Text
1–8	1,364 = .49	4,012 = .034
9–	1,417 = .51	113,137 = .966
Total	2,781 = 1.00	117,149 = 1.00

A more comprehensive study in Reports 21 (1962) and 25 (1964) took all issues of 90 magazines published in 1956—a total of 227,000 pages—and by a "stratified cluster sampling plan" investigated 440,000 occurrences of full content words and some 100,000 occurrences of particles and bound auxiliaries. The results for the content words are reported as follows:

Sample Frequency	Different Words	Percentage of Running Text
1–6	32,782	.14
7–	7,234	.86
(50–)	(1,220)	(.63)
Total	40,016	1.00

The results for the characters:

Sample Frequency	Different Characters	Percentage of Running Text
1–8	1,333	.014
9–	1,995	.986
Total	3,328	1.00

In the entire sample the number of different characters was 3,505. The figure of 1,995 characters includes 1,673 of the 1850 Tōkyō-Kánji.

About 500 characters accounted for 80 percent of the running characters in the newspaper Asahi-Shímbun for the year 1950, according to Ōno [1967, p. 176], who estimates that a thousand characters would account for 90 percent, and the list of 1850 Tōkyō-Kánji for 96 percent. (It should be borne in mind that Asahi has made a conscientious effort to conform to the orthographic prescriptions of the Ministry of Education.) Ōno's study of 1953 showed that primary students actually acquired nearly 600 characters in rural areas, and about a hundred more in urban areas [Ōno 1967, p. 171].

Among the postwar orthographic reforms was the adoption of simplified shapes for many of the characters and elements within characters. Later, the Chinese Communists independently simplified their script [cf. DeFrancis 1967], but often with different results from the Japanese, so that the characters currently used in Peking and Tokyo have less in common today than they had at an earlier period.

Although vertical writing is still the norm in Japan, horizontally printed texts are not uncommon. The National Language Research Institute in its Report 24 (1964) examined the form of characters used in printing horizontally and came to the following conclusions: The easiest to read horizontally are rectangular characters, followed by square, and the most difficult are oblong characters; solid printing in rectangular characters can be read most rapidly and with the fewest pauses; word-separated printing in rectangular characters occasions the shortest pauses. In this connection it should be noted that the Japanese, like the Chinese, do not normally separate words; one of the important functions of the mixed script is to help word-like units stand out from their surroundings, so that word identification is on the whole easier than in a Chinese text, which provides no graphic clues to the appropriate groupings. (It would be interesting to study the appropriateness of various mixes to see what would be maximally effective in signaling word units.) In modern Korean an effort is made to space the words, but there is great variation in deciding what constitutes a word. Punctuation marks, a relative innovation in languages of East Asia, are used for logical and partly grammatical purposes, as when quotations are set off or questions are marked by "?". Traditionally, there was only a fat comma and a hollow period; these were used to signal major breaks, the period normally marking the end of a sentence. In modern texts, the comma is sometimes used to prevent a misreading: "2,3nichi" is to be read nisannichi 'two or three days,' but "23nichi" might be (and usually is) taken as níjū sannichi '23 days' or 'the 23rd of the month.'

We have described the kana systems as sets of symbols to write syllables. Properly speaking, we mean moras, which were probably identical with syllables in early Japanese but now are somewhat different, since longer syllables of two moras have developed from several different sources. In one respect, the kana system is componential and morphophonemic: to write moras with voiced initials, the appropriate symbol for the corresponding mora with voiceless initial is marked with a diacritic, two short strokes to the right that look rather like a ditto mark. When the voiced initial is basic, the notation is componential; when the voicing results from word compounding, the notation is also morphophonemic. A somewhat similar mark, a small circle like a degree sign (°) is put to the right of the symbol of a mora beginning with h- (or f-) to warn that the pronunciation requires a stop [p], the original sound of native Japanese /h/, which gradually weakened with time, except in some mimetic words and late loans, to a bilabial spirant and then lost its labiality; in some words, the notation is morphophonemic, the stop pronunciation having persisted after a mora pronounced as a consonant.[2] Once when strolling through Shinjuku I was startled to run across a neon sign that advertised an inn called Ii-jima, written with hiragana I and repetition mark followed by the Chinese character for 'island' (TŌ/shimá) accompanied by the voicing mark (〃). This is symptomatic of the ingenuity that Japanese display in playing with writing systems. In front of an eatery that specializes in eel you will sometimes see the word unagi 'eel' written with the first kana symbol shaped to resemble

---

[2] The symbols known as dakuten 'voicing mark' and han-dakuten 'half-voicing mark' were originally inspired by the little circle that Chinese philologists would put at one of the four corners of a character to indicate its tone class. The Japanese imitated this device but also started using one small circle (°) to mark a character having a voiceless initial and two (°°) to mark a character with a voiced initial. (But the voiceless initials were generally left unmarked.) The dakuten was first used with kana in 1035 in the form °°, and in the fourteenth century the mark was put to the upper right of the kana symbol and modified to look much the way it does today, that being the form in which it spread from 1600 on. The use of the han-dakuten (°) to mark the moras beginning with p- dates from the early 1600s; the term first appears in the Ongyoku-gokuen-shū of 1727. This diacritic is also used on occasion by modern linguists to indicate the nasal pronunciation of moras that begin with g-, replacing the dakuten that otherwise would mark the voicing of the velar initial. From as early as the eleventh or twelfth century, some scribes commendably marked the primary voiced sounds with a horizontal pair of circles °° and the secondary voiced sounds with a vertical pair °̥. (The prescribed way to write the little circle is to start at the bottom and go around clockwise, but individuals sometimes do it the other way.)

an eel. A gentleman with the family name of Edanashi, realizing that it can be taken as a pun 'branchless,' decides to write it with the character for 'tree' stripped of the downstrokes on either side [Shibata in Ōno 1967, p. 97]. Visual puns can lead to linguistic consequences. In Shikoku [Doi 1958, p. 337] a pawnshop is called nanatsu-ya 'seven shop' because the morpheme shichi in shichi-ya 'pawnshop' is taken as its homonym, the On reading of the character for 'seven.' Kunóichi is a widely known slang word for 'woman' that comes from taking the three component strokes of the character for 'woman' and reading the first as the hiragana KU that it resembles, the second as the katakana NO that it resembles, and the third as the Chinese character for 'one' with the On ICHI. An outrageous recent example is that of the aggressive Japanese businessmen abroad who describe themselves as striving for the image of misutā-irébun 'Mr. Eleven,' that is, one step shrewder than the Jew = jū, the On reading of the character for 'ten.'

The Japanese have not hesitated to make up new Chinese characters by analogy with the old ones.[3] A description of nearly 250 of these waséi-ji ('made-in-Japan characters') or kokuji ('vernacular characters'), as they are called, will be found in Alexander [1951], who notes that some (such as GAN 'cancer' and SUI 'pancreas') have been borrowed back into Chinese; others have been adopted in Korea, which has itself created a number of unique characters, noted as "Korea-made" in Korean character dictionaries, which are traditionally called okphyen after the 6th-century Chinese dictionary Yù Piān. Some of the made-in-Japan characters have only Kun readings (kómu 'enters,' tōge 'mountain pass,' tsuji 'crossroads'); some have only an On reading (GAN 'cancer'), and some have both: DŌ/hatara(ku) 'toil.' Modern creations, probably ephemeral, include a character for erebētā-gáru 'elevator girl' (the woman radical on the left with Symbols for 'up' and 'down' on the right) and one for hamu-ráisu 'ham and rice' that has the rice radical on the left and katakana HA on top of katakana MU on the right; both at first glance are very respectable-looking characters [Alexander 1951, p. 4). Lists of Japan-made Chinese compounds, such as shimpai 'worry,' mendō 'trouble,' sōdan 'conference,' kifu 'donation,' will be

---

[3] For example "fire" or "white" was combined with "(rice) field" to make two characters each read hata(ke) 'dry field'; a cue was probably taken from the Chinese terms "white (i.e., waterless) field" and "fire(-cleared) field," the latter a common phenomenon in primitive agriculture in Korea. "In inventing new characters to suit their own special needs, the Japanese did but follow the example set by every provincial Chinese dialect" [Chamberlain 1899, p. 127].

found in Kindaichi [1957, pp. 139, 142, 156–159. Some of these have been borrowed in Korean and Chinese.

I have spoken earlier of associations of a Chinese character with a Japanese word or morpheme. A more extravagant usage is to assign a single word (short or long) to a string of characters that are taken as a whole, assigned a meaning, and then translated into the word. Thus the character for 'earth' (= 'local') and that for 'product' are used to write miyage 'gift,' and the word samidare 'spring shower' is written with three characters that mean '5th-month rain.' These are but two of many common examples, long hallowed by popular usage. This device of arbitrary word assignments (sometimes called ate-ji) frees Japanese literary men to write down long Chinese words with the intention that they be read as Japanese or modern European expressions of quite different structure, a tour de force felt to be esthetically elegant as well as ingenious. In order to let the reader in on the game, of course, the author must somehow signal his intention. This is done by the use of furigana, tiny kana symbols put alongside, either to indicate the appropriate On or Kun reading for each individual character in a word or, when the word is written as ate-ji, to show the reading of the whole. Thus what you might want to read as aodake-iro 'green bamboo color' will perhaps turn out to be accompanied by furigana that tells you the writer had in mind the word shātorūzu 'chartreuse'; and an author describing foreign men's appreciation of Japanese women may want you to read Nihon-jósei as Japanīzu-gáru 'Japanese girl.'[4] The device is not limited to Chinese compounds. In

---

[4] Isemonger (1929: 10) refers to ate-ji as "guess words." We can visualize a similar

device in English that would let us translate the Japanese TAIJIN with ADULT ^(otona) ^(grownup), perch-

ing the "native" word atop the foreignism as a reminder notation. I have culled a

number of revealing examples from the pages of a highly colloquial author (Kubota

Mantarō): KONNICHI ^(kyō) 'today,' SAKUYA ^(yūbe) 'last night,' SAKUJITSU ^(kinō) 'yesterday,' MYŌNICHI ^(ashita)

'tomorrow,' KACHI ^(neuchi) 'value,' SHŌKO ^(akashi) 'proof,' SEIMEI ^(inochi) 'life,' KOKYŪ ^(iki) 'breath,' DŌJŌ ^(omoiyari)

'sympathy,' KUTSŪ ^(kurushimi) 'distress,' KOGAI ^(soto) 'outdoors,' CHUSHIN ^(mannaka) 'middle,' SHŪI ^(mawari) 'around,'

SHIHEN ^(atari) 'neighborhood,' ZEMPŌ ^(mae) 'ahead,' KŌKEI ^(keshiki) 'scenery,' JŌKYAKU ^(nori-te) 'rider,' SHUJIN ^(aruji)

'master,' NYŌBŌ ^(kamisan) 'wife,' RŌJIN ^(toshiyori) 'old person,' DŌHAN ^(tsure) 'companion,' SEISHITSU ^(tachi) 'char-

wake   koto   hakarazu   jika
acter,' RIYŪ 'reason,' JIJITSU 'fact,' HUTO   'unexpectedly,' CHOKUSETSU ni 'immedi-
bikkuri
ately,' KIKKYŌ 'startled.' Although typically the glossed word is a binom, longer
                    arashi   ototoi
compounds will also be found: there are three characters in BŌHŪU 'storm,' ISSAKUJITSU
          asatte
'day before yesterday,' and MYŌGONICHI 'day after tomorrow;' there are four characters
saki-ototoi   si-asatte
in ICHI-ISSAKUJITSU 'three days ago' and MYŌ-MYŌGONICHI 'three days from now.' Some-

times the characters give a more specific meaning to the native gloss: DOKUSHIN means

'alone' but hitori 'one person' has wider uses; SEMPŌ means 'ahead' but mukō means

'over there;' YŌJI means 'infant' but kodomo is a child of any age; ZUNŌ means 'brains'

(and is extended to 'intelligence') but atama 'head' has many additional meanings;

KIKAI is an 'opportunity' but orí 'an occasion' has wider uses. "Moto" is used as a gloss

both for IZEN 'formerly' and for GEN'IN 'cause.' The word itsu 'when' is used to gloss

both NANNICHI 'what day' and NANJI 'what time.' For shina 'quality' in the passage

musume-rashíi shina o mísete 'showing girlish qualities' the Japanese writer chose the

characters KYŌTAI because the word means 'coquetry.' Sometimes both words are

Chinese in origin, though usually one is heavily assimilated, as when hontō is written

in kana to explain SHINJITSU 'truth,' tenden to explain KAKUJI 'respectively,' or dandan
                 fudan   daiji
to explain ZANJI 'gradually.' I have an example of a sentence written HEIZEI ga TAISETSU

da 'What is important is the ordinary;' the binoms in kana are normally written in

characters. (Elsewhere in the same text HEIZEI is glossed with the native word tsune

'always.') Once an author has given you one of his favorite ate-ji with its gloss and let

you get used to it a few times, he may feel you can get along without the gloss thereafter,

bearing in mind that he wants you to read, say, okamisan every time you see O-NAIGI-san

'wife' in the work. (Since you can not be sure he really means it—there being no device

to turn the ate-ji off—occasions for reader discomfort are frequent.)

Shūkan Asahi (2651:24b) I came across an example of the word mihari 'look-out' written with the appropriate Chinese characters and kana— 'look' + 'stretch' followed by hiragana RI—but accompanied by the hurigana information that this string was to be read as répo, an abbrevia- tion of the English loanword repótā 'reporter.' And in another issue of the same weekly (2665:14) my eye was caught by an advertisement that translates as "New timer switch. Completely eliminates the cord." The word for 'cord' was the indigenous noun himo and it was written in large katakana but accompanied by smaller katakana—above the word, since this was horizontal writing—that told me to read it as kódo, the English loanword for 'cord.' But kódo is also an English loanword meaning 'code.' So we see that the Japanese are running into many of the same problems of neutralization and diversification with European loans as they did ear- lier with the Chinese, despite the many differences between the languages and the eras of borrowing.

European words too are borrowed with more than one reading, some- times little more than free variants but usually acquiring specialized sen- ses. The word garasu, early borrowed from Dutch, means 'glass' as a sub- stance; gúrasu was later borrowed from English to mean 'a glass.' Gómu from Dutch means 'rubber'; gámu from English means 'chewing gum.' Shítsu and shíto are both from English, but the former means a 'sheet (for a bed)' while the latter means 'tarp(aulin)' and conflicts with a homonym that means 'seat.' Since many European words are longish, as compared with Chinese, we might expect less danger of homonym con- flicts from their being borrowed into Japanese, but the Japanese like to shorten all longer words so that unanticipated homonyms are newly created within the loan stratum itself. The letters of the Roman alphabet are borrowed into Japanese and the name of a single letter can be used as the spoken acronym for any of several different words that begin with the letter. Thus "M" is read ému and used to mean either 'money' or 'penis'—the latter from 'membrum [virile],' it is said, though there may also be association with the older term mará that was taken as slang from a Buddhist term of Indic origin [Miller 1967, p. 248]. While the term M-bótan 'a trouser-fly button' is carried by Kenkyusha's Japanese-English Dictionary, only the accompanying picture would help you realize that the appropriate translation for a caption in Shūkan Asahi (2678:28c) that reads M-ken made okonau is 'They even give you a short-arm inspec- tion.' On the other hand katakana is normally used to write the recently popularized word étchi 'lewd, vulgar,' even though it seems to be bor- rowed from the name of the letter "H" for reasons unknown but perhaps having to do with the word harénchi 'shameless' which has enjoyed a semantic shift in the opposite direction, what with changing times and mores, as remarked upon in Atlas 16:37–38 (1968).[5] The letter Y has been put to use to write the first part of the word wai-shatsu, borrowed from 'white shirt' but now used more generally just to mean 'shirt,' shatsu alone being restricted to the meaning 'undershirt.' This is an odd phonetic use, rather than an example of morphemic writing, since Y also sometimes appears for the Sino-Japanese morpheme WAI 'obscene' found in waidan 'dirty story' and waisetsu 'obscenity.' The usual way of writing bijinesu-gáru 'business girl = female office worker' was BG, pronounced bījí, until it was replaced a few years ago by the euphemism OL (ō-éru) from ofisu-rédei 'office lady.'

There is one ideographic symbol that is in prominent use in Japan: a bold-looking sanserif "T" with an extra line across the top. This symbol, a straightened version of the katakana symbol TE, comes from an abbreviation of Teishin (-shō), the name of the old '(Ministry of) Communications,' now replaced by Yūsei(-shō) '(Ministry of) Postal Services,' and appears on Japanese letterdrops and mail boxes (called pósuto). But it is also used in texts to mean 'postage,' a concept that can be expressed by several different words. A vertically written text in Shūkan Asahi (2688:36c) recently contained the following stretch: the ideograph in question ("T" with an extra stroke) followed by the Chinese character KYŌ/tomo that means 'together,' the logograph for Yen ("Y" with equalsign superimposed), two Chinese numerals for '9' and '5' separated by a comma, and two Arabic zeros. The reading is . . . x tomo kyuusen gohyaku-en '9,500 Yen including postage,' but the x can be rendered as yūzei 'postage,' sōryō 'carriage,' kitte-dai 'stamp charge,' and possibly a few other ways; the passage was intended to be read silently and x appreciated at a higher level.[6]

One of the problems brought about by the wholesale borrowing of Chinese characters is the large number of homonyms that resulted from the Japanese inability to master many of the distinctions of classical Chinese, such as tones; further phonetic erosion within Japanese led to the convergence of even some of the distinctions that were earlier

[5] But Inagaki (1956: 65a) lists étchi as contemporary slang meaning 'queer' and says it comes from the romanized initial of hentai, the Sino-Japanese binom meaning 'queer.'
[6] I recently came across a passage presumably to be read Arabú-tai Isuráeru no kōsō . . . 'the dispute between the Arabs and Israel,' in which the conjunctional pseudosuffix -tai 'versus, against' (normally written with a Chinese character) was printed as a multiplication sign (sanserif X) between the two stretches of katakana used to write the foreign names. Or did the author perhaps want us to read the phrase as a nonce dvandva Arabu-Isuraeru 'Arab-Israel(i)?'

maintained. And so the syllable kō of Sino-Japanese corresponds to such diverse syllables of classical Chinese as ko, kau, kou, kang, kwang, and kong—each with aspirated vs. unaspirated initial and each with three different tones—as well as syllables like k(h)ap and k(h)op, to make a total of at least 38 different syllables, some of which already represented more than one morpheme in classical Chinese. Among the 881 essential "educational characters" there are 29 with the On reading KŌ. It does not necessarily follow, to be sure, that because a language has many morphemes that sound the same it also has many homonymous words. But the Japanese have freely borrowed Chinese bimorphemic compounds, called binoms, and they have been quick to make up new ones themselves, in utter disregard for the phonetic consequences. As a result there are at last eighteen fairly common words pronounced kōshō, undifferentiated even by accent; Kindaichi (1957:83) tells us that dictionaries carry over thirty words so read and reminds us that it is not uncommon to run across a phonetically bewildering array like shikaishikaishikai, to be interpreted as shi.ka-í.shi 'dentistry doctor' + kái 'meeting' combined with shi.kai 'chairing,' and used to mean 'chairman of the convention of dentists.' Such monstrosities, to be sure, seldom survive off the printed page; a skilled newscaster will rephrase the written words to make the meaning unambiguous to his listeners. And some homonyms are readily distinguished by context, especially those that differ in grammar, since a verbal noun or an adjectival noun will appear in constructions that differ from those enjoyed by an ordinary noun. Even so, there are frequent reports of oral comprehension problems that result from the conflict of homonyms. Kindaichi (1957:83) reports the case of the cabinet minister who began his answer to a question "What is the Minister's opinion on the public law?" with the words "The recent fire at Hōryū-ji was truly regrettable," having taken the word kokuhō to mean the 'national treasures' lost in that temple fire rather than the intended 'public law(s).' Under less formal circumstances, Suzuki [1963, p. 14] reports that he replied to his daughter's question "What is the national flower of France?" with "La Marseillaise," owing to the homonymity of kókka, which can be taken as 'national flower' or as 'national anthem.' An audience participant on a TV talk program gave his occupation as seika, and the puzzled master of ceremonies had to try out three different indigenous synonyms before he found out that the man before him was not a confectioner, a shoemaker, or a greengrocer, but a florist.

   A number of interesting questions can be raised about the Japanese language of today. To what extent are we to regard the long-standing associations of multiple readings as linguistic units, and on what stratum of the structure do they belong? We usually hesitate to assign allomorphs to a morpheme when they lack the phonetic similarity that bespeaks a common origin, except in those relatively rare cases (usually of grammatical elements) in which suppletion forces such a conclusion. The Korean subject marker is i after a consonant and ka after a vowel, but probably no other morpheme in the language (certainly no content morpheme) has allomorphs that are so totally lacking in phonetic similarity. When we put two disparate elements into a linguistic unit we are usually committing ourselves to a historical claim: that they will thenceforth operate as a unit, and this fact will manifest itself as the language changes. It is unclear to 'what extent such claims might be justified in the particular examples that Japanese poses. Perhaps Japanese has created a new breed of linguistic unit, a kind of *"hypermorpheme,"* for the reality of which we might seek evidence in psycholinguistic experiments. For example we can ask questions like these: To what extent are the character-based associations manifested in the language of preliterate children and of the congenitally blind? To what extent do decoding techniques differ for the congenitally deaf? For that matter, what sorts of decoding techniques are actually employed by normal readers and listeners? Many compounds have a unique directionality: the binom kokusai 'international' does not vie for attention with any ˣsaikoku 'nation-inter' and the characters in kokusai kōkū-jō 'international airport' could hardly be rearranged to make any sensible phrase. Are such strings of symbols usually grasped as units so that a printing error in arrangement might often go unnoticed or get automatically corrected? A few binoms permit the characters to appear in either order to yield synonyms: the word shíjū (also pronounced shótchū) 'from start to finish, always' has virtually the same meaning as the word shúshi, in which the characters for 'beginning' and 'end' are reversed. But if you reverse the characters in the binom shōhi 'consumption' you end up with hishō 'embezzlement,' which is not quite the same thing.

The National Language Research Institute has made several relevant studies such as Report 20 (1961) on Japanese homonyms and Report 28 (1965) on Japanese synonymy. The Japan Broadcasting Company (NHK) has also conducted some interesting research, with obvious practical aims in view. Future exploration would perhaps profit from a careful examination of the actual reading strategies and techniques employed by various kinds of readers, of the oral comprehension strategies of nonreaders or poor readers, and of the distribution of information cues in various kinds of written and spoken texts. Close cooperation between linguists and experimental psychologists would seem to be essential for a clearer understanding of the place of the written characters, and the associations they represent, in the overall language skills of the modern Japanese speaker. We also need studies of the relative quantity of Chinese compounds and of English loanwords in different kinds of Japanese text, both written and spoken. Modern Japanese is said (by Shibata in Ōno 1967:73) to contain about 60 percent Chinese vocabulary (called Kan-go) and 5 percent European (called Yō-go), but these figures seem to be based on dictionary entries, not on current texts.

I would like to see some statistics to back up the feeling many of us have that the same content takes up less space in printed Japanese than it does in English. Japanese translations of English books seem to be as much as a third shorter than the original texts and they may well read that much faster under the eye of a skilled reader. There are several explanations—aside from size of type—that might account for this discrepancy. English is overexplicit and requires the repetition of many redundant words that a Japanese translation will omit; the word "the" seldom survives translation, for example, and that omission alone must lead to the accumulation of a sizable hoard of saved space. Abstract words borrowed from French or Latin and Greek tend to be longer than the equivalent translations into Chinese characters, and that may be another factor.

A sociolinguistic study of some interest would be the conflicting Japanese attitudes toward proper names. Some parents prefer the simple and traditional when they name their children, others delight in arcane literary allusions and farfetched readings. I recall meeting a gentleman whose card presented the characters for his given name as '51'; challenged to read the name, I luckily ventured the archaic Isokazu, but I was unable to fathom the reason for the odd name until he revealed that his father had been 51 years old when he was conceived! The reluctance—or inability—of many Japanese to consult telephone directories may say something about certain areas of functional literacy that are overlooked in ordinary surveys.

References

Alexander, R. P., 1951. *Kokuji.* Supplement to *A Grammar of Formal Written Japanese* by W. P. Lehmann and Lloyd Faust, Cambridge, Mass.: Harvard University Press.

Alleton, Viviane, 1970. *L'Écriture chinoise.* ("Que Sais-je?" no. 1374.) Paris: Presses Universitaires de France.

Chamberlain, B. H., 1899. *Moji no shirube, or A Practical Introduction to the Study of Japanese Writing.* Yokohama.

Chang, Chung-Yuan, 1942. A study of the relative merits of the vertical and horizontal lines in reading Chinese print. *Arch. Psych.* p. 276.

Chao, Y. R., 1948. *Mandarin Primer.* Cambridge, Mass.: Harvard University Press.

Chaplin, H. I., and Martin, S. E., 1969. *A Manual of Japanese Writing.* 3 vols. New Haven: Yale University Press, rev. ed.

DeFrancis, John, 1950. *Nationalism and Language Reform in China.* Princeton: Princeton University Press.

————, 1967. Language and script reform. *Current Trends in Linguistics* 2:130–50. The Hague: Mouton.

Doi, Shigetoshi, 1958. *Tosa-kotoba.* Kōchi.

Dougherty, Ching-yi, S. M. Lamb, and S. E. Martin, 1963. *Chinese Character Indexes.* 5 vols. Berkeley: University of California Press.

Du Ponceau, Peter S., 1838. *A Dissertation on the Nature and Character of the Chinese System of Writing.* Philadelphia: The American Philosophical Society.

Edgerton, William F., 1941. Ideograms in English writing. *Language* 17:148–50.

Inagaki, Minoru, 1956. *Ingo jiten* [Argot dictionary]. Tokyo: Tōkyō-dō.

Isemonger, N. E., 1929. *The Elements of Japanese Writing.* London: Royal Asiatic Society, repr. 1943.

Kindaichi, Haruhiko, 1957. *Nihon-go* [The Japanese language]. Tokyo: Iwanami.

KKK = Kokuritsu Kokugo Kenyū-jo, 1966. *An Introduction to the National Language Research Institute: A Sketch of Its Achievements. Tokyo:* KKK.

Lee, Sang-Beck, 1957. *The Origin of the Korean Alphabet Hangul According to New Historical Evidence.* Publications of the National Museum of Korea, Series A, Vol. 3. Seoul: Tong-Mun Kwan. In Korean, with English summary.

Martin, S. E., 1952. *Morphophonemics of Standard Colloquial Japanese.* Language Dissertation no. 47. Baltimore: Linguistic Society of America.

Miller, R. A., 1967. *The Japanese Language.* Chicago: University of Chicago Press.

Morohashi, Tetsuji, 1955–1960. Dai Kanwa jiten. 13 vols. Tokyo: Taishūkan.

Muraishi, Shōzō, 1959. Dokusho-katei no bunseki [Analysis of reading stages], *KKK ronshū 1: Kotoba no kenky.* Tokyo: KKK.

Ōno, Susumu, et al., 1967. *Nihon-go o kangaeru* [Thinking about the Japanese language]. Tokyo: Yomiuri-shimbunsha.

Ramming, Martin, 1960. Bemerkungen zur problematik der schriftreform in Japan. Sitzungsberichte der Deutschen Akademie der Wissenschaftern zu Berlin: Klasse für Sprachen, Literatur und Kunst, no. 4.

Soothill, W. E., 1942. *The Student's Four Thousand* [character] *and General Pocket Dictionary.* London: Kegan Paul, 16th ed.; original ed. 1899.

Suzuki, Takao, 1963. *A Semantic Analysis of Present-day Japanese: With Particular Reference to the Rôle of Chinese Characters.* Tokyo: The Keio Institute of Cultural and Linguistic Studies, 1963.

Wang, William S.-Y., 1971. Review of Liu: Chinese characters and their impact on other languages of East Asia. *Modern Language J.* 15:187–188.

JOHN B. CARROLL

The Case for Ideographic Writing

A Discussion of Martin's Paper

The two characteristics of nonalphabetic writing systems that are most likely to astonish the user of an alphabetic system are, first, the apparent complexity of the characters, and second, the apparently large number of different characters that the reader must be able to recognize in order to be able to read ordinary texts written for mature readers. That these characteristics do indeed present considerable difficulty for native speakers of Chinese, Japanese, and Korean is signaled by the fact that writing-system reforms for at least two of these languages have been directed at (1) simplifying characters (for example, by reducing the number of strokes), and (2) limiting the number of characters to be used.

It is revealing, however, to turn the tables and see how an alphabetic writing system might look to a user of a nonalphabetic system. Let's imagine a dialogue that might have taken place, let's say, in the court of Peiping in the mid-19th century between the Chinese Minister of Education (a Mandarin scholar) and the ambassador from Great Britain, during a period when the relations between China and Great Britain were relatively peaceful:

MANDARIN: Tell me about your writing system; I'm wondering whether it's something we ought to adopt for Chinese. I'm looking at one of your books, and I see you print spaces between your characters. We save a lot of space by not doing that.

AMBASSADOR: Well, yes, but we don't call them characters; we call them words. And we can hardly do without the spaces between the words.

MANDARIN: Whatever they are, those words look as complicated to me as our characters. Sometimes they use many more strokes than any of our characters do!

AMBASSADOR: I suppose they look complicated to you, but please notice, Sir, that they are composed of separate letters. We have only 26 different letters in our alphabet, and it takes no more than two or three strokes to write each letter. More important, the letters give us a key to the sound of the words.

MANDARIN: But our Chinese characters are composed of parts, too, and each part can be written with a small number of strokes. Sometimes the parts give a clue as to the sound, but we don't care so much about the sound—we care about the meaning. Most often the parts of the character give us a key to the meaning of the character as a whole, and there aren't too many different kinds of parts.

AMBASSADOR: In our system, we assume that if you can get the sound of the word, you get the meaning.

MANDARIN: I beg your pardon, but do you mean to say that all readers of English pronounce your characters in the same way? We have many dialects of Chinese, and a given character may be pronounced in quite different ways in different dialects. In that way the speakers of all our dialects can read the same writings, even if they can't understand one another when they speak.

AMBASSADOR: Yes, we have many dialects, but the pronunciations don't differ greatly, and the dialects are generally intelligible to one another. We find that speakers of different dialects can still learn to read, at about the same pace, by applying their own system of pronunciation to the letters of the words.

MANDARIN: That may be, but I suspect, Sir, that there is more difficulty caused by dialect differences than you are aware of. Now, let me turn to another aspect of the problem. I have been told that there is a great deal of inconsistency in your spelling system, so that a child may have trouble learning to read even if he speaks what you call "the Queen's English." In effect, he has to learn the way every single word is to be read and spelled, just as our Chinese children have to learn the way every different character is to be read and written. To be sure, your English child may be helped by certain cues in the characters just as our Chinese children are helped by recognizing what we call our "radicals" and our "phonetics," but he still has to learn every word as a separate thing. Isn't that true?

AMBASSADOR: Certainly there's some truth in what you say, I suppose.

MANDARIN: And yet another point: I've heard that many of your words have the same sound, but are printed with different letters depending upon the meaning. It is somewhat the same in Chinese; in fact, we have only a fairly small number of different syllables, but a given syllable may be represented by a number of different characters.

AMBASSADOR: You are right: we do have words that have the same sound but are spelled differently. But I don't think we have as many of these variations as you have in Chinese. In any case, this probably causes more difficulty in spelling than in reading. By Jove! You've made me realize something: when a word has different spellings, the different spellings help our children get the meanings, once they learn them, just as your Chinese children learn the meanings of the characters.

MANDARIN: Ah so! . . . Indeed, quite so. But now consider: I understand that in your language, a given printed word may have several different pronunciations. If you take any one dialect of Chinese, like my Mandarin dialect, you find very little of that sort of thing. Each character generally has only one pronunciation, if you ignore certain variations of tone and inflection. Those Japanese devils across the Yellow Sea, who have borrowed so much of our writing system, were stupid enough to use the same character for many different pronunciations. It seems to me that you English have made the same mistake.

AMBASSADOR: I shan't speak for the Japanese, but I don't really think our system is as defective in this respect as you suppose. Nevertheless, you have put your finger on something that has caused our educators much anguish.

MANDARIN: If you will allow me to say so at this point, Honorable Sir, it seems to me that your "alphabetic" spelling system is not so different from our character writing after all—at least in the way it truly functions. And isn't it the case that you have a very large number of words in your language—many more words than we have characters? In fact, you English pride yourselves on the number of words you can print in your dictionaries! It must take a very long time, does it not, for people to learn to read all those words?

AMBASSADOR: Yes, we have a great many different words, but we make out with only about 10 to 20 thousand words for ordinary purposes, and that's not much more than the number of characters you need to print most of your books. Our more educated classes learn to read these ten or twenty thousand words, and more, by the time they reach the university. But we teach only a limited number of words in the first school year, and gradually increase the vocabulary as the child grows older.

MANDARIN: Precisely! That's the way we teach characters, too. If your spelling system were as good as you claim, you could have children reading any word they know in speech, as soon as you teach them to read the letters.

AMBASSADOR: I don't believe it's quite that simple. I'll grant that our spelling system gives us problems, but still it works. Maybe you should talk with the Spanish ambassador. I've heard that the spelling system in his country is more regular than ours. But I must take leave of you now.

MANDARIN: I am so sorry that we cannot talk longer, for this discussion has been most interesting. But from what you have told me, I see little advantage in changing our system of writing; indeed, it might cause much difficulty if we were to do so. Nevertheless, I think your notion of an alphabet could help us; I shall put our scholars to work on composing a phonetic key that may assist our people to learn the sounds of our characters. Thank you very much, Sir, and Good day!

In this imaginary dialogue I have tried to suggest that the problems of teaching the reading of an alphabetic system may not be very different from those of a nonalphabetic system. The learning of the quick and easy recognition of words or wordlike units is a process that must take account of the fact that the graphic representations of those words are complex, and that there are relatively large numbers of such units that must be recognized. This is true whether or not the words are represented by an alphabetic principle, and whether or not the alphabetic principle is applied in some sense of the term "regularly." A perfectly regular alphabetic system may *facilitate* word-recognition processes, but its use does not alter the fact that the learning of reading entails the acquisition of skills in composing word-units from their separate graphic components, and practice—large amounts of it—in recognizing particular word units. One sees here the operation of what might be called a "universal" in the acquisition of writing systems.

In the time-worn, dreary controversy between "phonic" and "look-say" methods of teaching English-speaking children to read (a controversy that has its parallels even in countries whose writing systems are more "regular"), critics of the "look-say" method have sometimes complained that it treats the English writing system as if it were a nonalphabetic system like Chinese, requiring the child to learn the recognition of thousands of separate, unanalyzed word forms. Although I would be the last to support any pure "look-say" method, I think we should not forget the role of rapid word recognition in skilled reading. In this respect an alphabetic writing system cannot help resembling a nonalphabetic one. In a nonalphabetic system, recognition of characters depends on the total configuration of parts. In an alphabetic system, skilled recognition of words depends not so much on the recognition of individual letters as on the recognition of the total configuration of letters. This is what the tachistoscopic word recognition studies of Erdmann and Dodge, J. M. Cattell, and others told us long ago. The "look-say" reading-teaching methods that were in vogue in the 1920s and 1930s in this country overgeneralized this result in such a way as to ignore the role of individual components in word recognition. From our present perspective, we would be tempted to say that word recognition depends on a matching of the stimulus with some deep, abstract representation of graphic configuration that is stored in memory. The fact that a skilled reader can recognize words even when they are badly mutilated or written in a distorted way seems to support this idea. It works this way also in a nonalphabetic system, as I recently had occasion to observe. We had bought an elaborately carved Chinese desk that had a few Chinese characters etched into one corner of it. I copied off these characters as best I could in order to show them to some Chinese friends and get an interpretation. It turned out that my copy was far from an exact representation of the original characters, because the carving was faint and partly obliterated or worn, so that many of the proper strokes were lacking. Yet my friends had only a little trouble recognizing what had been intended.

Some of the papers at this conference are concerned with how sound is represented in alphabetic writing systems. But we can learn much from the characteristics of systems that minimize the representation of sound, or so-called "nonalphabetic" systems. (Parenthetically, I draw your attention to how much Martin's paper was concerned with sound representation even in nonalphabetic systems.) Consider Classical Chinese, which made very little use of sound representation at least in its early history. Some years ago I became acquainted with problems of teaching Chinese to non-Chinese speakers. There have been, apparently, two schools of thought about this. One school (represented by the work of Professor Creel at the University of Chicago) attempted to teach Chinese by starting with Classical Chinese—teaching the characters, and their histories and meanings, with little if any attention to the sounds (which are in any case not completely known for ancient Chinese). It was even possible for students to learn to read Chinese (i.e., get its meaning) by a kind of character-for-character translation into English. The other school (as represented more generally throughout American universities) believed that the best road to learning Chinese (even if Classical Chinese was the objective) was through teaching the modern spoken vernacular, only gradually introducing the structure and writing of Classical Chinese. Now, Classical Chinese is at least as different from vernacular Chinese as Old English is from present-day English (in some ways I'm exaggerating the differences, in other ways oversimplifying them). In any case, I would have liked to ask Sam Martin, if he were here, to confirm or disconfirm the opinion, that I frequently heard from experienced teachers of Chinese, to the effect that students who learned by the first method were rarely able, even after long study, to attain fluent command of written Chinese (whether classical or modern), in contrast to those who learned by the second method. It would seem as if those who learned the spoken language had a better command of the deep structure of the language and were better able to apply it in reading Chinese in various styles including "newspaper Chinese" and Classical Chinese. To use the theory proposed by Mattingly in the paper that he will be presenting, we might say that these latter students were better able to read Chinese by using the graphic representation to arrive at a kind of internal reconstruction of the spoken form of what was written, and from this to derive the meaning.

Yet reading Chinese does not call solely upon internal representations of sound, for it happens that the spoken form of Chinese often fails to communicate the entire meaning. One must appeal to particular meanings of particular characters. Chinese speakers, even speaking the same dialect, frequently have to write out characters in the air in speaking to one another, to avoid ambiguity or even complete confusion. The Chinese linguist Y. R. Chao once concocted a Chinese story all of whose spoken syllables were identical (except for differences in tone), which would have been almost completely unintelligible in speech but was perfectly intelligible in written characters. For an educated speaker of Chinese, the internal representation clearly consists of much more than sound and meaning; it has a graphic counterpart. I wonder whether this may not also be the case for literate speakers of alphabetic languages. Would not the internal representation of "The sun's rays meet" be somehow different from that of "The sons raise meat," not only in meaning, of course, but also in graphic counterparts? I find myself to some extent having images of printed words as I speak and hear language, just as I also tend to experience auditory images as I read, and I take it that I am not alone in this.

Note also that graphic symbols can under some circumstances mask their sound representation. One example: "Pas de leur Rhône que nous," as a concealed spelling of "Paddle your own canoe." Apparently this sort of thing happens all the time in Japanese, and the Japanese have to become skilled in deciphering such anomalies.

In planning the present discussion, I thought of a number of possible topics that might be pertinent. For example, I considered reviewing the evidence assembled for UNESCO by the late William S. Gray [1956] to the effect that reading behavior, and the learning of reading, are in most respects similar across a wide variety of languages, both alphabetic and nonalphabetic. There is in fact a rather voluminous literature of experimental psychological studies on the reading of Chinese and

Japanese, both in this country and in the Far East, although much of it is inaccessible to one who does not read Chinese and/or Japanese. I thought of recounting the fascinating history of the so-called "RAL" method developed in Red China in the late 1940s to teach literacy to the large mass of the Chinese people by a kind of "forced learning" technique—a method that presents large numbers of characters in very short periods of time and that relies on group competition and confidence-building procedures to achieve rapid learning. I pondered whether to comment on the claim of Makita [1968], a Japanese neuropsychiatrist, that there is a low incidence of reading failure among Japanese children due to the structure of the Japanese writing system (actually, he had reference to the phonetic regularity of the *kana* syllabary systems). I even thought of presenting some data about the frequency distributions of Chinese and Japanese characters and words, analyzed by new mathematical techniques that I have developed under an NICHD grant (HD01762) at the Educational Testing Service. But discussion of any one of these topics could have occupied the whole time at my disposal, and I am not sure how relevant they would have been. Therefore I content myself with reading them into the record, so to speak, hoping that what I chose to say instead would be provocative, or at least diverting.

References

Gray, W. S., 1956. *The Teaching of Reading and Writing*. Paris: UNESCO; Chicago: Scott Foresman.

Makita, K., 1968. The rarity of reading disability in Japanese children. *Amer. J. Orthopsychiat.* 38:599–614.

WAYNE O'NEIL

Our Collective Phonological Illusions: Young and Old

A Discussion of Klima's and Martin's Papers

That alphabetic writing systems are more principled than is generally granted, that their principles lie deeper in language than surface phonology has been recognized from time to time in the past. For example, Edward Sapir [1949, p. 54], as he went about explaining why his American Indian informants couldn't hear that certain sound segments were identical or different, argued the following in 1933: "John's certainty of difference in the face of objective identity is quite parallel to the feeling that the average Englishman would have that such words as *sawed* and *soared* are not phonetically identical. It is true that both *sawed* and *soared* can be phonetically represented as *sɔ'd*, but the -ing forms of the two verbs (*sawing, soaring*), phonetically *sɔ'-iŋ, and sɔ'r-iŋ*, and such sentences and in forms as "Saw on, my boy!" and "Soar into the air!" combine to produce the feeling that the *sɔ'd* of *sawed* = *sɔ'*-d but that the *sɔ'd* of *soared* = *sɔ'r*-d. In the one case zero = zero, in the other case zero = r. Among educated but linguistically untrained people who discuss such matters differences of orthography are always held responsible for these differences of feeling. This is undoubtedly a fallacy, at least for the great mass of people, and puts the cart before the horse. Were English not a written language, the configuratively determined phonologic difference between such doublets as *sawed* and *soared* would still be 'heard' as a collective illusion, as a true phonetic difference."

Klima has now proposed with admirable clarity five letter assignment conventions and four criteria from which to consider our collective illusions and within which to frame the notion "adequacy of orthography." What I shall do is look at two spelling systems, relating them to the conventions that Klima has proposed; but the question that I shall be asking is not what is an adequate orthography in some abstract sense but rather what do people do that they think is adequate.

In the first instance let us consider the standard orthography of Modern Faroese,[1] a West Scandinavian language spoken in the Faroe

[1] See O'Neil (In press) for a full discussion of the phonological basis of Faroese orthography.

Islands. This is an interesting case to examine, for there was no Faroese orthography until the middle of the 19th century[2] and thus no reason to believe that the orthography had any historical fetters on it. For one often hears, as he attempts to lay out the sweet reasonableness of English or French orthography, But isn't it that way because the printers got together in 17th or 18th century England or France and decided to do it that way? So rather than go off on a long thing about printers' being human too and about the relationships between historical change and synchronic grammar, it's just easier to have Faroese.

About the middle of the 19th century V. U. Hammershaimb [1891] put together an orthography for Faroese that he called etymological, that is, one in which morphemes are generally represented in one and only one way, as long as they are regular, and from which pronunciation can be predicted by the phonological rules of the language.[3] Clearly, then, Faroese orthography in large part, and like English orthography, falls under Klima's third convention, wherein the dominance of underlying phonemes is presupposed. This is of course true only insofar as the morpheme in question is regularly affected by the phonological rules. Irregularities are written down to the point where they fall into regular positions. Thus, for example, [turrur], 'dry (adj.),' is spelt *turrur* and [tɔdna], 'dry (v.),' is spelt *torna:* the underlying /r/ of the stem /tur-/ is preserved in the spelling of the verb because of a general assimilation rule in Faroese (viz.: $r \rightarrow d/-n$) but the underlying /u/ is not, since $u \rightarrow o$ is a rule in Faroese limited to vowel-graded stems and not a general phonological phenomenon.

Further support for the general claim about Faroese orthography lies in the Faroese use of the letter ð which nowhere turns up [ð] in surface phonology: *bráður,* 'sudden,' rimes with *bláur,* 'blue,' rimes with *lágur,* 'low': [brɔəvur]: [blɔəvur]: [lɔəvur]. However, an underlying segment /ð/ is needed because of such forms as *bráðliga,* 'suddenly,' pronounced [brɔdlija]. Moreover, this segment cannot be underlying /d/, for it shows up as [d] in intervocalic positions. Thus there is a rule of Faroese phonology that deletes /ð/ in intervocalic position and one that otherwise assimilates it to [d]. Faroese spelling represents the input to these rules, not their output.

There is then convincing support for the claim that Faroese orthography falls under Klima's third convention. This fact, together with similar observations about English—Chomsky and Halle [1968], O'Neil

---

[2] Earlier attempts to set language down were meant for non-Faroese eyes and ears; see Svabo [1966] and Haugen [1968].

[3] For discussion of Faroese phonology, see O'Neil (1964) and Anderson (1969).

[1969], C. Chomsky [1970], etc.—and other orthographies, suggests that there may be something quite natural about the tendency for underlying phonemes to be what is represented in orthography. The notion "adequacy of orthography" should not in fact be framed outside what it is that human beings do as they go about writing their languages. And what they seem to do first is what Klima did third.

Let us now turn to a second, quite different case. Late in the 19th century—less than fifty years after Faroese was given an orthography—the Faroese linguist Jakob Jakobsen [1957] proposed certain reforms for the orthography that would have pushed it in the direction of Klima's first and second conventions (Klima, this volume). His arguments for reform were quite simple: although the standard orthography was adequate for Faroese adults, that is, people who knew the language, it was too difficult for children, that is, people still learning the language (p. 32). And since it was as a child that one learned to read and write, the task could be made easier by adopting an orthography that presupposed the dominance of surface phonemes.

Jakobsen's suggested reforms—which of course did not succeed: why should adults give up a system which does so well by them—depend on certain presuppositions about children's phonological perceptions, their collective illusions: that they are quite different from, more phonologically superficial than those of adults. Jakobsen provided no evidence for his claim, his conclusion being based presumably in the fact that Faroese children did indeed have difficulty learning to read and write.

Is there any evidence for such a claim? Recently, Charles Read [1970] has examined the unschooled writing of 20 children aged 3 to 6.[4] These children had worked up orthographies based on the letter names (for vowels) and letter names minus their vowel parts (for consonants). In other words they wrote FIN, RIT, FEL, DEN, MAN, AT, etc. for *fine, write, feel, dean, main, ate,* etc.[5] And because of their letter names they at first used H for [č], Y for [w], W not at all, C & S for [s], but J only for [ǰ]; thus HAN, YEL, CAK or SAK, JAL, etc. for *chain, wheel, sake, jail,* etc. They subsequently learnt (presumably from the adults about them) to use G for [g] and C for [k] sometimes; thus GAM for *game* and JACC for *Jake's.*

Letter names finally run out and the helpful suggestions that adults offer are useful only up to a certain point. What then does the child do when he wants to represent some sound for which he has no letter name?

---

[4] What follows is abstracted from Read (1970), but also see Read (1971) and C. Chomsky (1971a, b).
[5] Following Read, I use upper case letters to indicate children's spellings.

For the lax vowels he proceeds to use the letter whose name can be said to contain the sound he is after. That is, since [a] is included in [āy], [i] in [īy], and [e] in [ēy], he writes DAN, PIT, FEN, etc. for *den, pot, fin,* etc. When that strategy runs out (as it soon does) he uses the letter whose name contains the vowel he wants if the feature [low] is ignored; he thus writes I for [ʌ] and A for [æ]: RAN, YIZ, etc. for *ran, was,* etc.

For consonants he employs a similar strategy, using (e.g.) H or S for [š]: FEH or FES for *fish* and G for [ŋ#]: SEG for *sing.* In addition, he also learns (again, presumably, from his adults) to use certain letters and combinations of letters in the conventional way: W, CH, TH, SH, etc. for [w], [č], [θ] and [ð], [š], etc. And finally—an indication of how closely his ear is to the phonetic surface—the child identifies initial *t* and *d* before *r* ([t] and [d]) not with T or D but with H (or CH,—sometimes spelt HC) and J: (C) HRA, (C) HREK, (C) HRIBLS, JRAGN, JRADL, etc. for *tray, trick, troubles, dragon, dreidel,* etc.

There are of course some things that he cannot write because he cannot associate them with any letter name. For him there is no phonetic relationship between simple nasals (written *m, n,* and *g*) and the nasals in postvocalic nasal clusters. So he characteristically does not write the latter and allows BIPE, FEGR, WAT, HACC, etc. to stand for *bumpy, finger, went, Hank's,* etc.

Clearly these children hover close to the phonetic ground as they seek to write what they hear. It would be more clear were they not constrained to operate within the limits of an alphabet of 26 letters, some of which are of no use at all to them. Just as clearly the writing they finally come up with is multiply ambiguous and dead wrong from the viewpoint of adult phonological perceptions and standard orthography. However, the child does go beyond standard orthography in abstractness in eliminating certain sequential redundancies. For example, he writes syllabic [r, l, m, n] simply R, L, M, N: SATR, LABL, BITM BITN, etc. *center, label, bottom, button,* etc. And some few children leave out the vowel in initial, unstressed cv syllables if what results is a consonant cluster that is not an initial cluster in English: PTATO, DVIN, etc. for *potato, divine,* etc. but BvLO for *below* (where v = any vowel letter, that being the child's solution to the problem of writing unstressed vowels).

The facts that I have summarized here are consistent across all 20 cases that Read examined. Their consistency is not, however, limited to just those children who for one reason or another pick up on writing, for the mistakes all children make in their early school attempts at spelling are many of them consistent with Read's facts. These mistakes include, inter alia, reverse errors such that, for example, once children have learned that *i* is to be used for [i] they begin using it for [iy]: sɪk for *sick* and *seek*.

Collective illusions about the phonology of English are thus different for children and adults, different in the ways that Klima's first and third conventions differ. For the child's phonology seems to be quite separate from his morphology, whereas the orthography reflecting adult phonology relates them in nearly optimal ways. And this difference may in fact be where the difficulties (insofar as these are linguistic) in children's learning to read may lie. For if standard orthography presupposes phonological perceptions that children have not yet acquired, then it is not going to be easy for them to associate standard spellings with the right things in their perception. Trouble will certainly follow. One solution to such problems would be for children to learn to read in a more superficial orthography, perhaps of their own creation—see C. Chomsky [1971a, b]. Another would be to delay the teaching of reading until such time as they have developed the phonological perceptions of an adult.[6]

References

Anderson, S. R., 1969. West Scandinavian vowel systems and the ordering of phonological rules. Doctoral dissertation, Massachusetts Institute of Technology.

Chomsky, C., 1970. Reading, writing, and phonology. *Harvard Ed. Rev.* 40:287–309.

——, 1971a. Invented spelling in the open classroom. Unpublished ms.

——, 1971b. Write first, read later. *Childhood Education,* 47:296–299.

Chomsky, N., and M. Halle, 1968. *The Sound Pattern of English.* New York: Harper and Row.

Hammershaimb, V. U., 1891. *Færøsk Anthologi I.* Copenhagen: Møller and Thomsen.

Haugen, E., 1968. Review of Svabo (1966). *Scandinavian Studies* 40:159–163.

Jakobsen, J., 1957. *Greinir og Ritgerðir,* C. Matras (ed.), Tórshavn, The Faroe Islands: H. N. Jacobsens Bókahandil.

O'Neil, W., 1964. Faroese vowel morphophonemics. *Language* 40:366–371.

——, 1969. The spelling and pronunciation of English. In *the American Heritage Dictionary of the English Language,* W. Morris (ed.), Boston: Houghton Mifflin.

[6] In Shankweiler and Liberman's paper (this volume), figure 2 suggests that third grade children have acquired adult perceptions. However, much research on these matters is required before one can speak with any certainty about them.

————, in press. The phonological basis of Faroese orthography. In *Studies for Einar Haugen,* E. S. Firchow, K. Grimstadt, N. Hasselmo, W. O'Neil (eds.), The Hague: Mouton.

Read, C., 1970. Children's Perceptions of the Sounds of English: Phonology from Three to Six. Doctoral thesis, Harvard University.

————, 1971. Pre-school children's Knowledge of English phonology. *Harvard Ed. Rev.* 41:1–34.

Sapir, E., 1949. *Selected writings of Edward Sapir,* D. G. Mandelbaum (ed.), Berkeley and Los Angeles: University of California Press.

Svabo, J. C., 1966. *Dictionarium Færoense: Færøsk-Dansk-Latinsk Ordbog,* C. Matras (ed.), Copenhagen: Einar Munksgaard.

JOHN LOTZ

How Language Is Conveyed by Script

A Discussion of Klima's and Martin's Papers

Before beginning my comments on Klima's and Martin's presentations on how language is conveyed by script, I would like to express my pleasure that script is accepted here at this conference as a normal mode of communicating language. Script was excommunicated for a long time in American linguistics as nonlanguage. This conference will help to put writing back into the mainstream of language research.

Although the program is admirably conceived, I would like to offer two minor points of criticism with reference to the formulation of the two topics concerning the relationship between speech and script. First, the relationship and transfer of speech to script is not a simple one. It is not just a question of the relation between speech on the one hand as a single well-defined basic medium of language to be transduced into alphabetic or logographic script on the other. It is rather something wider. Script is more than letters or logograms, though these are the most important elements of script. Script also includes other elements and principles, such as punctuation signs, abbreviations, hyphenations, numbers, etc. For example, one can distinguish through hyphenation the following two stretches in Hungarian which are identical in speech: *fel-ül* 'he sits up' and *fe-lül* 'above.' The use of capitals is also particular to script, as in German, where they indicate a special word class, namely, nouns. These examples represent elements in script that cannot be coordinated with units in spoken language. Speech, on the other hand, also contains phenomena that are not present, or that are very incompletely reflected, in script, for example, intonation patterns. Therefore an internal analysis of both media is required before anything can be said about the isomorphism between them that is relevant for the problem of reading.

Second, the formulation of the opposition between script systems as one between alphabetic and nonalphabetic systems is not entirely accurate. Although such an opposition is on the whole correct, a better distinction would be that between writing systems that represent morphemes, and literal writing systems that represent sounds. Besides alphabetic systems, the literal systems also include the purely consonantal Semitic script, which is the basis of all literal script, and a few marginal syllabaries. Thus the real dichotomy is between literal systems using letters—of which the alphabet is a later development introduced, according to Herodotus, by King Cadmus and his son—and what might be called "global" or morphographic systems, that is, what is generally called logographic.

In using the term "global" I mean a symbol that is not analyzable into its component parts that then could reoccur in meaningful units. Such global elements do occur in speech as emotive exclamation; for example in English [ṭsḵ] is a linguistically unanalyzable sound gesture. The difference between the occurrence of global elements in speech as opposed to those in script is that in speech they are always interjections and marginal and cannot be interpreted phonemically. In script, on the other hand, they are abstract elements of the system, occurring also in literal systems, for example, % for 'percent' and & for 'and,' or the number signs.

At the end of my comments on the two papers, I will return to the more general problem of reading and of script and speech in general.

Within the framework of this basic opposition between literal and global writing systems, Martin's paper dealt only with one logographic script tradition, namely, that of Chinese that extended south (Vietnamese), north (Korean), and east (Japanese), but not West, where Altaic peoples did not adopt it. It should be noted that in the history of script there were other logographic systems. Sumerian-Akkadian cuneiform script and Egyptian hieroglyphs were of enormous significance in the history of script and civilization. Today, of course, Chinese script represents the only logographic system of importance.

In considering logographic systems, the basic correlation is not between the logographic symbol and the individual sound unit—although there are some relationships in this respect, as Martin has demonstrated—but rather between the morpheme, the minimal formal unit, and the logogram. When speaking of logographic systems it should be kept in mind that a logogram is not an ideogram referring directly to meaning. It is rather a written symbol corresponding to the spoken morpheme. For example, the Chinese symbol 日 refers not only to SUN but also to DAY and other semantic extensions that are not solely restricted to the primary representation of the sun disc, originally ⊙. It corresponds to the entire semantic spectrum of the spoken unit. But the symbol has nothing to do with speech; it refers directly to the morpheme and its reference.

Correlation with phonological structure can also be bypassed in another way. For instance, often at the end of a word in Sumerian or Egyptian there was a symbol that in script looked exactly like the others but that referred to a semantic category such as DEITY and not to any feature of speech. These symbols are called "determiners," and they exemplify graphic symbols that do not correlate either to the morphemic structure or to the phonemic-phonological structure of the communication process, but only to its semantic aspect.

In literal script systems there is a direct relationship between speech segments and the letters, between the sound and the visual symbol. In general the letter and the phoneme (or whatever one prefers to call the sound unit) can be considered the corresponding sound-graphic units that serve as the basis for literal systems of writing, though the interrelation can be quite complex, as it is, for instance, in English. In some cases one visual sign represents more than one phonemic sound, for example, Greek $\psi = $ /ps/, and there are other conventions which use more than one visual sign for a single sound. But these more complex cases are generally marginal phenomena.

There have also been some syllabaries used as writing systems. It has been claimed, and probably with justification, that the syllable is a very important concept in speech, but syllabaries are unusual in the history of writing and have generally disappeared quickly. For all practical purposes, then, literal script systems currently in use consist of letters referring to shorter stretches of auditory expression.

Actually all script systems are mixed in that they contain both literal and global elements. The significant difference is, I think, in the mixture of them. In our English literal system we have 26 letters and about 20 or 30 global elements, or logograms if you wish. I am referring to script in general use, not to technical publications, which often contain many more. But in logographic systems there can be tens of thousands of global elements and the occurrence of phoneme-like script elements is more of a marginal nature. In other words, the individual units of the spoken pattern are not basic to the system.

Of course, as Martin has already shown, symbols for sound segments do occur in logographic systems. The solution of the hieroglyphs came from units representing letters and not from the logographic part. But because of the primacy of global elements, the total number of symbols in a logographic system runs into the tens of thousands as compared with the relatively small number needed in a literal system where the number of symbols hardly ever exceeds a few dozen. This difference in number of symbols obviously has implications for the learning process, the reading process and the writing process, as well as for any evaluation as to the effectiveness of an orthographic system.

When I first read Klima's paper I was somewhat baffled because I thought it had little bearing on the reading process itself and had more to do with general theories about how alphabets relate to phonological systems. On listening to his presentation I changed my mind and I am impressed by his systematic presentation of how what I call literal orthographic systems can relate to phonological systems of speech on various levels beginning with the surface representation, which essentially is a phonetic transcription, to closer and closer approximations to morphemic writing, using mainly English as an example. I think it is very important that we investigate the relationship of abstract phonological systems to script at various levels in addition to the total system itself.

In the correlation of English speech sounds to possible orthographic representations, in principle one has access to the entire gamut of phonological levels that Klima mentioned. It was interesting to follow his presentation of principles that can be used to set up orthographic systems based on different assumptions.

His first convention starts with a phonetic transcription that would yield an "ideal" orthography in the sense of closely reflecting sound, thus facilitating easy reconstruction of the linguistic units by direct and consistent correlation of the graphic and sound unit. This, of course, is useless for an orthography that by definition is a normatively regularized use of graphic symbols within a script system. The variation and change of phonetic transcriptions reflecting dialectal and social usage would be impractical as the basis of an orthography.

Klima's conventions then move to more and more use of morphophonemics through opacity, that is, highly predictable forms, to more abstract, semisystematic levels of general phonological deducibility of the orthography from underlying lexical-phonological representations. Finally, one could abandon the representation of the direct phonological form altogether and simply have access to meaning, as in some Chinese characters. Thus the ultimate outcome of Klima's conventions, if pursued, would be a morphographic, that is, a logographic, script where the morphemes are represented, and it is left to the native competence of the reader to interpret the predictable phonological realization. Literal systems can also approach this kind of morphographic script as in the Semitic consonantal roots, for example, Arabic $\sqrt{qtb}$ 'write.'

It is due to Chomsky's and Halle's work that new emphasis has been placed on the paradigmatic ties among words that sound differently, whereas previous analyses of English orthography emphasized mostly the sound-letter aspect. In spite of their authority, however, I consider the now fashionable view that the general principles of English orthography are good as not very convincing. The claim that English orthography reveals the underlying morphophonemic system rather than representing surface appearances is a dubious one. In my opinion, most of the examples given do not represent abstract synchronic underlying forms from the point of view of reflecting a grammatical mechanism of Modern English. English orthography obviously reflects—as do most writing systems—an earlier *phonetic* orthography of the language. Therefore, there is necessarily something "underlying" it. But this has nothing to do with the systematic correlation between phonology and orthography. The well-motivated phonological rules in question could be better interpreted diachronically. The concept of underlying forms in this instance only disguises a pseudohistory.

Further, the assumption that somehow these "underlying" forms live in the native speaker is contradicted by the fact that the supposed "ties" do not materialize for the learner in school, and it takes at least a decade for him to achieve sufficient intellectual sophistication to attain a mastery of the vagaries of English orthography. And only after this rather intensive training period can he be regarded as an "ideal language-knower." There are certain levels of language structure which are never accessible to a language learner except by conscious intellectual effort, not because of their abstractness, but rather because of their historical nature.

The question of an optimal orthographic representation of English is a relative question. One can also view optimality of a writing system in terms of its effectiveness in achieving continuity in time and comprehension in space. The optimal orthography of a writing system would then be the one which secures literacy for large numbers of people through a long period of time. In practice a writing system that secures literacy demands a constancy in orthography that cannot reflect fluctuations of language within social and regional dialects, or reflect too rapidly fluctuations due to historical change.

In my opinion, English comes closer to effectiveness in this sense than it does in having an effective orthography for native language learners of reading. A literate English speaker of any Anglo-Saxon country can successfully read Shakespeare, thus giving English continuity in time and space. From the same point of view, Chinese has been even more successful for a longer period of time and for more people, including even those whose speech represents mutually unintelligible dialects. At the same time, the learning of script and reading in these writing systems, in general, presupposes many years of learning at enormous cost.

It seems factually not convincing that English possesses a near optimal orthographic system for native learners of reading in the sense of providing an effective system for reconstructing linguistic units. Otherwise the teaching of reading would not cost the Anglo-Saxon world billions of dollars a year simply to maintain classrooms and instruction for reading. Other writing systems are more effective from this point of view.

If one wants to tackle the reading problem realistically in a general sense, one has to take into account various types of alphabetic writing systems. In Finnish, for example, the fit or correlation between script and sound is nearly isomorphic, and initiation into the reading-writing process is a relatively painless matter. A Finnish child of seven can read without any difficulty because the very close correlation between the phonemic system and the orthography minimizes an involved morphophonemic interpretation. For instance, writing *äidin* with *d* for the genitive of *äiti* 'mother' reflects a morphophonemically predictable form, yet this causes no difficulty in either morphemic identification or semantic interpretation of the stem for the language learner.

Finnish represents a very simple alphabetic orthography. Other languages would illustrate growing differences between the correlation of orthography and phonology. In Serbo-Croatian the timbres are very well indicated but the tone is missing, thus presupposing native competence. Hungarian presents a very close sound-letter fit using only predictable morphophonemic forms as underlying representations, somewhat comparable to Klima's Convention II of opacity. The correlation between sound and script is fairly good in German, but with significant deviations. Finally, English probably represents the most irregular system of all. However, whichever language one chooses to analyze, the basic problem remains the same in that one has on the one hand some visual marks and on the other certain sound waves, and these two media have to be correlated to meaning within language.

A last remark on English orthography would be the interesting fact that English as a first reading and writing experience is very bothersome. On the other hand, English as a second language poses no problem. Although English pronunciation does create some difficulties, it is very easy for foreigners to learn to read and spell English. So it is not the intricacy of the spelling but rather some kind of initiation in the writing-reading processes which seems to pose the relevant problem.

In conclusion I would like to point out that the focusing of this conference on reading alone tends, I am afraid, to encourage viewing the total script-problem atomistically. I am not saying that reading cannot be investigated as a special and a very important problem in itself, only that it must be kept in mind that it is not a self-contained process, but only a component in a larger, more general framework. It is the end phase of a total visual language process that begins with writing. Every single reading event presupposes permanent marks or glyphs made somewhere by some hand, even in printing. These glyphs can then be perceived and interpreted through reading.

The visible language process, including reading, is anchored in the writing system within the framework of the total language structure; and, at the same time, the visual process is correlated to the auditory speech process of the same language.

The role of script within the total framework of the structure of language can be represented by Figure 1. (1) Script refers directly to speech in literal script systems; (2) script represents morphemes in logographic script or indicates syntactic arrangements through interpunctuation signs; and (3) script relates to meaning directly as in the determiners of mixed logographic scripts, such as Egyptian hieroglyphs. The visual language process, which includes reading, might be symbolized as illustrated by Figure 2, parallelling the auditory language process, speaking. The relationship among these various components is, in my opinion, by no means as clear as has been generally assumed at this conference. In the script

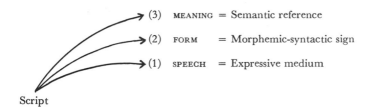

(3) MEANING = Semantic reference

(2) FORM   = Morphemic-syntactic sign

(1) SPEECH   = Expressive medium

Script

Figure 1. Script in relationship to other components of language.

		Process		
		Production	Product	Reception
Medium	Visual	Writing	Script	Reading
	Auditory	Articulation	Speech	Speech perception

Figure 2. Factors in speech and writing.

process the ability of writing clearly implies the ability to read, but not vice versa. Handwriting and printing introduce further problems. I can, for instance, read German in Gothic script perfectly well and also write it cursively, but I would be hard put to produce printed Gothic letters.

Also the relationship of reading in particular, and of the script process in general, to speech seems to me more complex than simply assuming that the visual language process is always converted into speech and ultimately projected upon articulation in the speech chain. Though admittedly such a conversion does take place—the persiflage of Sinclair Lewis comes to my mind, "The American businessman hates anybody who can read without moving his lips"—I doubt very much that in reading telephone numbers, for instance, one necessarily has spoken sound images. Also, one can recognize visual symbols without knowing how to pronounce them.

We can see from these models that the reading process is dependent on an underlying script system in much the same way as the speech process presupposes an underlying phonological system. In approaching the reading problem it is interesting to note that the Haskins investigators, in their efforts to determine speech invariants at the receptive end of the speech process via manipulable stimuli and perception models, turned more and more to the production end of speech. They now maintain that articulation is the basis of the speech process.

In order to approach the reading problem more adequately one should take into account the additional complicating problems which are raised in these models.

General Discussion of Papers by Klima, Martin, Carroll, O'Neil, and Lotz

Miller said that if learning to read takes advantage of the child's knowledge of his spoken language, then there may be a problem in teaching reading to children whose dialect is different from their teacher's. The teacher will correct the child in ways that are inconsistent with the child's intuitive knowledge of his own dialect. Black children in New York are being taught to read aloud with a pronunciation that is not theirs at all, and to say things they would not naturally say. There have been several proposals to overcome the difficulty: (1) to teach these students standard English as a second language, postponing reading until they have learned this kind of English. But this would probably take too long. (2) To teach the child to read in his own dialect with appropriate readers and spelling books. This is being tried, but there is a good deal of social pressure against it. (3) To let the child read in his own dialect and to train the teacher to understand and respect it, so that she can distinguish dialect differences from actual errors in the child's performance. This seems the most promising approach. If it is true that English spelling reflects a fairly abstract level of phonology underlying both dialects, the child with a divergent dialect should have no more trouble in relating his speech to this level than a normal child does. They will differ only in their performance at the surface level. However, it is possible, as Labov and others have suggested, that the difference between standard English and black English is much deeper. In that case the child will be unable to relate his speech to a spelling system matched to an abstract phonology that is not his own. Thus there seemed to be both linguistic and social questions involved.

O'Neil distinguished three issues: (1) the linguistic question—is there, in fact, a sharp divergence in the underlying phonology of the two dialects? (2) How much of the phonological knowledge that one can attribute to an adult is available to the child learning to read? (3) Since English spelling is only *near* optimal—there are many nonsystematic exceptions—how much difficulty does this cause?

Halle said that while English spelling, as suggested in *Sound Pattern of English* [Chomsky and Halle, 1968], corresponds to a fairly high phonological level, most closely approximating Klima's Letter Assignment Convention 3, it indeed has many difficulties and inconsistencies. Some of these arise from the fact that there are only five vowel letters, and digraphs are used inconsistently. Moreover, though there are certain principles for some parts of the vocabulary of English, there are no general principles. A large part of the vocabulary is of Romance origin, and is subject to phonological rules that do not apply to the rest of the vocabulary. If it were possible to eliminate these inconsistencies, many problems in reading instruction would likewise be eliminated, but it is doubtful that the problem of dialect pronunçiation would be lessened.

A related question, Halle said, is the age at which people learn to read. Halle recalled that, like Lotz, he found that spelling was no problem when he learned English as a second language at the age of 12. He thought that this was consistent with O'Neil's observation that young children hear more phonetically, and only later are able to tap a deeper phonological level. Halle also remarked that there is an underlying presumption in our culture that reading and writing should be made as easy as possible. In other countries, such as ancient Egypt, acquisition of reading and writing was made difficult for professional reasons.

Lotz said that the first acquisition of a writing system, like the acquisition of one's native language, is a unique event. The acquisition of a second writing system may not cause as much difficulty.

Carroll referred to a study of Lambert's [1970] in which English-speaking children were taught French, given their first grade teaching in French, and then taught to write in French. These children had no difficulty in transferring into English.

Mattingly questioned the assumption that a child does not acquire all of his phonology until a fairly advanced age. Even a very young middle-class child might know the rule for *rotate* and *rotation*.

O'Neil replied that little evidence is available on this point, but recalled one child who began by writing the past-tense markers as *t*, *d* or vowel +*d*. Later she gave this up and just wrote *d*. Clearly, in this case, the child began with a phonetic orientation and only later learned the morphophonemics of English, and learned that [t], [d] and [ɨd] are phonologically conditioned variants of one morpheme, and that there is a systematic relationship underlying pairs like *divine: divinity*. Liberman suggested that this might be a question of degree of awareness rather than actual intuitive knowledge.

Kolers remarked that Huey [1908] had recommended that reading instruction be delayed until age 10, not only to give the child time to master the phonological system of his language, but also to avoid confusion between words and things.

In response to a question from Kolers, Klima tried to clarify the notion of "optimal representation." It depends on which levels of language are most directly accessible to the consciousness of the reader and writer.

Lotz distinguished two questions that one can ask about any writing system: how efficiently an educated person can use it, and how easy it is to learn. There seems to be no great difference in performance among trained Chinese or English or Russian readers, but there is a great deal of difference in the time and effort required to learn the writing systems of these languages.

Cooper said that if preservation of the morphology makes no difference to the skilled reader, as Lotz's comment implied, then the only issue is whether a morphological writing system is more nearly optimal for someone who is learning to read. Miller said that the question involves more than just learning to read. He suggested that a writing system that reflects morphology affects the way one's knowledge of the language is organized. "You think about words very differently after you know how to write them than before you know how to write them." Being literate has extensive effects upon one's cognitive processes that should be investigated.

To illustrate Miller's point, Halle recalled his experiences as a child in learning to spell German, in which word-final /d/ and /t/ are both pronounced [t]. In order to spell correctly one has to think of a form of the word in which the /d/ or /t/ was nonfinal and prevocalic. He also referred to a colleague who claimed that his spelling had improved as a result of reading *The Sound Pattern of English*.

Gibson said that elementary instruction in reading should take account of its later use as a cognitive tool. For example, it was claimed for the Initial Teaching Alphabet (which disguises morphology to some extent), that children could learn to read more quickly, and transfer easily to conventional orthography. But follow-up studies have shown that by fifth grade children trained with ITA were no better, and perhaps a little worse off, than other children, because they had not learned to take advantage of the morphological information in conventional orthography [Gillooly 1971].

Cooper asked whether there was any evidence that writing systems that are more phonetic, like that of Finnish, and reflect the morphology of the language to a lesser degree, cause difficulty for readers. Lotz did not believe that any long-term cognitive effect can follow from having learned to read in a phonetic rather than a morphological orthography.

Miller said that in distinguishing between the learning of phonetic and of morphological orthographies, he did not mean that the difference would affect the performance of the adult reader, but that the adult reader who had been taught a morphological orthography might know more about the structure of his language. "One of the things you should keep in mind is what possible cognitive differences you are introducing other than the ability to make the right sound when you see the right wiggle." He was interested in the more general question of the psychological differences between literate and illiterate peoples. The difference is hard to isolate because the advent of literacy is usually accompanied by many other social changes.

Halle said that linguistic decisions are often politically motivated. He quoted Max Weinreich's definition of the difference between a language and a dialect: "a language is a dialect with a navy and an army." Halle said that Byelorussian, which is considered to be a separate language in the Soviet Union, has a spelling system very close to Klima's Convention 1. But if Klima's Convention 3 were used instead, written Byelorussian would be almost identical with written Russian. The difference in spelling reflects a political and cultural difference.

Cooper commented that from what had been said, it appeared that most writing systems deal in units about the size of a word. There are no languages with characters for sentences, and there are only a few syllabary writing systems. It also appeared that the representation of a word usually provides information about both sound and meaning. Thus a Chinese character may have a "radical" (i.e., semantic) element and a "phonetic" element. A written word in English carries semantically distinctive morphological information as well as information about its pronunciation. He concluded that writing systems have converged on a pretty narrow zone. "Does this tell us something?"

Klima and Halle pointed out that while not every writing system separates words by spaces, other devices are likely to be used. Sanskrit writing indicates phonetic variations at word boundaries, and Greek, Hebrew, and Slavic have used special characters for some letters in final position. Kolers suggested that not as much information is provided by word boundaries as might be supposed. He referred to an experiment by Miller and Friedman (1957) in which subjects read aloud unspaced English. Rate of reading for unspaced English proved to be about half the rate for normal spaced text. Kolers considered this to be a high rate, at least by comparison with rates for geometrically transformed text. Stevens pointed out, however, that word spacing gives a decided advantage to the learner.

Gough asked if all writing systems are linear. Apart from early pictographic writing, the group agreed that this was the case.

Kavanagh found it hard to believe that rapid reading had to await the invention of printing. Mattingly cited Augustine's account (*Confessions*, Book VI) of how astonished he was to find his master, Ambrose, reading a book silently, without moving his lips.

References

Chomsky, N., and M. Halle, 1968. *The Sound Pattern of English*. New York: Harper and Row.

Gillooly, W. B., 1971. The influence of writing system characteristics on learning to read, Parts I and II. Papers presented to the American Educational Research Association, Feb. 6, and the International Reading Association, April.

Huey, E. B., 1908. *The Psychology and Pedagogy of Reading*. New York: Macmillan. Reprinted Cambridge, Mass.: MIH Press, 1968.

Lambert, Wallace E., M. Just, and N. Segalowitz, 1970. Some cognitive consequences of following the curricula of the early school grades in a foreign language. *Georgetown University Monograph Series on Languages and Linguistics*, 23:229–279.

Miller, G. A., and E. A. Friedman, 1957. The recognition of mutilated English texts. *Information and Control*, 1:38–55.

PART II

Speech Perception and Reading as Converging Processes

IGNATIUS G. MATTINGLY

Reading, the Linguistic Process, and Linguistic Awareness

Reading is a rather remarkable phenomenon. The more we learn about speech and language, the more it appears that linguistic behavior is highly specific. The possible forms of natural language are very restricted; its acquisition and function are biologically determined [Chomsky 1965]. There is good reason to believe that special neural machinery is intricately linked to the vocal tract and the ear, the output and input devices used by all normal human beings for linguistic communication [Liberman, Cooper et al. 1967]. It is therefore rather surprising to find that a substantial number of human beings can also perform linguistic functions by means of the hand and the eye. If we had never observed actual reading or writing we would probably not believe these activities to be possible. Faced with the fact, we ought to suspect that some special kind of trick is involved. What I want to discuss is this trick, and what lies behind it—the relationship of the process of reading a language to the processes of speaking and listening to it. My view is that this relationship is much more devious than it is generally assumed to be. Speaking and listening are primary linguistic activities; reading is a secondary and rather special sort of activity that relies critically upon the reader's awareness of these primary activities.

Comparison of Reading and Listening
The usual view, however, is that reading and listening are parallel processes. According to this view, written text is input by eye and speech by ear, but at as early a stage as possible, consistent with this difference in modality, the two inputs have a common internal representation. From this stage onward, the two processes are identical. Reading is ordinarily learned later than speech; this learning is therefore essentially an intermodal transfer, the attainment of skill in doing visually what one already knows how to do auditorily. As C. C. Fries [1962, p. xv] puts it, "Learning to read . . . is *not* a process of learning new or other language signals than those the child has already learned. The language signals are all the same. The difference lies in the medium through which the physical stimuli make contact with his nervous system. In 'talk' the physical stimuli of the language signals make their contact by means of sound waves received by the ear. In reading, the physical

stimuli of the same language signals consist of graphic shapes that make their contact with his nervous system through light waves received by the eye. The process of learning to read is the process of transfer from the auditory signs for language signals which the child has already learned, to the new visual signs for the same signals."

Something like this view appears to be shared by many who differ about other aspects of reading, even about the nature of the linguistic activity involved. Thus Bloomfield [1955], Fries and others assume that the production and perception of speech are inversely related processes of encoding and decoding, and take the same view of writing and reading. They believe that the listener extracts the phonemes or "unit speech sounds" from speech, forms them into morphemes and sentences, and decodes the message. Similarly, the reader produces, in response to the text, either audible unit speech sounds or, in silent reading, "internal substitute movements" [Bloomfield 1955, p. 103] which he treats as phonemes and so decodes the message. Fries's model is similar to Bloomfield's except that his notion of a phoneme is rather more abstract; it is a member of a set of contrasting elements, conceptually distinct from the medium which conveys it. This medium is the acoustic signal for the listener, the line of print for the reader. For Fries as for Bloomfield, acquisition of both the spoken and written language requires development of "high-speed recognition responses" to stimuli which "sink below the threshold of attention" [Fries 1962, p. xvi) when the responses have become habitual.

More recently, however, the perception of speech has come to be regarded by many as an "active" process basically similar to speech production. The listener understands what is said through a process of "analysis by synthesis" [Stevens and Halle 1967]. Parallel proposals have accordingly been made for reading. Thus Hochberg and Brooks [1970] suggest that once the reader can visually discriminate letters and letter groups and has mastered the phoneme-grapheme correspondences of his writing system, he uses the same hypothesis-testing procedure in reading as he does in listening (Goodman's [1970] view of reading as a "psycholinguistic guessing game" is a similar proposal). Though the model of linguistic processing is different from that of Bloomfield and Fries, the assumption of a simple parallel between reading and listening remains, and the only differences mentioned are those assignable to modality, for example, the use which the reader makes of peripheral vision, which has no analog in listening.

While it is clear that reading somehow employs the same linguistic processes as listening, it does not follow that the two activities are directly

analogous. There are, in fact, certain differences between the two processes that cannot be attributed simply to the difference of modality,
and which therefore make difficulties for the notion of a straightforward
intermodal parallel. Most of these differences have been pointed out
before, notably by Liberman, Cooper, Shankweiler and Studdert-Kennedy [1967] and by Liberman at an earlier conference on "the Reading
Process" [Kavanagh 1968]. But I think reconsideration of them will
help us to arrive at a better understanding of reading.

To begin with, listening appears to be a more natural way of perceiving
language than reading; "listening is easy and reading is hard" [Liberman,
in Kavanagh 1968, p. 119]. We know that all living languages are spoken
languages, and that every normal child gains the ability to understand
his native speech as part of a maturational process of language acquisition. In fact we must suppose that, as a prerequisite for language acquisition, the child has some kind of innate capability to perceive speech.
In order to extract from the utterances of others the "primary linguistic
data" that he needs for acquisition, he must have a "technique for
representing input signals" [Chomsky 1965, p. 30].

In contrast, relatively few languages are written languages. In general,
children must be deliberately taught to read and write, and despite
this teaching, many of them fail to learn. Someone who has been unable
to acquire language by listening—a congenitally deaf child, for instance—will hardly be able to acquire it through reading; on the contrary, as Liberman and Furth [Kavanagh 1968] point out, a child with
a language deficit owing to deafness will have great difficulty learning
to read properly.

The apparent naturalness of listening does not mean that it is in
all respects a more efficient process. Though many people find reading
difficult, there are a few readers who are very proficient: in fact, they
read at rates well over 2000 words per minute with complete comprehension. Listening is always a slower process: even when speech is artificially
speeded up in a way which preserves frequency relationships, 400 words
per minute is about the maximum possible rate [Orr, Friedman et al.
1965]. It has often been suggested [e.g., Bever and Bower 1966; Bower,
1970] that high-speed readers are somehow able to go directly to a deep
level of language, omitting the intermediate stages of processing to which
other readers and all listeners must presumably have recourse.

Moreover, the form in which information is presented is basically
different in reading and in listening. The listener is processing a complex
acoustic signal in which the speech cues that constitute significant linguistic data are buried. Before he can use these cues, the listener has

to "demodulate" the signal: that is, he has to separate the cues from the irrelevant detail. The complexity of this task is indicated by the fact that no scheme for speech recognition by machine has yet been devised that can perform it properly. The demodulation is largely unconscious; as a rule, a listener is unable to perceive the actual acoustic form of the event which serves as a cue unless it is artificially excised from its speech context [Mattingly, Liberman et al. 1971]. The cues are not discrete events well separated in time or frequency; they blend into one another; we cannot, for instance, realistically identify a certain instant as the ending of a formant transition for an initial consonant and the beginning of the steady state of the following vowel (see Cooper's paper, this volume).

The reader, on the other hand, is processing a series of symbols that are quite simply related to the physical medium that conveys them. The task of demodulation is straightforward: the marks in black ink are information; the white paper is background. The reader has no particular difficulty in seeing the letters as visual shapes if he wants to. In printed text, the symbols are discrete units. In cursive writing, of course, one can slur together the symbols to a surprising degree without loss of legibility. But though they are deformed, the cursive symbols remain essentially discrete. It makes sense to view cursive writing as a string of separate symbols connected together for practical convenience; it makes no sense at all to view the speech signal in this way.

That these differences in form are important is indicated by the difficulty of reading a visual display of the speech signal, such as a sound spectrogram, or of listening to text coded in an acoustic alphabet, for example, Morse code or any of the various acoustic alphabets designed to aid the blind [Studdert-Kennedy and Liberman 1963; Coffey 1963]. We know that a spectrogram contains most of the essential linguistic information, for it can be converted back to acoustic form without much loss of intelligibility [Cooper 1950]. Yet reading a spectrogram is very slow work at best, and at worst impossible. Similarly, text coded in an acoustic alphabet contains the same information as print, but a listener can decode it only if it is presented at a rate which is very slow compared to a normal speaking rate.

These facts are certainly not quite what we should predict if reading and listening were simply similar processes in different modalities. The relative advantage of the eye with alphabetic text, to be sure, may be attributed to its apparent superiority over the ear as a data channel; but then why should the eye do so poorly with visible speech? We can only infer that some part of the neural speech processing machinery must be accessible through the ear but not through the eye.

There is also a difference in the linguistic content of the information available to the listener and the reader. The speech cues carry information about the phonetic level of language, the articulatory gestures which the speaker must have made—or more precisely, the motor commands which lead to those gestures [Lisker, Cooper et al. 1962]. Written text corresponds to a different level of language. Chomsky [1970] makes the important observation that conventional orthography, that of English in particular, is, roughly speaking, a morphophonemic transcription; in the framework of generative grammar, it corresponds fairly closely to a surface-structure phonological representation; Chomsky uses the term "lexical representation." I think this generalization can probably be extended to include all practical writing systems, despite their apparent variety. The phonological level is quite distinct from the phonetic level though the two are linked in each language by a system of phonological rules. The parallel between listening and reading was plausible in part because of the failure of structural linguistics to treat these two linguistic levels as the significant ones: both speech perception and reading were taken to be phonemic. Chomsky [1964] and Halle [1959], however, have argued rather convincingly that the phonemic level of the structuralists has no proper linguistic significance, its supposed functions being performed either at the phonological or the phonetic levels.

Halwes observed at the conference on the Reading Process [Kavanagh 1968, p. 160] "It seems like a good bet that since you have all this apparatus in the head for understanding language that if you wanted to teach somebody to read, you would arrange a way to get the written material input to the system that you have already got for processing spoken language and at as low a level as you could arrange to do that, then let the processing of the written material be done by the mechanisms that are already in there." I think that Halwes' inference is a reasonable one, and since the written text is not, in fact, a representation at the lowest possible level, the problem is with his premise, that reading and listening are simply analogous processes.

There is furthermore a difference in the way the linguistic content and the information which represents it are related. As Liberman [Kavanagh 1968, p. 120] observes, "speech is a complex code, print a simple cipher." The nature of the speech code by which the listener deduces articulatory behavior from acoustic events is determined by the characteristics of the vocal tract. The code is complex, because the physiology and acoustics of the vocal tract are complex. It is also a highly redundant code: there are, typically, many acoustic cues for a single bit of phonetic information. It is, finally, a universal code, because all human vocal tracts have similar properties. By comparison, writing is in principle a fairly simple mapping of units of the phonological representation—morphemes or phonemes or syllables—into written symbols. The complications that do occur are not inherent in the nature of what is being represented: they are historical accidents. By comparison with the speech code, writing is a very economical mapping; typically, many bits of phonological information are carried by a single symbol. Nor is there any necessary relationship between the form of written symbols and the corresponding phonological units; to quote Liberman once more [Kavanagh 1968, p. 121], "only one set of sounds will work, but there are many equally good alphabets."

Linguistic Awareness

The differences we have listed indicate that even though reading and listening are both clearly linguistic, and have an obvious similarity of function, they are not really parallel processes. I would like to suggest a rather different interpretation of the relationship of reading to language. This interpretation depends on a distinction between primary linguistic activity itself and the speaker-hearer's awareness of this activity.

Following Miller and Chomsky [1963], Stevens and Halle [1967], Neisser [1967], and others, I view primary linguistic activity, both speaking and listening, as essentially creative or synthetic. When a speaker-hearer "synthesizes" a sentence, the products are a semantic representation and a phonetic representation that are related by the grammatical rules of his language, in the sense that the generation of one entails the generation of the other. The speaker must synthesize, and so produce a phonetic representation for, a sentence which, according to the rules, will have a particular required semantic representation; the listener, similarly, must synthesize a sentence which matches a particular phonetic representation, in the process recovering its semantic representation. It should be added that synthesis of a sentence does not necessarily involve its utterance. One can think of a sentence without actually speaking it; one can rehearse or recall a sentence.

Since we are concerned with reading and not with primary linguistic activity as such, we will not attempt the difficult task of specifying the actual process of synthesis. We merely assume that the speaker-hearer not only knows the rules of his language but has a set of strategies for linguistic performance. These strategies, relying upon context as well as upon information about the phonetic (or semantic) representation to be matched, are powerful enough to ensure that the speaker-hearer synthesizes the "right" sentence most of the time.

Having synthesized some utterance, whether in the course of production or perception, the speaker-hearer is conscious not only of a semantic experience (understanding the utterance) and perhaps an acoustic experience (hearing the speaker's voice), but also of experience with certain intermediate linguistic processes. Not only has he synthesized a particular utterance, he is also aware in some way of having done so, and can reflect upon this linguistic experience as he can upon his experiences with the external world.

If language were in great part deliberately and consciously learned behavior, like playing the piano, this would hardly be very surprising. We would suppose that development of such linguistic awareness was needed in order to learn language. But if language is acquired by maturation, linguistic awareness seems quite remarkable when we consider how little introspective awareness we have of the intermediate stages of other forms of maturationally acquired motor and perceptual behavior, for example, walking or seeing. (The concept of "linguistic awareness" developed here is similar but not identical to the concept of "accessibility" discussed in Klima's paper in this volume.)

The speaker-hearer's linguistic awareness is what gives linguistics its special advantage in comparison with other forms of psychological investigation. Taking his informant's awareness of particular utterances as a point of departure, the linguist can construct a description of the informant's intuitive competence in his language which would be unattainable by purely behavioristic methods [Sapir 1949].

However, linguistic awareness is very far from being evenly distributed over all phases of linguistic activity. Much of the process of synthesis takes place well beyond the range of immediate awareness [Chomsky 1965], and must be determined inferentially—just how much has become clear only recently, as a result of investigations of deep syntactic structure by generative grammarians and of speech perception by experimental phoneticians. Thus the speaker-hearer's knowledge of the deep structure and transformational history of an utterance is evident chiefly from his awareness of the grammaticality of the utterance or its lack of it; and he has no direct awareness at all of many of the most significant acoustic cues, which have been isolated by means of perceptual experiments with synthetic speech.

On the other hand, the speaker-hearer has a much greater awareness of phonetic and phonological events. At the phonetic level, he can often detect deviations, even in the case of features which are not distinctive in his language, and this sort of awareness can be rapidly increased by appropriate ear training.

At the phonological (surface-structure) level, not only distinctions between deviant and acceptable utterances, but also reference to various structural units become possible. Words are perhaps most obvious to the speaker-hearer, and morphemes hardly less so, at least in the case of languages with fairly elaborate inflectional and compounding systems. Syllables, depending upon their structural role in the language, may be more obvious than phonological segments. There is far greater awareness of the structural unit than of the structure itself, so that the speaker-hearer feels that the units are simply concatenated. The syntactic bracketing of the phonological representation is probably least obvious.

In the absence of appropriate psycholinguistic data (see, however, Savin's paper in this volume), any ordering of this sort is of course very tentative, and in any case, it would be a mistake to overstate the clarity of the speaker-hearer's linguistic awareness and the consistency with which it corresponds to a particular linguistic level. But it is safe to say that, by virtue of this awareness, he has an internal image of the utterance, and this image probably owes more to the phonological level of representation than to any other level.

There appears to be considerable individual variation in linguistic awareness. Some speaker-hearers are not only very conscious of linguistic patterns but exploit their consciousness with obvious pleasure in verbal play (e.g., punning) or verbal work (e.g., linguistic analysis). Others seem never to be aware of much more than words and are surprised when quite obvious linguistic patterns are pointed out to them. This variation contrasts markedly with the relative consistency from person to person with which primary linguistic activity is performed. Synthesis of an utterance is one thing; the awareness of the process of synthesis quite another.

Linguistic awareness is by no means only a passive phenomenon. The speaker-hearer can use his awareness to control, quite consciously, his linguistic activity. Thus he can ask himself to synthesize a number of words containing a certain morpheme, or a sentence in which the same phonological segment recurs repeatedly. Without this active aspect of linguistic awareness, moreover, much of what we call thinking would be impossible. The speaker-hearer can consciously represent things by names and complex concepts by verbal formulas. When he tries to think abstractly, manipulating these names and concepts, he relies ultimately upon his ability to recapture the original semantic experiences they represent. The only way to do this is to resynthesize the utterance to which a name or formula corresponds.

Moreover, linguistic awareness can become the basis of various language-based skills. Secret languages, such as Pig Latin [Halle 1964] form one class of examples. In such languages a further constraint, in the form of a rule relating to the phonological representation, is artificially imposed upon production and perception. Having synthesized a sentence in English, an additional mental operation is required to perform the encipherment. To carry out the process at a normal speaking rate, one has not only to know the rule but also to have developed a certain facility in applying it. A second class of examples are the various systems of versification. The versifier is skilled in synthesizing sentences which conform not only to the rules of the language but to an additional set of rules relating to certain phonetic features [Halle 1970]. To listen to verse, one needs at least a passive form of this skill so that one can readily distinguish "correct" from "incorrect" lines without scanning them syllable by syllable.

It seems to me that there is a clear difference between Pig Latin, versification, and other instances of language-based skills, and primary linguistic activity itself. If one were unfamiliar with Pig Latin or with a system of versification, one might fail to understand what the Pig Latinist or the versifier was up to, but one would not suppose either of them to be speaking an unfamiliar language. And even after one does get on to the trick, the sensation of engaging in something beyond primary linguistic activity does not disappear. One continues to be aware of a special demand upon one's linguistic awareness.

Reading as a Language-Based Skill

Our view is that reading is a language-based skill like Pig Latin or versification and not a form of primary linguistic activity analogous to listening. From this viewpoint, let us try to give an account, necessarily much oversimplified, of the process of reading a sentence.

The reader first forms a preliminary, quasiphonological representation of the sentence based on his visual perception of the written text. The form in which this text presents itself is determined not by the actual linguistic information conveyed by the sentence but by the writer's linguistic awareness of the process of synthesizing the sentence, an awareness which the writer wishes to impart to the reader. The form of the text does *not* consist, for instance, of a tree-structure diagram or a representation of articulatory gestures, but of discrete units, clearly separable from their visual context. These units, moreover, correspond roughly to elements of the phonological representation (in the generative grammarian's sense), and the correspondence between these units and the phonological elements is quite simple. The only real question is whether the writing system being used is such that the units represent morphemes, or syllables, or phonological segments.

Though the text is in a form which appeals to his linguistic awareness, considerable skill is required of the reader. If he is to proceed through the text at a practical pace, he cannot proceed unit by unit. He must have an extensive vocabulary of sight words and phrases acquired through previous reading experience. Most of the time he identifies long strings of units. When this sight vocabulary does fail him, he must be ready with strategies by means of which he can identify a word that is part of his spoken vocabulary and add it to his sight vocabulary, or assign a phonological representation to a word altogether unknown to him. To be able to do this he must be thoroughly familiar with the rules of the writing system: the shapes of the characters and the relationship of characters and combinations of characters to the phonology of his language. Both sight words and writing system are matters of convention, and must be more or less deliberately learned. While their use becomes habitual in the skilled reader, they are never inaccessible to awareness in the way that much primary linguistic activity is.

The preliminary representation of the sentence will contain only a part of the information in the linguist's phonological representation. All writing systems omit syntactic, prosodic, and junctural information, and many systems make other omissions: for example, phonological vowels are inadequately represented in English spelling and omitted completely in some forms of Semitic writing. Thus the preliminary representation recovered by the reader from the written text is a partial version of the phonological representation: a string of words which may well be incomplete and are certainly not syntactically related.

The skilled reader, however, does not need complete phonological information, and probably does not use all of the limited information available to him. The reason is that the preliminary phonological representation serves only to control the next step of the operation, the actual synthesis of the sentence. By means of the same primary linguistic competence he uses in speaking and listening, the reader endeavors to produce a sentence that will be consistent with its context and with this preliminary representation. In order to do this, he needs, not complete phonological information, but only enough to exclude all other sentences which would fit the context. As he synthesizes the sentence, the reader derives the appropriate semantic representation, and so understands what the writer is trying to say.

Does the reader also form a phonetic representation? Though it might seem needless to do so in silent reading, I think he does. In view of the complex interaction between levels which must take place in primary linguistic activity, it seems unlikely that a reader could omit this step at will. Moreover, as suggested earlier, even though writing systems are essentially phonological, linguistic awareness is in part phonetic. Thus, a sentence that is phonetically bizarre—"The rain in Spain falls mainly in the plain," for example—will be spotted by the reader. And quite often, the reason a written sentence appears to be stylistically offensive is that it would be difficult to speak or listen to.

Having synthesized a sentence that fits the preliminary phonological representation, the reader proceeds to the actual recognition of the written text; that is, he applies the rules of the writing system and verifies, at least in part, the sentence he has synthesized. Thus we can, if we choose, think of the reading process as one analysis-by-synthesis loop inside another, the inner loop corresponding to primary linguistic activity and the outer loop to the additional skilled behavior used in reading. This is a dangerous analogy, however, because the nature of both the analysis and the synthesis is very different in the two processes.

This account of reading ties together many of the differences between reading and listening noted earlier: the differences in the form of the input information, the difference in its linguistic content, and the difference in the relationship of form to content. But we have still to explain the two most interesting differences: the relatively higher speeds that can be attained in reading and the relative difficulty of reading.

How can we explain the very high speeds at which some people read? To say that such readers go directly to a semantic representation, omitting most of the process of linguistic synthesis, is to hypothesize a special type of reader who differs from other readers in the nature of his primary linguistic activity, and differs in a way which we have no other grounds for supposing possible. As far as I know, no one has suggested that high-speed readers can *listen,* rapidly or slowly, in the way they are presumed to read. A more plausible explanation is that linguistic synthesis takes place much faster than has been supposed, and that the rapid reader has learned how to take advantage of this. The relevant experiments (summarized by Neisser [1967]) have measured the rate at which rapidly articulated or artificially speeded speech can be comprehended, and the rate at which a subject can count silently, that is, the rate of "inner speech." But since temporal relationships in speech can only withstand so much distortion, speeded speech experiments may merely reflect limitations on the rate of input. The counting experiment not only used unrealistic material but assumed that inner speech is an essential concomitant of linguistic synthesis.

But suppose that the inner speech which so many readers report, and which figures so prominently in the literature on reading, is simply a kind of auditory imagery, dependent upon linguistic awareness of the sentence already synthesized, reassuring but by no means essential to synthesis (any more than actual utterance or subvocalization), and rather time-consuming. One could then explain the high speed reader as one who builds up the preliminary representation efficiently and synthesizes at a very high speed, just as any other reader or speaker-hearer does. But since he is familiar with the nature of the text, he seldom finds it necessary to verify the output of the process of synthesis, and spends no time on inner speech. The high speed at which linguistic synthesis occurs is thus directly reflected in his reading speed. This explanation is admittedly speculative but has the attraction of treating the primary linguistic behavior of all readers as similar, and assigning the difference to behavior peculiar to reading.

Finally, why should reading be, by comparison with listening, so perilous a process? This is not the place to attempt an analysis of the causes of dyslexia, but if our view of reading is correct, there is plenty of reason why things should often go wrong. First, we have suggested that reading depends ultimately on linguistic awareness and that the degree of this awareness varies considerably from person to person. While reading does not make as great a demand upon linguistic awareness as, say, solving British crossword puzzles, there must be a minimum level required, and perhaps not everyone possesses this minimum; not everyone is sufficiently aware of units in the phonological representation or can acquire this awareness by being taught. In the special case of alphabetic writing, it would seem that the price of greater efficiency in learning is a required degree of awareness higher than for logographic and syllabary systems, since as we have seen, phonological segments are less obvious units than morphemes or syllables. Almost any Chinese with ten years to spare can learn to read, but there are relatively few such people. In a society where alphabetic writing is used, we should expect more reading successes, because the learning time is far shorter, but proportionately more failures, too, because of the greater demand upon linguistic awareness.

A further source of reading difficulty is that the written text is a grosser and far less redundant representation than speech: one symbol stands for a great deal more information than one speech cue, and the same information is not available elsewhere in the text. Both speaker and listener can perform sloppily and the message will get through: the listener who misinterprets a single speech cue will often be rescued by several others. Even a listener with some perceptual difficulty can muddle along. The reader's tolerance of noisy input is bound to be much lower than the listener's, and a person with difficulty in visual perception so mild as not to interfere with most other tasks may well have serious problems in reading.

These problems are both short-term and long-term. Not only does the poor reader risk misreading the current sentence, but there is the possibility that his vocabulary of sight words and phrases will become corrupted by bad data, and that the strategies he applies when the sight vocabulary fails will be the wrong strategies. In this situation he will build up the preliminary phonological representation not only inaccurately, which in itself might not be so serious, but also too slowly, because he is forced to have recourse to his strategies so much of the time. This is fatal, because a certain minimum rate of input seems to be required for linguistic synthesis. We know, from experience with speech slowed by inclusion of a pause after each word, that even when individual words are completely intelligible, it is hard for the listener to put the whole sentence together. If only a reader can maintain the required minimum rate of input, many of his perceptual errors can be smoothed over in synthesis; it is no doubt for this reason that most readers manage as well as they do. But if he goes too slowly, he may well be unable to keep up with his own processes of linguistic synthesis and will be unable to make sense at all out of what he reads.

Liberman has remarked that reading is parasitic on language [Kavanagh 1968]. What I have tried to do here, essentially, is to elaborate upon that notion. Reading is seen not as a parallel activity in the visual mode to speech perception in the auditory mode; there are differences between the two activities that cannot be explained in terms of the difference of modality. They can be explained only if we regard reading as a deliberately acquired, language-based skill, dependent upon the speaker-hearer's awareness of certain aspects of primary linguistic activity. By virtue of this linguistic awareness, written text initiates the synthetic linguistic process common to both reading and speech, enabling the reader to get the writer's message and so to recognize what has been written.

References

Bever, T. G., and T. G. Bower, 1966. How to read without listening. *Project Literacy Reports No. 6,* pp. 13–25.

Bloomfield, Leonard, 1955. Linguistics and reading. *Language Learning* 5:94–107.

Bower, T. G., 1970. Reading by eye. In *Basic Studies on Readings,* H. Levin and J. P. Williams (eds.), New York: Basic Books.

Chomsky, N., 1964. *Current Issues in Linguistic Theory.* The Hague: Mouton.

———, 1965. *Aspects of the Theory of Syntax.* Cambridge, Mass.: M.I.T. Press.

———, 1970. Phonology and reading. In *Basic Studies on Reading,* H. Levin and J. P. Williams (eds.), New York: Basic Books.

Coffey, J. L., 1963. The development and evaluation of the Battelle Aural Reading Device. *Proceedings of the International Congress of Technology and Blindness,* New York: American Foundation for the Blind.

Cooper, F. S., 1950. Spectrum analysis. *J. Acoust. Soc. Amer.* 22:761–762.

Fries, C. C., 1962. *Linguistics and Reading.* New York: Holt, Rinehart and Winston.

Goodman, K. S., 1970. Reading: a psycholinguistic guessing game. In *Theoretical Models and Processes of Reading.* H. Singer and R. B. Ruddell (eds.), Newark, Del.: International Reading Association.

Halle, M., 1959. *The Sound Pattern of Russian.* The Hague: Mouton.

———, 1964. On the bases of phonology. In *The Structure of Language,* J. A. Foder and J. J. Katz (eds.), Englewood Cliffs, N.J.: Prentice-Hall.

———, 1970. On metre and prosody. In *Progress in Linguistics,* M. Bierwisch and K. Heidolph (eds.), The Hague: Mouton.

Hochberg, J. and V. Brooks, 1970. Reading as an intentional behavior. In *Theoretical Models and Processes of Reading.* H. Singer and R. B. Ruddell (eds.), Newark, Del.: International Reading Association.

Kavanagh, J. F. (ed.), 1968. *Communicating by Language: The Reading Process.* Bethesda, Md.: National Institute of Child Health and Human Development.

Liberman, A. M., F. S. Cooper, D. P. Shankweiler, and M. Studdert-Kennedy, 1967. Perception of the speech code. *Psych. Rev.* 74:431–461.

Lisker, L., F. S. Cooper, and A. M. Liberman, 1962. The uses of experiment in language description. *Word* 18:82–106.

Mattingly, I. G., A. M. Liberman, A. K. Syrdal, and T. Halwes, 1971. Discrimination in speech and non-speech modes. *Cog. Psych.* 2:131–157.

Miller, G., and N. Chomsky, 1963. Finitary models of language users. In *Handbook of Mathematical Psychology,* R. D., Luce, R. R. Bush, and E. Galanter (eds.), New York: Wiley.

Neisser, U., 1967. *Cognitive Psychology.* New York: Appleton-Century-Crofts.

Orr, D. B., H. L. Friedman, and J. C. C. Williams, 1965. Trainability of listening comprehension of speeded discourse. *J. Ed. Psych.* 56:148–156.

Sapir, E., 1949. The psychological reality of phonemes. In *Selected Writings of Edward Sapir in Language, Culture, and Personality,* D. G. Mandelbaum (ed.), Berkeley: University of California Press.

Studdert-Kennedy, M., and A. M. Liberman, 1963. Psychological considerations in the design of auditory displays for reading machines. *Proceedings of the International Congress of Technology and Blindness,* New York: American Foundation for the Blind.

Stevens, K. N., and M. Halle, 1967. Remarks on analysis by synthesis and distinctive features. In *Models for the Perception of Speech and Visual Form,* W. Wathen-Dunn (ed.), Cambridge, Mass: M.I.T. Press.

MORRIS HALLE

On a Parallel between Conventions of Versification and Orthography; and on Literacy among the Cherokee

A Discussion of Mattingly's Paper

In preparing a comment on Mattingly's paper I found myself in the curious position of having nothing to criticize. Most of what Mattingly said seems to me not only just, but also extremely well put. My comments are, therefore, less directly tied to Mattingly's text than they might otherwise have been. In fact, I want to touch upon two quite disparate topics. On the one hand, I want to suggest an avenue through which it might be possible to obtain information about the accessibility of particular phonetic features of utterances to conscious introspection on the part of the speaker. On the other hand, I want to express some doubts about the practical (as opposed to the scientific) value of the approach that this conference has followed. I realize, of course, that these two topics have next to nothing in common, but now is the time allotted to me by the organizers of the conference. And if I do not speak now, these topics are not likely to be discussed here.

The first of my two comments deals with the kind of representation of an utterance that is especially accessible to the naive speaker. When speaking of different representations of an utterance, I have in mind a model of linguistic competence of the type that is found in *The Sound Pattern of English* [Chomsky and Halle 1968]. As those who are familiar with the book will recall, it is argued there that many of the phonetic properties of an utterance are due to the operation of various rules. It is, moreover, assumed that these rules apply in sequence so that the phonetic properties of the utterance emerge gradually, as illustrated in the example below.

English is subject to the following two rules: (1) Nasals assimilate the point of articulation from a following velar if the preceding vowel is stressed; e.g. *cóngress but congréssional; íncome but inchóate.* (2) After nasals, [g] is deleted at the end of the word (and in a few other places); e.g., *strong* and *young* have no [g], although they show this [g] in such forms as *stronger* and *younger* where rule (2) does not apply. The application of these rules is pictured as a derivation where the input is some abstract representation and the output a narrow phonetic representation of the utterance. Such a derivation is illustrated in (3) below (see also similar derivations in Klima's paper).

(3)	young	younger
Stress Rule	yóung	yóunger
Rule (1)	yóuŋg	yóuŋger
Rule (2)	yóuŋ	not applicable

No spelling system is identical with the narrow phonetic transcription; that is, every spelling system ever used in practice represents the sounds of the utterance while disregarding the effects of some rules. If we define the *abstractness* of an orthography as varying directly with the number of phonetic rules whose effects it fails to mirror directly, we can say that Chinese orthography is very abstract; Finnish orthography is quite concrete, while that of English is somewhere in between that of the former two.[1]

It is interesting that a similar disregard for the effects of certain phonetic rules is to be found in the way words are employed in metrical verse. For instance, in Russian, a rule governs the complementary distribution of [ɨ] (which is found only after "hard" consonants) and [i] (which is found elsewhere). The effects of this rule, however, are not taken into account in rime and poets often rime, for example [unɨlɨj] with [m,ílɨj] [Tomaševskij 1959, p. 410]. Similarly in Old English, the distribution of [g] and [y] was governed by rule, but the Old English poets—for example, the author of *Beowulf*—allowed words beginning with [g] to alliterate with words beginning with [y] (cf. for example A. J. Bliss [1958] p. 11].

This parallel disregard of the effects of certain phonetic rules found in metrical systems and in orthographies naturally leads one to inquire whether the rules that are being disregarded in the two cases have anything in common. For instance, one might ask whether these rules all occupy a particular position in the order of the rules (e.g., the end), or whether they affect special phonetic properties of the sounds. If it should turn out that rules disregarded by orthographies have certain

[1] It is a major discovery of Klima's paper at this conference that in practice orthographies are subject to such conditions that require them to take account of the effect of a given rule in the representation of some words, while disregarding systematically the effects of this rule in the representation of other words. This refinement, however, has only marginal consequences for the point under discussion; I shall, therefore, not take it into account here.

common features with rules disregarded by the conventions of metrical verse, this would suggest that the effects of such rules are less readily accessible to introspection on the part of the speaker than are those of other rules. This in turn might then shed new light on how orthographies might take advantage of this fact. Unfortunately this question has hardly been studied by anyone; in fact, to my knowledge, it has been raised only by Paul Kiparsky in his "Metrics and Morphophonemics in the Rigveda" [1972] and "What Metrics Shows About Phonology" [1971].

My second comment is in a way much more basic, for it means to question the practical validity of the enterprise that we are engaged in. I take it that an essential reason for holding this conference is concern about the fact that our schools fail to teach reading to many children so that a significant proportion of them are functionally illiterate upon leaving school. It is reasonable to suppose that an improvement in this sorry state might come, at least in part, as the result of a deepened understanding of the reading process, such as has been sought in the different papers contributed to this conference. While this is a perfectly plausible notion, it is no less conceivable that very little improvement in literacy will result from such efforts, for while there are significant differences among different writing systems, it is not to be ruled out that these differences may play only a very minor role in a person's ability to acquire command of this system, if compared to such other factors as the pupil's motivation, the attitudes of teacher and pupil to the subject matter and to each other, etc.

The first fact that I wish to bring to your attention is autobiographical. The first language that I was taught to read was German, and I was taught it in the first grade of a municipal elementary school. I recall clearly that by Christmas almost all children in the classroom could read, and that the few stragglers learned to read by the end of the first year. I do not recall any child who had a reading problem in second or third grade. I do not mean to argue that there were no dyslexic children in our school, but rather that their number was quite small, of the same order as the number of children who had a harelip, a club foot, or other congenital deformity. I shared this impression with my colleague Paul Kiparsky, who went to elementary school in Finland during the late 1940s, and he told me that his memories were rather similar to mine: reading problems among his schoolmates were fairly rare. Moreover, my wife tells me that she does not remember a great number of children having reading problems in her elementary school in Pittsfield, Mass. in the 1930s. These highly anecdotal reports lead me to ask an empirical question: am I correct in believing that massive reading problems in the school are a relatively recent phenomenon?

While puzzling about this fact it occurred to me that reading problems have long been said to be very serious in American Indian schools. The usual explanation for this is that the children in these schools have a much harder task than other children because they are being taught to read a language that they do not speak. In spite of its plausibility this explanation does not seem fully satisfactory to me. In Eastern Europe, where I grew up, Jewish children were for generations taught to read and write in Hebrew, a language of which very few had practical command, yet there are no reports that this ever led to the development of massive reading problems. This is especially striking since the teaching methods used in these schools were medieval in their coerciveness and the people to whom teaching was entrusted were, on the whole, held in low esteem by the community.

To return to literacy among American Indians, I had read about the writing system invented in the early part of the nineteenth century by Sequoya for the Cherokee language. When I inquired about the utilization of this writing system in more recent times I was told that in the 1960s the Carnegie Corporation had sponsored an educational program among the Cherokee, in which the teaching of reading in Sequoya's system was a major component. My colleague, G. H. Matthews, provided me with a primer published by the project [Walker 1965] as well as with a mimeographed paper by Professor Walker titled "An Experiment in Programmed Cross-Cultural Education: The Import of the Cherokee Primer for the Cherokee Community and for the Behavioral Sciences" [n.d.]. As this paper contains a number of observations that I believe illuminate the problem of literacy in a very significant manner, I shall quote from it at length.

Professor Walker tells us that "Cherokee society has a long tradition of literacy. It has been estimated that the Cherokee were 90 percent literate in their native language in the 1830's. By the 1880's the Western Cherokee had a higher English literacy level than the white populations of either Texas or Arkansas." [p. 3]

"Since the federal government took over the Cherokee school system in 1898, Cherokees have viewed the school as a white man's institution which Cherokee children are bound by law to attend, but over which their parents have no control. Most Cherokee speakers drop out of school as soon as this is legally possible. While in school, they learn relatively little due to the language barrier and also due to this unfortunate, but accurate, definition of the school as a white man's institution. As a further complication Cherokee parents are well aware that educated children tend to leave the community, either geographically or socially. To them the school threatens the break-up of the family and division of the community, precisely those consequences which no genuinely tribal society can tolerate." [p. 4]

Nonetheless quite a few Cherokees are literate in both Cherokee and English. It is significant that literacy in Cherokee is attained by many "late in life," and then almost without benefit of special courses, teachers, or teaching material. "It is thought of as a sudden revelation. A Cherokee will say, for example, that it is easy to learn to read Cherokee, that he learned it in two days, in a day, or even in an afternoon. Thus one Cherokee claims to have learned to read in an afternoon, stretched out under a tree alone with the Bible." [p. 5]

"It seems clear that the startling decline during the past sixty years of both English and Cherokee literacy in the Cherokee tribe is chiefly the result of the recent scarcity of reading materials in Cherokee, and of the fact that learning to read has become associated with coercive instruction, particularly in the context of an alien and threatening school presided over by English speaking teachers and controlled by English speaking superintendents and PTA's which conceive of Cherokee as a 'dying' language and Cherokee school children as 'culturally impoverished' candidates for rapid and 'inevitable' social assimilation. Indians and whites alike are constantly equating competence in the school with assimilation into the white middle class. . . . For the Cherokee community to become literate once again, Cherokees must be convinced that literacy does not imply the death of their society, that education is not a clever device to wean children away from the tribe." [p. 8]

Walker also remarks that "This is not a uniquely Cherokee situation. Identical attitudes towards education and the school no doubt can be found in Appalachia, in urban slums, in Afro-Asia, and indeed in all societies where the recruitment of individuals into the dominant society threatens the extinction of a functioning social group." [p. 8]

I have quoted at such length from Walker's paper because it seems to me that this conference on the relationship between language and learning to read should not be allowed to come to a close without having considered the possibility that learning to read is so powerfully influenced by social and cultural factors of the kind described by Walker that all other factors—and I refer here to orthographic systems, visual shapes of letters, proper sequencing of reading materials; in short, everything that a conference such as this could conceivably hope to influence—might at best have third-order or fifth-order effects and could, therefore, affect the success or failure of any literacy program only in a very marginal fashion.

References

Bliss, A. J., 1958. *The Metre of Beowulf*. Oxford: Oxford University Press.

Chomsky, N., and M. Halle, 1968. *The Sound Pattern of English*. New York: Harper and Row.

Kiparsky, P., 1971. What metrics shows about phonology. Paper presented at University of Illinois Symposium on Phonology, April.

————, 1972. Metrics and morphophonemics in the Rigveda. In *New Ideas in Generative Phonology*, M. Brame (ed.), Austin: University of Texas Press.

Tomaševskij, B., 1959. *Stilistika i stixosloženie*. Leningrad: Gosudarstvennoe učebno-pedagogičeskoe izdatel'stvo Ministerstva prosveščenija RSFSR.

Walker, W., 1965. *Cherokee Primer*. Tahlequak, Oklahoma, Carnegie Corporation Cross-Cultural Education Project of the University of Chicago.

————, n.d. An Experiment in Programmed Cross-Cultural Education: The Import of the Cherokee Primer for the Behavioral Sciences. Mimeo.

General Discussion of Papers by Mattingly and Halle

Mattingly's discussion of the phenomenon of high-speed reading drew a number of comments. Gough shared Mattingly's doubt that anyone really goes directly from print to meaning without linguistic analysis. Gray's [1956] studies of reading rates for different orthographies suggest that the time required for linguistic analysis, rather than the time required for visual processing, sets the upper bound on reading rate, and that this rate seemed to be around 800 to 900 words per minute.

Norman objected to Mattingly's suggestion that speed reading might be accounted for by analysis-by-synthesis of more than one sentence at a time, but he agreed that analysis-by-synthesis might well go very much faster than normal speaking rate. LaBerge, however, said that some experiments by Bjork and Estes [1969] with tachistoscopic presentation of letters suggested that some parallel processing is possible, at least at a low level. Miller pointed out that a further alternative to high-speed processing and parallel processing is partial processing. In certain reading tasks it is highly unlikely that complete linguistic processing is done. For example, searching a list for a particular target word probably does not require full-scale linguistic processing of all the unwanted words, though each of these words would have to be analyzed at least sufficiently to determine that it is not the target word.

Gibson described an experiment [Gibson, Tenney et al. 1972] related to Miller's point. Her subjects were asked to search for a target letter under two conditions. In the first condition the letter appeared in a pronounceable string. In the second condition the string was not pronounceable. She anticipated that letters in the pronounceable strings would be found more quickly because the unwanted material could be discarded more rapidly. Actually, reaction time for both groups was the same, presumably because the subjects made no attempt to process the stimuli linguistically but simply searched for the graphic features of the target letter.

Kolers described some of his unpublished reaction-time experiments similar to Gibson's. He had used hexagraphs, some of which were English words and some of which were "nonwords." The subject's task was to find a target letter. When words and nonwords were presented randomly during a test no advantage was found for the words. But when only words, or only nonwords, were presented, reaction time was faster for the words, a result that appears to disagree with Gibson's findings.

Lotz raised a number of questions bearing on the issue of immediate versus linguistically mediated semantic understanding. He wondered whether linguistic mediation is necessary to understand numerals, or the symbols on Continental traffic signs. Does one verbalize a telephone number during the interval between looking up the number in the directory and dialing it? These questions were not directly answered, but they served to bring the discussion back to high-speed reading. Norman attempted to place the matter in perspective: "Some of the discussion about speed reading reminds me of the apocryphal study of the bumblebee that is computed to be unable to fly. People do speed read, and they have very good comprehension. Yes, it is true that we can compute that maximum reading speed is someplace between 500 and 900 words per minute. And I have done the computation myself. I agree with it. Presumably, therefore, a speed reader is doing something different. He is not looking at all the words on the page. He is skimming. He is more selective. But he is, indeed, reading at a very rapid rate and passing a comprehension test at (usually) a level superior to that of a normal reader."

Gough was unwilling to accept this formulation, and alluded to some obviously fraudulent claims for high-speed reading. Penney said that the question cannot be settled until criteria for high-speed reading have been agreed upon.

O'Neil supported the comments in Halle's discussion about the destructive effects of American education on the cutures of minority groups like the Cherokees or the children of the ghettos. "I think that any book that comes out of this Conference ought to make it perfectly clear that all of what we talk about is for naught if in fact American education is going to proceed to be exactly what it has been, [a way of] drawing people away from their roots and cultures rather than a way of increasing their activity within those groups and cultures. And this, of course, extends across a whole range of problems in America, not just reading. The problem of teaching a second language, for example, . . . offers the same kind of threats. The solutions being proposed are exactly . . . the wrong kinds of solutions, with assimilatory positions, and positions destined to destroy the coherence of these groups."

Brewer added that no one at this kind of conference was prepared to deal with the main causes of reading disability. There are data that suggest that while teaching method seems to have little effect on reading performance, there is great variance from one classroom to the next. Since this must reflect the ability of individual teachers, someone should be trying to find out what these successful teachers are doing. Only after these social problems have been cleared up would an analysis of the reading process, such as was being attempted at this conference, prove useful.

Cooper said that Halle, O'Neil, and Brewer had made an important point, but that there are still many children with reading difficulties, and many children who have overcome such difficulties after remedial instruction, who do not belong to minority groups. It would be wrong to give up the attempt to understand the reading process just because there are serious social problems that are beyond the control of the members of the Conference.

Referring to Mattingly's discussion of Pig Latin, Jenkins described some experiments in teaching it to naive undergraduates which were interesting as reflections of the subjects' linguistic awareness. Some subjects removed the first letter of a digraph which represented a single sound (e.g., *haircay* for *chair*). Others applied the Pig Latin rule before adding inflectional endings.

Liberman noted that so far, the group had insisted on the importance of linguistic awareness, and on the necessity for devising writing systems which tapped in at the appropriate level of awareness. He hoped that the members of the Conference would also consider what can be done to *improve* someone's linguistic awareness.

References

Bjork, E. L., and W. K. Estes, 1969. Detection and placement of redundant signal elements in tachistoscopic displays of letters. In *Communications in Mathematical Psychology,* New York: Rockefeller University.

Gibson, E. J., Y. J. Tenney, R. W. Barron, and M. Zaslow, 1972. The effect of orthographic structure on letter search. *Perception and Psychophysics* 11:183–186.

Gray, W. S., 1956. *The Teaching of Reading and Writing.* Paris: UNESCO.

MICHAEL I. POSNER, JOE L. LEWIS, AND CAROL CONRAD

Component Processes in Reading: A Performance Analysis

Introduction

A detailed analysis of the internal structures and mental operations involved in the process of reading might help us understand problems in acquiring the skill. This is a point that our keynote speaker [Gibson 1965] made several years ago. In the last few years there has been a considerable advance in the development of techniques used to isolate stages of processing and their interrelationships [Neisser 1967; Posner 1969; Sternberg, 1969]. This paper is an effort to review both the techniques and the results that might aid in elucidating the component processes in reading.

Most work on human performance has been with adults, and this situation is reflected in our paper. We believe that many of the phenomena that we report will be magnified when studied in detail with children. The adult ability to acquire and to transfer information rapidly makes it necessary to develop techniques of study that are more sophisticated than might be necessary with children. However, there is reason to suppose that the logic of these techniques and analyses will apply to children. Moreover, most of the studies reported in this paper involve letters or words rather than more complex material. The hope is that their simplicity will allow us to develop an analysis of the basic components of the skill.

ISOLABLE SUBSYSTEMS

Let us be quite concrete. A young child who has never before seen the symbol "A" must be aware primarily of the visual form of the letter. But this is not so with an adult. Consciousness of the letter is suffused with past experience: its association to other visual forms (e.g., "a"), the phoneme /a/, its status as a vowel, and as the first letter of a list called the alphabet. Yet, even in the skilled reader, by appropriate experimental technique, we can isolate the visual system processes from these other influences. We can, in fact, argue that the visual processes represent in the adult an isolable subsystem the properties of which can be studied.

Experiments showing that the visual process is an isolable subsystem of letter processing in the adult [Posner 1969] suggest that there are important psychological problems involved in passing from one subsystem to another (e.g., visual to name). Perhaps it is at the boundaries between any two isolable subsystems that special difficulties in cognitive processing lie. Indeed, the problem of coordinating modality-specific subsystems may represent one explanation of the difficulty in the seemingly simple translation from a visual word to the word name.

The idea of an isolable subsystem is a complex one [Miller 1970]. In the recent experimental literature there have been many efforts to discover serial "stages" of processing [Clark and Chase 1971; E. E. Smith 1968; Sternberg 1969; Trabasso 1970]. These tasks tend to be ones in which one stage must depend directly upon the outcome of the previous stage. There is still dispute about the details of these models (e.g., whether the comparison stage is serial), but they have had sufficient success to show that internal mental operations can be isolated for study.

There is reason to believe that the successive and additive assumptions involved in these models are not general properties of adult performance [Posner 1969], especially in tasks like reading. The well-known eye-voice span suggests that complex visual processing moves ahead of, as well as being simultaneous with, other components of the reading task [Levin and Kaplan 1970]. Moreover, studies of visual scanning suggest that the processing of visual, phonemic, and semantic targets can overlap in complex ways [Cohen 1970]. Even in discrete tasks, considerable evidence exists to show that mental operations can overlap in time [Posner and Keele 1970]. Nonetheless, it is still possible to separate classes of mental operations that are performed upon different internal codes. For example, the visual or the acoustic properties of a message may be isolated from the common internal name codes of which we are usually conscious. Experiments can manipulate these codes independently, thus revealing their separate contributions to overall performance. In this sense, they are isolable subsystems whose outputs are combined in most complex tasks. Their isolability in the adult suggests that similar manipulations in children may be useful in diagnosing points of difficulty in reading [Calfee, Chapmen et al. 1970].

ORGANIZATION OF THE PAPER

The remainder of this paper will be concerned with the problem of isolability within three subsystems that are related to the task of reading. The next section discusses the visual processing system. The third section deals with the name code for reclassification of visually and aurally presented information. In the fourth section we deal with some aspects of the problem of meaning. We shall argue that certain operations that go on within isolable subsystems may proceed simultaneously with little or no interference. However, some operations do place a load on a single limited-capacity processing system. The properties of this system are dealt with in more detail in the concluding section. Translations among subsystems may be particularly demanding of the limited capacity mechanism, thus posing considerable problems for the learning of tasks that demand close coordination among subsystems. Within each section we deal only with a limited set of experiments that seem to relate most directly to the reading task. In many cases, the argument we make is rather sketchy. References are made to studies and summaries that present arguments in more detail, providing necessary controls and converging operations. Where possible, we attempt to show the relationship between our analysis and other treatments of the reading process [e.g., Gibson 1965; Gibson, Shurcliff et al. 1970; Kolers 1970; Neisser 1967]. In each section we attempt to indicate how the ideas presented may bear more directly upon the problems of acquiring skill in reading.

Visual Codes

The words that you are presently reading are unique configurations of print. The names that these words represent are abstractions in the sense that they stand for a variety of perceptually different visual forms (e.g., "PLANT, plant") and auditory patterns (e.g., the word *plant* spoken by a male or a female). The name of a word gains its meaning from the semantic structure to which it is related. The word *plant* may be related to a structure dealing with living things, or to one dealing with labor unions and assembly lines [Quillian 1969]. At one level the word is a visual code, at another a name, and at still another, an aspect of the overall semantic structure of which it is a part.

AN EXPERIMENTAL METHOD

The mental operations that transform one code into another can be observed in the time required for making classifications. Suppose that the subject is shown a pair of items and is asked to press, as quickly as possible, one key if they are "same" and another if they are "different." Figure 1 (left diagram) illustrates the results from an experiment in which items were letters and the definition of "same" was "both vowels" or "both consonants" [Posner and Mitchell 1967]. If the letters were identical in physical form ("A A"), the reaction time was faster than if they had only a name in common (e.g., "A a"), which in turn was faster than when items shared only the same class (e.g., "A e," both vowels). A similar result [Schaeffer and Beller 1970] is shown (right

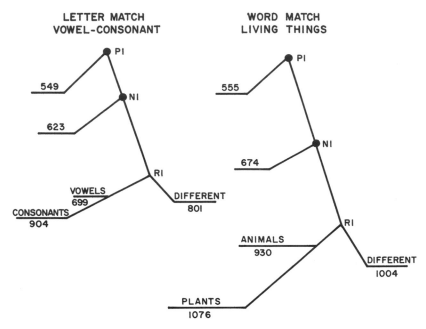

LETTER MATCH
VOWEL-CONSONANT

WORD MATCH
LIVING THINGS

Figure 1. Reaction times for physical (PI), name (NI), and rule (RI) level matches for letter pairs (left) and word pairs (right).

diagram) for an experiment in which word pairs were used and the subject was required to press the key when both words were "living things" or both were "nonliving things." These figures illustrate the method measuring mental operations by the amount of time they require.

ISOLABILITY

Can we isolate operations that are performed on visual information? The problem is how to determine if the operations performed on letters or words use visual representations rather than letter names or semantic information. Suppose that a pair of items is presented simultaneously. The subject is then required to press one key if the two items have the same name and another key if the names are different. If the two are physically identical (e.g., "A A") it is logically possible to base the match upon the visual form. On the other hand, for letters like "A a," which are not similar in physical form, the match is more likely to be based upon a learned correspondence between the visual forms such as the letter name.

Experimental data show that these logical distinctions apply to actual performances of subjects. The time for matching identical letters (e.g.,

"A A") is faster than for upper and lower case forms of the same letter (e.g., "A a"). Moreover, the times to make physical matches are systematically affected by visual factors such as the visual similarity of the forms [Chase and Posner 1965; Posner, 1969], while the name matches are affected primarily by factors related to the letter name, such as the number of letter names held in short-term store [Posner 1969]. Physical matches are unaffected by name level information (e.g., it takes no longer to say "different" to letters of different form that have the same name) and name matches for already encoded letters are not affected by visual similarity [Posner 1969]. Finally, omitting all physical matches from a list does not affect the time for subjects to make matches at the name level.

Any model that suggests that a match of letters with identical physical and name properties involves a pooling of redundant physical and name information (redundancy model) would have to predict that the time for physical matches would be increased by a manipulation that increases the time for naming. Since this assumption is false [Posner 1969], we argue that visual (physical) and name codes are isolable subsystems in the sense that it is possible to manipulate them quite independently. Figure 2 illustrates some of the means of manipulating the times for

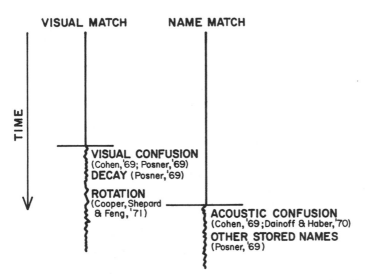

Figure 2. Some of the factors that have been shown by various investigators to affect physical and name matches. The two lines represent assumed parallel processes. The times for each kind of match can be manipulated by the factors listed.

matches based upon visual and name codes. Our data do not agree with a serial stage model in which all the visual level processing preceeds name level processing. Such a model would suggest that omitting all physical matches from a list, or increasing the time for a physical match, would vary the time for name level processes, neither of which is true. Rather, Figure 2 indicates two parallel processes which are isolable. Of course, the naming process may begin only after a visual stage common to both types of matches.

Two pieces of evidence suggest even more strongly the isolability of visual and name processes as internal codes. In one study [Posner 1969] a subject was shown three letters simultaneously, in alphabetical order (e.g., "ACE"). After sufficient time for him to name them, they were removed and replaced by a probe letter, either to the right or left of the previous letter triple. For physical matches (e.g., same case) responses were fastest if the probe matched the letter that was spatially adjacent to it. When the probe matched only in name, reaction times always showed a left-to-right processing order. These results suggest that the visual code preserved the actual spatial organization, but that the names were organized in a temporal list starting with the left letter. Since a subject never knew what kind of probe would be shown, this is strong evidence for independence between the two codes. Another result [Buggie 1970] that argues for separation between the two codes is obtained if one of the letters is physically rotated (e.g., "A ⊁"). Under these circumstances the time to match on the physical level is increased and we get effects of the name breaking through (e.g., it is now harder to say "different" to "A a"). Recently a study was reported in which a subject had to signify whether a single rotated form was an actual letter or a mirror image of that letter. In this case the time to perform the rotation is much longer than the time needed to know the letter name [Cooper, Shepard et al. 1971]. These data argue for separate visual and name processing which can be independently manipulated. The actual judgments of subjects may be based upon either of the codes alone, or both together, depending upon the task organization.

FAMILIARITY

The isolability of visual and name processes, even for letters, allows us to study properties of the visual code independently of names. For example, it is now clear that any number of letters may be matched simultaneously, as long as they are physically identical. This means that the contact between external letters and their internal pattern recognizers can go on in parallel and with no interference [Beller 1970; Donderi and Case 1970]. When the subject has only to judge whether a set of letters are all identical, it makes no difference how many there are ("AA" vs. "AAAA"). The limitation is not in the number of letters shown the subject, but in the number of different internal units they activate. If the letters are arranged into pairs, with physical differences between pairs $\left(\text{i.e., } \dfrac{\text{"ABCD"}}{\text{"a b c d"}}\right)$ it takes subjects 60 milliseconds longer per pair to respond [Beller 1970]. Thus as long as the letters activate the same internal recognizers there is no penalty in response time; but if they activate different internal units, time increases markedly. This finding is important because it suggests that there is no necessary time penalty for coding techniques that deal not with a single letter, but with groups of letters, provided that these letters activate a single internal representation (e.g., a single word).

In her 1965 paper, Gibson argues that the primary units of analysis for reading are spelling patterns rather than single letters. It is possible now to show that these familiarity effects occur within the visual code and do not depend upon feedback from the letter names. Recent experiments have allowed us to study the influence of past experience upon mental operations within the visual system. If a subject is required to match two strings of letters to determine if they are physically identical, he can do so much faster if they form a familiar word than if they are nonsense strings [Eichelman 1970; Krueger 1970]. The evidence indicates that this advantage for words is not due to naming but rather to the efficiency of the visual matching operation when the letter sequence is familiar. This point is confirmed by Gibson's [Gibson, Shurcliff et al. 1970] finding that word familiarity effects are as great in the deaf child as in the hearing child.

Moreover, the word appears to form a unit. If the subject has to identify a single letter from a brief exposure, he can do so as efficiently when a word is presented as when a single letter is presented [Reicher 1969; Wheeler 1970]. It thus appears that having had past experience with certain sequences of letters allows us to perform matching and other visual operations upon them with great efficiency.

A visual word can be seen as a very complex trace system that contains letters as elements but that does not depend upon any particular element for its activation. The activation of the internal unit depends both upon the external information and the context. The trace system is very flexible. In one study [Smith, Lott et al. 1969] it was found that subjects scanned a visual array just as rapidly whether the visual patterns were familiar ("PLANT, plant") or quite new ("pLaNt"), provided that the letters were equated for visibility. The scanning task is probably less sensitive than the matching task, but this result indicates the rather extreme flexibility of the internal recognition units.

Nothing we have said suggests a solution to the more general problem of pattern recognition. We simply do not know how the input is brought into contact with the internal system. What we are saying is consistent with the idea of analysis by synthesis [Neisser 1967] in that it is the internal memory system that is the crucial factor in our conscious experience. However, our data refine the notion by arguing for a separation of the visual and name characteristics of a letter or word. Familiarity can be shown to have an effect within the visual system independently of any feedback from letter names.

COMPLEX OPERATIONS

SPATIAL OPERATIONS: In an extensive series of studies, Kolers [1970] has shown that rotated and inverted words can be read by subjects but at a very reduced rate. These studies suggest that the visual system can recognize items despite very severe spatial distortion. They indicate a remarkable capacity for spatial operations. However, such techniques do not separate solely visual processes from feedback mediated by already named items. By using a pair of letters, one of which is rotated, it is possible to show that the time for physical match operations is affected more drastically by rotation than are the naming operations, so that it is possible for name information to disrupt physical matches [Buggie 1970].

In order to study visual spatial operations free from the use of names, it is often easier to use unfamiliar nonsense materials. One way of doing this is to ask a subject to respond "same" if two figures are equivalent despite rotation. For example, Shepard and Metzler [1971] showed subjects two complex forms which appeared to be three-dimensional. The subjects were required to respond "same" if the two figures could be made congruent by rotation. The time to respond was a linear function of the amount of rotation required. The authors suggest that the subjects had to rotate the figures mentally at a rate of about 50 degrees per second. This is striking evidence that subjects can perform complex manipulations upon visual representations. The time for such manipulations is an orderly function of the task requirements.

HIERARCHICAL OPERATIONS: It is not surprising that the visual system can perform complex spatial operations. What is more important for reading is that visual codes may undergo complex classifications that have a hierarchical form. Kolers [1970] discusses the complex relationships between a visual form and its meaning. In Chinese, certain stylized characters have meaning without regard to any correspondence with the spoken language. Moreover, pictures also are understood quite independently of their being named. We may know to eat or sit on something without knowing that it is named *candy* or *chair*. Free associations obtained to pictures are quite different from associations obtained to the names of the pictures [Karwaski, Gramlich et al. 1944]. The former contain many more responses having to do with manipulating the object pictured. Studies of pictorial memory [Bahrick and Boucher 1968; Frost 1971] argue that visual forms can be stored and retrieved quite independently of their names. Frost [1971] found clear evidence that recall of the names of pictures can be clustered by the visual shape of the pictures.

All these studies suggest that visual codes can have a complex associational structure. However, it is not clear whether, in fact, letters and words in languages such as English can lead directly to meaning, or whether they must first contact the units that code the letter or word names. Kolers [1970] deals with this question. He argues that fluent readers do not form representations of the word names. Rather he suggests that the visual forms themselves are related to complex meanings. We feel that this is still an open question that can best be approached by detailed empirical analysis. Consider two types of studies that relate to it. Posner [1970] has shown that subjects can proceed from the visual form of a letter (i.e., "J") to the classification "letter" without activating the internal units related to the letter name. That is, manipulations that affect name matches do not necessarily affect the classification "letter." However, by the same criterion a letter can be related to the concept "consonant" only by first activating a representation of the letter name. Second, scanning data [Brand 1971; Rabbitt 1967] also provides some indication that a visual form can be classified as a member of a complex subset (e.g., letter) without first activating its name. These data are encouraging for the idea of visual reading [Bower 1970; Kolers 1970], but they are a long way from being definitive.

GENERATION

Before leaving the discussion of visual and name codes it is important to consider briefly the generation of visual information from letter or word names. There is now quite good objective evidence that subjects can generate at least a crude visual code of a single letter [Boies 1971; Brooks 1968; Posner 1969]. The method has been extended with some success to faces and complex forms [Cohen 1969; Tversky 1969]. The process of developing a visual representation from a letter name appears to be relatively slow. A rough estimate might be half a second for an experienced subject [Boies 1971; Weber and Castleman 1970]. While the generated visual information may be scanned in much the same way as present or previous visual input [Boies 1971], there appears to be, at least in most adults, a relatively low capacity for the simultaneous generation of letters.

The ability to develop objective tests of generation appears to us to be extremely important for the understanding of difficulties in the reading process. Suppose that children tend to represent information, including their understanding of sentences, by a visual code. Indeed, Bruner, Oliver and Greenfield [1966] argue for the importance of iconic representation at the ages when reading is being taught. Simple sentences like *The boy hit the ball* may be recoded into something that resembles a visual representation [Huttenlocker 1968]. If children begin the reading task with this habit they may be at a great disadvantage. It has been shown in adult studies that the development of imagery is interfered with by use of the visual modality to take in new information [Brooks 1968]. In a highly visual task like reading, it would be very hard to use the visual system for comprehending. Many people have proposed that schools train out visualization as they develop the skill required to comprehend while continuing to take in information visually [Neisser 1967]. A detailed analysis of this process may be very fruitful in determining the consequences of learning to read for the internal cognitive state of the individual. An overemphasis on reading without compensatory training on visual operations could be detrimental to visual thinking [Arnheim 1969].

IMPLICATIONS

In this section we have reviewed some evidence on the visual system processing of letters and words. We have suggested that the visual code is an isolable subsystem that can be studied independently of other systems. Within the visual processing system, familiar units are developed that are activated by appropriate visual input. Usually we become conscious of the output of these units, although it is possible to be aware of input information when it is desired. These visual units are subject to complex spatial and classificatory operations within the visual system. Thus we agree with Kolers that visual processing constitutes a system of great complexity.

The view that the visual processing of letters and words is an isolable subsystem with a complex set of operations of its own has implications for teaching. It suggests that great respect needs to be given to purely visual skills. These are important cognitive components, in their own right, which should not be ignored in an effort to harness the visual system too closely to the skills needed for reading. Studies of the role of imagery in learning [Bower 1970] and thinking [Huttenlocker 1968; DeSoto, London et al. 1965] have also suggested this conclusion. It is a pity that many of our letters require distinctions (e.g., "p q") which are unnatural in visual tasks.

The isolability of visual skills has been demonstrated with children [Calfee, Chapman et al. 1970]. These studies show that visual matching tests are uncorrelated with tests of verbal performance (e.g., knowledge of the alphabet). Moreover, letter identification, which involves both visual and name factors, shows intermediate correlations with both visual and verbal tests. A related finding with brain-damaged adults is that physical matching is relatively or completely unimpaired in patients suffering from aphasia, while there is a severe loss in name and meaning level matches [Boies 1971]. It should be possible for schools to diagnose such difficulties and develop curricula that take advantage of the natural strengths of students whose cognitive preferences differ.

The complexity of visual system processes indicates that it would be possible for speakers of English to go directly from visual forms to meaning without reference to the word names. Presumably this is done in the visual perception of objects, in nonalphabetic languages [Kolers 1970], and perhaps in some cases by unusually skilled readers of alphabetic languages [Bower 1970]. However, most readers, particularly during learning, probably use a representation that relates to the word names as a mediator. Once we understand this process it will be easier to evaluate the claims for purely visual reading.

Name Codes

The concept of the name of a word or letter is an extremely important one for the psychology of reading. Many theories implicitly assume that the internal representation that stands for the name of a word is the same regardless of the modality through which the information was received [Morton 1969]. This assumption greatly simplifies an analysis of reading. The unique problem of reading would then involve mainly converting from a visual to a name code. From there on, comprehension would be based on mechanisms already present for listening. We have already reviewed one objection to this idea, namely, the view that meaning is connected directly to the visual forms. A second objection is that subjects can recall the channel of entry by which a stimulus was presented

[Murdock 1967]. This objection, however, can be met by recognizing that the activation of a name code does not obliterate information about the past history of the input [Posner 1969].

In order to understand the sense in which visual and auditory input converge on the same internal units, it is first useful to examine the similarities and differences in the extraction of name information from visual and from auditory material. The performance method we have described to separate visual and name codes of letters can be applied directly to auditory input with somewhat comparable results [Coltheart and Allard 1970]. Matching two letters presented in the same voice is consistently faster than when one is in a male voice and one is in a female voice. Coltheart and Allard argue that the two letters are represented both in a physical code, which does preserve the frequency differences in the input, and in a name code, which does not. They find that the "different" judgments are not faster when the voice differs in frequency, as would be expected by an overall similarity redundancy model. Thus their data argue for the isolability of the physical and name components. The greatest difference between their data and those obtained with visual stimuli is that with the auditory presentation the difference between physical and name matches is preserved over a six-second interval. This finding corresponds to the idea, very familiar to students of short-term memory, that aurally presented information has a higher persistence in memory, particularly in conditions where recoding of the visual information is difficult [Posner 1967].

MOTOR THEORY OF SPEECH PERCEPTION

The argument that both auditory physical information and recoded name information are available for matching responses may at first seem to run counter to some of the results obtained in experiments on speech perception, results that indicate that only recoded information is available to consciousness [Liberman, Cooper et al. 1967; Studdert-Kennedy, Liberman et al. 1970; Liberman 1970]. However, we believe that a careful analysis of the experiments and theory in this area reveals some important similarities between the process of categorical perception as developed in these experiments on speech recognition, and the idea of physical and name codes of visually presented letters.

It is clear that the motor theory would not be embarrassed by the fact that subjects are sensitive to differences between male and female voices and other characteristics of the acoustic signal not crucial to the distinction between internal categories (e.g., phonemes). As Liberman [1970] points out in discussing the motor theory, "we would prefer now to apply this hypothesis only to the encoded sounds, not necessarily to those aspects of the speech signal that are not highly encoded." Thus categorical perception applies only to certain dimensions of the speech signal.

There is a sense in which the same analysis applies to visual letters. In Figure 3 we show an outline letter "E" transformed in steps until it becomes a letter F. At some stage in this process one would be likely to identify the figure by the name *e* and at other stages, *f*. The doctrine of categorical perception seems to us to propose two testable consequences of this classification. The first [Halwes 1969] is that we may perceive the output of the classification without consciousness of the input. With the visual material this implies that one can become aware of the letter name without being aware of the details of the figure that was presented. Later on in this paper we will refer to evidence that subjects can extract a letter name without involvement of the limited capacity mechanism. The second idea is that we are unable to become conscious of differences between letters that are within a class boundary (e.g., both *e*). This assertion would clearly be false for visual material. Careful comparison of two figures within a class will surely lead to an awareness of their difference.

However, it is possible that this second consequence of classification does not apply strongly either to visual or acoustic input. Let us consider the method used for demonstrating categorical perception within phoneme classes [Liberman, Harris et al. 1957], as it might be applied

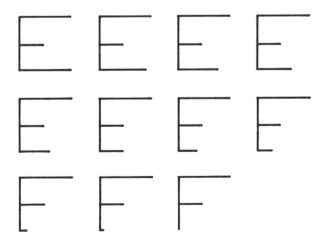

Figure 3. The letter "E" being deformed into the letter "F" by systematic deletion of lower bar.

to our visual continuum. The subject would first be shown a 300-milli-second flash of one letter, followed after a one-second delay by a 300-millisecond flash of a second letter, followed after another second by another 300-millisecond flash of one of the two letters (ABX method). Under conditions of similar memory load, our experiments using letters [Posner 1969] suggest that a subject's judgments would be based almost entirely upon the name code. Thus a subject would show nearly perfect discrimination across name boundaries but would do poorly within them. However, we would certainly not want to conclude from such a result that subjects cannot be conscious of small differences between the letters. Rather we would suggest that the physical code is difficult to maintain as a salient feature once the classification is made. This analysis can apply to both visual and acoustic input.

Some experiments have attempted to study the categorization of visual materials using the ABX method [Cross, Lane et al. 1965; Parks, Wall et al. 1969]. The results, however, have not been very illuminating. In both cases, only four stimuli were used, so that subjects might have verbal reclassification for each of them, although the authors intended for them to develop a learned distinction only between a particular pair. In the Cross study, since the instructions emphasized the learned distinction, subjects probably tended to use that information and thus showed evidence for categorical perception. In Parks's study, feedback was given during discrimination so that subjects probably were more sensitive to the visual form and/or developed reclassifications of all four forms. Thus, in this study, the data show little evidence for categorical perception.

One recent study of an auditory continuum has attempted to reduce reliance on memory in testing whether subjects can make discriminations within a category [Barclay 1970]. The evidence for categorical perception in this study was weaker than that shown using the ABX procedure, and is in line with what we would expect for visual materials.

Our suggestions should not be taken as being against the motor theory of speech perception. Rather, they are intended to clarify it, and to show that there are many similarities between the categorical perception of speech and the classification processes that occur with visually presented letters and words.[1] An important contribution of the motor theory of speech perception is the finding that complex classifications, which

---

[1] Evidence presented by Crowder at this conference of the storage in a precategorical acoustic store (PAS) of vowels and not consonants is clearly in support of a crucial difference between auditory and visual recoding. Still we feel that it is of some value to stress the similarities as well.

relate input to phoneme, *may* be performed unconsciously. This seems to us more crucial and more convincing than the idea that there is a total loss of encoded information that was available in the acoustic message but not in the classification. Similarly, we have argued [Posner and Boies 1971] that, for the skilled reader, visual letters may be named without conscious involvement, although there is retention of both the physical code and the name code. Of course, the experimental status of these ideas would be enhanced by an operational measure of conscious processing, a question to which we will turn later.

HEMISPHERIC TRANSFER

Another similarity between visually and aurally presented information has arisen in recent studies that have involved presenting information primarily to one cerebral hemisphere [Klatzky 1970; Klatzky and Atkinson 1970; Kimura 1967; Studdert-Kennedy and Shankweiler 1970]. Studies of visual presentation are particularly interesting here because of the clear separation of visual pathways between the two hemispheres. In one study [Klatzky and Atkinson 1970] a number of visually presented letters were followed by a probe letter that went only to one hemisphere. In this task, which involved physical matching, subjects showed faster response times when the probe was presented to the right hemisphere. In a second task, subjects were shown faces that they had to name, extract the first letter, and then match it to a stored list of letters. The results showed a definite left-hemisphere bias for this task. Although not all the data obtained in various studies are completely consistent [Rizzalatti, Umiltá et al. 1971], the majority seem to agree that matches involving physical codes do better with probes presented to the right hemisphere, while those that involve a name code do better with probes presented to the left hemisphere. Since letters can be matched on either a physical or a name basis, some of the discrepancies in results may well arise from different memory loads and subjects' coding preferences. Nonetheless, the data obtained so far can be viewed as providing additional support to the isolability of physical and name matches.

Even more interesting is the finding of similar results in listening tasks. Despite the complexity of auditory system projections, it has been known for some time that there is a right ear (left hemisphere) advantage for speech-related sounds, and a left ear (right hemisphere) advantage for nonspeech auditory stimuli [Bryden 1967; Kimura 1967; Satz 1968]. More recent studies have attempted to separate the various components of the speech signal [Studdert-Kennedy and Shankweiler 1970]. The conclusions of the last-named authors bears a striking resemblance to the theory advanced by Klatzky and Atkinson. They say, "we have tentatively concluded that, while the general auditory system may be equipped to extract the auditory parameters of a speech signal, the dominant hemisphere is specialized for the extraction of linguistic features from those parameters. The laterality effect would then be due to a loss of auditory information arising from interhemispheric transfer of the ipsilateral signal to the dominant hemisphere for linguistic processing" (Studdert-Kennedy and Shankweiler 1970, pp. 592–593].

We do not wish to force an unduly strong argument from the hemispheric studies. The various experiments differ greatly in method, and many details can and will be hotly disputed. However, the basic pattern of the hemispheric studies reinforces our conclusions, reached by other methods, that physical and name codes are separable. Moreover, they suggest that the name codes involve a common system regardless of their source, a question that will be examined further in the next section.

The hemispheric results and the theoretical structure in which we have embedded them become even more relevant to the problem of reading when coupled with the challenging, but highly speculative, analysis advanced by Gazzaniga [1970]. Gazzaniga proposes that the child has a functional disconnection between the two hemispheres that is reduced as one hemisphere gains dominance. This speculation may show that the isolability of physical and naming processes has far more significance for the child than for the adult.[2] It would explain some of the problems involved in a close coupling of the visual system processes to naming, such as occurs in reading.

CROSS-MODAL STIMULATION

We have argued that studies of reading and of listening to verbal stimuli suggest that both physical information and name information are stored in memory. The question that naturally arises is whether name information is coded in terms of the same internal system regardless of whether the stimulus was presented visually or aurally. We believe that the available evidence favors a common name code regardless of input modality.

One of us has investigated this question in a series of experiments involving concurrent stimulation of eye and ear [Lewis 1970]. There were two groups of subjects. One group named words presented visually and was instructed to ignore all auditory stimuli, while the other group

[2] Some more direct evidence on this issue has been presented by Bryden [1967].

did the reverse. Both groups were instructed to name the attended modality words as quickly as possible. On five-sixths of the trials there was a word on the "unattended" modality, and on one-sixth of the trials that word was the same as on the attended modality. The time relations between the two words were systematically varied so that the unattended word might lead by as much as 300 milliseconds or lag by as much as 150 milliseconds. Figure 4 shows the response time to trials on which the attended and unattended words were the same, subtracted from the response time trials on which there were no unattended words.[3] This value represents the degree of facilitation in response time due to the same word being on the "unattended" modality. When the same word occurs on the "unattended" modality the speed at which subjects can name the attended word is improved for both groups. The improvement increases quite rapidly as the time by which the "unattended" word leads is increased. There is some effect even for simultaneous presentation. The same basic result has also been reported by Greenwald [1970], in a task involving the naming of digits.

These results suggest that at some stage the visual input and the acoustic input are meeting in such a way as to improve the naming of the attended message. However, it is possible that the meeting is very far on the output side, that each message is independently giving rise to an overt response, and as a result the time to emit the name is reduced.

An argument against this explanation is provided by Warren [1970]. In this study subjects were given several words aurally. They were then shown a single visual word, which may or may not have been presented in the previous list. The visual word was printed in colored ink, and the task was merely to name the color of the ink. Their naming of the ink color was retarded if the visual word was one presented in the previous aural list. It is hard to imagine an interpretation of this effect, which does not require the visual word to make contact with a unit already activated by the previous auditory message.

LEVEL OF NAME CODE

What characteristics does a name code have? This question might be approached in several different ways. One might want to know the unit of code used at any level. At the visual level this might be a letter, syllable, spelling pattern, or word. At the name level a linguist might

---

[3] Separate control blocks run with no irrelevant input confirmed the control baseline obtained from the mixed blocks.

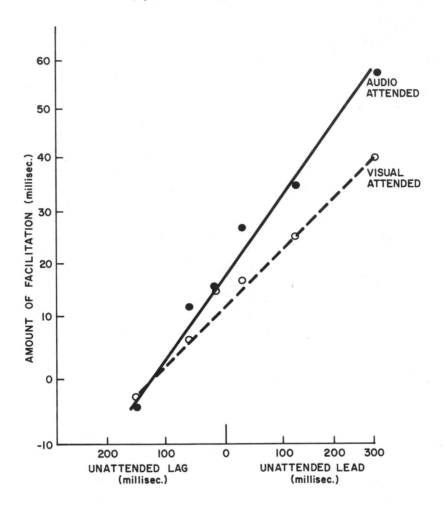

Figure 4. Improvement in response time to repeating an aurally (solid) or visually (dotted) presented word when the same word is presented either leading, simultaneously, or lagging on the opposite modality [after Lewis 1970b].

suggest a phonemic, morphemic, or lexical unit. Perhaps our experimental findings will provide some constraints on the proper unit.

However, the question that seems to be more related to psychological analysis concerns the qualitative characteristics of the code. For example, it has been shown [Posner 1969] that the name abstracted from the visual input of a letter is placed in a system that is affected by the number of letter names presented aurally. The response time for physical matches is not affected by the stored letter names. These results confirm our view that the names of visually and aurally presented letters are in the same system. However, it does not tell us very much about the system itself. Should we think of its form as sensory (perhaps closely related to audition), or motor (articulatory), or abstract [Wickelgren 1969]? Early work in memory was taken as evidence for the first [R. Conrad 1964], while the motor theory of speech perception stresses the second.

Both the distinction between physical and name codes and the evidence that favors the view that the name code for visually and aurally presented letters is the same argue against an acoustic representation of the name code. It is more difficult to decide between an articulatory code and an abstract code. Since there can be little doubt that in some cases subjects articulate the names of individual words, the real question then becomes, how minimal can the involvement of articulation become as skill develops?

The task of separating the decision processes that lead to the activation of a motor program from the motor program itself is familiar to students of motor skills [Posner and Keele 1971]. The processes of selecting a movement and of executing a movement are isolable systems that can be manipulated almost independently [Fitts and Peterson 1964]. The logic of this analysis is also applicable to name codes. If the location of the internal representation of a word name is isolable from the articulation, it would seem reasonable to call the name code abstract. The greater the degree of isolability, the freer from articulation the name code would be. For example, if the name code is isolable, all other things being equal, it should take no longer to activate the internal code of a long word than a short one, but execution time will be greater for the former. Thus if name codes are affected by the length of the word (all other things being controlled) this would be evidence for the name code involving a motor program.

A recent study [Eriksen, Pollack et al. 1970] reported that the response time for visual number identification (i.e., "6" vs. "7") is affected by the length of the digit name. Some control experiments suggested that this occurs only when the subject is uncertain about which item will appear. Thus, it might be possible to argue that the extra time was in locating the name code and not in executing it. If this were true the location of the name code would be affected by its length. This would be evidence against isolability and for an articulatory code. However, the use of a verbal response and other factors in the experiment raise doubts about the results of this particular study.[4] Another operation that can help on this issue would be clear evidence that acoustic confusability (which is a property of the motor program) affects all tasks requiring internal location of letter names. Although there is some evidence that this is true [Cohen 1969b; Dainoff and Haber 1970] there is also some evidence against it [Posner and Taylor 1969]. Thus, the issue remains uncertain. However, we believe that in any particular instance the issue can be resolved by experimental analysis with current techniques.

IMPLICATIONS

This section has pointed out similarities between listening and reading. We have reviewed evidence arguing for similarities between the extraction of the name codes from auditory and visual stimuli. Moreover, we have suggested that the name code involves the same units, regardless of the source of the message. However, because physical information is not entirely lost, subjects have additional information with which to distinguish two experiences that are given the same name, even at a later time.

The child may have some special difficulties in dealing with the name code when it arises from visual information, and these difficulties are likely sources of problems in learning to read. Perhaps the most interesting possibility is that close coordination between visual and language subsystems is difficult in a period in which hemispheric rivalry is intense. However, even without specific reference to hemispheric coordination, our review suggests that the separability of the codes is likely to cause special difficulty in their coordination. Moreover, the activation of the name code is probably quite different in rate, rhythm, and intensity when the stimuli are visual and the reader must painfully sound out the name. Thus a child undoubtedly needs to invest his limited processing and memory capacity both in the translation from visual to name codes and in an attempt to keep in memory the activated name units. This

---

[4] Recently Klapp [1971] has reported a study that suggests that matching of digits is longer for digits whose names involve more syllables. This study provides additional evidence favoring a close relationship of the name code to articulation.

makes it difficult for him to free capacity to deal with the integrative information that leads to comprehension.

Meaning

The idea of analyzing human performance by reference to isolable subsystems was made in a paper on the subjective lexicon [Miller 1970]. Miller discusses the subjective lexicon for nouns in terms of "first a designation of the superordinate class to which the concept belongs, and then a relative clause that describes how this member of the class differs from all others." He recognizes that in this sense, lexical information is a restricted part of meaning that he refers to as intrinsic meaning. As we understand it, the idea that the subjective lexicon might be an isolable subsystem does not imply that perceptual context is unimportant in the actual use of terms by subjects [Olson 1970], but only that judgments based on information in the subjective lexicon might be studied independently by appropriate experiments. Recently there have been many attempts to study information in the subjective lexicon using experiments which resemble those discussed previously for isolating physical and name codes [Collins and Quillian 1969; Conrad 1971; Schaeffer and Wallace 1970].

Name Codes and Meaning

It is obvious that knowing the name of a word is not the same as knowing its meaning. James [1890] commented on this point (Vol. I, p. 263), "it is more difficult to ascend to the meaning of a word than to pass from one word to another; or to put it otherwise, it is harder to be a thinker than to be a rhetorician, and on the whole nothing is commoner than trains of words not understood." It is well known that the word associations of children often involve similarity of word sound, a type of association that is reduced in frequency later in life. If subjects are asked to signify that they have read a word, they respond much more quickly than when required to signify that they understand it [Wickens 1970]. These time differences were obtained by introspective reports, but they can be observed in a more objective way by reference to the tree structures obtained for levels of word classification such as those shown in Figure 1. There remain difficult questions concerning the relationship between a word name and its lexical meaning. For example, it might be that the name code is located in the nervous system in a way that is directly organized by meaning. This would mean that the location of a word name would necessarily be affected by its meaning even though we may not be conscious of the meaning. On the other hand, it is also possible that word names form an isolable subsystem that can be activated and studied separately from the associative structure that determines their meaning.

There is some evidence on this issue from studies of word matching. In one study [Schaeffer and Wallace 1970], subjects were presented with pairs of words and asked to judge whether or not they were both trees, flowers, birds, or mammals. If both words were members of one of these categories, subjects were to respond "same," and if not, "different." Different judgments were longer when both words of a pair were animals (e.g., *wren–fox*) or plants (e.g., *daisy–elm*) than when one was a plant and the other an animal. This finding suggests that subjects are indeed influenced by the superordinate commonality among words when trying to make judgments concerning a subclass. However, when one word of a pair was a specific instance (e.g., *wren*) and the other an immediate superordinate of another category (e.g., *tree*) the response time to respond "different" did not vary with overall semantic similarity. That is, it took no longer to respond different to *daisy–tree* than to *wren–tree*, even though the former pair are both plants. In the case of these judgments, the authors argue that subjects extract the name of the superordinate category from the specific instance and match it against the superordinate name.

In short, the authors suggest that subjects can operate in either of two ways. They can make matches that involve the network of associations in which the name is embedded (concept), or they can use only the word names in isolation. Neither the data nor the theory provides any account of exactly what will be done in an individual case. Note that in judgments of two specific instances (e.g., *wren–fox*) it would be possible for subjects to derive each subclass name (namely, *bird* and *mammal*) and make the match accordingly; but for some reason they do not seem to do this. While current data suggest that subjects can operate on the names in isolation from their associations, they do not tell us very much about the kinds of isolability that are implied. For example, we do not know whether superordinate lexical information concerning a visually presented word is directly available from the physical code, or whether meaning judgments can be made without activation of the name code. The degree of separability between name code and meaning may be much greater when one discusses the comprehension of entire sentences rather than single words. Thus the principle of separability between name code and meaning may be more important for the analysis of reading than it might seem, based upon studies of word matching.

The suggestion that subjects can match word names without influence from superordinate categories must not be taken as evidence that either awareness or intent is necessary to retrieve superordinate lexical information. Although subjects can respond to visual or auditory information based upon a physical code, it does not follow that obtaining the name requires conscious processing. Indeed, we have previously argued the reverse (p. 173). The same basic relationships may apply to word meaning. Warren [1970], using the Stroop technique of color naming (see p. 175), has shown that superordinate categories are activated by a word even when such activation is destructive to the primary task. He presented three words aurally (e.g. *elm, oak, maple*) and showed a greater disruption in naming the ink color of a subsequent visually presented word when it was the superordinate category of the word list (e.g. *tree*) than when it was a control word (e.g. *fire*). Moreover, studies of recognition memory for words [Anisfield and Knapp 1968; Underwood 1965; Wickens 1970] also suggest that there are implicit associations activated at the time of presentation that can interfere with correct memory judgments. These data suggest an automated process that activities some parts of the overall meaning structure. However, much work remains to be done to determine the mechanism and limits of such an automatic activation of meaning units.

ISOLABILITY OF MEANING LEVELS

Collins and Quillian [1969] have suggested a hierarchical model of lexical meaning that serves to relate a word to its superordinate and to its properties. In its strongest form this model proposes that each level is an isolable subsystem. Moreover, the model contains a feature of "cognitive economy" such that each property is stored only at one level. Thus, judgments of canary based upon the properties "yellow" or "sings" are direct, while judgments related to the properties "can fly" or "can move" are inferred through other levels (i.e., bird and animal).

Support for this theory comes from response time data for true sentences in which the subject of a sentence is described by a superordinate or a property, either at its own level or at a higher level. The greater the distance in the hierarchy between the sentence subject and the superordinate or property assigned to the subject, the longer the response time. However, data from other sources raise serious questions about some aspects of this model. We have already noted that Schaeffer and Wallace found that "different" responses were affected by superordinate categories in cases where judgments rested upon a comparison of the word concepts. This finding raises difficult problems for the isolability of meaning levels. Moreover, when the frequency with which subjects assign a property to a noun is controlled, the evidence for the idea of "cognitive economy," at least for high frequency words, is lost [Conrad 1971].

These findings suggest that levels of lexical meaning do not serve as isolable subsystems. That is, there is a tendency for judgments of meaning to be based on several levels, and it is difficult to find evidence for separation, as least with current techniques. These features contrast strongly with the findings using physical and name matches, where isolability is readily achieved. Nonetheless, there is some reason to believe that experiments will be able to separate the automatic activation of related lexical units from the conscious transformations involved in the inference process [Clark and Chase 1971; Trabasso 1970]. The ability to do so can help us gain an understanding of the process of comprehension.

The data reviewed in this section are perhaps even more tentative than those discussed previously. They do suggest, however, that psychological techniques can investigate problems of isolability in the subjective lexicon. Probably none of the data so far speak to the complex and difficult issues of comprehension that intrigue linguists and that play a prominent role in Miller's [1970] paper. However, the use of techniques for studying the subjective lexicon, which have been so fruitful in lower levels of analysis, does appear to us to give hope that Miller's faith in the inventiveness of experimental psychologists might be justified.

Consciousness

At many points in this paper we have referred to the intuitions of the reader concerning which processes are conscious. We argued that, for the adult, neither the processes that lead to the name of a letter, nor those that produce the recoding of speech, need be conscious. Further, we suggested that even superordinate categories may be activated with neither intent nor awareness. The use of the term "conscious" without an explicit operational analysis would be a violation of the mores of the experimental psychologist. Unfortunately, any operational account of a term that has been used in such a variety of ways is likely to appear arbitrary and incomplete.

Nevertheless, one of us [Posner and Boies 1971] has reported results that provide some encouragement for one such operational definition. The term "consciousness" is viewed as one component of attention. This component involves a mechanism that is capable of integrating signals from different modalities. Because this mechanism is of limited capacity, interference occurs between signals that demand this limited capacity system. This idea is similar to the "p" system first proposed by Broadbent [1958]. What is new is that many complex mental operations involving long-term memory are carried out without the involvement of the system. It is this property [Posner and Boies 1971; Posner and Keele, 1970] that makes the system more specifically related to conscious processing.

PROBE METHODS

The operation of the limited capacity mechanism can be investigated through the interference between a primary task and a secondary task. The idea is a very old one in psychology [Welch 1898]. Some more recent studies have employed letter matching as the primary task and a probe response time task as secondary. The probe stimulus is embedded in the primary task and the subject is instructed to report where it occurs. The time to process the probe is used as a measure of the conscious attention demands of the primary task [Posner and Boies 1971; Posner and Keele 1970].

Probe experiments using the letter matching task have indicated that mental operations such as extracting the name of a letter may go on with little or no interference with the probe task. However, other mental operations, such as rehearsal, transformations, and response selection, do demand processing capacity [Posner and Keele 1970]. The former operations are ones that involve the contact of input with highly over-learned structures in long-term memory, while the latter tend to be operations performed upon the information retrieved from memory. Moreover, other results obtained with this method suggest that the limited capacity system can be inserted rather flexibly into a processing sequence, depending upon task demands. Thus the mechanism can be directed toward the encoding processes or withheld to operate after encoding is complete [Posner and Keele 1970]. The possibility of performing complex operations without conscious processing fits with other recent findings in experimental psychology. For example, it appears that semantic processing can be done on input information when a subject's conscious attention is held elsewhere [Lewis 1970a], though the subject is unable to report the "unattended" stimulus. Many results suggest parallel encoding of different aspects of external input [Beller 1970; Hawkins 1969; Keele in press; Reicher 1969] with little indication of interference. These properties are in agreement with the arguments that we have made in earlier sections of this presentation on the extraction of name information from visually and aurally presented letters.

The evidence cited above is still fragmentary and subject to other types of interpretation. Moreover, in order to know if this operational account of conscious processing is appropriate, it will be necessary to explore the relationship between the limited capacity mechanism as studied by the probe technique and other intuitive uses of the term involving intent, awareness, and storage.

ATTENTION DEMANDS OF SENTENCES

All material presented so far has been concerned with the presentation of single letters, phonemes, or words. The hope is that the principles can be applied to more complex stimuli. William James [1890] speculated upon the role of consciousness in the production of a simple sentence. His method was introspective and his results were presented in a graph showing the degree of conscious involvement at each point in a sentence. This graph is reproduced in the upper panel of Figure 5. James summarized his view of our conscious content during sentence production as follows: "Immediately after 0 [see Fig. 5], even before we have opened our mouths to speak, the entire thought is present in our mind in the form of an intention to utter the sentence. . . . Again immediately before 0′, after the last word of the sentence is spoken, all will admit that we again think its entire content as we inwardly realize its completed deliverance." In principle the probe response time method can be used to obtain functions that relate to the attention demands of a task such as producing a sentence. Although no exactly comparable data have been published, the lower panel of Figure 5 shows the attention demands of executing a 150-degree movement to either a large or small target as obtained by the probe response time method [Posner and Keele, 1969]. Somewhat analogous to James's introspections, both the time before the movement is initiated and the time when the target is approached appear to be particularly demanding of attention.

The probe reaction time method has been applied during the task of listening to and comprehending a sentence [Foss 1969; Foss and Lynch 1969; Hakes and Foss 1971]. In these studies the subject listens to a sentence which he must repeat or comprehend. He is instructed to press a key whenever he hears the initial phoneme /b/. The results of these studies have shown that the probe response time is related to aspects of sentence difficulty. The probe speed appears to reflect the transition probabilities between successive words [Foss 1969], position in the sentence [Foss 1969; Hakes and Foss 1971], and some aspects of the syntactic form of the sentence [Foss and Lynch 1969]. Although it is clear that the probe technique is sensitive to the processing of the sentence, there are some special problems in these studies. The probe used is a part

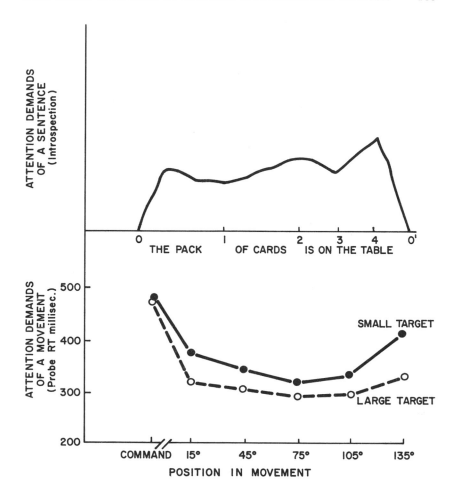

Figure 5. Top: Graph adapted from William James's introspective speculation on the time course of consciousness during the production of the sentence "The pack of cards is on the table." Bottom: A result of probe response times obtained during the selection and execution of a motor movement in which subjects move to a large or small target [Posner and Keele 1969]. Although the tasks are quite different, the probe response time method has been applied to sentence processing (see text) and may be useful in obtaining objective data relating to James's introspective account.

of the sentence itself [Savin and Bever 1970], and thus the independent variables might be having their effect by means of changes in word predictability rather than by changes in attention demands. This problem can be eliminated by making the probe completely independent of the sentence, as has been done in the letter matching studies.

One result of these studies, of particular interest to the problem of consciousness, is the effect of sentence ambiguity on probe time. Subjects who were instructed to repeat the sentence and respond to the probe responded more rapidly when the sentence was not ambiguous than when it was ambiguous. A second group, instructed to attend to ambiguity, took longer to respond to the probe only for sentences that they later classified as ambiguous. Although the data are neither entirely consistent nor conclusive, they indicate that ambiguity does affect probe time, and they suggest that this might be so only in cases when the ambiguity rises to consciousness. In further studies this finding would be an important confirmation of the theoretical account of probes as a means of measuring conscious operations.

Relatively few studies have used the probe technique with linguistic materials, and there are many methodological problems [Posner and Boies 1971; Posner and Keele 1970; Savin and Bever 1970]. Nor can it be assumed that the probe response times reflect only the processing demands at the instant they are presented. Nevertheless, the data obtained so far give hope that techniques are available to study a number of important questions concerning the role of the limited capacity mechanism in reading and listening. Perhaps many of the principles discussed in the studies of letter and word processing can be transferred to the processing of sentences.

Conclusions
What are the implications of this research for the learning of reading? Perhaps we should be grateful that they are neither very obvious nor very direct. Many errors have been made in the enthusiasm to apply research findings directly to the task of learning to read [Chall 1967]. Our results are more in the direction of emphasizing the variation in the component skills that may underlie reading and other cognitive processes. We must avoid the human predilection for single orderings [DeSoto 1961] by recognizing that different children may find their strengths in different subskills. Moreover, as important as is learning to read, there are other, equally respectable, skills that should not be neglected. Tests can be devised to find specific deficits in the abilities of children that block their progress [Calfee, Chapman et al. 1970].

New exercises should be designed not only to remedy those specific deficits but to probe for strong points so that each child can best develop his inherent strengths.

The improvement of skilled performance may be accomplished in three ways. Either the personnel who perform the skill may be more carefully selected (selection), the task may be redesigned (human engineering), or a training program may be instituted (see Posner and Keele [1971] for examples). While it is useful to find some area of strength for each child and to recognize that some children may become more expert readers than others, it is probably important to try to ensure that all children learn to read as well as possible. For this reason, personnel selection methods such as are involved in highly competitive grading and testing are not very useful. Perhaps our analysis of components of reading will suggest those skill components for which a combination of task design and training might prove most fruitful.

References

Anisfield, M., and M. Knapp, 1968. Association, synonymity, and directionality in false recognition. *J. Exp. Psych.* 77:171–179.

Arnheim, R., 1969. *Visual Thinking.* Berkeley: University of California Press.

Bahrick, H. P., and B. Boucher, 1968. Retention of visual and verbal codes of the same stimuli. *J. Exp. Psych.* 78: 417–422.

Barclay, J. R., 1970. Noncategorical perception of a voiced stop consonant. In *Proceedings of the 78th Annual Convention of the American Psychological Association,* pp. 9–10.

Beller, H. K., 1970. Parallel and serial stages in matching. *J. Exp. Psych.* 84:213–219.

Boies, K. G., 1971. An experimental study of aphasia: An investigation of the naming process in brain damaged populations. Doctoral dissertation, University of Oregon.

Boies, S. J., 1971. Memory codes in speeded classification tasks. Doctoral dissertation, University of Oregon.

Bower, G. H., 1970. Analysis of a mnemonic device. *Amer. Scientist* 58:496–510.

Bower, T. G. R., 1970. Reading by eye. In *Basic Studies in Reading,* H. Levin and J. Williams (eds.), New York: Basic Books.

Brand, J., 1971. Classification without identification in visual search. *Quart. J Exp. Psych.* 23:171–186.

Broadbent, D. E., 1958. *Perception and Communication.* London: Pergamon Press.

Brooks, L. R., 1968. Spatial and verbal components of the act of recall. *Canad. J. Psych.* 22:349–368.

Bruner, J. S., R. R. Oliver, and P. M. Greenfield, 1966. *Studies in Cognitive Growth.* New York: Wiley.

Bryden, M. P., 1967. An evaluation of some models of dichotic listening. *Acta Oto-Laryngol.* 63:595–604.

————, 1970. Laterality effects in dichotic listening: Relations with handedness and reading ability in children. *Neuropsychologia* 8:443–450.

Buggie, S., 1970. Stimulus preprocessing and abstraction in the recognition of disoriented forms. Master's thesis, University of Oregon.

Calfee, R. C., R. S. Chapman, and R. L. Venezky, 1970. How a child needs to think to learn to read. Technical Report No. 131, Wisconsin Research and Development Center for Cognitive Learning.

Chall, J., 1967. *Learning to Read: The Great Debate.* New York: McGraw-Hill.

Chase, W. G., and M. I. Posner, 1965. The effect of visual and auditory confusability on visual and memory search tasks. Paper presented to the Midwestern Psychological Association, Chicago.

Clark, H. H., and W. G. Chase, 1971. On mental comparisons of sentences and pictures. Unpublished manuscript, Carnegie Mellon University.

Cohen, G., 1969a. Pattern recognition: Differences between matching patterns to patterns and matching descriptions to patterns. *J. Exp. Psych.* 82:427–434.

————, 1969b. Some evidence for parallel comparisons in a letter recognition task. *Quart. J. Exp. Psych.* 21:272–279.

————, 1970. Search times for combinations of visual phonemic, and semantic targets in reading prose. *Perception and Psychophysics* 8:370–372.

Collins, A. M., and M. R. Quillian, 1969. Retrieval time from semantic memory. *J. Verbal Learning and Verbal Behavior* 8:240–247.

Coltheart, M., and F. Allard, 1970. Variations on a theme of Posner: Physical and name codes of heard letters. Paper presented to the Psychonomic Society.

Conrad, C., 1972. Cognitive economy in semantic memory. *J. Exp. Psych.* 92:149–154.

Conrad, R., 1964. Acoustical confusions in immediate memory. *Brit. J. Psych.* 55:75–83.

Cooper, L. A., R. N. Shepard, and C. M. Feng, 1971. Mental manipulation of rotated symbols: Forming and transforming mental images. Paper presented to the Western Psychological Association, April.

Cross, D. V., H. L. Lane, and W. C. Sheppard, 1965. Identification and discrimination functions for a visual continuum and their relation to the motor theory of speech perception. *J. Exp. Psych.* 70:63–74.

Dainoff, M. J., and R. N. Haber, 1970. Effects of acoustic confusability on levels of information processing. *Canad. J. Psych.* 24:98–108.

DeSoto, C. B., 1961. The predilection for single orderings. *J. Abnorm. Soc. Psych.* 62:16–23.

DeSoto, C. B., M. London, and S. Handel, 1965. Social reasoning and spatial paralogic. *J. Person. Soc. Psych.* 2:513–521.

Donderi, D., and B. Case, 1970. Parallel visual processing: Constant same-different decision latency with two to fourteen shapes. *Perception and Psychophysics* 8:373–375.

Eichelman, W. H., 1970. Familiarity effects in the simultaneous matching task. *J. Exp. Psych.* 86:275–282.

Elkind, D., and J. H. Flavell, 1969. *Studies in Cognitive Development*. New York: Oxford University Press.

Ericksen, C., M. Pollack, and W. Montague, 1970. Implicit speech: Mechanism in perceptual encoding? *J. Exp. Psych.* 84:502–507.

Fitts, P. M., and J. R. Peterson, 1964. Information capacity of discrete motor responses. *J. Exp. Psych.* 67:103–112.

Foss, D. J., 1969. Decision processes during sentence comprehension: Effects of lexical item difficulty and position upon decision times. *J. Verbal Learning and Verbal Behavior* 8:457–462.

————, 1970. Some effects of ambiguity upon sentence comprehension. *J. Verbal Learning and Verbal Behavior* 9:699–706.

Foss, D. J., and R. H. Lynch, 1969. Decision processes during sentence comprehension: Effects of surface structure on decision times. *Perception and Psychophysics* 5:145–148.

Frost, N. A., 1971. Clustering by visual shape in free recall of pictorial stimuli. *J. Exp. Psych.* 88:409–413.

Gazzaniga, M. A., 1970. *The Bisected Brain*. New York: Appleton-Century-Crofts.

Gibson, E. J., 1965. Learning to read. *Science,* 148:1066–1072.

Gibson, E. J., A. Shurcliff, and A. Yonas, 1970. Utilization of spelling patterns by deaf and hearing subjects. In *Basic Studies in Reading,* H. Levin and J. Williams (eds.), New York: Basic Books.

Greenwald, A. G., 1970. A double stimulation test of ideo-motor theory with implications for selective attention. *J. Exp. Psych.* 84:392–398.

Hakes, D. T., and D. J. Foss, 1971. Decision processes during sentence comprehension: Effects of surface structure reconsidered. *Perception and Psychophysics* 8:413–416.

Halwes, T., 1969. A note on the motor theory of speech perception. Unpublished paper, University of Connecticut.

Hawkins, H. L., 1969. Parallel processing in complex visual discrimination. *Perception and Psychophysics* 5:56–64.

Huttenlocker, J., 1968. Constructing spatial images: A strategy in reasoning. *Psych. Rev.* 75:6, 550–560.

James, W., 1890. *Principles of Psychology*. Vol. 1. New York: Holt.

Karwaski, T. F., F. W. Gramlich, and P. Arnott, 1944. Psychological studies in semantics I: Free association reactions to words, drawings and objects. *J. Psych.* 20:233–247.

Keele, S. W., in press. Attention demands of memory retrieval. *J. Exp. Psych.*

Kimura, S., 1967. Functional asymmetry of the brain in dichotic listening. *Cortex,* 3:163–178.

Klapp, S. T., 1971. Implicit speech inferred from response latencies in same-different decisions. Paper presented at Western Psychological Association, April.

Klatzky, R. L., 1970. Interhemispheric transfer of test stimulus representations in memory scanning. *Psychonomic Sci.* 21:201–203.

Klatzky, R. L., and R. C. Atkinson, 1970. Specialization of the cerebral hemispheres in scanning for information in short-term memory. Institute for Mathematical Studies in the Social Sciences, Tech. Report No. 167, Stanford University.

Kolers, P. A., 1969. Clues to a letter's recognition: Implications for the design of characters. *J. Typogr. Res.* 3:145–167.

———, 1970. Three stages of reading. In *Basic Studies in Reading,* H. Levin and J. Williams (eds.), New York: Basic Books.

Krueger, L. E., 1970. Visual comparison in a redundant display. *Cog. Psych.* 1:341–357.

Levin, H., and G. J. Kaplan, 1970. Grammatical structure and reading. In *Basic Studies in Reading,* H. Levin and J. Williams (eds.), New York: Basic Books.

Lewis, J. L., 1970a. Semantic processing of unattended messages using dichotic listening. *J. Exp. Psych.* 85:225–228.

Lewis, J. L., 1970b. Activation of "logogens" in an audio-visual word task. Doctoral dissertation, University of Oregon.

Liberman, A. M., 1970. The grammars of speech and language. *Cog. Psych.* 1:301–323.

Liberman, A. M., F. S. Cooper, D. Shankweiler, and M. Studdert-Kennedy, 1967. Perception of the speech code. *Psych. Rev.* 74:431–461.

Liberman, A. M., K. S. Harris, H. S. Hoffman, and B. C. Griffith, 1957. The discrimination of speech sounds within and across phoneme boundaries. *J. Exp. Psych.* 54:358–368.

Miller, G. A., 1970. The Subjective lexicon. Paper presented to the American Psychological Association, September.

Morton, J., 1969. The interaction of information in word recognition. *Psych. Rev.* 76:165–178.

Murdock, B. B., 1967. Auditory and visual stores in short-term memory. *Acta Psych.* 27:316–327.

Neisser, U., 1967. *Cognitive Psychology.* New York: Appleton-Century-Crofts.

Olson, D. R., 1970. Language and thought: Aspects of a cognitive theory of semantics. *Psych Rev.* 77:257–273.

Parks, T., C. Wall, and J. Bastian, 1969. Intercategory and intracategory discrimination for one visual continuum. *J. Exp. Psych.* 81:241–245.

Posner, M. I., 1967. Short-term memory systems in human information processing. Proceedings of the Symposium on Attention and Performance. *Acta Psych.* 27:267–284.

———, 1969. Abstraction and the process of recognition. In *Advances in Learning and Motivation,* G. Bower (ed.), New York: Academic Press.

———, 1970. On the relationship between letter names and superordinate categories. *Quart. J. Exp. Psych.* 22:279–287.

Posner, M. I., and S. W. Boies, 1971. Components of attention. *Psych. Rev.* 78:391–408.

Posner, M. I., and S. W. Keele, 1969. Attention demands of movements. In *Proceedings of the 16th International Congress of Applied Psychology,* Symposium on Work and Fatigue, Amsterdam, 1969.

Posner, M. I., and S. W. Keele, 1970. Time and space as measures of mental operations. Paper presented to the American Psychological Association, September.

Posner, M. I., and S. W. Keele, 1972. Skill learning. In *Handbook of Research on Teaching,* R. W. Travers (ed.), American Educational Research Association. In press.

Posner, M. I., and R. F. Mitchell, 1967. Chronometric analysis of classification. *Psych. Rev.* 74:392–409.

Posner, M. I., and R. L. Taylor, 1969. Subtractive method applied to separation of visual and name components of multi-letter analysis. *Acta Psych.* 30:104–114.

Quillian, M. R., 1969. The teachable language comprehender: A simulation program and theory of language. *Communications of the Association of Computer Machines,* 12:459–476.

Rabbitt, P. M., 1967. Learning to ignore irrelevant information. *Amer. J. Psych.* 80:1–13.

Reicher, G., 1969. Perceptual recognition as a function of meaningfulness of stimulus material. *J. Exp. Psych.* 81:276–280.

Rizzalatti, G., C. Umilta, and G. Berlucchi, 1971. Opposite superiorities of the right and left cerebral hemispheres in discriminative reaction time to physiognomical and alphabetical material. *Brain* 94:431–442.

Satz, P., 1968. Laterality effects in dichotic listening. *Nature* 218:277–278.

Savin, H. B., and T. G. Bever, 1970. The nonperceptual reality of the phoneme. *J. Verbal Learning and Verbal Behavior* 9:295–302.

Schaeffer, B., and H. K. Beller, 1970. Unpublished study, University of Oregon.

Schaeffer, B., and R. Wallace, 1970. The comparison of word meanings. *J. Exp. Psych.* 86:144–152.

Shepard, R. N., L. Cooper, and C. Feng, 1971. Mental manipulation of rotated symbols with time control of advance information. Paper presented to the Western Psychological Association, San Francisco, April.

Shepard, R. N., and J. Metzler, 1971. Mental rotation of three-dimensional objects. *Science* 171:701–702.

Smith, E. E., 1968. Choice reaction time: One analysis of the major theoretical positions. *Psych. Bull.* 69:77–110.

Smith, F., D. Lott, and B. Cronnell, 1969. The effect of type size and case alternation on word identification. *Amer. J. Psych.* 82:248–253.

Sternberg, S., 1969. The discovery of processing stages: Extension of Donders' method. In *Attention and Performance II,* W. G. Koster (ed.), Amsterdam: North-Holland.

Studdert-Kennedy, M., A. M. Liberman, K. S. Harris, and F. S. Cooper, 1970. The motor theory of speech perception: A reply to Lane's critical review. *Psych. Rev.* 77:234–249.

Studdert-Kennedy, M., and D. Shankweiler, 1970. Hemispheric specialization for speech perception. *J. Acoust. Soc. Amer.* 48:279–294.

Trabasso, T., 1970. Reasoning and the processing of negative information. Invited address to the 78th convention of the American Psychological Association, September.

Tversky, B., 1969. Pictorial and verbal encoding in a short-term memory task. *Perception and Psychophysics* 6:225–233.

Underwood, B. J., 1965. False recognition produced by implicit verbal responses. *J. Exp. Psych.* 70:122–129.

Warren, R. E., 1970. Stimulus encoding and memory. Doctoral dissertation, University of Oregon.

Weber, D. J., and J. Castleman, 1970. The time it takes to imagine. *Perception and Psychophysics* 8:165–168.

Welch, J., 1898. On the measurement of mental activity through muscular activity and the determination of a constant of attention. *Amer. J. Psych.* 1:288–306.

Wheeler, D. D., 1970. Processes in word recognition. *Cog. Psych.* 1:59–85.

Wickelgren, W. A., 1969. Auditory or articulatory coding in verbal short-term memory. *Psych. Rev.* 76:232–235.

Wickens, D. D., 1970. Encoding categories of words: An empirical approach to meaning. *Psych. Rev.* 77:1–15.

PAUL A. KOLERS

Some Problems of Classification

A Discussion of Posner, Lewis, and C. Conrad's Paper

With great energy and enthusiasm, Posner and his colleagues have sent up a shower of sparks that no twenty-minute commentary of mine can hope to capture and contain. They have brushed against, alluded to, or discussed most of the important topics in the study of reading, almost in the field of cognitive psychology itself. The experiments and Posner's interpretations of them have aroused wide interest, both here and among psychologists generally. Clearly, he and his coworkers are dealing with important issues.

The assertions of greatest interest to this meeting come later in the paper. They have to do with consciousness, comprehension, meaning, and related topics of some complexity. In making their assertions, Posner and his colleagues build upon the discussion earlier in their paper, and upon a still earlier paper by Posner and Mitchell [1967], so that the claims in the later one depend upon the claims in the earlier. I confess, however, that although I am impressed with Posner's activity and en- thusiasm, I suffer from a considerable disquiet regarding his claims, for I have not been able to put the pieces of his work together into a coherent or consistent whole. This failure may of course be due to my own misreading entirely, or to my ignorance, for I am not an expert on studies of reaction time. I think that I can best serve our common purpose, and resolve the matter, by describing some of these sources of disquiet. I propose to do this by examining some of the assumptions that seem to underlie the experiments themselves.

Most of my remarks will be directed to the notion of classification, but I will also raise a point about the model of the reader that Dr. Posner seems to have in mind. I add, however, that the literature on speed of reaction has blossomed in the past decade (indeed, the study of information processing has become, for reasons I do not fully under- stand, almost synonymous with studies of speed of reaction), and I am not conversant with all of this complicated literature. I apologize in advance for any misinterpretations my ignorance has induced. I discuss these matters from the point of view of a student of perception interested in the perception of written language.

The Problem

Posner is concerned with what many thinkers have taken to be the fundament upon which cognition is built: classification. An important subtheme in his work is to specify how classifying is carried out. Here he describes differences between what might be called pictorial or graphemic encoding, and nominal or linguistic encoding. The relevance of these concerns to a theory of reading can hardly be missed, both at the level of description of what the child learning his alphabet must accomplish, and at the level of concern for reading disability ("dyslexia"). In the latter case, for example, the disability is thought by some researchers to be due to a failure to merge in memory a pictorial representation of a stimulus and its linguistic encoding.

Classifying is regarded as the fundamental cognitive activity precisely because the world is in continuous change and no two events are exactly alike. One question of deep significance is how two objects or events of notable difference come to be regarded as instances of the same "thing"; another is how linguistic and nonlinguistic encodings affect each other. Posner's experiments are directed at these distinctions. They fall within the framework of the problem enunciated by Heraclitus and commented on by William James. Heraclitus taught that existence is synonomous with continuous change. James, 2500 years later, recognized in the development of that lesson that perceiving identities despite variations in their surface appearance is the basis of cognitive life. Dr. Posner's contribution to this topic is the idea that classifying is not a single process but is composed of a number of constituents that can be isolated.

His main assertion is that at least two aspects of classification can be distinguished, one involving linguistic mediation and the other free of it. Linguistically mediated classifications are further distinguished according as whether they are performed on the basis of "names" or of "rules." He refers to these three kinds of classifying as nodes of processing and as isolable subsystems, and means thereby, as I read him, that linguistically mediated classification requires the subject to draw upon stored knowledge; but linguistically free classification is made on the basis of the stimulus itself, upon what Posner refers to as its "physical identity." So let us consider this first topic, the basis of classifications.

The Basis of Classification

If it is true that classifying is the basis of cognitive life, it is true because events differ so much from each other. But not only events differ; all their minor clusterings that we refer to as objects of experience also differ. Posner has focused down upon three features, which he calls "physical identity," name identity, and rule identity (as in Figure 1 of his paper). The evidence for these distinctions is found in experiments in which subjects take varying amounts of time to make judgments or comparisons according to which of the three kinds of instructions they have received. It is important to note here that no theory predicts that the different judgments should vary in time; rather, the differences in time are used to create a theory. The basis of the difference is therefore of some significance, and is itself worthy of examination.

When two letters are exposed, say two capital ays, the subjects are requested to respond "same" or "different" according to whether on one test the letters have the same "physical identity," on another test whether they have the same name, and on a third test whether they are both vowels or both consonants. The differences in time to respond average out to about 15 percent between conditions, or between seven and eight hundredths of a second absolutely. Although small, the differences are said to be reliable.

Now, speaking strictly, the *only* correct response that can be made when one is judging a pair of objects for their "physical identity" is that they are different. The reason is of course that the two objects differ in location, they differ in details of their manufacture, they differ in their chemical and physical composition (being composed of different atoms, for example), and in an infinite number of other ways besides. Hence the choice of phrase "physical identity" is unfortunate; what is meant, I think, is something like graphemic, pictorial, or physiognomic features. But this change of name does not change the fact, which is that any two objects are different. Hence we must ask what subjects might be doing—what, indeed, we ourselves would be doing—when, as we would, we judge two letters to be the same in respect to their graphemic or physical identities.

Posner seems to imply that some pictorial representation of the letters is formed and compared, and that comparisons on the basis of these pictorial representations are carried out necessarily more rapidly than comparisons on the basis of name. The argument is not well made, however, as I understand it. Consider first that typically only four or six letters in upper and lower case are used, and that the subjects are given a large number of trials. Consider also what it means to compare things for their physiognomic similarity. The main feature, I should think, would be shape; but contrast, color, and other features could enter in. Hence what we would be doing in making the judgment is ignoring all the ways in which the two letters are different while selecting out from the two instances the set of features that we implicitly use to make up our category "physiognomic" or "pictorial" identity. In a word, this judgment of "physical identity" is no less abstract and no less free of stored information than is a judgment based on name, on vowel, or on any other comparison; for example, on whether two letters are derived from the Semitic or the Greek alphabet. Name, physical identity, and historical derivation are based on different clusters of features of the letters; these clusters may be overlapped or partially correlated. They are not, I should think, different "nodes of processing."

How then can one account for the difference in time required to respond? There are at least three ways that might be important. First is the general observation that people are more experienced in comparing objects on the basis of physiognomic than of linguistic properties. We are far more likely to note, and are more skilled in noting, that two people, two pictures, or two letters "look alike" than we are in noting that they have the same name as *man, picture,* or *ay.* Dr. Posner, I think, does not sufficiently consider the role of skills acquired prior to the experiment and brought to it by the subject. Indeed, he tries to exclude particular experience as the basis for some of these differences in performance, but I shall show in a moment how I think it might be important nevertheless.

A second possible explanation is based on the options available to the subject. In one experiment the letters ay, bee, cee, ee in upper and lower case were used. In this alphabet of eight letters there are only eight possible pairs that share a "physical," or graphemic identity: that is, when each letter is paired with itself. Taking position into account so that "A a" and "a A" are two pairs, there are, however, sixteen pairs that share a name. And there are 32 pairs that are vowels or consonants. In studies of reaction time a familiar finding is that the speed of reaction decreases with an increase in the number of alternatives among which subjects must choose. Hence, as one goes from graphemic identity, to name, to rule identity, the number of possible positive responses increases from 8 to 16 to 32; a corresponding decrease in speed of reaction accompanies this increase. Dr. Posner reports that the actual sample of positive instances was kept constant across trials, but that is an experimenter's control and not necessarily a test of the subject's reality. With such a small alphabet and with the large number of trials provided, subjects may very well have inferred the entire set—or even may have been shown it prior to the experiment. We do not know for sure, therefore, that the subjects were not actually making their choices from the "positive sets" carried in mind. If they were doing that, then their performance does not need a concept like "nodes of processing" to explain it. The more familiar relation that I mentioned between size of the positive set and speed of reaction is sufficient.[1]

The third possibility to account for differences in speed again considers the subject's knowledge of the familiar set of stimuli used. Is it a necessary finding that classifications by name or by rule take more time than comparisons on the basis of physiognomy? What if the letters were made so that they differed from trial to trial in an unpredictable way? What if, every time a capital ay appeared, a small but discriminable feature were varied: say the angle of one of the legs was varied slightly, or a little scalloping was imposed on one side, or a disk of one millimeter was dropped out of its shape, or the like? Any two instances would still both be vowels, still have the same derivation from the Semitic alphabet, still both be capital ays in many respects, and yet certainly be different in their physiognomic or physical identity. Moreover, such differences could unquestionably be made to take longer to find than the letters would take to be named. Thus by proper experimental manipulations comparisons by physical identity can be made to take more or less time than comparisons by name. Which judgment takes longer is therefore partly an artifact of method. Whether comparisons based on pictorial features, names, or set membership take more or less time depends upon the construction of the stimuli and the subject's knowledge. It is the stereotypy and familiarity of the letters in Posner's experiment— their artifactual invariance—that, I think, can account for the greater speed in judging their "physical identity" than their name. If Posner were to turn his experiment around so that variations in appearance became crucial features for judgment of physical identity (as they are for name and rule), he might well find different temporal relations in the data. The difference of 70–80 msec separating the responses to the various types of classification, to which Posner attaches so much importance for theory, may be tied more tightly in this and other experi-

---

[1] These relations for the possible positive set are independent of the size of the alphabet used. With N upper case and n lower case letters as stimuli, there are $(N + n)$ possible matches for physical identity, and $2(N + n)$ matches for name. When upper and lower case vowels (V, v) and consonants (C, c) are used, there are $(V + v)^2 + (C + c)^2$ matches for rule.

ments to his particular stimuli than he considers. Whether judgments based on physiognomic, nominal, historical, or other features take more or less time must need to depend upon the conspicuity of the critical feature, the subject's knowledge, and, indeed, upon his skill in making the particular classifications. The differences in time that Posner reports are restricted to the data obtained; they do not necessarily distinguish between types of classifications.

This point, at the risk of belaboring it, can be viewed in another way. In their Table 6, Posner and Mitchell show the times taken to respond to pairs of letters all of which were judged for their "physical identity." Extracting values from the table, illustrated here in Table 1, we find that for the pairs "A A, B B, C C, E E" the reaction times were 397 msec, 421 msec, 465 msec, and 452 msec respectively, a range of 68 msec; and for the lower case pairs "a a, b b, c c, e e," the measurements were 459 msec, 422 msec, 409 msec, and 388 msec, respectively, a range of 71 msec. (The near-perfect increase in time among capital letters and decrease among lower case letters, found as one pro-

Table 1
From Posner and Mitchell [1967], Table 6

Same			Disparate	
AA	397		cB	395
BB	421		eB	410
EE	452		cb	421
CC	465		bE	434
ee	388		EA	442
cc	409		BA	449
bb	422		eA	457
aa	459		bA	462
			ec	472
			ba	477
			aC	487
			eC	489
			ca	492
			ea	504
			EB	527
			CB	547

ceeds through the subsets, is itself quite interesting, although unexplained.) Consider now another ranking of the data, from the same Table 6. These are the disparate pairs, which differ from fastest to slowest not by 71, but by more than twice that, or 152 msec. The pairs, moreover, cluster in interesting ways. In some cases they cluster irrespective of size, as "E A, B A, e A, b A"; but in another case not, as when "c B" and "e B" are the two fastest but "C B" and "E B" the two slowest. The clustering suggests, moreover, that different features or combinations of features are used in these different judgments, such as size, curvature (or angularity), and the like. If such different clusters of features are used for this one classification of physical identity, one cannot, I think, meaningfully separate these judgments as a class from any other as a class. All of these judgments are based on different sets of nameable features. And, to repeat, features such as shape, size, and angularity—or hooks, bars, arches, and loops—are no less abstract, and no less dependent upon memory and skill in classifying, than are features such as name or rule or historical derivation.

Posner bases his argument for a difference in node of processing upon a measured difference in speed of reaction of 70 to 80 msec between physical identity and name identity. His data reveal at least as large a variation between pairs of items all judged following the same instructions—to match for physical identity. Here we have an example of the conceptual dangers, in the absence of a supportive theory, of using differences in time as an index of differences in processing. Two might be pointed out.

First are the facts that speed of nervous conduction from retina to primary visual cortex is about 25 to 30 msec; and that the simple reaction time to a flash is about 160 msec. Hence, when we measure reactions that take 300, 600, or even 1,000 msec, we are dealing with responses whose initial encoding has occurred in small fractions of the total time, and with responses that are between two and six times the duration of the simple reaction. Undoubtedly, many operations on the input occur during those intervals; but taking about 10 percent of the reaction time, that is, about 70 to 80 msec, as an index of so important a difference as a node of processing that distinguishes among types of classifications, seems to me to be a little wanton.

Second is the fact that there are always at least four interpretive possibilities available when one measures a difference in time. They are (1) that one is measuring an extension in time of essentially the same process or event, as for example, the difference in time between walking 10 feet and 10 yards at the same pace; (2) that one is measuring substantially different processes, as for example, the difference between walking and crawling 10 yards; (3) that one is measuring the same process on which an additional burden has been imposed, as for example, walking 10 feet normally or carrying a weight; and (4) that one is measuring a simple or atomic process in one case and a compound in another. It is not exactly clear to me which if any of these four the notion of "isolable subsystems" should be equated with, but the data do not yet lend themselves to supporting any of them, I fear.

The confusion is confounded, I fear further, when Dr. Posner and his colleagues use a tree graph to represent the results as "nodes of processing," but say, at the same time, that the processing at the different nodes is not an entailed serial chain. Normally, as I understand the matter, one expects a tree graph to represent some continuity of relationship or rule of descent, as in family trees or parsing trees. The only relation common to the nodes of Dr. Posner's tree, however, is a linguistic accident: the presence of the word "same" as it is used to indicate that two letters have the same shape, or have the same name, or are both vowels. Of course a diagram used as a conceptual aid does not have to have a logical motivation: it may have only some intuitive appeal or for that matter simply be a convention. But I do find this tree graph misleading, especially when, as Dr. Posner argues, the various encodings diagrammed are not to be thought of as performed serially and, as I have argued, they lack a common relation. Actually, a more apt representation of the data, I think, would be something like partly overlapping circles to indicate that each of the encodings is based on a subset of the test object's features, and that the various subsets may be partially correlated. It is not clear to me what the diagram as it stands is intended to represent, and indeed it may intend more than it represents.[2]

An Implicit Model
Some of the difficulty here may rest with the model that Dr. Posner seems to have in mind. It is one that a perception psychologist would

[2] In the version of their paper that appears in this volume Posner, Lewis, and Conrad have moved so far away from the notion of serial processing implied earlier as to include Figure 2. This figure illustrates the idea that geometric and linguistic properties (visual and name codes) of letters or other objects may be processed in parallel. If these features are processed in parallel, what of other features such as historical derivation and means of manufacture? Moreover, if these and other features are thought of as processed in parallel, the whole notion of isolable subsystems decomposes, it seems to me, into nothing more than a feature list. One would then have as many "isolable subsystems" as features, and be none the more knowledgeable about how classifying occurs.

call an "inflow model," that is, one that assumes that the person acts primarily as an analytic detector and that the flow of information is always from the environment sequentially inward, "data" and "program" fixed and distinct. In studies of perception it is found that inflow models as a class do not do justice to the remarkable amounts of record-keeping and command and control functions that characterize perceiving, or to the remarkable interactions between "data" and "program" that are found. Several alternatives have been proposed, some called "outflow models," others called "feedback models." The distinguishing feature of the latter two as compared with the first is that they regard a person as an active gatherer of information rather than its passive detector: information processing is found to be a two-way rather than a one-way street.

The same is implied when we find that the syntactic and semantic features of a text are more important to a subject's reading than the graphemic features are; or that bilingual subjects will sometimes actually "misread" a linguistically mixed passage in a way that preserves its semantic but not its lexical features. From these cases we are obliged to realize that the subject is usually doing more than allowing shapes to enter his visual system to which at some stage he adds meaning. Indeed, what could it mean to add meaning, even if we knew what "meaning" meant? One sometimes speaks of ostensive definition, again of operational definition, and sometimes of syntactic definition, among others. Surely whatever meaning is, it is not the same thing for words like *four, because, pencil,* or *Michael Posner.* I doubt that it can be adequately specified in the way Posner intends.

Pictorial experience and linguistic experience, or pictorial and linguistic encodings, are substantially different in some respects, both experientially and in the way the brain seems to process them; but we do not yet know much about these differences. We do know from some tests that sometimes pictures are recognized more rapidly than words, and sometimes words are recognized more rapidly than pictures. If differences in time to respond do not restrictively imply serial or parallel processing, as Posner's data seem to show is the case, then they imply only what they show, which is that some judgments take longer than others.

The way in which linguistic experience affects pictorial experience—so that, having had something named, we see it differently; and the way pictorial experience affects linguistic experience so that, having seen something, we find we need a name for it—is a major problem for some areas of research. As Posner has pointed out, our understanding of these kinds of encodings would contribute greatly to our understanding of perception in general and, most particularly, to our understanding of reading.

Reference

Posner, M. I., and R. F. Mitchell, 1967. Chronometric analysis of classification. *Psych. Rev.* 74:392–409.

General Discussion of Papers by Posner, Lewis, and Conrad; and Kolers

Posner responded to Kolers's criticisms. He agreed that "physical identity" is a misleading label for what is undoubtedly a very complex and abstract process, and that reaction time for physical identity depends a great deal on the stimulus set. The distinction between physical identity and name identity depends on findings other than a simple comparison of the reaction time for the two tasks; for example, that reaction time is affected by the number of items in short-term memory for the name identity task but not for the physical identity task; or that the same pair of letters "AB" require a longer reaction time for the name-identity task than for the physical identity task. As for the objection that subjects might have greater familiarity with a physical identity task than with a linguistic task, he said that no significant change in reaction time had been observed for either task after long practice.

With respect to Kolers's point about the options available to the subjects, Posner said that in the name identity task, pairs of the type "AA, aa" had not been used, so that the number of actual stimuli (if not the number a subject might conceive of) was the same as in the physical identity task. The number of stimuli used in the vowel-consonant task was admittedly greater but there is other evidence [Posner 1970] that the number of alternatives is not important for this task. He agreed that the tree graph might be a confusing way to display his data, but that no suggestion of serial processing had been intended. He did not intend to reject "outflow" and agreed that more attention might have been given to this aspect of the perceptual process.

Much of the rest of the discussion was concerned with the concept of "active" perception. Gibson suggested that perception, and reading in particular, is "an active gathering of information." Posner said that "active" might be defined in a number of ways. To the extent that a subject sets himself to follow the instructions of the experimenter, his perception is active, that is, purposeful. Or "active" might refer to the functioning of the operational model of consciousness proposed in his paper: a limited capacity processor capable of integrating signals from different modalities. The "look-up" operation required to identify shapes or names of letters would not be active in this special sense; consciousness may be otherwise occupied but look-up can still continue. Nor would an analysis-by-synthesis process that does not take up any attention be active, even though analysis-by-synthesis is often referred to as an active model. Thus, if information presented to the unattended ear in a dichotic listening experiment is stored in memory unconsciously, the processing would not be active, in Posner's sense.

Gibson said that the active aspects of Posner's model represents only a small part of the reading process. Posner said that the active processor is needed to extract meaning from sentences, and actual reading is a highly active process. But he did not pretend to offer his particular approach to information processing as a model of reading, though he thought his results were related to reading. Nor was he proposing a theory of pattern recognition. Before one could make a model of reading one would like to know, for example, whether a subject attending to the right ear looks up a word presented at the left ear, and if so, whether he can get the meaning from a sentence under the same conditions. Assuming that a subject could not perform these tasks, the role of an active processor with limited capacity would become very important.

LaBerge asked whether, if adults perceive speech automatically and unconsciously, using analysis-by-synthesis, infants also learn to perceive speech using analysis-by-synthesis, but at a level of conscious awareness. The implication of the dichotic experiments at Haskins Laboratories [Studdert-Kennedy and Shankweiler 1970] was that speech must be learned in some genetically determined way. If speech were indeed learned consciously, and later became unconscious, different children would learn to speak in different ways, and these differences would be preserved after speech became unconscious and automatic. Posner said that Konorski [1967] had observed that the way in which a first language is learned has an influence on the effects of later brain damage.

References

Konorski, J., 1967. *Integrative Activity of the Brain.* Chicago: University of Chicago Press.

Posner, M. I., 1970. On the relationship between letter names and superordinate categories. *Quart. J. Exp. Psych.* 22:279–287.

Studdert-Kennedy, M., and D. Shankweiler, 1970. Hemispheric specialization for speech perception. *J. Acoust. Soc. Amer.* 48:579–594.

Speech and Reading

For a very large number of children the first word they learn to read is their own name—and one can think of no more meaningful word. Some time may elapse before a second word is confidently added to the reading repertoire. But this first word marks the attainment of a concept of immense intellectual importance: the child accepts the idea that an untidy nonrepresentational pattern of lines in some way symbolizes a name. We say to children, "What does this word say?" In so doing, we intuitively link reading with speaking, dramatically distinguishing between the identification of printed pictures of objects and printed names of objects. Never, in Western culture, would we point to the picture of a dog and ask, "What does this picture say?"

If we examine this intuition in more detail, there is an implication that the printed word says something to the child; the child listens to what is said and then repeats it out loud. But it is not hard to accept that the child, looking at the word, says something to himself, listens to himself, and then repeats what he has heard. In this analysis we are at least within the realm of theoretical possibility. But this does not make it correct, and in this chapter we shall examine evidence concerning the role of certain processes—and their interrelationships—involved in reading.

In no sense is this chapter a broad survey of reading processes. Quite the contrary. We shall be concerned only with the transduction problem of a visual input transformed into a speech-motor output when we read aloud. But the main emphasis will be to consider the speculation that has continuously intrigued students, that the identical transduction necessarily occurs when we read silently to ourselves. We shall consider codes and memories—those systems required for viably maintaining the substance of perceptions during the addition of subsequent perceptions so that higher-order manipulations are possible and textual meaning is achieved. In the first section we shall consider the mature adult with long-established reading skill. In the next we shall go back to the beginning, trying to relate the elements of adult reading skill to those of the child struggling with the wonder that little black lines are mysteriously endowed with familiar meaning. In all of this, we shall never be able to evade the intrusive presence of speech. Then in the last section we shall turn round on our own speculations and discuss the nature of the transduction for profoundly deaf children who have little and poor-quality vocal speech.

Speech and Reading in Adults

Does all reading involve speech, and does reading aloud merely add sound? Or does reading aloud crucially change the nature of key operations, bypassing or transforming many of those involved in silent reading? We know that reading in its ordinary sense, that is, reading with intent to comprehend the material read, must include a very great deal more than making a speech sound each time we look at a word. We can then pose as a primary question, do the processes involved in comprehension occur before the sound is made? In this case, speaking aloud would merely be fulfilling the behavior requirement to read aloud. Or do we make the speech sounds, listen to them, and comprehend what it is we have heard? What we are asking here is whether comprehension of printed material—reading—is possible directly from the visual input. Or do we have to say words, whether covertly or overtly, in order to understand their meaning? Certainly the latter possibility has a conceptual elegance, since it would fit reading and listening to speech into a single behavioral framework, the only difference being the source of the speech—oneself or another person. But since behavioral mechanisms rarely fall into simple patterns, a discussion of the evidence is necessary; and the reader might just as well be warned at this point that it will not be conclusive.

At the outset, we might just as well place our cards and our prejudices on the table, and try to indicate what we mean by silent speech. In the present context this term covers a wide range of phenomena. At one extreme, the most obvious, we can think of reading with almost full articulation; that is, all articulatory processes are involved except those required for making sounds. Although nothing is heard, lips visibly move to form speech sounds and movement of the speech organs can easily be felt with the fingers. In one sense this is unquestionably silent reading. The continuum then moves toward less directly observable behavior. (Lips may be closed and apparently unmoving, movements in the throat may be too attenuated to be felt. Nevertheless, articulation may still be detected by electromyographic (EMG) and related techniques.) Here, the fact that reading is accompanied by electrical activity in muscles required in the production of speech sounds, though no movement is visible to the eye, is taken as evidence for the occurrence of silent articulation of speech during reading. This line of investigation began with Curtis [1900] and reviews are to be found, for example, in Edfeldt [1960] and McGuigan [1970].

Rarely questioned, it usually remains an implication that the silent articulation shown by the EMG record does in fact refer to the material actually being read, and is not merely an irrelevant accompaniment. There are ways around this as well. Locke and Fehr [1970] required subjects to read silently (for subsequent recall) two classes of word— those that did, or did not, include labial phonemes. Using surface electrodes, they also recorded activity of the labial musculature. Though the results were not entirely unambiguous, they seemed to indicate that "labial" words, silently read, do show more movement of the labial muscles than do "nonlabial" words. At any rate the procedure is novel and highly promising.

But even the complete absence of detectable speech-motor activity does not preclude the occurrence of silent speech in the form of speech imagery. We are not saying here that this ever happens, only that it can happen. If auditory imagery is a genuine biological phenomenon, then the sounds of speech must be included in its definition, and silent reading can be accompanied by a succession of auditory speech images that might have the same psychological function in the reading process as does silent articulation. Granted auditory imagery in this context, then speech-motor imagery, even though unresponsive to EMG recording, must be included in this definition as well. (If in imagination we can move a leg, then there is no reason why in imagination we should not be able to move a tongue and so image the feel of silent speech without articulation and without imaged sound.) All these phenomena would be silent speech. The fact that no visible lip movement is observed does not preclude the presence of silent speech in reading. EMG silence equally does not preclude silent speech. As always, it is easier to prove the presence of a phenomenon than its absence.

We can turn now to a critical, but brief, review of the evidence relating to our specific question. But instead of discussing in detail the very numerous studies that have been reported on this topic, we shall comment on categories of study, exemplifying where necessary. The original discussion in scientific form arose toward the end of the nineteenth century, opinion dividing on the basis of introspections. We do not know how reliable the introspections were. (Paulhan [1886] denied silent speech; Stricker [see Edfeldt 1960] insisted on it. Lepley [1952] asked some 200 undergraduates whether they silently spoke words (while writing rather than reading); introspections were about equally divided.) It may be that some people do silently speak when reading and others do not.

But it may also be that undergraduates divide equally into those who can detect their own imagery and attenuated muscle movements, and those who cannot. We cannot ignore this possibility, and the evidence from introspection must be considered inconclusive. It is a great pity that few studies have checked the reliability of introspection in this area by simultaneously taking EMG recordings. An early one by Reed [1916], using a rather primitive recording device, showed a number of mutual discrepancies between data from introspection and data from EMG.

Another discontinued line of enquiry may be exemplified by studies by Pintner [1913] and by Reed [1916], who had subjects silently read a text while simultaneously saying something else, such us counting. Both authors reported comprehension to be unimpaired by the vocalizing activity and concluded that silent speech could not therefore be occurring during the silent reading. It is perfectly true that one cannot speak two different words concurrently. But silent speaking of every word may be no more essential for comprehension during reading than is eye fixation of every word; and in the same way that vision is unquestionably necessary for reading, so too by analogy can silent speech be. We shall return to this analogy later. We do not know the rate at which the distracting words were spoken. When an interpolated counting task is used in a short-term memory paradigm (read test material: interpolated counting: recall test material; Peterson and Peterson [1959]), the counting rate determines amount recalled. Presumably verbal rehearsal can be accommodated during counting, depending on the rate of the latter [Conrad and Hull 1966]. A second point with this type of experiment, is that the interfering counting task need not interfere with speech imagery. It is perfectly easy, as anyone can test for himself, to utter a continuous vowel sound while reading silently using silent speech. In this situation, the silent speech sounds of reading can be "heard" quite clearly. It is tempting to believe that these are auditory images, adequately lending themselves to comprehension of the text. The fact that silent reading and counting aloud can appear to occur together need not exclude the possibility of silent speech during reading. This type of study, then, is also inconclusive.

A third category that continues to flourish [McGuigan 1970] uses EMG recording. As we have said, this category has a history going back to the beginning of this century; and almost without exception, results show more EMG response from speech muscles during silent reading than during rest. One of the most comprehensive and carefully controlled studies is that of Edfeldt [1960], who reported articulation during silent reading with almost all of 84 subjects. (Perversely, Edfeldt does not report whether any of these subjects gave negative introspections). There are indeed so many good studies reporting the presence of articulation during silent reading, that we might be justified in concluding that the case is proved. But of course, the case that appears to be proved is that silent reading is accompanied by articulation. What is far from proved is that articulation is *necessarily* involved in silent reading. This kind of imperative seems most unlikely. No one has convincingly shown comprehension to be seriously impaired directly as a result of preventing articulation in some way. This latter is not easily accomplished by mechanical means [Novikova 1966]. Indeed, the contrary may be true. Hardyck, Petrinovich et al. [1967], using a conditioning procedure, reported the complete inhibition of articulation during silent reading with unimpaired comprehension. A later report qualified this [Hardyck and Petrinovich 1970]. In any case, absence of articulation does not preclude the use of speech imagery, so that comprehension when there is no EMG response could still be based, as a requirement, on silent speech.

Even when EMG response does accompany silent reading, it is rarely evident that the response is related to the words read. The study of Locke and Fehr [1970] referred to earlier would be of considerable importance here. The crucial point is that their technique demonstrates that (at least) those speech muscles from which they recorded showed activity directly related to the words being silently read. Chin-lip response was more marked for words like "map" than for words like "hat." Promising though this approach appears to be, caution is required since there was in fact some chin-lip response from nonlabial words, and in some experimental conditions the labial-nonlabial difference was not found. But the major logical limitation of EMG procedures remains: though articulation clearly does occur during silent reading, it may not be necessary, and it remains possible from this evidence that silent reading is basically sustained by other processes.

If silent reading depends on articulation, it can be argued not very convincingly that the speed of silent reading would be comparable to that of vocal reading. Indeed Landauer [1962] reported that subjects (n = 4) could recite number sequences, for instance, at the same speed whether the recitation was vocal or subvocal. The case of reading, though, is rather different. In reading aloud, every word is enunciated. In silent reading, we cannot know whether this is true. It is well known that with suitable training, silent reading speeds of up to 500 words per minute can be achieved with no loss of comprehension [Poulton 1963]. McLaughlin [1969] reports a case study of a girl who read at about 2000 words a minute. In these cases, it is extremely unlikely that every word would be enunciated. But this does not imply that in this case, comprehension is based on (e.g.) visual imagery.

Poulton [1963] suggests that in rapid reading, or skimming, better selection of crucial items is made, with an implication that no more words are individually visually or subvocally read per unit time than in conventional reading. We must suppose that in rapid reading, eye saccades are longer in terms of number of words covered by one saccade, and eye fixations fewer per passage of text than in vocal reading. We might then suggest that (articulation occurs only at eye fixations, and that at those points enough words can be both seen and articulated to provide an input adequate for comprehension.) There seems no reason why more information should be available from vision than from articulation. The close association between eye fixation and articulation is further supported by the fact that silently read text that is difficult, either syntactically or through unfamiliarity or through poor legibility, shows increased articulation, as compared with simpler or easier material [Edfeldt 1960; Hardyck and Petrinovich 1970; Novikova, 1966].

Summing up the evidence provided by EMG studies on the question, Does comprehension in silent reading depend on an articulatory input? we have to say that articulation almost always occurs, that it is probably task-relevant, but that sound evidence that it is necessary is lacking. Other inputs may be equally useful, and possibly concurrent.

There are other, less direct, ways of approaching this problem. In a short-term memory (STM) task for visually presented verbal items, it is possible to suppress articulation effectively. Recall is then severely impaired when a visual input into memory is clearly available [Murray 1967]. Also, when in verbal STM tasks there is a clear penalty for articulating visually presented items, subjects seem unable to make use of the visual information, and their performance accordingly suffers. It will be convenient to discuss the latter case first.

A number of authors have shown that when verbal items (words, consonants, etc.) are visually presented for immediate recall, or for recall delayed by several seconds, the material is encoded in phonological form [Baddeley 1966; Conrad 1962; Hintzman 1967; Murray 1966; Sperling 1963; Wickelgren 1965]. Thus far, this merely confirms EMG work using a quite different technique. What would happen, though, in STM experiments were subjects required to read silently test items which phonologically were very similar? If they persisted in using a phonological code, using either articulation or auditory imagery, we would expect severe impairment of recall. However, if subjects could with facility switch to another code such as visual,[1] the phonological similarity of items would be irrelevant and—assuming that the visual code was efficient—recall need not suffer. In fact a number of experiments suggest that subjects do persist in using a phonological code with impairment to serial recall [Baddeley 1966; Conrad 1963, 1965; Murray 1967], to probe recall [Murray 1968], and to recognition [Felzen and Anisfeld 1970].

As a matter of fact, we have no conclusive empirical evidence in these experiments to refute the possibility that subjects do switch to visual coding of phonologically similar items—and that it is a relatively inefficient code. But subjects' introspections are consistently negative on this point.

We have one other set of data, as yet unpublished and relevant here, which may be worth mentioning. These come from conventional immediate recall of visually presented letters chosen to be phonologically confusing, namely, "B,C,D,P,T,V." We have an error matrix from this study, which we can relate to a matrix of shape confusions for certain letters of the alphabet presented by Thomasson [1970]. Thomasson displayed single letters for identification. He used several procedures (distance, brief exposure, visual noise); all gave effectively the same results and justified pooling of data. We can therefore ascertain whether our recall errors suggest shape confusions rather than phonological confusions. Inspection then shows clear evidence of phonological rather than visual coding. For example, "D" confuses much more with "T" than with "B."

Our hesitancy in reporting these data in this context stems from the fact that the subjects were aged 10 to 11 years. In the course of the experiment it was evident that the subjects were aware of the special difficulty of this letter-set, compared with a phonologically dissimilar control set that typically showed much better recall, but it was fairly certain that visual coding was not generally attempted. We incline to the view therefore that these STM studies indicate so marked a preference for phonological coding in situations that make such coding penal, that they might almost be taken to support the view that speech coding is necessary in silent reading.

The evidence from experiments that attempt to suppress articulation of items read, by requiring subjects to speak a different verbal item concurrently with presentation of the test item, is somewhat tantalizing. Murray [1967] reported reduced memory span. This result has been

[1] Were there enough time, a semantic recoding might be possible, but this would again suggest the need for phonological storage.

confirmed by the present author in a hitherto unpublished study that in principle repeated Murray's procedure. But in addition the nature of recall errors was examined. There are a number of possible guesses at the reason for the reduced span in this situation. Subjects deprived of the easy use of articulation may use a code dependent on auditory imagery. Or they may switch to a quite different strategy and use visual coding. Both codes would probably be not only less effective but also unpracticed. Third, subjects might in fact attempt to use an articulatory code and accept heavy interference effects from the irrelevant articulation. By comparing the error matrix with those obtained in other studies, we might hope to decide among these alternatives.

In the experiment, 4 consonants (Murray used 7) were presented visually and singly at a rate of 120 letters per minute. They were drawn from the set of 10 letters: "B,C,P,T,V,F,M,N,S,X," which we had used in other studies. Forty-one adult subjects, tested individually, were instructed to say "the" in unison with the letters as they appeared on a Bina-View display. They then immediately wrote down their recall in correct serial order. After initial practice there were 40 trials. The percentage of correctly recalled letters was 66.5. This may be compared with about 75 percent correct obtained, with comparable subjects, using 6-letter sequences but with ordinary silent reading of items and in otherwise similar conditions [Conrad and Hull 1964]. It is safe to say that without "suppression" of articulation, in this experiment, recall would have been close to 100 percent. Murray [1967] also reported more than double the number of wrong letters when his subjects "suppressed" compared with reading aloud the same number of letters per sequence. This justifies the conclusion that "suppression" markedly reduces span.

A number of collapsed error matrices are shown in Table 1. Using the matrix shown below as a grid, collapsing was based as follows:

a b

c d

Cell a shows the percent wrong responses that were "B,C,P,T,V" (consonant followed by /i/) when the correct letter was "B,C,P,T,V." Cell b shows the percent wrong responses that were "B,C,P,T,V" when the correct letter was "F,M,N,S" (/e/ followed by consonant). Cell c shows the percent wrong responses which were "F,M,N,S" when the correct letter was "B,C,P,T,V." Cell d shows the percent wrong responses which were "F,M,N,S" when the correct letter was "F,M,N,S." In all of the

Table 1
Collapsed Confusion Matrices from Various Sources

35.6	79.1		79.2	19.8		57.6	57.8
64.4	20.9		20.8	80.2		42.4	42.2
(1a)		(1b)		(1c)

58.2	58.1		50.0	62.5
41.8	41.9		50.0	37.5
(1d)		(1e)

(1a) Shape confusions:after Thomasson [1970]
(1b) Immediate recall confusions:after Conrad [1964]
(1c) "Suppression" confusions
(1d) Delayed recall confusions:after Conrad [1967]
(1e) Chance (equiprobable) confusions

STM experiments from which Tables 1b, 1c and 1d are derived, the letter "X" was also one of the set used. But Table 1a is based on the carefully conducted study of letter shape confusions by Thomasson [1970], who unfortunately did not use "X," and we have accordingly excluded it from the other collapsed matrices.

Table 1b is derived from Conrad [1964]. In this study subjects silently read 6-letter sequences and immediately reported them in writing. This table strikingly brings out the role of vowel similarity in STM errors. Table 1c shows comparable data from 4-letter sequences when each visually presented letter is "read" aloud as "the" instead of its correct name. Table 1d comes from an experiment reported by Conrad [1967]. In the particular experimental condition, subjects read aloud 4-letter sequences, again visually displayed one at a time by Bina-View. This was immediately followed by 18 digits (requiring 7.2 sec) which subjects also read aloud. Following this, recall was made. Table 1e merely shows what the chance values would be if, when a letter was wrong, all other letters were reported equally often. (Note that "X" was not included).

Comparing these subtables, it is immediately clear from Tables 1b and 1c that "suppression" has almost entirely disrupted the phonological coding represented in Table 1b. The extent of the disruption of the code is closely paralleled by the effect shown in Table 1d when rehearsal is prevented for a few seconds. Nevertheless this massive disruption apparently does not tempt subjects into general use of shape coding in order to memorize the material. The error distribution in Table 1a is very different from that of Table 1c (suppression). In fact Thomasson's complete matrix [1970, p. 189] shows that the main effect of shape confusion for these letters is felt in two specific confusions: "B" and "S", and "F" and "P". The full "suppression" matrix (not shown here) shows both of these pairs to confuse less than would be expected by chance. We are therefore led to conclude that even when silent speech in reading is made extremely difficult, subjects still do not use shape coding. The evidence is that they remain firmly attached to an ineffective code and performance accordingly suffers. Here too, then, it seems as if a (speech code not only is commonly used in this type of reading task, but also must be used, since no other apparently is available.)

A crucial test against a shape-coding hypothesis in this situation can be made. Subjects in a "suppression" condition would have to memorize letters drawn from either of two different letter-sets, one set having a high similarity in phonological features but of low visual similarity, the second having high visual similarity and low phonological similarity. Shape coding would show as an advantage for the first set, when similarity in speech characteristics would be irrelevant. Murray [1967] reports another experiment in the same study that comes close to this description. He used 7-letter sequences of either high or of low "acoustic" confusability, drawn from most letters of the alphabet. Unfortunately not enough details are given to determine the degree of visual similarity within the two sets (Murray's hypothesis did not need this). However, if in spite of "suppression," subjects still manage to use phonological coding, one would expect the phonologically similar sequences to be most affected by "suppression." In fact, Murray reported no difference between these two conditions. Superficially, then, this suggests that phonological coding can be eliminated from the silent reading of to-be-remembered material. But by using 7-letter sequences, overall about 65 percent of letters were wrong in both conditions; at that part of the sequence—items 3, 4, 5, and 6—most sensitive to changes in experimental conditions, errors appear to be around 90 percent. The test therefore, regrettably, was probably too insensitive to permit valid comparison.

Another approach to the question of the use of the speech code in silent reading is represented in some experiments by Corcoran [1966, 1967]. In the first of these, subjects were set the essentially visual task of rapidly examining a section of printed prose, with instructions to mark each occurrence of the letter *e*. It was found that a silent *e* (as in *hope*) was missed nearly four times as often as a pronounced *e* (as in *seat*). In Corcoran's second experiment, *e*'s were systematically deleted from a text and the subject's task was to detect absence of *e*. Again, significantly more silent *e*'s were undetected than were pronounced missing *e*'s. Here is an almost pure visual task, but using verbal material, and with neither a need to memorize nor to comprehend meaning. The evidence is that just the same, silent speech, perhaps compulsively, again occurs, again detrimentally to performance. This is a study that badly needs to be repeated in a developmental context.

This section should not be concluded without some reference to a body of data that ought to be relevant to this discussion. These data concern the difference in performance between reading material silently or aloud—the nature of the performance depending on the nature of the material. There is wide common experience that for certain tasks, such as adding columns of figures, or reading syntactically difficult prose, vocalizing appears to be an aid. Intuitively support for this would come from the established fact that STM performance is enhanced when the material is heard or is vocalized by subjects, as compared with silent reading [Atkinson and Shiffrin 1968; Conrad and Hull 1968; Corballis 1966; Craik 1969; Murdock 1967; Murray 1965]. Since many other reading tasks must involve substantial degrees of short-term memorizing, it is possible that the STM component provides the basis that can support the intuition. However, empirical tests do not lend convincing support to this hypothesis.

Conrad [1971], Poulton and Brown [1967], and Rogers [1937] all reported no real effect on prose comprehension of reading aloud. It seems possible that under everyday conditions, reading aloud simply acts as an arousing device. This would not be needed under rigorous test conditions, and the STM modality component may be relatively trivial, though it is undoubtedly present. The added acoustic information, supplementary to the articulatory, appears to contribute too little to detect. If in fact reading aloud helps us to unravel tangled prose, it may do so by nothing more fundamental than making sure that we do in fact read it.

It is evident that the EMG studies discussed earlier are by definition concerned with the occurrence of articulation in silent reading—but they in no sense exclude the possibility of concurrent, and perhaps functionally supra-auditory imagery. In the case of the STM and "proofreading" experiments, the distinction cannot so easily be made, and for this reason we have used terms like "speech code" or "phonological code," with the implication that we prefer not to be forced to choose between the roles of speech imagery and speech-motor activity. Indeed, empirically there is little to go on.

Thomasson [1970] has presented an extremely thorough review of the problem as it concerns memorizing; he particularly draws attention to the apparent role of place of articulation in determining STM errors. Certainly it is clear from Thomasson and from Hintzman [1967] that material read silently and encoded for immediate recall depends to a large extent on articulatory features. But we already know from EMG studies that articulation is rarely absent from silent reading, and so phonetic feature analysis in this case could hardly contribute to the question of the ultimate representation of the coded material.

Furthermore, ordinary experience as well as empirical evidence compel us to accept that codes other than motor speech-based codes may be valuably involved in remembering material initially read. Baddeley [1966] and others have shown that semantic features of words can underlie a memory code in appropriate conditions. Indeed it must be recognized that most, but not all, of the STM experiments discussed above have been so designed as to preclude the likelihood of detecting the presence or absence of other than speech codes. Readers might like to consider for themselves, for instance in remembering a long telephone number, how far, between reading and dialing it, they make use of "semantic" features (e.g., 456), and visual features. The concept of a multicode system, hierarchically organized, is intuitively attractive as being biologically adaptive.

Not one of the studies cited in this discussion has required a subject to perform a task for a duration of practice even remotely resembling the experience we have accumulated for reading procedures in ordinary life. When an experimental reading task is presented that can be performed more effectively using a visual, or other nonspeech, code, we have no idea whether subjects could or would develop this strategy if they could practice for extended periods of time.

In drawing the threads of this section together, we must certainly hold these caveats in mind, but we can consider only the evidence that we have. This evidence tells us that normal adults, using vision to take in verbal information, go to what appears to be considerable neurological bother to recode it out of the input state. Though there are the inevitable anecdotal accounts of other procedures, documentation is utterly lacking. Yet all of our common sense tells us that we do detect the presence of misspelled words when there is no phonological clue. In the Concoran [1967] experiment, although more missing silent *e*'s were undetected, nevertheless about 60 percent of them were in fact detected. Common sense impels us to the view that reading must involve parallel phonological and visual inputs, and perhaps others, though they may not all go the same neurological distance. We may note in this connection the fascinating description of the behavior of a professional memory man by Luria [1969]. Why then do we so seem to need to "listen" to what we have read?

There is a very obvious and simple—perhaps oversimple—explanation. Our initial experience of language is aural; words come to us as sounds, and we may forever after need to hark back to auditory referents. Just the same, many of the new words that we learn, we initially read; yet when we meet them again we recode them phonologically along with all the others. Perhaps more likely, our initial reading experience is of vocal reading. Parents and teachers want to *hear* what we see. Can this relatively short exclusively vocal reading experience so condition us to say the words we see, that in spite of a subsequent much greater silent reading experience, we never change? Hardly likely. Where nurture fails to explain, can nature help?

We can rephrase the problem. Why do we need to name each word we read? Were we certain that, for whatever biological reason, serial recall of shapes is poorer than serial recall of phonological names, we would have an explanation. But this cannot be reliably tested in a valid context. Test words, or the phonemes used to construct nonsense words, would be familiar; test shapes—unless they could be named—would not be. Nor could we control the informational stimulus equivalence of the two sets of test material. This test just cannot be made, though the difference might still be real. But whatever biological evidence can be adduced, it clearly cannot show that memory for visual form is impossible, since we all know it exists. In that case, we are left manipulating relative quantities of perceptual performance. In a later section we will show that when speech is not available, quite high levels of performance at tasks involving reading may still be achieved.

Genesis of the Speech Code in Short-Term Memory

In discussing the role of speech when mature adults read, although there are serious gaps even at a descriptive level, such as the relationship between eye fixations and subvocalizing, there is overwhelming evidence of an association. But the reason why pictures (of words) are recoded in this way remains obscure. In this section we shall consider certain aspects of reading at its origins to see whether in the child beginning to read we can observe the genesis of the adult pattern.

Many authors have analyzed the elements of reading and discussed the nature of the prerequisite abilities. A very detailed breakdown is given by Staats [1968]. Although Staats's analysis of the processes is based on strict instrumental conditioning theory, the names of the processes—so far as they go—are hardly in doubt. Thus in order for a child to learn to read, he must be able to perceive the visual difference between letters of the alphabet. We know for example that the "b"–"d" distinction may be one of the last to fall into place, and we can assume that at an early enough age large numbers of letters look alike. Subsequently the child will learn that each letter has a name (or sound). The ability to enter names into a long-term memory store and retrieve them at will has an early development, and once a child can see the difference between two letters he will be able to memorize their different sounds. There is a later necessary stage in this transfer of seen-to-named information when the child learns that, according to context, the same letters may have different sounds, and different letters the same sound. So the child goes on to learn the names of whole words, which he can and does name aloud—and on to phrases.

But there are other abilities required that do not fit so easily into an instrumental conditioning framework, and that probably depend more on neurological maturation, since no formal training ever gets involved. These include the ability to accept a picture as a symbol for the real thing. It may not be until around 2 to 3 years before a child is able to point to a picture of a dog, especially if the picture is small, even though a real dog would have presented no problem. The concept that a printed word is a symbol for an object must come later still—and again not by formal training.

At which stage can we say that the child can read? Making motor responses to picture stimuli is no great biological achievement, and uttering a sound is a motor response. Rats can easily learn to respond to pictures that are not part of their natural environment. Children learn to respond to a printed word by saying its name. The trick of course is to understand the meaning of the sound—that is, to be able to transfer it correctly into other semantic contexts. When a child can correctly associate a printed word with an object, he can read. However if the child is to get beyond the single-word stage, then a quite separate ability must be brought in, and this again not subject to formal training, namely, short-term memory (STM). The child must remember for a short while what it was that sat on the mat, because it could have been other things than the cat. At the end, there is not true comprehension of the sentence unless the beginning can still be remembered. Without a massive STM operation, comprehension of prose would be impossible.

Yet there is a curious puzzle in this. Numerous authorities have stated an age for the development of the ability to learn to read. Edfeldt [1960] puts it at 6½ years; Gesell and Ilg [1946] at around 6 years; Lovell [1968] at 5½ to 6 years. Yet all of the above prerequisite abilities seem to be available well before the age of 5 years. Only one item is perhaps in doubt, and this is the STM role. Yet at one level it appears quite straightforward. At 4½ years, a child has a digit span of 4 on the Stanford-Binet scale. At 5 years he can repeat back quite long sentences. But this is verbal response to auditory input, and some of it may well be no more than an echoic response with little value for comprehension. At the same time, initial reading is always word-by-word aloud, and it also might provide no more than an input suitable for echoic response. But this is conjecture, and on the face of it, all the bits seem to be there long before the child can in fact usefully begin to learn to read in the full sense of comprehending the matter. But it doesn't happen.

In all of this chain of events from perception to evident comprehension, there are certain corners of significant promise into which we do not have experimental access. One of these concerns the STM code during the earliest phases of learning to read. Once a child-subject can fluently read the test material, as we have seen earlier, we have useful investigative procedures. But the child who cannot yet read our test material cannot be used in an experiment requiring reading. This, to say the least, is frustrating since by the time a subject can read well enough—and developmental time is rushing by—we may have missed these elusive critical stages, leaving us just where we were with our puzzle. By 4 years or so, the child is through all the necessary stages of visual perception, his vocabulary is large, his language is fluent enough, and his memory span for heard words is quite adequate for comprehending simple sentences, an ability he demonstrates throughout the day. Yet authority tells us that he is not old enough to begin to learn to read—and reading is not something that is spontaneously learned. What has been added by the age of 6 years that makes so great a difference? Let us look rather closely at the question of the STM code.

What appears to happen with the child who can just about read simple prose, is that he names each word aloud and, we presume, transfers them in phonological form into his STM store. Now let us suppose that for some obscure maturational reason this does not happen. That is, the child is faced with a visual stimulus, he can name it as a simple learned motor response, but that for this purpose he does not yet have availability into a phonological store. To remember the word, while looking at and naming the next word, it has to stay in a visual store. At this point there would be two good reasons why comprehension (i.e. reading) might be difficult. First a visual code might be a poor vehicle for storing percepts in this situation of rapidly changing temporary storage. Second, the act of vocalizing words at this early stage of reading might be so absorbing that even simple visual coding is impaired. Recapitulating this hypothesis in its barest form, the child at this stage can name words of running prose, but cannot remember the names.

What he must try to remember is the strange picture of the words—the pattern the print makes. The efficiency of a visual code in this context is then a separate question. What we need empirically to determine as a developmental brick, is whether a word read is held in a phonological or a visual STM store.

We have already pointed out that we cannot wait to study this question until developmentally the child can read. We need to know what it is that changes during the period when the child passes from unable to read to able to read. It turns out that using pictures of familiar objects, the names of which are well known to the child, reveals an intriguing growth trend which could be highly relevant to the reading problem, and it is perhaps worth describing one germane study [Conrad, 1971] in some detail.

The rationale is based on the adult studies referred to in the previous section [Conrad 1963, 1965]. These demonstrated the preferred use of a penal phonological STM code, by comparing recall for like-sounding and unlike-sounding verbal items presented visually. Although items in the former lists were visually quite different (e.g., "B, T," or "rays, raise"), this information was apparently ignored and adult subjects had great difficulty in serially recalling items of this kind. In adapting this paradigm for young children we used two sets, each of 8 colored pictures, the names of which we ascertained were familiar to all subjects. One set, the homophone (H) set, consisted of *cat, rat, bat, hat, mat, man, tap, bag.* The second set, the nonhomophone (nonH) set, used *fish, girl, bus, spoon, horse, train, clock, hand.* All children were first given the English Picture Vocabulary Test, which is a British standardization of the Peabody Picture Vocabulary Test, and in the rest of the description and discussion of this study, age will mean mental age as determined by the English Picture Vocabulary Test. Subjects were aged 3 to 11 years.

After appropriate practice, 16 trials proceeded as follows. A complete set of pictures, alternating H and nonH, were laid out face up and at once covered over. The spatial order of these sets was different for each trial. Then n cards drawn from a duplicate set were placed face up before a child, and the experimenter, in order, named a card and turned it over face down until all of the n cards were turned over. The vocabulary set of 8 was then uncovered and the child tried to match from memory the cards still face down, to the appropriate ones in the vocabulary. The n value, the number of cards a child had to remember, was determined individually for each subject during practice, on the basis that on average there were 50 percent correctly matched cards when the H set was used.

Table 2
Percentage of Correctly Matched Cards (After Conrad [1971])

Mental age (years)	3–5	5–6	6–7	7–8	8–11
No. subjects	21	20	16	20	18
H set correct (%)	52.4	52.0	51.9	52.1	52.4
NonH set correct (%)	52.8	59.1	64.0	69.1	75.3
Mean no. items presented	3.2	3.8	4.1	4.4	5.9

The results are shown in Table 2, which essentially compares recall of the H sets and nonH sets for each age group. It also gives the number of subjects per group and the mean number of cards used with each group. It will be seen that correct matches on the H set were in fact held at just over 50 percent for all groups. In other words, on that criterion the groups are matched, and this justifies our using the nonH set results to examine age effects.

Up to 5 years there is clearly no difference in recall of the two sets. If this youngest group is split into two smaller subgroups aged 3–4 and 4–5 years, the picture is the same: no difference. At this age then the fact that the H set pictures have like-sounding names, and the nonH set pictures do not, is irrelevant to STM performance. Since recall is a good deal above chance level, this would be likely to occur only in the absence of a phonological code. Although there is no internal evidence to indicate that a visual code was used, it is difficult to see what else is available in this material, and at this age. Beyond 5 years there is a consistently increasing advantage for the nonH set that is already significant for the 5–6 year group ($p < 0.02$). This is exactly that we would expect from subjects who were saying the names to themselves and using that phonological information as a memory code.

These differences were also reflected in the children's overt behavior. For one thing, the older children often whispered or mouthed the names and were visibly disturbed when the names were like-sounding. They tended to match in strict serial order so that each name was tagged to a location in the test cards. The youngest children, on the other hand, were much more likely to match in haphazard order. Their overt verbal behavior took one of two forms. Either it was completely absent without the slightest sign of lip movement, or in some cases, children did say names during matching that were clearly irrelevant to task performance. For example, a child might say, "bat goes with cat," while correctly matching hat with hat. This seems to be a kind of word babble referred to by Weir [1966], who regarded it almost as playing with the sounds of words, more interesting for the child than nonverbal sounds, but nevertheless used with little semantic significance.

The evidence of this study throws some speculative light on the problem of fitting together the various psychological bits that go to make up maturational readiness to learn to read. It is just about at the age which educators point at, that children move over to a preference for using a phonological STM code. When all other specified necessary abilities seem to be present, certainly by about age 4 years, this one is still absent. When this one final bit arrives, reading begins. Incidentally, it is easy to see how once use of phonological coding has occurred, instrumental conditioning might further its entrenchment since it seems to be efficient. It is hard to believe that its occurrence in the first place, so universally, and in such a short space of developmental time, is purely by chance.

Can the behavior we have observed, when young children try to remember a sequence of pictures of objects that have familiar names, also describe what happens when the pictures are abstract symbols with names? We might speculate that even though a child of, say, 4 years could easily distinguish the visible difference between "cat" and "dog," and know what a cat was and what a dog was, he might still have fundamental difficulty in comprehending the *printed* sentence, *The dog bit the cat*. We are suggesting that this can occur if the words when read (even aloud) do not pass into a phonological STM store, and if a visual code based on shape is less efficient for remembering verbal material than is a phonological code.

The fact that for perhaps two years or so a child may have been quite fluent in using and comprehending spoken language is possibly irrelevant when it comes to language visually perceived. We do not doubt that a child of 3 to 4 years could be taught to say the names of many printed words, as he can learn the names of the objects themselves. But though we certainly do not understand the mechanisms involved, we can appreciate a phenomenological difference between the acquisition of a repeated association over many "trials" helped by the formal and especially informal reinforcements of daily life, and the immediate recall of a familiar word in a novel context, such as in reading. Faced with immediate recall of pictures, whether of objects or words, the 4-year-old codes in a manner qualitatively different from that of a 6-year-old. The maturing of this quality may be a crucial prerequisite for learning to read.

Considerable research has been concerned with just this question of whether the use of phonological coding by young children does in fact help recall [Flavell 1970]. There are a number of experiments that report that when children name out loud a sequence of pictures, they recall more than when they do not name them [Bernbach 1967; Rosenbaum 1962; Weir and Stevenson 1959]. But this is only the nominal comparison, since there is an implied premise that in the silent condition the child is not naming to himself. This premise is untenable. In the non-naming condition, the experimenter does not know whether or not the child names. If he does name, the comparison becomes one between vocalizing and naming silently, both involving a phonological code. Or the child may not name when looking silently at pictures, which is the underlying assumption of the paradigm, and sometimes the instruction. In this case the vocal condition permits comparison only of nonnaming with naming plus vocalizing.

The latter two effects cannot be untangled. There is a third possibility, to which we have already referred, that in the vocal condition true semantic naming is not occurring; the child is merely uttering word-like sounds. In this case no effect of naming need be expected, and this may account for reports of absence of effect [Hagen and Kingsley 1968]. For this paradigm to be effective there must be independent confirmation of nonnaming in one condition, and confirmation in the vocal condition that naming is in fact mediating recall.

It is certain that visual coding is a biological reality. Nevertheless, when it comes to memorizing words, there is a good deal of circumstantial—but no direct—evidence of the superiority of a phonological code over a visual one. But we have seen that in the equivocal case where a child has a "choice" between memorizing a picture and memorizing the name of the picture, for a long period of developmental time it is the picture code that dominates. Though we cannot assess its relative efficiency, it is a viable and effective code—the child does memorize. We have nowhere in this discussion been able to assert with confidence that a phonological code is better than a visual one for reading—only that it is very widely used, and even in circumstances where it is clearly handicapping. In the next section, therefore, we will look at the extreme case of people for whom speech is either absent or extremely imperfect, a condition found in people who have been profoundly deaf from an age too young to have acquired any spoken language.

Reading without Speech

Since this paper is directly concerned with the role of speech in reading and in learning to read, it is certainly pertinent to consider the nature and the effectiveness of reading skill in the deaf, who have had no experience of aural speech. There are of course, other pathologically handicapped populations who do not speak, such as certain aphasics. But unless deafness is present, opportunity to hear speech has been present. We have seen how tenaciously the normal hearing person clings to his phonological code when he reads material that he is to remember; and we have seen the way young children appear spontaneously to come to use a phonological name-code when they memorize a series of pictures. When, through experimental manipulation, the phonological code becomes difficult to use, STM is gravely impaired. We have therefore suggested that there is a close association between silent reading and silently speaking because comprehension requires memory. The STM involved seems best supported by phonological coding.

Only among the deaf can we find people with no speech experience— or at any rate with relatively little—who for our present purposes therefore provide an invaluable control. We can simply ask the question: can the deaf learn to read? Were the answer an emphatic negative much of our enquiry would come to a comfortable end, since we would be very close to proving that reading is possible only when phonological coding is available. But of course the truth is not as simple as that, and most deaf children do, to some extent, learn to read. That immediately tells us that for hearing people, phonological coding is a preference, not a necessity. Knowing the versatility of man, this is what we would have expected. But since it has turned out to be exceedingly difficult to get hearing subjects to abstain from their predilection for phonological coding, we might hope that studies of the deaf would give us clearer insight into the rules governing the development and use of reading codes in general. By this we refer to the kinds of transductions that occur between seeing a printed item and storing it in a form in which it is available for future use, so that we can say: an item is remembered; a phrase is comprehended.

The paradox of a "normal deaf" population is too great for the term to be meaningful. In the first place, anyone whose hearing does not fall within defined "normal" limits is deaf. In the studies to be discussed, we are concerned with a category of profound deafness. Over the range of useful speech frequencies between 250 and 4000 Hz, our subjects, mostly children, had hearing losses of not less than about 75 dB in their better ear. These children, even with hearing-aid amplification, would have very little awareness of different speech sounds. Unless they can see lips moving, they would not know that someone in a room was speaking. They are profoundly deaf. Second, their medical records would show that they were either born deaf—sometimes of deaf parents—or became profoundly deaf within the first year or so of life; they have never used normal speech. These are features common to any person who can loosely be described as "congenitally and profoundly deaf." All of the deaf subjects of the studies to be discussed are in this category. But by the time a deaf child is likely to take part in reading experiments, variations in home background, intelligence, other pathology, and particularly in the educational theories that have guided his school training, will become important sources of experimental "noise." In using these subjects in experiments we have to confine ourselves to relatively simple questions and be content only with large experimental effects.

Probably in most schools for the deaf some attempt is made to teach deaf children to speak. There are some schools where no other mode of communication is used, come what may, between teachers and pupils. Other schools regard communication by no matter what means, as essential. Even less then, than with normal children, can we talk of deaf children "on average." But no matter how speech oriented a school might be, children who are profoundly deaf from an early age exceedingly rarely attain a quality of speech that can be readily understood by strangers. It is exceedingly rare that a hearing person can address such a deaf person normally, even though making sure that his lips can be seen, and get normal comprehension of his speech at normal speeds. It is exceedingly rare to see two such deaf children speaking to each other using the language that hearing persons would use. All of these things do occur, but they are levels of speech and language skills that certainly fewer than one in a hundred profoundly deaf children achieve.

If then speech is a skill acquired by the deaf with immense difficulty when acquired at all, from all that has gone before we would expect reading also to present grave difficulties to the deaf. Apart from anything else, this would be due to severe vocabulary deficiency and to the handicap of never having acquired the easy use of the innumerable rules of grammar that the rest of us pick up through hearing before we usually begin to learn to read. But there is something else also. There is the fact of only partial, or even of complete absence of, availability of phonological coding as an aid to comprehension. And indeed there is very good evidence that profoundly deaf children have great difficulty in learning to read. Myklebust [1960] reports on a number of studies of reading ability in the deaf.

For example, on the Columbia Vocabulary Test, at 9 years the mean score for normal children is about 20; for deaf children it is just over

3. At 11 years the respective values are 33 : 6; at 13 years, 43 : 10; at 15 years, 63 : 11. Not only is the difference huge, but it increases with age. The 15-year-old deaf child has a much poorer vocabulary than a 9-year-old normal child. In every aspect of the grammatical handling of words the deaf child is many years behind the hearing child on attainment tests. It is not therefore surprising that similar discrepancies are reported when memory span for verbal material is examined. Blair [1957], Furth [1964], Olsson and Furth [1966], and others have shown that deaf children are grossly inferior in digit span to hearing children. But when the material to be remembered consists of shapes that do not readily have names, deaf and hearing children have the same span. Furthermore the Olsson and Furth data show that whereas for hearing subjects the difference in span between digits and shapes is substantial, for the deaf it is quite small. It is not impossible then, that for the deaf, digits are just another set of shapes. There is no internal evidence in the Olsson and Furth study to indicate whether the deaf group did in fact code digits by shape. Olsson and Furth suggest that they could have finger-spelled them; there is uncertainty. The point is that there is some suggestive evidence here that phonological coding has unique advantages for STM over certain other codes, and among these we must include visual codes. This is unquestionably a loose argument since we do not know for certain what kind of codes in this experiment either group used with any of the test material. Then, as Furth [1966] points out elsewhere, any direct comparison of cognitive abilities between deaf and hearing must be taken with great caution because of innumerable differences that cannot be taken into account when matching groups.

Since many studies show deaf and hearing to have similar span on material not easily verbalized, but inferiority of the deaf when nameable items are used, the need is emphasized for a clearer understanding of the STM code used by the deaf when presented with words and other items having familiar names. We have continuously pointed out the important role that phonological coding has in reading: but we are equally clear that the deaf do read. They could be using a phonological code very ineffectively, or they could be using some other code or codes that are in themselves less efficient for the purpose than is a phonological code.

At the outset we can say that the few published studies of EMG recording using deaf subjects are unhelpful here. For reasons given when discussing EMG with reading adults, it cannot provide conclusive evidence. Just the same, there is a sizeable gap in knowledge here. Max [1935], in a pioneer study, reported that his deaf subjects showed EMG activity in their fingers when having dreams with "verbal" content. Unfortunately Max did not also record from the speech muscles—though hearing subjects in the same situation did not show finger activity. Novikova [1966] did record both from the speech muscles and from the fingers of deaf children during (among other tests) a digit span test. There was activity in both sets of muscles (presumably during presentation of the task: it is not clear in the report). But Novikova states that the subjects had specifically been taught speech as well as finger-spelling, and also that response was verbal.

A less direct, but in some ways less equivocal, procedure has been used in two studies by the present author [Conrad 1970; Conrad and Rush 1965] to study the nature of the code used when reading verbal material for immediate recall. In both studies, consonant sequences were visually presented followed by immediate written recall. The resulting data were represented in the form of error matrices showing the frequency with which letters were wrongly reported instead of the correct letter. Recapitulating the rationale of this procedure [Conrad 1964], if systematic confusions emerge they may be taken to provide an indication of a main code used in the memorizing process. For example, if the letter *B* when wrongly recalled is fairly consistently represented as *T*, we infer the use of a phonological code. Were *B* to be frequently reported as *R*, we would infer the use of shape coding. The inference, although having some face validity, is not necessarily correct, since we cannot ignore the possibility that other codes, of which we may be unaware, may throw up certain similar confusions. In the English finger-spelling alphabet, for instance, some signs are close figurative representations of the printed form of the letters. So this is inevitably an "on the whole" type of analysis.

The two experiments cited above differed in certain important respects. That by Conrad and Rush [1965] used profoundly deaf children at a State School for the Deaf in the U.S.A., and also used American hearing controls. The school was eclectic in its teaching procedures, speech, signing (a system of expressive mime) and finger-spelling (an alphabet using only the fingers of one hand) were all used where appropriate. A pooled error matrix was reported for a group of deaf children with the best recall performance, and another for a group of hearing children with matched recall performance, who in fact comprised the worst subgroup of hearing subjects. Further pooled error matrices were also shown for the remaining (the worst) deaf subjects and for the remaining (best) hearing subjects. The principal conclusions drawn from examination of these matrices are that the hearing children are predominantly using a phonological memory code. Main confusions are, for example, "B–V;" "B–P;" "F–X." The errors of the deaf subjects show, superficially, a less clear picture. For example, the better deaf subjects erroneously report "T" most often when "B" is the correct letter; for the worst deaf subjects, though, "R" is the commonest error for "B." Again, the best deaf, like the hearing group, are most likely to report "X" when "F" is wrong; the worst deaf are most likely to report "P" or "R." For all deaf subjects the most likely error for "X" is "V," strongly suggesting visual coding here, and certainly not a speech-based code; hearing subjects most frequently give "F" for "X." A particularly cautionary confusion that occurs substantially with all groups is "T–V." The phonological basis seems evident here, yet for the worst deaf subjects this would be quite paradoxical, since their error matrix shows no other evidence of speech-based coding. But since the original article was published, a study by Locke [1970] has appeared on confusions in finger-spelled letters, showing that the letters "T" and "V" are highly confusing in the American finger-spelling alphabet.

What was easily seen during the test was the overt use by a number of subjects of finger-spelling both during presentation of test material and during recall. We also did see some children mouthing letters, and we also saw children who, during presentation, "wrote" letters in the air, which could have been the basis for a manual kinesthetic code or an alternate visual code. The variety of codes apparently used by the deaf children is striking—and indeed alarming from a pedagogic viewpoint. Nor can we be sure that every child either consistently, or even predominantly, used a single code.

The code used by the hearing children after the letters were read is without much doubt largely phonological in character. A rank order correlation between recall errors and errors of perception when letters, spoken singly, are identified [Conrad 1964] is significantly at better than the .001 level for both best and worst groups. This is in line with all of our other evidence. But the correlations between recall and listening errors for the deaf groups were close to zero. It is clear that for this group of deaf subjects the use of speech-coding is small when reading material to be memorized. It may have been used by a few subjects, but we have no direct evidence of this.

The second study referred to [Conrad 1970] extended this procedure to permit a closer examination of individual coding performance. It took place in a private school for profoundly deaf children in England, which was characterized by its insistence on oral communication between pupils and teachers. All teaching was conducted by speech, and good speech and language skill was a condition of acceptance into the school at 11 years. In general the children came from socially more privileged homes and were all distinctly above average intelligence. This latter is crudely reflected in the fact that the U.S. deaf children used in the experiment described above, had a mean age of about 16 years, and presented with 5-letter sequences, averaged about 40 percent wrong letters. The U.K. subjects who were given 5-letter sequences had a mean age of 15 years, and averaged 17 percent wrong letters. This difference reflects selection criteria, and is important in the context.

Basically the same test procedure was used as in the American study, though some modifications were made in the 9-letter vocabulary from which sequences were constructed. The main difference was in the treatment of the results. This time an error matrix was set up for each subject individually. Because of the relatively few entries per cell, the matrices were then classified on a rather ad hoc basis, into those showing evidence of speech-based coding ("B–C–T" and "H–X" confused) and those more suggesting shape coding ("K–X–Y–Z" confused). When this was done, 21 subjects fell into the first category and 15 into the second. For convenience we can label the groups respectively articulatory (A) and nonarticulatory (nonA). A group of 75 hearing adults provided control data. A summary of the main recall confusions of these three groups is given in Table 3, which shows the level of significance with which certain letter clusters confused beyond chance level for each subject group.

Table 3
Frequency of Confusion by Hearing Controls, Deaf Articulators and Nonarticulators, Showing Observed and Chance Values, and Significance Level of the Difference (After Conrad [1970])

		O	E	
	BCT	676	408	0.001
Controls	HX	245	149	0.001
	KXYZ	866	825	n.s.
	BCT	193	95	0.001
A group	HX	62	38	0.01
	KXYZ	242	233	n.s.
	BCT	83	78	n.s.
Non-A group	HX	40	38	n.s.
	KXYZ	310	248	0.001

As a result of this procedure we have been able to identify two distinct coding groups of deaf subjects. One group we can be fairly confident are using a speech-based code, which because of the known degree of deafness can have no effective acoustic component. Accordingly we have designated it as articulatory. The second group seem most likely to be using a visual-shape code. Thomasson's [1970] matrix of shape confusions does not include 4 of the 9 letters used in this experiment, and so we cannot be more certain than this—hence the designation "nonA." We would rather the reader himself judge, than be argued into, whether "K–X–Y–Z" have more common shape characteristics either than the other letters used ("B–C–H–L–T") or than any other common characteristic. Granted this division, the way is open to us to see what differences there are between these two groups on other relevant criteria.

As conducted, the experiment required the subjects to read half of the sequences aloud and half silently, suitably counterbalanced. Of the 36 subjects taking part, 24 of them memorized 6-letter sequences, and we shall consider the differences between reading silently and aloud for these subjects only. Results for the remaining 12 subjects who were given 5-letter sequences were very similar. Table 4 shows the percentage wrong letters for the A and nonA groups according to the reading mode. For the A group it makes no difference to recall whether the material is read silently or aloud. It may be noted in passing that this is at variance with the behavior of hearing subjects, who invariably in this situation show an advantage when reading aloud [Murray 1965; Conrad and Hull 1968]. This discrepancy would fit the general run of 2-component STM models where one is a benign acoustic echoic component [e.g., Morton 1970]. Since the deaf do not have this second component available to them, we would on these models, expect no modality effect. But Table 4 shows the nonA group to be highly significantly handicapped ($p < 0.001$) when reading verbal material aloud. The two groups, which are effectively, though fortuitously, matched in performance when reading silently, are markedly different ($p < 0.001$) when articulation is

Table 4
Error Rate for Deaf Articulators and Nonarticulators When Reading Sequences Silently or Aloud (from Conrad [1970])

	Percentage Wrong Letters	
	Silent Reading	Loud Reading
A Group	23.8	24.1
NonA Group	22.8	29.9

required. The analysis supports the reliability of the original classification. We seem to have distinguished two clinically different groups of subjects, and we feel justified in asserting that the nonA group do not articulate when reading silently. When the subjects in the nonA group are made to read aloud, articulation is forced upon them, and we might imagine that it is behavior that not only is difficult for them (when reading silently they do not do it), but also contributes nothing to the task of transducing the visually perceived letters into a form that can later be recalled. We should add here that the reading mode does not at all affect the nature of recall errors.

Granted the relatively high level of recall performances, we can say now with confidence that there are effective ways of transducing printed verbal material other than phonological, and that these need not be based on articulation at all. This leads us to wonder about the relative merits of articulatory and phonological codes in this situation. In the silent-reading condition the two groups are effectively equal in performance, though apparently using different coding strategies. They are also very close in terms of intelligence and degree of hearing loss; the nonA group is only months older than the A group. The implication then is that articulatory coding is no more effective than the use of some other nonarticulatory codes. The difference between articulatory and phonological codes, as we are using these terms here, is that the former excludes accompanying acoustic imagery, which may be present in the latter. When hearing subjects read silently, this additional feature may still give them an advantage over those deaf subjects who articulate when reading.

In the STM experiments, referred to earlier, that show an advantage for reading aloud over silent reading, it is almost certain that in both conditions most subjects use phonological coding, the advantage being attributed to "echo" available only for final items. This should not be confused with effects of acoustic imagery available throughout a sequence. Murray [1965] reports that "mouthing" letters during visual presentation gives no better recall than silent reading, a finding that is consistent with this speculation. In both cases, his subjects would have used phonological coding. They showed significant improvement in recall only when they vocalized, and then only on the final items [Murray 1966].

It was pointed out earlier that profoundly deaf children are far behind hearing children in reading ability. We have also drawn attention to the warning by Furth [1966] on the inherent problems of matching deaf and hearing children in order to make this kind of comparison. A quantitative difference in performance on some aspect of reading ability merely describes an outcome into which many factors have gone, some unknown, others known but not considered. All factors may be generated by the fact of the deafness. But between that and the results of a formal reading test, lies a wilderness of intangibles which may just the same be contributory. To dip at random into this wilderness, are we sure, when comparing reading ability of deaf and hearing children, that they have had equally good teachers, using equally good teaching techniques? We have no evidence to substantiate difference; yet we know of no study which has controlled for this factor. In other words, are deaf children backward readers because they are deaf, or because their deafness has led to social and pedagogic "treatments" that result in reading backwardness? The last study to be discussed can be taken as an *essai* into this area of enquiry.

The experiment follows from the reported effects of reading aloud, which depend on whether deaf subjects use articulatory coding or not. The subjects used comprised all of those still at the school who took part in the letter-sequence experiment, and whom we have been able to classify into A and nonA subjects. There were, respectively, 12 and 11 subjects. In this study [Conrad 1971] we considered the effect of reading aloud on comprehension of printed prose.

Six prose passages, each of about 300 words, were selected from published standard school exercises. For each of them, 8 questions were drawn up to probe subjects' comprehension of the text. The questions were accompanied by four alternative answers, only one of which could possibly be correct, and the subject's response required no more than one tick per question. The questions were particularly aimed at minimizing effects of recognition memory, and avoided questions (and answers) of the form: Was the boy's name . . . Tom, Dick, Bob, John? Alternative answers tried not to repeat words appearing in the text, and in general, without comprehension, performance would have been little better than chance. All subjects read all 6 passages, 3 silently and 3 aloud. Order of test presentation and reading mode were counterbalanced, as far as possible, separately for the A and nonA groups. The passages were subsequently given to a group of hearing children whom we tried to match for comprehension performance on the silent reading condition. That the match is poor reflects the fact that as we reached down to younger and younger hearing children, we hit a reading barrier before comprehension was impaired to the level of very much older deaf children. The control group remains valid because the main effect is between reading silently and aloud, and for this, subjects served as their own control. The results are in Table 5. The hearing subjects

Table 5
The Effect on Comprehension of Prose of Reading Silently or Aloud: Percentage of Wrong Answers (from Conrad [1971])

	Silent Reading	Read Aloud
Hearing Subjects	41.6	37.2
Deaf Articulators	58.0	51.4
Deaf Nonarticulators	61.0	69.7

and deaf A group were little affected by reading mode, showing a nonsignificant improvement aloud. But comprehension of the nonA group was impaired when reading aloud ($p < 0.05$). In the silent reading mode, the two deaf groups show similar comprehension performance. When reading aloud, the nonA group is significantly worse ($p < 0.001$).

The results for the hearing children are in broad agreement with Poulton and Brown [1967] and with Rogers [1937], and clearly indicate that vocalizing—the addition of sound to articulation—has little value for comprehension. That this is different from the modality effects found in STM experiments and discussed earlier confirms that those are relatively short-lived. It is not then surprising that the A-group deaf subjects are also unaffected by reading mode. The small nonsignificant advantage for hearing and A-group deaf when reading aloud probably reflects no more than that they took more time over it. It is the effect of forced articulation when the nonA group read aloud which is so interesting here.

Unlike the A group, reading aloud leads to a significant loss of comprehension. This supports the view that when these children read they bring to bear on the task certain cognitive processes that are fundamentally different, and that are disrupted by the requirement to articulate. But different though these processes may be, they achieve the same result. In silent reading there is only a little difference in comprehension between the two groups. We have to accept that reading, and the comprehension that justifies use of that word, can occur with minimal, if any, employment of speech muscles and by the same logic, without speech imagery. For these children, vocalizing words with its concomitant articulation seems to be independent of the cognitive act of reading. We saw earlier that preliterate children can memorize pictures and ignore the names of the pictures. Now we see older children who read and understand printed prose while ignoring all of the speech-based attributes of the words. Their comprehension is not quite as good as that of the A group deaf—they give slightly more wrong answers during silent reading, though they are, on average, one year older. But they are not dramatically worse. Whatever reading codes they use, they are not grossly inferior to the articulatory code almost certainly used by the A group. True, the evidence for the use of nonarticulatory coding is circumstantial. It remains possible, for instance, that the alleged nonA group subjects are in fact using a very noisy articulatory code, which becomes even more noisy during vocalization. But were this so, it would be counter to the results of the analysis of errors in the STM experiment, and it would ill fit the fact of silent reading performance, closely similar to that of the A group, who—we are as near certain as we can be—do use articulatory coding.

It is this reasonable certainty of comprehension without articulation that prompted the homily about the effects of teaching technique. Applied in this case, it can mean that a possibly large proportion of deaf children who are either unable or unwilling to transduce printed material into speechlike forms are being taught reading skills based on incompatible assumptions about their underlying cognitive processes that are much less easy to discern than deafness. When the deaf come to be compared with hearing children, it may be not only their deafness as such that is responsible for their reading backwardness—though it must be responsible to a considerable extent. What we do not know is how far inappropriate teaching is responsible—inappropriate only in the sense of making false assumptions about the child's available cognitive abilities.

Now we have tended to discuss codes used by the deaf when they read printed verbal material as if we believe that when an articulatory code is not used, then a visual code is used. This is not our belief. It so happens that a good deal of the data we have used in this discussion can be taken to support this view. But this is largely because tasks have been designed that would favor visual coding were it available to the deaf. We are quite sure that other codes are also available to most of the deaf that are based on finger-spelling, signing, and lip-reading at the least. On present knowledge it is much harder to construct reading test material that could greatly benefit, for example, a finger-spelling code. Indeed it seems plausible that with reading skills, since the deaf do not have available what seem to be the most efficient codes, they could very well make extensive use of multiple coding, no one code being particularly efficient, to a much greater extent than do those of us with normal sensory experience.

If many deaf children, when they read, really are using codes very different from those used by hearing children—and this seems probable now—the educational hazards could be great. This can perhaps best be illustrated by reference to a simple task such as a digit span test.

This has frequently been used to compare deaf and hearing children, invariably showing the deaf to be worse [Furth 1964]. But if we look more closely at this test, one questions whether in fact it is memory that is being tested and compared. Because of their deafness, this kind of test has to be made in visual form. Now what do we know about the visual discriminability of printed digits, as compared with the auditory discriminability of the names of digits? There is much evidence [Cornog and Rose 1967], that the curvature of many digit shapes—"2, 3, 5, 6, 8, 9"—may lead to perceptual confusion. We have already pointed out that when a phonological code is used in STM, letters that sound alike are difficult to recall. We must then also assume that when using a visual code, digits that look alike will be difficult to recall. There is no simple way of comparing the visual confusability of printed digits with the phonological confusability of spoken digits. But the effect of difference here could be serious for recall. In an unpublished study, the author compared the auditory intelligibility of spoken digits with that of the 10 least interconfused letters. To obtain similar perceptual error rates, 10 percent more white noise had to be added to the digits than to the letters. Used in a phonological memory code, digits would have more staying power than letters, and we know that memory for digits is generally greater than for any equal-sized set of consonants [Mackworth 1963]. It is probable also that digits in visual form have poor durability. When deaf subjects use visual coding in digit span tests, they are almost certain to appear worse than hearing subjects. But whether because their memory is worse, or because they are obliged to use a code that the nature of the test material then renders ineffective, is doubtful.

By analogy, words have been "designed" to provide high auditory discriminability. When we read we continue to take advantage of this fact. The visual appearance of words has limited relevance. The deaf try to read a language perfectly adapted for the use of hearing people. They are faced with many commonly used words of the same length and general configuration; the majority of words begin with a minority of different consonants, usually followed by a vowel, all of which sound different but which in print, except for i, look quite similar.[2] Just as we try to teach the deaf a spoken language that permits them to use only minimally those cognitive abilities that are intact, so too we try

[2] Data presented by Baddeley, Conrad et al. [1960] show that in ordinary prose, 80 percent of all words begin with only 10 different letters; 23 percent of all words begin with one of 7 consonants followed by either a, e, o, u; and 70 percent of all words end in only 6 different letters.

to teach them a written language, making the tacit assumption that when a deaf child sees a printed word he will cognitively "do" with it just what a hearing child will.

In summary, what this section has tried to do is to show that speech or speech-based codes are not necessary for reading. We have agreed that deaf children who do not use speech-based codes are poor readers. But we have argued that the reasons for this are far from simple. In particular it may be that nonspeech codes, when developed by training to the extent that speech codes are, would not in themselves be inefficient. But when used to transduce printed words that derive from spoken forms, then they are bound to be at a disadvantage.

A Conclusion

In this paper we have taken a speculative look at the relationship between reading and speech. Though reading has meant reading silently to oneself, we have also presented the paradox that there are some profoundly deaf children who can "read aloud" without speech. The evidence is that speechlike sounds for these people do not carry phonetic significance. Instead of mediating communication, in this case they obstruct it. What this has shown is that, in spite of the extremely common intervention of speech behavior in silent reading, this behavior cannot be accepted as necessary in the sense that reading cannot occur without it. As a matter of fact, at one time there was a vigorously defended theory in educational circles, that children should be discouraged from subvocalizing during reading on the grounds that this would reduce silent reading to the speed of articulation (see Edfeldt [1960] for a review of this work). The theory has not been empirically supported with conviction possibly because the rate of silent speech in reading is more dependent on eye-movement patterns than on speech-motor patterns.

Silent speech, and this does include speech imagery, may never be used by a few normal people. No one knows whether the rest might dispense with it after training. At present we have to accept that silent speech in reading is a near universal in cultures where alphabets are used. Earlier we discussed some possible reasons for this, but since this is the way we all necessarily start, and later there seems no good reason for stopping, it could be that this is sufficient explanation. It is hard to think of a more parsimonious one.

But the present author cannot evade the feeling of intuitive improbability about so sparse a view. Man, on the whole, does not leave well alone. So we have introduced into the question two other related phenomena. We have urged the significance of STM in reading: the need to hold on to one or more words, or to a group of words condensed to an idea, while considering the related implication of subsequent words or ideas. We do not see how linguistic understanding can proceed without this step. This lets us out of the problem of intuitive improbability. It makes us wonder whether speech might not be the best possible code for remembering words. If it is, we are rescued from our disbelief that man, in this case, has uncharacteristically left well alone. Not at all; we use a speech code in reading because it best sustains the necessary STM processes. Here we are on safer ground. There is abundant evidence that STM thrives on a speechlike input. The fact of necessarily learning to read in vocalized speech then becomes fortuitous. We could perfectly well abandon speech in reading if we had a better STM code for the purpose. We seem not to, though we do have ancillary supporting codes.

Many of the deaf are forced to manage without the opportunity to use speech-based codes. But because of the theoretical obstacles in this case to comparing the relative efficiency of well practiced speech and nonspeech STM codes, we cannot say with certainty that nonspeech codes are just as good. The Olsson and Furth data imply that they are not. Our own data show little difference between deaf articulators and nonarticulators. But it is possible that good deaf readers who do not articulate have exceptional, rather than average, visual memory.

We have also seen that young children appear spontaneously to abandon pictorial STM coding in favor of phonological STM coding. We do not need to teach them to do this, but neither do they rush into it as soon as they can speak. This ability needs to mature; and until it does, educators think it not worth trying to teach them to read. Here is another biological leg. We need speech in learning to read not just to provide information on progress to teachers, but because it would be difficult without it for the beginning reader as well as for the highly skilled adult.

In the end then, our view is that reading is most certainly possible with no phonology involved at all, but that with phonology it is a great deal easier. Our written language is a system for describing and distinguishing the sounds of spoken language. Informationally, printed words are far more economic than figurative descriptions. Perceptually they are far more discriminable as speech sounds than as pictures. In our view this begins to add up to reasonable grounds for all of that neurological bother involved in transducing the little lines on paper into the language of that "inward ear" which is the next door neighbor to the "inward eye."

References

Atkinson, R. C., and R. M. Shiffrin, 1968. Human memory: A proposed system and its control processes. In *The Psychology of Learning and Motivation; Advances in Research and Theory*, K. W. Spence and J. T. Spence (eds.), New York: Academic Press.

Baddeley, A. D., 1966. Short-term memory for word sequences as a function of acoustic, semantic and formal similarity. *Quart. J. Exp. Psych.* 18:362–365.

Baddeley, A. D., R. Conrad, and W. E. Thomson, 1960. Letter structure of the English language. *Nature* 186:414–416.

Bernbach, H. A., 1967. The effect of labels on short-term memory for colors with nursery school children. *Psychonomic Sci.* 7:149–150.

Blair, F. X., 1957. A study of the visual memory of deaf and hearing children. *Amer. Ann. of the Deaf*, 102:254–263.

Conrad, R., 1962. An association between memory errors and errors due to acoustic masking of speech. *Nature*, 193:1314–1315.

———, 1963. Acoustic confusions and memory span for words. *Nature*, 197:1029–1030.

———, 1964. Acoustic confusions in immediate memory. *Brit. J. Psych.* 55:75–84.

———, 1965. The role of the nature of the material in verbal learning. *Acta Psych.* 24:244–252.

———, 1967. Interference or decay over short retention intervals? *J. Verbal Learning and Verbal Behavior*, 6:49–54.

———, 1970. Short-term memory processes in the deaf. *Brit. J. Psych.* 61:179–195.

———, 1971. The effect of vocalizing on comprehension in the profoundly deaf. *Brit. J. Psych.* 62:147–150.

———, 1971. The chronology of the development of covert speech in children. *Developmental Psych.* 5:398–405.

Conrad, R., and A. J. Hull, 1964. Information, acoustic confusion and memory span. *Brit J. Psych.* 55:429–432.

Conrad, R., and A. J. Hull, 1966. The role of the interpolated task in short-term retention. *Quart. J. Exp. Psych.* 18:266–269.

Conrad, R., and A. J. Hull, 1968. Input modality and the serial position curve in short-term memory. *Psychonomic Sci.* 10:135–136.

Conrad, R., and M. L. Rush, 1965. On the nature of short-term memory encoding by the deaf. *J. Speech and Hearing Disorders*, 30:336–343.

Corballis, M. C., 1966. Rehearsal and decay in immediate recall of visually and aurally presented items. *Canad. J. Psych.* 20:43–51.

Corcoran, D. W. J., 1966. An acoustic factor in letter cancellation. *Nature* 210:658.

———, 1967. An acoustic factor in proof reading. *Nature* 214:851–852.

Cornog, D. Y., and F. C. Rose, 1967. *Legibility of Alphanumeric Characters and Other Symbols*. II. *A Reference Handbook*. Washington, D.C.: National Bureau of Standards.

Craik, F. I. M., 1969. Modality effects in short-term storage. *J. Verbal Learning and Verbal Behavior,* 8:658–664.

Curtis, H. S., 1900. Automatic movements of the larynx. *Amer. J. Psych.* 11:237–239.

Edfeldt, A. W., 1960. *Silent Speech and Silent Reading.* Chicago: Chicago University Press.

Felzen, E., and M. Anisfeld, 1970. Semantic and phonetic relations in the false recognition of words by third- and sixth-grade children. *Developmental Psych.* 3:163–168.

Flavell, J. H., 1970. Developmental studies of mediated memory. In *Advances in Child Development and Behavior,* Vol. 5, H. W. Reese and L. P. Lipsitt (eds.), New York: Academic Press.

Furth, H. G., 1964. Research with the deaf: Implications for language and cognition. *Psych. Bull.* 62:145–164.

————, 1966. *Thinking Without Language.* New York: The Free Press.

Gesell, A., and F. L. Ilg, 1946. *The Child From Five to Ten.* London: Hamish Hamilton.

Hagen, J. W., and P. R. Kingsley, 1968. Labelling effects in short-term memory. *Child Development,* 39:113–121.

Hardyck, C. D., and L. F. Petrinovich, 1970. Subvocal speech and comprehension level as a function of the difficulty level of reading material. *J. Verbal Learning and Verbal Behavior,* 9:647–652.

Hardyck, C. D., L. F. Petrinovich, and D. W. Ellsworth, 1967. Feedback of speech muscle activity during silent reading: Two comments. *Science,* 157:581.

Hintzman, D. L., 1967. Articulatory coding in short-term memory. *J. Verbal Learning and Verbal Behavior,* 6:312–316.

Landauer, T. K., 1962. Rate of implicit speech. *Perceptual and Motor Skills,* 15:646.

Lepley, W. M., 1952. The participation of implicit speech in acts of writing. *Amer. J. Psych.* 65:597–599.

Locke, J. L., 1970. Short-term memory encoding strategies of the deaf. *Psychonomic Sci.* 18:233–234.

Locke, J. L., and F. S. Fehr, 1970. Young children's use of the speech code in learning. *J. Exp. Child Psych.* 10:3, 367–373.

Lovell, K., 1968. *Educational Psychology in Children,* London: University of London Press.

Luria, A. R., 1969. *The Mind of a Mnemonist,* London: Jonathan Cape.

McGuigan, F. J., 1970. Covert oral behavior during the silent performance of language tasks. *Psych. Bull.* 74:309–326.

McLaughlin, G. H., 1969. Reading at "impossible" speeds. *J. Reading,* 12:449 ff.

Mackworth, J. F., 1963. The relation between the visual image and postperceptual immediate memory. *J. Verbal Learning and Verbal Behavior,* 2:75–85.

Max, L. W., 1935. An experimental study of the motor theory of consciousness. III. Action current responses in deaf-mutes during sleep, sensory stimulation and dreams. *J. Comparative Psych.* 19:469–486.

Morton, J. A., 1970. A functional model for memory. In *Models of Human Memory*, D. A. Norman (ed.), New York: Academic Press.

Murdock, B. B., 1967. Auditory and visual stores in short term memory. *Acta Psych.* 27:316–324.

Murray, D. J., 1965. Vocalization-at-presentation and immediate recall, with varying presentation rates. *Quart. J. Exp. Psych.* 17:47–56.

———, 1966. Vocalization-at-presentation and immediate recall, with varying recall methods. *Quart. J. Exp. Psych.* 18:9–18.

———, 1967. The role of speech responses in short-term memory. *Canad. J. Psych.* 21:263–276.

———, 1968. Articulation and acoustic confusability in short-term memory. *J. Exp. Psych.* 78:679–684.

Myklebust, H. R., 1960. *The Psychology of Deafness.* New York: Grune and Stratton.

Novikova, L. A., 1966. Electrophysiological investigation of speech. In *Thinking: Studies of Covert Language Processes*, F. J. McGuigan (ed.), New York: Appleton-Century-Crofts.

Olsson, J. E., and H. G. Furth, 1966. Visual memory span in the deaf. *Amer. J. Psych.* 79:480–484.

Paulhan, F., 1886. Le langage intérieur et la pensée. *Revue Philosophique,* 21:26–58.

Peterson, L. R., and M. J. Peterson, 1959. Short-term retention of individual verbal items. *J. Exp. Psych.* 58:193–198.

Pintner, R., 1913. Inner speech during silent reading. *Psych. Rev.* 20:129–153.

Poulton, E. C., 1963. Rapid reading. *J. Documentation,* 10:168–172.

———, and C. H. Brown, 1967. Memory after reading aloud and reading silently. *Brit. J. Psych.* 58:210–222.

Reed, H. B., 1916. The existence and function of inner speech in thought processes. *J. Exp. Psych.* 1:365–392.

Rogers, M. V., 1937. Comprehension in oral and silent reading. *J. General Psych.* 17:394–397.

Rosenbaum, M. E., 1962. Effect of direct and vicarious verbalization on retention. *Child Development,* 33:103–110.

Sperling, G., 1963. A model for visual memory tasks. *Human Factors,* 5:19–31.

Staats, A. W., 1968. *Learning, Language and Cognition.* New York: Holt, Rinehart and Winston.

Thomasson, A. J. W. M., 1970. *On the Representation of Verbal Items in Short-Term Memory.* Nijmegen: Drukkerij Schippers.

Weir, M. W., and H. W. Stevenson, 1959. The effect of verbalization in children's learning as a function of chronological age. *Child Development,* 30:143–149.

Weir, R. H., 1966. Some questions on the child's learning of phonology. In *The Genesis of Language,* F. Smith and G. A. Miller (eds.), Cambridge, Mass.: M.I.T. Press.

Wickelgren, W. A., 1965. Distinctive features and errors in short-term memory for English vowels. *J. Acoust. Soc. Amer.* 38:583–588.

DAVID LABERGE

Beyond Auditory Coding

A Discussion of Conrad's paper

Conrad has given us a very interesting and clearly presented review of his efforts to test a hypothesis that is of importance to all investigators of the reading process. The hypothesis can be cast in a strong form or a weak form. In its strong form it asserts that written material must be coded into phonological form to be comprehended. In its weak form it states that written material is *preferably* coded in phonological form to be comprehended. I share Conrad's enthusiasm for the view that considers the acoustic mechanism central to reading, since after all it is a sensory avenue to the uniquely powerful device by which language was initially acquired by the child, and therefore we are quite naturally led to expect it to continue to play a critical role when language skills are expanded to include reading.

I am impressed with the way Conrad's experimental methods in memory can illuminate if not resolve some crucial issues in reading. It is heartening to the experimental psychologist to see a current laboratory method such as the STM recall task taken into the reading world with the success that Conrad has achieved with it.

The evidence he marshals to support his answer to the question of the role of acoustic coding in reading is drawn from studies with adult readers, both those with normal hearing and those who are profoundly deaf, as well as with children who are in the early stages of learning to read. I agree wholeheartedly with his desire to extract from the data a consistent story concerning the dominant role of the acoustic code in STM experiments, but I do not share with him the confidence that the conclusion drawn from STM experiments can be generally applied to experiments involving fluent reading of textual material.

My remarks will be concerned with the question of the type of code dominant in STM experiments, the role of visual coding in fluent reading, and the hypothesis of mixed code strategies in reading. Finally, I would like to comment on the suitability of current experimental designs and models for the investigation of possible productive strategies that involve confirmation of expectancies.

Conrad's main question can be cast within the framework of a linear flow model. Imagine that visual inputs journey through visual analyzers into a system of memory, made up of STM and LTM components. Parallel to the visual inputs are the auditory inputs and analyzers that converge with the visual channel at the memory system. The hypothesis probed by Conrad is that in reading there is a crossover from the visual processing stages to the auditory ones prior to entering the memory system. More specifically, it is at the level where sounds are coded into speech that the output from the visual system enters the auditory system. Thus learning to comprehend what is read should be a rather simple affair once spoken language is understood. One merely transduces graphemic stimuli into subvocal speech and listens to the inner voice as if it were the voice of a friend reading the text.

I would like to suggest that the code in which visual written material eventually is cast enroute to the comprehension processes need not be exclusively auditory *or* exclusively visual for a given individual reader. It is conceivable that both the auditory and visual codes may make contact with comprehension processes, and that during reading they may make this contact in parallel, or one at a time by fluctuating in some fashion between the two modalities.

Conrad tests the strong version of the hypothesis with data from the profoundly deaf, who were classified by him into articulators and non-articulators by the kinds of confusions they made in recall from STM. The fact that "reading aloud" reduced the comprehension of the non-articulators more than that of the articulators (who showed a reduction similar to that of normals) serves as indirect, but persuasive evidence that nonarticulating deaf persons are using something besides a phonological code when they read—probably a visual code. He concludes that reading can occur in the absence of a phonological code, and therefore the strong hypothesis is rejected. Thus, the remaining question is concerned with the preference that a person with normal hearing has for the phonological code over the alternative of keeping the written input in the visual system to the point of entry into the memory systems.

Conrad's emphasis on the STM code in recall experiments as an indicator of the code used in reading has some indirect justification from the fact that in reading sentences we assume that results of successive processing of words or word groups must be stored in STM until the pattern or sense of the whole sentence is achieved. However his experimental procedure, as we have implied, typically does not require the subject to comprehend the material seen, as is the general intent when reading, but rather simply to recall each discrete item just seen or heard.

Therefore, conclusions with respect to the type of code used should be restricted to tasks where the intent is to store and retrieve directly from STM. We should be cautious when generalizing these findings to comprehension tasks.

To me, the most interesting use of the STM recall experiment in the investigation of reading involved homophonic and nonhomophonic words to determine the age at which the child is apparently first able to enter phonological codes of pictures into STM. That this age is very close to the age that he begins to learn to read seems to me more than coincidence. Quite possibly, the initial scaffoldings necessary to build advanced reading skills are dominated by phonological coding, so that the beginnings of reading training must wait for the child to learn to control and manipulate this code, segmenting syllables into phonemes as well as efficiently recoding visual items into phonological form and transferring and retrieving them from STM. If indeed it is the case that the child may easily name a picture but he cannot at the same time put its name code into STM, then an intriguing question arises as to what additional things he must learn about the phonological code and his memory system in order to readily store names he gives to objects. A related problem stems from the observation that some children have no trouble reading aloud a line of text word by word (e.g., "the boy hit the ball"), but after they finish saying the last word they cannot recall the initial words or the general meaning of the sequence. Yet when they listen to the same sentence spoken to them, they have little difficulty repeating it back. Thus they can indeed store in STM phonologically coded material under some conditions, while under other conditions they apparently cannot. One speculation is that word-by-word reading focuses attention on the decoding process at the expense of other necessary operations such as retention. Another reason for this discrepancy may be that the heard sentence is perceived as a familiar unbroken phonological sequence in which word boundaries are perhaps not yet significant to the child, while the read sentence has been broken into components that are less familiar to the child.

This view is analogous to that of Savin, who maintains that syllables may be familiar to the child while the component phonemes of the syllables are not at all well discriminated. What is being stressed here is the possibility that when a child sounds out a simple sentence word by word, the sound of each word he constructs is not perceived in the same way (i.e., at the same level) as when he hears these words spoken in a familiar sentence delivered in the usual rhythm and tempo. Moreover, once the child has perceived the words as having new sound content, he still has to learn to perceive the order of these new sounds. All of this requires considerably more storage space in STM than the heard sentence, and it would be no surprise to find that when he is reading strings of words, the new words are bumping the old ones out of STM [Atkinson and Shiffrin 1968].

On the surface this analysis would seem to suggest two general training procedures. One method would train him to discriminate phonemic units in speech, into which corresponding visual material could be decoded. The other method would train him to take in whole visual words or even phrases that correspond to the larger phonological units he can now hear. The latter method is flawed because the person cannot decode words he has never seen before [Jeffrey and Samuels 1967], and therefore he must learn to identify an enormous number of visual patterns before he can read typical text. The former method, on the other hand, seems more manageable in terms of the size of the set of visual patterns to be learned, but seems to tie down the reader to processing a succession of small units, a procedure which will soon have him needlessly processing redundant information. Hopefully, continued exposure with the right kind of discriminatory alternatives will induce him to blend or rechunk the sounds his decoder puts out as he learns to chunk visual material into larger patterns. Thus he ends up with the capability to choose the level at which he will decode the visual into the phonological. For new words he may decode at the phonemic or syllabic levels. For familiar words, he may decode at the word level.

Conrad's emphasis on the widespread preference for the phonological code is appealing on at least two counts over and above the fact that subjects prefer it in STM experiments. We learned our language in this mode, and presumably the deeper wirings are already attached to it in a special way [Liberman, Cooper et al. 1967]. Second, even if the visual code were comparable to the phonological code in almost all other respects, the fact that we can rehearse in this mode much more effectively than in the visual mode would compel a person to choose the phonological code over the visual code when he has the choice.

But the auditory and visual codes may not be comparable in most other respects when one looks beyond STM recall tasks into tasks which require fast comprehension processing such as fluent reading. The STM experiments, which use arrays of letters or words, are valuable for telling us if a person can indeed code phonologically, and also if he prefers this code over other available codes in this situation; but these findings do not force the same conclusion on tasks that involve syntactically and semantically structured items. When the subject reads with the intent simply to recall the string of words he has just seen, he is quite likely to perform as he does in the standard STM recall task. But when he reads with the intent to comprehend, he may process and encode material in quite different ways. Consider an attempt to comprehend quickly the following sentence given to me by Jay Samuels: "The bouy and the none tolled hymn they had scene and herd a pear of bear feet in the haul." If visual words were coded into word sounds before they made contact with linguistic comprehension levels, then there should be no disruptive effect due to the spelling variations of the sentence, so long as the familiarity of the visual words is controlled.

My final remarks are concerned with the possibility that the fluent reader may use a mixture of coding strategies, depending upon the momentary demands of the written material. First of all, there is evidence that the way the reader uses articulatory mechanisms varies as a function of the difficulty of material. Hardyck and Petrinovich [1970] used an audio signal that was activated by an increase in muscle tension in the larnyx to train the subject to inhibit his vocal responses during reading. When subjects read easy material comprehension was not affected by this procedure. However, when subjects read difficult material, comprehension was considerably reduced, as compared to control subjects who showed no appreciable change in comprehension when they went from easy to difficult material. On the basis of these findings one would conclude that a person uses a good deal of subvocalization *when needed* for making effective contact with semantic levels, and uses little, if any, when it is not so needed. Thus it appears that the fluent reader may vary the amount of articulatory coding over a considerable range when he reads material which fluctuates widely in difficulty.

Another way the reader may vary his coding strategies occurs at the perceptual analyzers where he may select among various levels of processing. There is some evidence from experiments with simple tones and lights that indicates that the subject may tune his perceptual analyzers according to the sort of a stimulus he expects to receive, and that, in addition, he can adjust himself to process that stimulus at a chosen level [LaBerge 1971a, b]. When the expected stimulus arrives the person produces a faster response time than when an unexpected stimulus arrives. In other words, he saves himself processing time when he has some preparation for the expected stimulus. In the reading situation, for example, we assume that the alternative perceptual levels that can be primed by deeper expectancies are letters, words, phrases, etc. During the reading of continuous text, the person is not always tuned to perceive the same sort of thing; he searches for a variety of things, depending on the task. Sometimes he is ready only for the next word, sometimes for a capital letter to mark the beginning of the next sentence or to signal a proper name, sometimes for a certain size of phrase. We assume that he sets these levels through an attention mechanism that opens the gates of perceptual analyzers to read out the coded input into STM. The capacity of attention is limited, and during early phases of pattern learning, we assume that a good deal of attention space is allocated to assembling the distinctive features into units. Later on the person learns to see a letter as a whole, which requires less attention space. Similarly, in associating the letter pattern to a name or its sound, attention space is needed to monitor the flow of information, but later it may become automatic in the sense that little attention capacity is used. A similar line of reasoning is applied to learning to identify and sound words, phrases, and other patterns.

So far we have been concerned with the way attention contributes early and late in training to the efficient flow of information into the deeper levels of the system. Let us now conjecture that the role of the attention mechanism may change analogously when we *reverse* the direction of information flow, that is, when information proceeds from deep linguistic structures toward the perceptual levels to translate an expectancy into the appropriate perceptual readiness at a given moment in the reading of text. Suppose, for example, that in the processing of the sentence "the dog chased the cat" the reader anticipates the sort of thing that the dog is chasing. This expectancy is generated by structures in LTM and sent via the attention system to the appropriate perceptual level to reduce processing time of the expected input by making a match between the appropriately coded input and the predicted image. The prediction could be "the cat" or "the rabbit" in visual form, but less detailed expectancies are probably possible. We have found, for example, that a person can be prepared for a tone match at varying levels of a specific pitch, at a wide range of pitches, as a tone opposed to noise, or as any auditory event [LaBerge 1971a].

In the case of processing information inward from receptors through perceptual levels to STM and LTM it is assumed that initially considerable attention space is devoted to monitor the inward flow of information. With sufficient practice, this control seems to become relatively automatic, requiring little attention, so that the organism can devote his attention capacity to other matters. In like fashion, the expectancy generated by memory systems initially requires attention space to make the proper perceptual settings, and when the stimulus arrives, to make the match in some storage location. With further training, this control of outward flow of information may take place relatively automatically, that is, with little or no involvement of attention. Thus the change in amount of attention needed to process information flowing outward from memory to perceptual levels over the course of learning is analogous to the change in attention requirements during learning to process information flowing inward from receptors to memory systems.

One implication from this model is that once the reader is freed from controlling the strategies of information uptake from the page he can put his attention capacity to operation on meanings, making inferences from them, and manipulating them into forms for efficient storage. If he is attending exclusively to the flow of meanings or ideas, he may not be aware at all of the way he reads, that is, of the way he takes up the information from the page, such as the continuous predicting ahead to the sort of thing that he next expects to see. The best readers may be the least aware of how they are doing it.

One of the important issues facing the researcher in the field of information processing, or any field, is whether or not the methods he is using will tell him how the system works. Flow diagrams with chains of processes leading from sensory surfaces into structures of LTM too often seduce the experimenter into the notion that all information is flowing in the inward direction during a perceptual activity such as reading. Many investigators in the Donders [1868–1869] tradition use response time data in additive and subtractive models to reveal the properties of stages between the stimulus input and the response output. STM models of simple retention tasks can also lead to this way of thinking about information flow. What we are becoming slowly aware of in our attention experiments is that there must be important information flows from higher processes outward to the perceptual levels that allow the organism to tune his ear or eye to the sort of stimulus he expects, and thereby significantly cut down his processing time from what it would be were he to receive information at a constant state of perceptual preparation, that is, in a linear—take it as it comes—manner.

I think that the sorts of experiments Conrad is doing may constrain the subject to process stimuli in a linear way, because the experimental items are presented in small discrete chunks (a letter or word at a time) so that the subject gains no advantage by varying his expectations of the sorts of stimuli to come next. As it turns out, the dominant code that the subject uses in these tasks is a phonological one. Indeed, Conrad's work may be more relevant to the building of initial reading skills that may stress the inward flow of information, that is, from receptors toward memory systems. However, if we can invent experimental tasks that challenge the subject to do what he does when he fluently reads written material, we may begin to see new and interesting properties of information flow when it is directed outward toward the receptors. I suspect that such tasks will show us that the visual code plays a much stronger role in monitoring the contacts between the input of printed page and the comprehension of the inner systems.

References

Atkinson, R. C., and R. M. Shiffrin, 1968. Human memory: A proposed system and its control processes. In K. W. Spence and J. T. Spence (eds.), *The Psychology of Learning and Motivation: Advances in research and Theory*. Vol. II. New York: Academic Press.

Donders, F. C., 1868–1869. Over de snelheid van psychische processen. Onderzoekingen gedaan in het Psysiologisch Laboratorium der Utrechtsche Hooge School, 1868–1869. Second series, II, 92–120. Translated by W. G. Koster, in *Attention and Performance II, Acta Psych.* 30:412–431 (1969).

Hardyck, C. D., and L. F. Petrinovich, 1970. Subvocal speech and comprehension level as function of the difficulty level of reading material. *J. Verbal Learning and Verbal Behavior,* 9:647–652.

Jeffrey, W. E., and S. J. Samuels, 1967. The effect of method of reading training on initial reading and transfer. *J. Verbal Learning and Verbal Behavior,* 6:354–358.

LaBerge, D., 1971a. Effect of type of catch trial upon generalization gradients of reaction time. *J. Exp. Psych.* 87:225–228.

————, 1971b. On the processing of simple visual and auditory stimuli at distinct levels. *Perception and Psychophysics,* 9:331–334.

Liberman, A. M., F. S. Cooper, D. P. Shankweiler, and M. Studdert-Kennedy, 1967. Perception of the speech code. *Psych. Rev.* 74:431–461.

General Discussion of Papers by Conrad and LaBerge

Liberman said that the inability of deaf children to read well is of great significance. The fact that they cannot take in the necessary linguistic information by eye—a better channel than the ear—calls for an explanation. Liberman also remarked, in connection with Conrad's observation that the shapes of the letters in the Roman alphabet might be a source of confusion, that Donna Erickson had recently conducted an experiment on the visual, phonetic, and semantic confusability of the Kanji characters used by the Japanese. In her experiment, subjects were presented with a series of characters and then asked to name the character that followed a "probe" character. When the series of characters was phonetically similar, confusion was far greater than when they were visually or semantically similar. The relative absence of visual confusions suggests that the Kanji might be more distinctive than Roman characters. The evidence of phonetic confusions indicates that people resort to the speech code even in situations where a visual coding might be expected. The speech code was evidently extremely efficient, both in production and perception, no doubt because it had become adapted to human requirements over a long period of evolution.

Liberman also alluded to the "shortcuts" in linguistic processing—in which familiar, clearly anticipated material does not receive complete linguistic processing—that an experienced reader might be expected to employ. He said that these shortcuts are common to all linguistic processing, and in particular to the processing of colloquial speech. However, it is just as unlikely that a reader responds directly to print, short-circuiting phonetics and phonology altogether, as that the listener responds directly to the acoustic speech signal. Lotz said that if there are shortcuts in speech perception and reading, there should be shortcuts in speech production and writing as well.

In answer to a question by Klima, Conrad said that the reading of deaf children may be accompanied by both mouthing and finger-spelling. Klima suggested that these activities may be considered as analogous to the articulatory movements of normal readers rather than as shortcuts.

Gibson emphasized that for a skilled reader, if not for a child learning to read, the strategy selected depends largely on the task. For some tasks phonetic coding in short-term memory is appropriate, but not for others. In search tasks, potential phonetic confusion in the context does not slow down an adult at all, though it does slow down a seven-year-old. Graphic confusability does slow down a subject: evidently he uses a graphic strategy for the search task. She referred to an experiment by Cohen [1970] using meaningful paragraphs. When subjects were asked to locate and cross out words that belong to the same taxonomic category as a given word, they found this task easy. Finding words that are graphically similar to the given word was more difficult; finding homophones for the given word was the most difficult task of all. The point is that if a subject's task requires him to consider meaning, acoustic confusability may not make any difference.

Liberman replied that in search tasks the reaction of a subject depends on both processing and "accessibility" as defined in Klima's paper. Poor performance on tasks similar to Cohen's might mean simply that the processes being called for took longer to bring to consciousness. Good performance on the semantic similarity task does not mean that phonetic or phonological processing did not take place.

Reference

Cohen, G., 1970. Search times for combinations of visual, phonemic, and semantic targets in reading prose. *Perception and Psychophysics,* 8:370–372.

ROBERT G. CROWDER

Visual and Auditory Memory

It may be taken for granted that short-term memory plays a crucial role in the understanding of both written and spoken language. Even simple linguistic forms would be poorly understood, if at all, by a receiver who was forced to process each unit in a message fully at its time of arrival. Granted the centrality of memory to understanding language, an interesting conjecture occurs that memory has partially different functions in reading and in listening. The reader, for example, can ordinarily backtrack over previous material for a second look, whereas the listener can do so only rarely, and then at the expense of a rude "What?" The plausibility of different memory factors, or of different memories, for reading and listening does not ensure, unfortunately, that experimental demonstrations of visual-auditory memory differences for artificial verbal materials are instructive about real language in the natural setting. However, in view of our ignorance of observational techniques for the study of language comprehension in vivo, experiments with simpler materials should at least serve as a source of working hypotheses.

One of two major themes in recent research on memory (the other is the concept of organization, e.g., Tulving and Donaldson [1972] is the examination of how sensory, nonverbal information survives the stimulus to influence storage and retrieval. This focus on nonverbal coding amounts to rejection of the concept of a memory trace as abstract and neutral in favor of a concept of the trace as composed of features that result from some selective encoding process. The particular features of memory stimuli getting increased attention are those that derive from modalities such as vision, hearing, speech, kinesthesis, etc. These bodily functions have conspicuous roles in theory across the following diverse research areas: (a) short-term sensory stores in vision [Averbach and Coriell 1961; Sperling 1960] and in audition [Crowder and Morton 1969; Eriksen, Johnson et al. 1964; Massaro 1970]; (b) recoding of visual materials along audiospeech dimensions [Conrad 1964; Wickelgren 1965; Sperling 1960]; (c) kinesthetic memory, such as has been established in certain situations [Posner and Konick 1966]; (d) demonstration of a "medium short-term" visual code that outlasts verbal recoding [Posner, Boies et al. 1969]; and (e) long-term visual imagery, both in traditional learning paradigms [Paivio 1969] and also in long-ignored (by academics) mnemonic devices [Bower 1970; Norman 1968]. To these examples of how sensory processes have invaded recent thinking on memory must be added Luria's [1968] report of a man with pathological memory endowments. A salient theme of Luria's study is how this individual's aberration was linked to imagery and synesthesia running berserk.

Given renewed interest by students of memory in sensory forms of coding, it is perfectly natural that comparisons of visual and auditory presentation in immediate memory should have made their way (back) into the literature. The main purpose of this paper is to describe and explain the differences which exist between memory for *seen* and *heard* stimuli. First there will be a quick sketch of the results establishing this modality difference. Second, I will describe a model of short-term acoustic memory that is adequate to cover the modality difference. This model will then be extended and tested in other contexts. Finally, some rather recent evidence will be presented bearing on the type of information held in auditory storage. Direct comparisons between the visual and auditory modes will be drawn where appropriate; however, since (as seems invariably to be the case) visual work is considerably farther advanced than auditory, most of my talk will be directed to the properties of auditory memory.

Visual versus Auditory Presentation: The Data to Be Explained

Figure 1 shows the distribution of recall errors across serial positions in an experiment [Crowder 1970] where subjects remembered lists of nine digits under three input conditions. In each of these three input arrangements, the subject saw the digits serially on a screen at a rate of two per second. In the Silent condition he was instructed to read each digit to himself as it appeared on the screen. In the Active Vocalization condition he was instructed to read each digit aloud as it appeared on the screen. In the Passive Vocalization condition he was to remain silent, but the experimenter's voice was heard on a synchronized tape recording pronouncing each element as it appeared on the screen. Thus in two of the conditions (Active Vocalization and Passive Vocalization) the visual input was accompanied by auditory input, whereas in the Silent condition it was not. Figure 1 shows that it mattered *relatively* little (but see Crowder [1970]) which vocalization condition was used, but it mattered a great deal whether or not there was acoustic information. In particular substantially more errors were made on the last three serial positions when input was silent than when information entered the ears. Mode of presentation had little effect on the early serial positions.

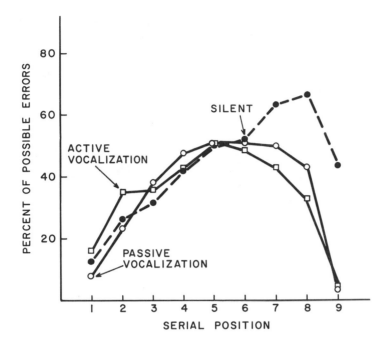

Figure 1. The relation between serial position and errors under conditions of varied modality. From Crowder [1970], Fig. 3.

Similar data from Murray [1966] and Corballis [1966] first brought the modality effect to general modern attention, although it is perhaps unfair to claim these individuals "discovered" the phenomenon. Washburn [1916, p. 74], for example, gave the following summary: "The superiority of the auditory memory after-image to the visual is implied by many investigations. Calkins . . . found that the most recent of a series of auditory impressions which were to be immediately recalled had more advantage on account of its recency than the last of a series of visual impressions similarly recalled: the recent impression must derive its advantage in immediate recall from the memory after-image, so this result would indicate that the auditory memory after-images were clearer than the visual ones. Muller . . . says that short intervals between learning and testing verbal materials lead to an auditory method of learning, because of the tendency to use the auditory memory after-image, which he thus implies is more striking than the visual after-image." I have quoted Washburn at some length because besides an apt summary of the empirical contrast between visual and auditory presentation she gives us also an anticipation of why the difference exists—a more persistent sensory store in audition than in vision. There is no particular advantage in a term such as Precategorical Acoustic Storage (see below) over her "auditory memory after-image."

Incidentally, history does not provide a clear picture on the modality difference. Both Woodworth [1938, p. 41] and McGeoch [1942, p. 169] were skeptical that any conclusion could be drawn from the literature as a whole, the latter even somewhat sarcastic about the amount of effort that had been invested in the topic.

Although my own coverage is going to be limited to the memory-span situation (immediate ordered recall for supraspan lists presented fairly rapidly) the modality difference occurs with satisfactory regularity in other experimental paradigms [Cooley and McNulty 1967; Craik 1969; Murdock 1971; Madigan 1971].

Precategorical Acoustic Storage (PAS)

Several years ago John Morton and I [Crowder and Morton 1969] proposed a theory of short-term memory in the acoustic mode whose purpose was to unify data concerning (a) serial position effects in immediate memory, (b) the difference between auditory and visual presentation, and (c) the effects of redundant elements on immediate recall. To account for the modality difference we assumed that when verbal materials arrive through the ears an extra source of information is set up beyond what is available through visual stimulation only. Associated with this claim, that the auditory advantage comes from the presence of extra information, is responsibility for stating the type of information involved and why this extra information affects only the recency portion of the serial position curve. The Washburn-Crowder-Morton hypothesis is that the extra information is held in a Precategorical Acoustic Storage (PAS) system similar to the sensory-storage systems proposed some years ago for the visual modality [Averbach and Coriell 1961; Sperling 1960]. The visual and auditory stores are held to be fundamentally similar in that they both hold information in a primitive or prelinguistic form. The two sensory stores are different in that the acoustic store lasts for a second or two while the visual store is usually held to persist only for a quarter-second [Averbach and Coriell 1961]. The difference in persistence for storage in vision and audition is almost a qualitative difference when one considers the timing of immediate memory experiments (where items are usually delivered at rates of around two per second). Having PAS for up to two seconds means that the subject could postpone classification of some items momentarily, recheck his categorization of others, and, generally, transcend the strict pacing imposed upon the task by the experimenter. A visual sensory store would allow exactly the same sort of freedom if only it lasted more than a fraction of a second.

Why does the PAS advantage occur only for the last few items in the series? The answer to this question depends on the factors believed to limit the duration of information in PAS. Crowder and Morton assumed that there are two such limiting factors, a fixed spatial or numerical capacity and a limited temporal capacity determined by decay. If there is a numerical limit on the information that can occupy PAS, then each new presentation, after the limit has been surpassed, must result in the displacement of previously entered items. The only items that would be relatively free from degradation by subsequent input would be those which ordinarily are not followed by subsequent input—the last items in the list. The early list positions benefit from only very transient storage in PAS since new inputs are always following closely on their heels.

Granted the availability of PAS information concerning the terminal items the question of access to this information remains. There are basically two solutions [see Routh 1971], one which assumes an autonomous continual readout of information from PAS into the perception (categorization) mechanism and another which assumes a directed readout from PAS under the subject's control. Since there are data to show that subjects can be instructed to direct their attention to selected portions of auditory space (see below) it appears that at least the latter and at most both types of transfer occur. The most likely time for directed readout to occur is during the brief interval separating auditory presentation and recall. It has been proposed [Crowder and Raeburn 1970] that the subject engages in a subvocal "dress rehearsal" during this interval of time. Given subvocalization rates of between five and ten items per second, PAS information concerning the last few items would still be present in PAS when these items get covertly articulated. The most reasonable assumption is that the PAS traces are then compared with the subject's subvocalizations and that the former are used to correct discrepancies. The *logogen* system proposed by Morton [1970] would be the locus of such comparison since the units in that system have precisely the function of correlating evidence of different types in the service of perceiving verbal units (letters, words).

There are compelling a priori reasons for the existence of some system such as PAS or, to use Neisser's term, Echoic Memory. As he has observed [Neisser 1967, pp. 199–200] the great majority of sounds with biological significance are defined by changes over time (see also Worden [1971])—changes such as time-of-arrival differences permitting sound localization, frequency modulation, and formant transitions in human speech. To encode such transient signals the auditory system needs mechanisms capable of simultaneous registration for things occurring at different points in time. This means that memory at a relatively peripheral acoustic level is an absolute logical necessity. At the neural level, both dramatic variation in conduction times within auditory pathways and also the presence of many feedback loops provide a possible basis for such simultaneous registration [Worden 1971]. The very fact of frequency analysis argues for buffer storage in audition, as Guttman and Julesz [1962] have observed in their experiments showing perception of periodicities in recurrent segments of white noise. Given these arguments that buffer storage must occur in audition, it furthermore makes excellent sense that such acoustic storage should be more persistent than in vision. For one thing, the reception of stimuli in vision depends in large part upon the voluntary direction of attention (gaze) and thus the human being can often arrange for the persistence of the *stimulus itself* without needing a persistent stimulus trace. More generally, there is the frequently cited proposition that audition is inherently spread out in time whereas vision is inherently spread out in space [Jakobson 1967]. Insofar as perception depends crucially upon the availability of contextual information, then vision capitalizes on parallel availability of context from a wide spatial array and audition capitalizes on wide temporal array furnished by memory.

PAS in Other Situations

Having one theoretical mechanism (PAS) to match one empirical phenomenon (the modality effect) is not worth much as "explanation." It should be possible to observe the properties of PAS in other situations and thus converge several phenomena upon a single unifying theory. According to the theory each element of a serial auditory list exerts an inhibitory or masking effect on previous items due to the limited capacity of PAS for holding information. This process could potentially be observed by comparing recall for the ninth element of a nine-element series with recall for the ninth element of a ten-element series. However, lengthening the list by one item has another unfortunate consequence beyond its presumed inhibitory effect on the PAS traces—it adds to the subject's memory load. We can dissociate these two effects of an additional item by referring to a situation where a redundant item, called a "stimulus suffix," is added to the end of a memory list. The special feature of the suffix is that it is perfectly predictable by the subject both as regards its occurrence and its identity, which are constant over a large block of trials. One way, in fact, of describing the suffix to the subject is to say that it is a cue indicating to him when to begin recalling the series he just heard. The comparison of interest is thus between error functions for an n-element list and the same list to which a redundant suffix has been added just in the position which would be occupied by an $n + 1$st item.

The consequence of presenting a redundant *zero* at the end of a nine-digit series is shown in Figure 2. These data come from an experiment in which lists of nine digits produced by a speech synthesizer were presented at a rate of four digits per second. In the control condition there was a 1,000 Hz tone occurring at the end of the list (i.e., in time with the "tenth" serial position) while in the experimental suffix condition the same temporal location was occupied by the word *zero*. (It will be established below that the tone control condition is not different from a control condition in which no additional sound at all is presented; the advantage of having some cue in the control condition is to control for such factors as signaling the end of the series and cueing recall.)

The data of Figure 2 permit observation of the PAS-displacement mechanism without the confounding influence of an added memory load. Since in both the experimental and control conditions presentation was auditory, the subject is presumed to have had equivalent PAS information following occurrence of the ninth memory item. According to the model, subjects in the control condition then went on to carry out a dress rehearsal of the whole list, or of the last portion of it, matching

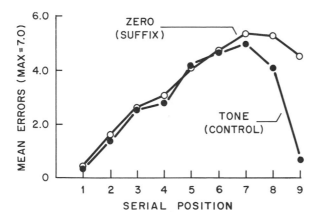

Figure 2. The effect of a stimulus suffix on the distribution of errors across serial position. Data from Crowder [1971a].

whenever possible their subvocalizations against still-lingering traces from PAS. The experimental subjects, on the other hand, presumably went through their dress rehearsal without benefit of corroboration from PAS; essentially, the suffix left them with only the type of information they would have received from visual presentation. And, as can be seen from comparing Figures 1 and 2, the suffix produces a serial position function characteristic of visual rather than of auditory presentation. A bit of practical advice emerges: one should obviously pronounce telephone numbers aloud while consulting the phone book but then, at all costs, remain silent on the way to dial.

That the suffix effect is indeed occurring at a stage of information processing prior to the ultimate combining of vision and audition is attested by experiments of Crowder and Morton [1969 Exp. II] and of Morton and Holloway [1970] showing that an auditory suffix does not affect the recency portion of serial position curves derived from visual presentation.

Naturally the similarity between Figures 1 and 2 does not necessarily argue in favor of a common theoretical interpretation. As I have suggested previously, administration to naive subjects of a karate chop during the presentation of the last item in a memory series would probably produce a specific impairment in recall of the recency part of the list resembling the suffix curve of Figure 2. No one seriously believes this particular distraction hypothesis of the suffix effect; however, somewhat more sophisticated hypotheses can be offered to explain the suffix effect independently of the modality difference. For reasons such as these it seemed desirable to develop an independent way of demonstrating PAS, especially one that depended on a selective *improvement* in performance rather than a selective *impairment*. Fortunately Moray, Bates, and Barnett [1965] developed an experimental technique that filled the bill. In experiments on "the four-eared man" they distributed four verbal messages across two headphones such that the subject heard the messages in four spatial locations—one each at the right and left ears and one each partway "inside the head" on the right and left sides. The four messages (letters of the alphabet) were delivered *simultaneously* and a visual cue was given just after the stimuli indicating to the subject which channel to report. These cue lights were arranged to match the geometry of the apparent message locations. It will be recognized that the Moray-Bates-Barnett technique is a direct application to audition of Sperling's [1960] visual poststimulus cueing experiment. The critical operation is overloading the subject with more simultaneous information than he could handle ordinarily, then determining whether he can selectively "rescue" portions of the input after stimulus termination. Like Sperling, Moray et al. showed an advantage of partial report over whole report. The inference to be drawn from this advantage of partial over whole report is that the limiting factor in uncued performance is not on the amount of information held in the auditory system but rather is the slow rate at which information can be identified. Experiments on the "cocktail-party" phenomenon [Moray 1969] have shown that spatial location is an unusually effective cue on which to base selective attention when selection is anticipated *before* the stimulus; that similar spatial selectivity can be exercised *after* the stimulus has already occurred supports the idea of some acoustic memory where localization cues survive.

Collaborating with Christopher Darwin and Michael Turvey of Haskins Laboratories, I undertook to replicate the Moray et al. finding and hopefully to show that the poststimulus cue must be given soon after stimulus termination to be effective, thus estimating the decay time for PAS. Strictly speaking, the simple advantage of partial over whole report is not enough to establish a transient sensory memory because partial report conditions are by definition less subject to output interference, on the average, than whole report conditions.

Darwin, Turvey, and I arranged for three simultaneous utterances, one played on the left headphone only, one on the right headphone only, and a third through both headphones such that it sounded in the middle of the head. Each utterance consisted of a "minilist" of three elements run together from a set of letters and digits. The three minilists began and ended together; thus, there were nine elements presented on a trial, distributed in three spatial and three temporal locations. After 0, 1, 2, or 4 seconds following stimulus offset, a visual cue appeared on a screen. The cue was a vertical bar occupying the left, right, or center of the screen and cueing, respectively, partial report of the left, right, or center minilist. All such partial-report trials were run together in blocks, although the delay of cue and the channel to be reported were nonpredictable for the subject. Control series, in which whole report of all nine elements was required, were presented also and the comparison between partial and whole report was balanced against practice. A total of 15 subjects was tested, with the results shown in Figure 3. The three serial positions within a minilist have been tallied separately, as have the cue delays and the whole-report baseline. The results from the terminal item in each minilist are of primary interest since earlier positions' residence in PAS would have been degraded by the terminal items. The findings for the third minilist position indicate a sharp partial-report advantage that completely dissipates between simultaneity and a cue

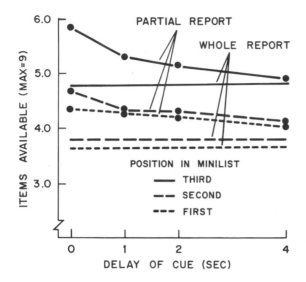

Figure 3. Estimated number of items available in acoustic memory as a function of delayed partial-report cues with ordinal position as the parameter. Whole-report performance is given by horizontal lines.

delay of 4 seconds. The first two minilist positions show a similar partial-report advantage and a similar dissipation with time. The estimate of PAS decay from Figure 3 is something over 2 seconds, a figure which is consistent with earlier estimates based on delaying the occurrence of a stimulus suffix [Crowder 1971a].

By way of summary it has been claimed that PAS is more or less directly observed in three experimental situations, (a) the comparison of visual and auditory presentation of memory series, where the last few elements are dramatically facilitated by the auditory mode; (b) the addition of a redundant suffix word to the end of a series, where the advantage seen in (a) is lost; and (c) the poststimulus cueing experiment showing that the subject can direct his attention to a portion of acoustic space after stimulus offset provided the instruction to do so comes soon enough.

The Type of Information in PAS: I. Varying the Suffix

The joint presence of masking (the suffix effect) and cueing in auditory memory, and the fact that these operations apparently share the same time parameters, is comparable to the first demonstrations of a prelinguistic store in vision. Actually, these data speak more to the presence of *some* system of storage than they speak to the precategorical nature of such a store. Another class of experiments is almost incomparably more powerful in evaluating the level of information processing involved in the masking and cueing studies. Techniques that permit inference as to coding levels are based on variation in the types of stimuli that will serve as adequate masks or cues. Sperling [1960] was well aware of how critical such experiments are when he showed that poststimulus cues calling for partial report of verbal classes (digits versus letters) did not reveal a partial-over-whole-report advantage as did cues selecting on spatial location. Others since [Dick 1969; von Wright 1968] have produced a reasonably orderly set of data showing selection as being possible for prelinguistic dimensions (color, brightness, size, location) and impossible for cues calling for selection based on postcategorical (linguistic) ones (verbal class, title). An extreme example makes the logic clear; if asked to select from iconic or echoic memory only those elements that are prime numbers, the subject should not show a partial-over-whole-report advantage since this classification requires previous identification of elements.

Generally speaking, the type of dimension according to which a precategorical storage system is organized—so as to permit effective cueing or masking—should be the type of dimension salient to a prelinguistic infant. Thus color, brightness, size, and possibly angularity should play important selective roles in the visual sensory store, while pitch, voice, quality, location, and loudness should play comparable roles in PAS. Verbal class, semantic characteristics, language nationality, vowel-consonant distinctions, and comparable dimensions ought to be just as absent from these precategorical systems as they are absent from the world of a prelinguistic infant. Showing that this is the case affords the best type of evidence for specific coding within memory systems.

Two parallel programs of research are implied by these arguments. The first is a direct analog to the Sperling, Dick, and von Wright demonstrations in vision—testing for various types of selection in the poststimulus cueing situation. Since the "three-eared man" has only recently become operational in New Haven, these investigations are yet to be performed. The second program of research is based on the suffix experiment, and in particular on how the suffix effect is governed by relations between the suffix word and the stimulus list. If the suffix effect is occurring precategorically, then postcategorical dimensions of similarity should not influence its magnitude; by the same token, determination of which dimensions do affect the suffix phenomenon should help locate the level of storage in PAS.

The results of a number of experiments are summarized in Figure 4. Each of the seven experiments portrayed there has two conditions

FOLLOWING INPUT OF 8-9 DIGITS,
THE SUFFIX EFFECT:

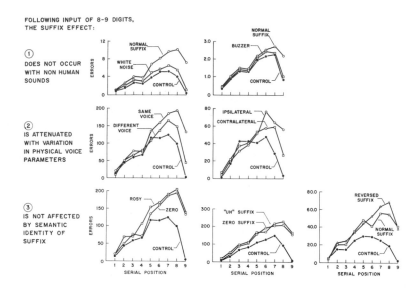

Figure 4. The effect of various manipulations on the size of the stimulus suffix effect.

in common—a control condition in which a list of eight or nine digits was presented at a two per second rate, and a standard suffix condition in which the word *zero* was spoken after the last memory item (by the same voice) in time with the presentation rate. In each of the panels of Figure 4 the third serial position function represents an additional, critical suffix condition in which the suffix utterance was varied from the standard in some way. Each experiment is based on repeated measurements on approximately 20 subjects, with conditions balanced against both practice and individual memory stimuli.

Morton and I originally considered the possibility that PAS occurred at such an extremely peripheral level that *any* acoustic signal would be effective in displacing previous traces given certain limits on timing and amplitude. The topmost pair of studies shows how wrong this initial guess was. In one of these studies a burst of white noise (comparable in subjective intensity to the verbal *zero*) was given as the critical condition and in the other a doorbell-type buzzer was used in place of the standard suffix. The results are quite clear in showing no selective effect whatever when these two nonspeech sounds are used as suffixes. In fact, such stimuli can be used as controls for verbal suffixes since they make conditions exactly comparable with regard to recall delay.

In the second pair of experiments in Figure 4, the critical suffix conditions are normal speech like the standard suffix condition, except that two physical parameters are varied: voice quality and laterality. In the left-hand experiment the memory series were recorded in a female voice, as was the standard suffix; the other suffix condition was the same except that a male voice delivered the *zero*. As the figure shows, the switch to a male voice gave results intermediate between the control and standard suffix conditions. The mismatched-voices suffix condition was reliably different both from the control and the matched-voices conditions. An intermediate suffix effect is obtained also when laterality is the parameter distinguishing the two suffix conditions, as shown in the righthand experiment. In this particular study laterality cues were based on signals occurring in either of two loudspeakers, one directly to the left and the other directly to the right of the subject. Morton [1970] has elegant data that indicate that this type of laterality effect derives not from a lateralized PAS but rather from the use of location as a distinguishing cue.

The three experiments shown at the bottom of Figure 4 show that given suffixes that are qualified by the criteria above (speech from the same voice as gave the stimulus and in the same place), the semantic content of the utterance is quite immaterial. In the experiment on the far left the word *zero* was compared with the word *rosy*. In the middle experiment the comparison was between the standard *zero* and the phoneme /ʌ/—a sort of neutral vocalization designed to convey as little in the way of "articulatory features" as possible. In the final panel [Crowder and Raeburn 1970] the forward *zero* was compared with the same utterance reversed. The tape for the normal word was simply cut out and spliced in upside-down. The variations accomplished in these three experiments cover considerable distance in both the "meaning" of the suffix and indeed in whether or not the suffix possesses meaning. However, in these three studies the acoustic properties of the suffixes are always comparable to the standard condition. The independence of the suffix effect from similarity along this dimension is a necessary condition for the precategorical nature of PAS.

A different perspective on the data of Figure 4 is suggested by thinking of the suffix experiments as tests of how well the subject can *ignore* a distracting signal at the end of the list. As such, the data just described fall into place alongside the literature on selective attention in audition, particularly studies in multichannel listening (see reviews in Garner [in press]; Treisman [1969]). The empirical generalizations coming from these two situations are strikingly similar: those variables that affect the amount of disruption caused by the suffix are the same variables that affect the amount of disruption caused by a competing message.

The Type of Information in PAS: II. Varying the Nature of the Stimulus Vocabulary

The stimuli in all of the research described so far have been natural-language vocabularies such as digits and letters. For some purposes these are ideal stimuli, for after all, it is to such events that we wish our theories ultimately to generalize. For other more analytic purposes, these stimuli are less attractive. Actually, the grounds for dissatisfaction with natural digits are the same as the advantages they possess in their real-life communication function—their redundancy. Considering just the nine digits, there are several sources of redundancy. For example, with the exception of the *five-nine* confusion, knowing only its vowel sound suffices to identify a digit. With other pairwise confusions excepted, initial phonemes are likewise a reliable cue. Stress, length, number of syllables, and other features also help facilitate communication in this sense. The disadvantage of this redundancy for present purposes is that a phenomenon like the modality effect could in principle occur if *any one of these features* received special processing such as PAS. Naturally, it is possible that PAS, or some similar system, carries a "tape recording" of acoustic input limited in fidelity only by random noise and the resolving power of the receptor itself. If, however, the tape recorder model is false and the auditory-memory effects depend on certain selected features of the signal, then it would be impossible to tell which features are the important ones so long as they are always covarying in the stimulus ensemble.

This problem can be overcome by using artificial stimulus vocabularies whose members differ on *only one* of the possible acoustic dimensions. Consider series of consonant-vowel syllables that differ from one another only in their vowel sound. Stimuli such as these should produce results typical of auditory memory (i.e., the recency advantage of auditory over visual presentation, the suffix effect, and poststimulus cueing effect) if the tape recorder model is true. Also, the recency and suffix effects would occur if vowels are among those selected features which are stored at the level of PAS. If sets of artificial stimuli are devised that, one after another, tap all the plausible dimensions of acoustic stimuli (phoneme classes, pitch, stress, length, etc.) and if all these vocabularies produce results that are characteristic of auditory presentation, then the tape-recorder model will begin to look like a possibility; that is, it will begin to look as if auditory presentation is both a necessary and a sufficient condition for the modality effect. If any one dimension does not yield such results however, then it will appear that auditory input is a necessary but not sufficient condition for "auditory memory results."

It should be added that this strategy is valid even if the PAS hypothesis is totally wrong. *Something* produces the advantage of heard over seen memory series, and it is reasonable to ask whether this unknown mechanism handles the entire auditory input or rather only certain features of it.

I have recently completed several experiments involving auditory presentation of memory stimuli assembled from the vocabulary, /ba, da, ga/. These items were prepared on the Haskins Laboratories speech synthesizer and thus differed from one another only in the feature of interest. Series of seven such items in random order were presented at a two per second rate. In one condition a tone followed the last memory item, while in another the suffix /gou/ was presented in the same place. Fifteen subjects were tested under these conditions, and then another ten under conditions that were identical except the presentation rate was slowed down to one per second; these two experiments are shown as Experiments I and II in the upper portion of Figure 5. In a third study involving 12 new subjects, the same conditions were tested as in Experiment I except that the list length was shortened to six times instead of seven. Notable in the results for each of these three studies (Experiments I, II, and III of Figure 5) are (a) the lack of a recency effect, and (b) the lack of a suffix effect that is selective on the late serial positions. Along with the poststimulus cueing method, which has not yet been extended to stimuli from restricted sets, (a) and (b) are the defining criteria for auditory memory; therefore, it appears that auditory memory does not carry information about stop consonants. In a descriptive sense the data of the first three panels in Figure 5 offer results typical of visual memory experiments even though they were collected under conditions of auditory presentation.

The data for these /ba, da, ga/ stimuli probably do not depend on the overall difficulty of the task, for when the 15 best subjects from Experiments I and II were examined separately they showed the same result. Nor do these data result from something peculiar about (a) using synthetic speech, (b) using a restricted vocabulary of three items, (c) using

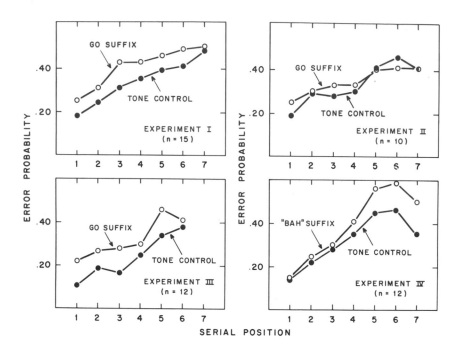

Figure 5. The effect of the stimulus suffix in four experiments with vocabularies of three synthetic consonant-vowel syllables. In the first three experiments the consonant contained the memory information and in the fourth, the vowel did. From Crowder [1971b].

computer-assembled lists with monotonous presentation, or other novel features of the study. This exclusion is permitted by a companion experiment in which all conditions were identical with those of Experiment I in Figure 5 except that the syllables /gæ, ga, gʌ/ were substituted for /ba, da, ga/ and the suffix /ba/ for the suffix /goʊ/. The lower right-hand panel of Figure 5 shows that with this vocabulary both the marked recency effect and the suffix effect have returned. Notice that overall the error probabilities are not out of line with the other three studies. Thus, at the empirical level, there seemed data to allow the conclusion that while PAS (or some comparable mechanism) does not carry information about stop consonants, it does about vowels.

The same conclusion was independently verified in an experiment on vocalization of visually presented memory items. In each condition of this experiment the stimuli were series of seven syllables shown on a screen, written out, for 2 seconds. After this study period the subject was required under all conditions to write out the items he had just seen in left-to-right order. Four experimental treatments were defined by two orthogonal comparisons; the subject read the items either silently or aloud as he read them from the screen, and he wrote them down either silently in the recall phase or spoke them aloud as he wrote. Every subject served in each of the four resulting vocalization conditions. Sixteen subjects saw stimulus slides in which the to-be-remembered items were from the set "BAH, DAH, GAH," and another 16 subjects saw items from the set "BEE, BIH, BOO." These items, in series of seven, were typewritten on hand-mounted slides from the upper left corner down toward the lower right in a stairstepped fashion. The results are given in Figure 6, where for comparison the far right-hand panel shows results from a similar study in which the stimulus materials were arabic digits. For the most part, the vowel-varied syllables, "BEE, BIH, BOO" behave like the digits, showing a sharp advantage of input vocalization (the modality effect) and interference from output vocalization. The syllables that differed only in their initial consonants ("BAH, DAH, GAH") do not show either of these effects, thus reinforcing the earlier conclusion that what distinguished auditory from visual memory in previous work is not an *inevitable* consequence of auditory input. It appears that stop consonants are excluded from PAS but that vowels are included. At least we may with some confidence reject the tape-recorder model for auditory memory.

There are three outside sources of data which sustain my conclusion that the PAS system is receptive differentially to vowels as opposed to

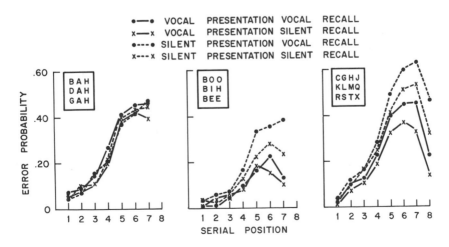

Figure 6. The effect of presentation and recall vocalization on immediate memory for items from three different vocabularies—consonants, vowels and letters of the alphabet. From Crowder [1971b].

stop consonants. First, Ronald Cole (personal communication) has compared memory for acoustically presented strings of artificial syllables differing either in initial consonant, terminal vowel, or both. His findings indicate a substantially greater recency effect for vowels than for consonants. Second, a recent study by Smallwood and Tromater [1971] effected comparisons between alphabet letters with high or low "acoustic similarity." Letters used by these authors with high similarity, "b c d g p t v z," are of course mainly distinguished by initial consonantal features while the letters in their experiment with low similarity, "h j l n r x q y," permit many different distinctions including terminal vowels. Separate scoring of the high and low similarity letters permitted comparisons showing a much larger recency effect with the low-similarity vocabulary than with the high-similarity vocabulary.

Finally, Fujisaki and Kawashima [1970] provide data from an entirely different setting that reinforces the vowel-consonant distinction. The Fujisaki-Kawashima experiment treats ABX speech-discrimination performance as a function of whether or not a vowel "context," or reference point, is provided after each stimulus. Without context, vowel discriminations in their experiment would have sounded to their subjects as follows: /i/—pause—/e/—pause—/e/—pause and decision. With context the routine would have been altered as follows: /i/—/a/—pause—/e/—/a/—pause—/e/—/a/—pause and decision. With respect to the to-be-discriminated items, the vowel context may be likened operationally to a *stimulus suffix,* (personal communcation with Alvin Liberman) since it was formally redundant and occurred shortly after the item which had to be retained. Consistent with this interpretation was the finding that context increased the categorical nature of vowel perception (on the /i/–/e/ continuum), as one would expect if the context (suffix) presentations reduced the availability of acoustic information. In another part of their experiment, however, Fujisaki and Kawashima performed the same context manipulation on ABX discrimination of consonants, in this case fricatives along the /ʃ/–/s/ continuum. With consonant stimuli the addition of context had no effect. Thus, just as Figure 5 shows that a suffix removes the acoustic component in serial memory for vowels but not for consonants, likewise, a suffix-like element added to ABX trials is shown here to affect vowel discriminations but not consonant discriminations.

Two possibilities underlying the vowel-consonant difference have some a priori plausibility. One is that registration of information in PAS simply requires some nonnegligible time for burning in, just as some kinds of visual after-images result more reliably from a prolonged gaze than from a fleeting glimpse. The acoustic cues for distinguishing the stop consonants are established by formant-frequency transitions lasting only around 50 msec [Liberman 1970] while the cues for vowels are steady-state and ordinarily (certainly in the present case) last much longer.

Perhaps more interesting is the possibility that the different auditory-memory results found with vowels as opposed to stop consonants are manifestations of laterality differences in the perception of speech [Studdert-Kennedy and Shankweiler 1970]. The recent data on later speech-perception effects indicate that whereas the dominant hemisphere (left) receives such "highly encoded" phonemic information as stop consonants best (i.e., a right-ear effect), other stimuli such as vowels and music are best received by the nondominant hemisphere (left-ear effect). In these experiments (reviewed and expanded by the Studdert-Kennedy–Shankweiler paper) the laterality effects depend on dichotic stimulation; therefore, further studies should permit replication of the phenomena in a trichotic situation. However, the really tempting hypothesis is that *PAS is a property of the nondominant (right) hemisphere.* Scrutiny, in further studies, of (a) where "PAS effects" occur, (b) where laterality effects occur, and (c) whether the two tend to co-vary, will provide information relevant to the laterality hypothesis.

Concluding Comments: PAS and What It Is Good For

It is curious that in this presentation, where my stated task was to elucidate differences between auditory and visual information processing in memory, I have been at some pains to argue for similarities between these two modalities. I have, for example, claimed that the suffix experiment bears some relationship to visual masking, that the experiments on cueing the "three-eared man" correspond roughly to Sperling's seminal poststimulus cueing studies, and that the evidential basis for a precategorical store comes ultimately in both modalities from the nature of stimulus dimensions to which the masking and cueing operations are sensitive. It was necessary to do this, because establishing comparability is in some sense a necessary prerequisite to the comparison itself. This point can be amplified by considering for a moment the type of model that Morton and I sought to reject in proposing PAS.

The main alternative to a separate acoustic store which is comparable to the visual one is a theory which many many writers seem to endorse vaguely but which Sperling [1960, 1967; also Sperling and Speelman 1970, p. 172] has taken care to state with precision. The major assumption of this model is that short-term memory is basically auditory. Further, whereas auditory input enjoys direct access to the auditory store, visual input has to pass through a visual store and then get translated into auditory form. According to this model (see also Morton and Holloway [1970]) there is not a fundamental difference between auditory imagery resulting from direct stimulation through the ears and auditory imagery resulting from recoding of visual input. Sperling and Speelman [1970] state this proposition most clearly when they answer the following question in the affirmative (p. 179): "Are rehearsed (visual) letters stored in the same memory as unrehearsed auditory letters?" The advantage of auditory over visual input in memory experiments is explained by observing that visual input has an extra information-processing stage to pass through as compared with auditory. Additional assumptions can be made to cover the specificity of the modality effect to the last serial positions. The main point of the recoding hypothesis, however, is that vision and audition are simply not comparable. Visual memory for language items is an extra, derivative process feeding indirectly into a storage system that is designed for audition. It is possible to assume (Sperling, personal communication) that residence in the "same memory" does not require storage in the exact same form of coding; however, without such an extension the Sperling-Speelman position seems to imply that audition entails no extra processes above and beyond vision, just possibly more vivid imagery. In hopelessly, possibly even perversely, simplified form, they seem to be saying that seeing or reading memory stimuli is essentially an indirect way of hearing them.

Others authors, notably Neisser [1967, p. 226] and Atkinson and Shiffrin [1968, p. 92] hold open the possibility of an "echoic" store for audition which is not activated by visual input, but they assign little or nothing to such a store in the way of evidence or theoretical responsibilities. Thus, the essence of the PAS model is more clearly seen in contrast with other models: there are separate, parallel, and therefore comparable sensory storage systems in vision and audition.

Granted comparability between visual and auditory prelinguistic stores, I would emphasize two prominent differences between the two. The first has to do with time parameters. The data on delayed suffixes and stimulus cues in the Moray-Bates-Barnett procedure both suggest that PAS traces last around two seconds. This estimate is not far from others that have been reached [Guttman and Julesz 1963; Neisser 1967], which is comforting; but more importantly, this estimate differs literally by an order of magnitude from those which have emerged from masking or cueing experiments in vision (with one exception to be noted presently). Now of course the setting of "critical intervals" in masking is a tricky business and one can enter the literature with any favorite interval and find evidence for it. For example, von Békésy [1971] summarizes the literature as indicating backward masking delays of 60 msec across the major sensory modalities. Other evidence [Elliott 1962] shows minimal or absent backward masking in audition beyond about 25 msec when noise bursts and tones are used. But the same intervals with speech materials have been reported to give maximum masking effects so long as the target and mask are presented to contralateral ears [Studdert-Kennedy, Shankweiler et al. 1970]. These intervals in auditory masking are of course far shorter than the two-second period which I have been trying to associate with PAS. It is most likely that fundamentally different stages of information processing account for these different estimates of masking effectiveness, just as monoptic and dichoptic masking in vision give quite different results [Schiller 1965].

The main point remains that whereas one can find short-interval masking in both vision and audition, it is only for PAS that storage times anywhere near the order of seconds have been proposed. The possible exception to this generalization is provided in work by Posner, Boies, Eichelman, and Taylor [1969]. These authors show apparent survival of authentically visual information from single letters that lasts on the order of seconds; however, the sensitivity of their results to voluntary rehearsal, to interference from central information-processing demands, and the insensitivity of their storage mechanism to visual interference, suggests a considerably more central form of storage than we have been considering here.

The data assembled here in support of PAS suggest also a more central form of storage than that associated with the masking obtained (at 25 and 60 msec, respectively) by Elliott [1962] or by Studdert-Kennedy, Shankweiler, and Shulman [1970]. However, for the reasons given above in some detail I must insist on a form of coding which is basically sensory or prelinguistic. Nonetheless, the *relative* centrality of PAS (relative, that is, to the systems responsible for the rapid masking) is compatible with its selectivity to certain features of acoustic signals, viz., vowels rather than consonants. Lack of fidelity by PAS to the acoustic stimulus is the second major basis for distinguishing the visual and auditory precategorical stores. The particular way in which PAS handles incomplete information about the stimulus is of less importance than the major point that some selective information reduction has occurred before PAS. There is of course a trivial sense in which all sensory representation in memory must be nonveridical since the receptor itself has limited resolving power, and since it is safe to assume the introduction of random noise in later systems. The selective nonveridicality in audition seems a step beyond these obvious limitations and seems to have no analog in vision, where, if the icon fades [Neisser 1967] it is usually assumed to fade evenly.

The selectivity of PAS to classes of acoustic information emphasizes the relation of sensory storage to sensory analysis. If I am correct in interpreting the Studdert-Kennedy, Shankweiler, and Shulman [1970] "lag effect" as representative of a shorter-term, more peripheral holding mechanism than PAS, it would be expected that exclusion of certain types of signals such as stop consonants would not be found in that situation. Still, escalating the number of prelinguistic storage systems seems counterproductive since the range of cueing and masking results is quite wide and depends so critically on the stimuli employed. Perhaps a better viewpoint is that precategorical storage in either modality is a property of the analysis system for the modality, as Morton [1970] has recently made explicit. In this light the finding that stop consonants appear excluded from PAS is less puzzling. Categorical decisions about certain phonemes, about all phonemes possibly, get made immediately but the raw materials for certain of these decisions linger in the acoustic system. This lingering of incomplete information provides context; just as the visual system includes a region of sharp acuity in the fovea and a somewhat vaguer periphery, so in audition we may say that the "present" is a temporal region of sharp acuity, supported by a somewhat vaguer temporal periphery.

Beyond the general usefulness of context information, there are two specific uses to which a PAS system saving information only about vowels might be put. One is in the perception of suprasegmental features. These features, notably stress, depend acutely on changes in the acoustic signal over time and are furthermore quantized at least in segments of seconds, particularly when the stress pattern ranges across a whole sentence or phrase.

The second specific use to which a PAS holding only vowels might be put is the diagnosis of vocal-tract parameters. Ladefoged and Broadbent [1957] have laid out in general form the nature of the problem: our perception of vowels is necessarily based on relative judgments rather than on absolute judgments since the vocal-tract machinery produces such wide variance in the acoustic cues for vowels. These relative judgments, in turn, must involve the existence of an acoustic comparator receiving input both from the present and the past. This must occur precategorically, naturally, since vowel identification depends on setting estimates of the vocal cavity based on output from the comparator. Broadbent, Ladefoged, and Lawrence [1956] have performed an experiment which is tantalizing with regard to the role of PAS in this process.

These authors showed that identification of words of the form /b/–(vowel)–/t/ depends very critically on the formant frequencies used in the context sentence, "Please say what this word is . . . " When two utterances contained exactly the same critical word but different-sounding voices in the context sentence, 14 of 15 subjects identified the critical word as being a different word in the two cases. When the same experiment was repeated with a silent interval of 10 seconds between the context sentence and the critical word, only 7 of a new set of 15 subjects reported a difference, a significant interaction. Apparently, the raw acoustic information provided by the context sentence could not be maintained by rehearsal in this situation, as one would expect of information stored in PAS.

References

Atkinson, R. C., and R. M. Shiffrin, 1968. Human memory: A proposed system and its control processes. In K. W. Spence and J. T. Spence (eds.), *The Psychology of Learning and Motivation.* Vol. 2. New York: Academic Press, pp. 90–197.

Averbach, E., and A. S. Coriell, 1961. Short-term memory in vision. *Bell System Technical Journal,* 40:309–328.

Bower, G. H., 1970. Analysis of mnemonic device. *Amer. Scientist* 58:496–510.

Broadbent, D. E., P. Ladefoged, and W. Lawrence, 1956. Vowel sounds and perceptual constancy. *Nature,* 178:815–816.

Conrad, R. Acoustic confusions in immediate memory. *Brit. J. Psych.* 55:75–84.

Cooley, R. K., and J. A. McNulty, 1967. Recall of individual CCC trigrams over short intervals of time as a function of mode of presentation. *Psychonomic Sci.* 9:543–544.

Corballis, M. C., 1966. Rehearsal and decay in immediate recall of visually and aurally presented items. *Canad. J. Psych.* 20:43–51.

Craik, F. I. M., 1969. Modality effects in short-term storage. *J. Verbal Learning and Verbal Behavior,* 8:658–664.

Crowder, R. G., 1970. The role of one's own voice in immediate memory. *Cog. Psych.* 1:157–178.

Crowder, R. G., 1971a. Waiting for the stimulus suffix: Decay, delay, rhythm, and readout in immediate memory. *Quart. J. Exp. Psych.* 23:324–340.

———, 1971b. The sound of vowels and consonants in immediate memory. *J. Verbal Learning and Verbal Behavior* 10:587–596.

Crowder, R. G., and J. Morton, 1969. Precategorical acoustic storage (PAS). *Perception and Psychophysics,* 5:365–373.

Crowder, R. G., and V. P. Raeburn, 1970. The stimulus suffix effect with reversed speech. *J. Verbal Learning and Verbal Behavior,* 9:342–345.

Dick, A. O., 1969. Relations between the sensory register and short-term storage in tachistoscopic recognition. *J. Exp. Psych.* 82:279–284.

Elliott, L. L., 1962. Backward masking: Monotic and dichotic conditions. *J. Acoust. Soc. Amer.* 34:1108–1115.

Eriksen, C. W., H. J. Johnson, and J. F. Collins, 1964. Storage and decay characteristics of nonattended auditory stimuli. *J. Exp. Psych.* 68:28–36.

Fujisaki, H., and T. Kawashima, 1970. Some experiments on speech perception and a model for the perceptual mechanism. *Annual Report of the Engineering Research Institute,* Faculty of Engineering, University of Tokyo, Vol. 29.

Garner, W. R., in press. Attention: The processing of multiple sources of information. In E. C. Carterette and M. P. Friedman (eds.), *Handbook of Perception,* in press.

Guttman, N., and B. Julesz, 1962. Lower limits of auditory periodicity analysis. *J. Acoust. Soc. Amer.* 35:610.

Jakobson, R., 1967. About the relation between visual and auditory signs. In W. Wathen-Dunn (ed.), *Models for the Perception of Speech and Visual Form.* Cambridge, Mass.: M.I.T. Press.

Ladefoged, P., and D. E. Broadbent, 1957. Information conveyed by vowels. *J. Acoust. Soc. Amer.* 29:98–104.

Liberman, A. M., 1970. The grammars of speech and language. *Cog. Psych.* 1:301–323.

Luria, A. R., 1968. *The Mind of a Mnemonist.* New York: Avon Books.

McGeoch, J. A., 1942. *The Psychology of Human Learning.* New York: Longmans, Green.

Madigan, S., 1971. Modality and recall order interactions in short-term memory for serial order. *J. Exp. Psych.* 87:294–296.

Massaro, D. W., 1970. Perceptual processes and forgetting in memory tasks. *Psych. Rev.* 77:557–567.

Moray, N., 1969. *Listening and Attention.* Baltimore: Penguin Books.

Moray, N., A. Bates, and T. Barnett, 1965. Experiments on the four-eared man. *J. Acoust. Soc. Amer.* 38:196–201.

Morton, J., 1970. A functional model for memory. In D. A. Norman (ed.), *Models of Human Memory.* New York: Academic Press.

Morton, J., and C. M. Holloway, 1970. Absence of a cross-modality "suffix" effect of short-term memory. *Quart. J. Exp. Psych.* 22:167–176.

Murdock, B. B. Jr., 1971. Short-term memory. In G. H. Bower and J. T. Spence (eds.), *The Psychology of Learning and Motivation: Advances in Research and Theory.* Vol. 5. New York: Academic Press.

Murray, D. J., 1966. Vocalization-at-presentation and immediate recall, with varying recall methods. *Quart. J. Exp. Psych.* 18:9–18.

Neisser, U., 1967. *Cognitive Psychology.* New York: Appleton-Century-Crofts.

Norman, D. A., 1968. *Memory and Attention.* New York: Wiley.

Paivio, A., 1969. Mental imagery in associative learning and memory. *Psych. Rev.* 76:241–263.

Posner, M. I., S. J. Boies, W. H. Eichelman, and R. L. Taylor, 1969. Retention of visual and name codes of single letters. *J. Exp. Psych.* Monograph 79 (No. 1, Part 2).

Posner, M. I., and A. W. Konick, 1966. On the role of interference in short-term retention. *J. Exp. Psych.* 72:221–231.

Routh, D. A., 1971. Independence of the modality effect and amount of silent rehearsal in immediate serial recall. *J. Verbal Learning and Verbal Behavior,* 10:213–218.

Schiller, P. H., 1965. Monoptic and dichoptic visual masking by patterns and flashes. *J. Exp. Psych.* 69:193–199.

Smallwood, R. A., and L. J. Tromater, 1971. Acoustic interference with redundant elements. *Psychonomic Sci.* 22:354–356.

Sperling, G., 1960. The information available in brief visual presentations. *Psych. Monographs* 74 (No. 498).

Sperling, G., 1967. Successive approximations to a model for short-term memory. *Acta Psych.* 27:285–292.

Sperling, G., and R. G. Speelman, 1970. Acoustic similarity and auditory short-term memory experiments and a model. In D. A. Norman (ed.), *Models of Human Memory.* New York: Academic Press, pp. 151–202.

Studdert-Kennedy, M., and D. Shankweiler, 1970. Hemispheric specialization for speech perception. *J. Acoust. Soc. Amer.* 48:579–594.

Studdert-Kennedy, M., D. Shankweiler, and S. Shulman, 1970. Opposed effects of a delayed channel on perception of dichotically and monotically presented CV syllables. *J. Acoust. Soc. Amer.* 48:599–602.

Treisman, A. M., 1965. Strategies and models of selective attention. *Psych. Rev.* 1969, 72:89–104.

Tulving, E., and Donaldson, W. (eds.), 1972. *Organization and Memory.* New York: Academic Press.

von Békésy, G., 1971. Auditory backward inhibition in concert halls. *Science,* 171:529–536.

von Wright, J. M., 1968. Selection in visual immediate memory. *Quart. J. Exp. Psych.* 20:62–68.

Washburn, M. F., 1916. *Movement and Mental Imagery.* Boston: Houghton Mifflin.

Wickelgren, W. A., 1965. Acoustic similarity and retroactive inhibition in short-term memory. *J. Verbal Learning and Verbal Behavior,* 4:53–61.

Woodworth, R. S., 1938. *Experimental Psychology.* New York: Holt.

Worden, F. G., 1971. Hearing and the neural detection of acoustic patterns. *Behavioral Sci.* 16:20–30.

DONALD A. NORMAN

The Role of Memory in the Understanding of Language

A Discussion of Crowder's Paper

Once upon a time, in the never-never land of psychological theories, all worked smoothly and simply. There were three different kinds of memory: visual short-term memory (sometimes called sensory information store); short-term memory (or primary memory); and long-term memory (sometimes called secondary memory). The long-term memory contained the knowledge of the long since past. Short-term memory was a transient memory of the events of the present. And the sensory information store seemed capable of holding an accurate rendition of the visual physical input for a span measured in a few tenths of a second. Presumably, there was a sensory information storage (SIS) system for each sensory modality, and there was some evidence for such systems in vision, audition, and for tactile sensation.

It seemed sensible that the sensory information store would feed directly into the more normal short-term memory (STM) and that, with language-based material at least, recoding took place in the transition from one memory to the other. The evidence for this came from the nature of errors made in the short-term memory experiments: the experiments of Conrad, Baddeley, Sperling, and Wickelgren showed them clearly to be sound-based (I use the neutral term "sound" to circumvent the differences among acoustics, articulation, and phonetics). Obviously, no one ever believed that nonlinguistic information was recoded into acoustical format before storage in long-term memory, but it was (and is) commonly accepted that linguistically based material—printed words—entered the visual system and then was transformed into an auditory or articulatory form in the short-term memory. From there, by processes unknown, they made contact with their semantic equivalents and were finally stored in the long-term memory system.

Things are now not nearly so simple. Posner and his colleagues find a form of visual memory that may last for several seconds, apparently a visual memory that is neither the sensory information store nor the normal short-term memory so heavily studied by others. Crowder and Morton discuss an acoustical memory with a time constant of several seconds, their precategorical acoustical store (PAS). This is not the short-term memory of before. Where does it go into the system? Moreover, Crowder's PAS has peculiar properties—it is not affected by the meanings of sounds, but it is also not affected by meaningless sounds.

Warrington and Shallice have discovered a patient who appears to have impaired short-term memory and a normal long-term memory, yet he functions normally [Shallice and Warrington 1970; Warrington and Shallice 1969, in preparation; Warrington and Weiskrantz 1972]. This could mean that it is possible for material to enter long-term memory directly, without going through short-term memory: a notion that goes against almost every contemporary theory. Of course, it is always possible that this patient simply has a very much reduced short-term memory which he uses normally. At the present time no one knows.

Finally, to add more bits and pieces to the puzzle, there are peculiar results with the differences between memory for attended and nonattended materials. Nonattended auditory inputs can be recovered from a temporary memory store if they are tested for immediately after presentation (Norman [1969a]; replicated and expanded by Glucksberg and Cowen [1970]). Bryden [1971] finds evidence that auditory material that is attended to seems to be stored differently from material not attended to: in some ways, the latter material comes out better when there is a delay in time before it can be accessed. Corballis and Luthe [1971] argue not only for differences between visual memories for attended material and nonattended material, but also that items stored preattentively may be labeled individually, but not organized into sequence.

Now what? What do we do with all these memories? Can we make sense out of this apparently ever increasing drive to find new properties for memory, each demanding its own new separate system? Let us now examine in detail the evidence for the precategorical acoustical storage system (PAS) postulated by Crowder, and then see whether an analysis of the processing steps required to understand language might help us understand the dilemma posed by all these different results.

Precategorical Acoustical Storage

Primarily, the evidence for PAS comes from one form of experiment: the stimulus-suffix experiment. Here, a list is presented to the subject for him to remember and then, at the conclusion of that list, an irrelevant item is presented. This latter item, the suffix, is known by the subject to be irrelevant to the experiment, and ideally it should be completely ignored by him. The fact that the suffix cannot be ignored leads to the postulate that it must enter memory along with the other items, and the nature of the interference caused by the suffix as the characteristics of both stimulus items and the suffix are varied leads to the postulated properties of precategorical acoustical store. The experiment is an important one, for it is reasonably sensitive to experimental manipulation, so that properties of the system can be tested with some efficiency. It is somewhat unfortunate that almost all the evidence for PAS comes from this single paradigm, but meanwhile, until more experiments get done, we will have to make do with what we have. So, what are the properties of PAS?

We find PAS to be neither a memory for sensory features nor one for meaningful ones. It lies somewhere in the middle. Precategorical would appear to be too strong a label, for certainly some categorization has already taken place. It is not simply a sensory store, for we find that a simple tone presented as a suffix has no effect. It is not a meaningful store, for we find that semantic variations have no effect: a word played backwards over a tape recorder has as much interfering effect as does a word spoken normally; it cannot simply be that the proper auditory frequencies must be present, for a burst of white noise has no interfering effect. When the suffix is presented in a voice different from that of the stimulus material, or presented so that it is localized in a different spatial location than the stimulus material, then we find halfway interference, neither as little interference as a tone nor as much interference as the normal suffix effect. Finally, we find that the PAS would appear to have in it information about the sounds for vowels, but not for the stop consonants. Whether this reflects a real difference between storage for vowels and consonants (as Crowder suggests), or simply reflects the fact that the critical features of a stop consonant occur over a very small duration of time and so may not be stored as firmly as vowels, or even that the PAS does not contain any information about temporal sequence (and, hence, no information about stop consonants) cannot yet be determined from the existing data. This result, I discover, pleases the Haskins Laboratories contingent, for they have long argued for a difference in processing between consonants (especially stop consonants) and vowels.

There is a strong similarity between the aspects of material that interfere with storage in PAS and those aspects of auditory information that are known to affect the attentional process (see the reviews by Norman [1969b] and Treisman [1969]). All of these factors argue that PAS must exist at a reasonably high level of processing, not simply at the sensory level. In fact, one might argue that it exists either after the process of selective attention has already taken place, or it may, in fact, be a part of the process of selective attention. Unfortunately, this rules out PAS as a mechanism for the auditory memory studied by Norman [1969a] and Glucksberg and Cowen [1970], for these memories hold auditorily presented material for a short time, even though that material was *not* attended to. Thus, someone is wrong. Unfortunately, in the arguments that follow, I am going to say that it was probably I who was wrong.

Pattern Recognition

What should we make of it all? Precategorical acoustical store is too selective in its nature to be sensory, not selective enough to be cognitive. Where does it stand with regard to the normal short-term memory? We have noted a strange similarity in its properties to those of the attention mechanism. Where does it fit with regard to all the other memory systems that have been proposed: a pure sensory visual or auditory memory, a precategorical visual or auditory memory, the normal short-term memory, the long-term memory? Maybe it is time to back up a bit, to reconsider the necessity for postulating so many memory systems, and take another look at what is necessary in the processing of incoming language-based sensory material. Maybe these memories do not exist in such isolated, separable units, but simply are results of the process of recognizing the incoming patterns.

What do we know for certain? (1) The results of seeing and hearing enter the information-processing sequence as sensory-oriented signals. (This is true by definition.) (2) The lexicon and the semantic space of language are independent of sensory modality. (This is true by acclamation. It follows from logic, and no one has seriously ever entertained the notion that we have entirely independent meaning systems based upon the sensory system through which that meaning was originally acquired. The fact that we can or cannot remember the sensory modality in which linguistic material was presented is irrelevant to this discussion.) (3) The internal processing language is organized around a representation that is either (a) input oriented (e.g., a sensory representation, such as acoustical); (b) output oriented (a motor representation, such as articulatory); (c) abstract (i.e., anything else); (d) all, some, or none of the above.

Moreover, we know that language cannot be understood by interpreting each word or phrase as it arrives. For example, whenever one wishes to, against all the rules of good grammar and against the protests of cranky editors, split an infinitive, then, as in the example given within this sentence, all the words in the phrase between "to" and "split" must be temporarily shunted aside in a storage location so that the processing of the main theme of the sentence can continue without disruption.

It is an interesting exercise to perform a memory analysis of written English. To do this, one simply analyzes written sentences word by word, shunting aside to memory locations words that cannot yet be interpreted but that must wait for later parts of the sentence. Such an analysis not only shows the great importance of short-term memory in such activity, but also tends to indicate, against all better instincts, that many of the "arbitrary" rules of grammar are in actuality quite sensible: the rules of good grammar tend to minimize the load on short-term memory.

If one is to take Fillmore's [1968, 1969] case grammar at all seriously, then the process of understanding sentences is in large part simply that of identifying the action and the role of the various actors and locations of that action. One can view sentences as descriptions of scenarios, and the problem of the listener or reader is to fit together all the various pieces. (I steal this abbreviated and simplistic description from Rumelhart, Lindsay et al. [1972].)

Consider hearing or reading the sentence

The boy was bitten by the . . .

Bite, in *my* meaning-store, is defined as an action which requires an animate actor (agent), an object to be bitten, and a time and place. The instrument of the action is obligatorily required to be *mouth.* With the sentence received so far, the animate actor is missing. What one does in the processing of language is to attempt to put together the pieces, so that in this case the animate actor is missing, and it must be discovered. If the next few words in the sentence are *big ferocious,* then things must be stored away temporarily until the actor is completed. Things must be held in the storage until finally the proper word *butterfly* is received. Then things are finished.

Most of the linguistic rules of language seem designed to help the receiver determine the relationships of the parts of the sentence to the scenario. Different languages symbolize the cases differently, but the problem of communication remains much the same: the speaker or writer of a language has a complex, multidimensional representation he wishes to communicate. He must translate this into a sequential string of words or symbols. He must do this in such a way that makes it possible for the receiver of the language to reconstruct an internal image that is in some way isomorphic to the structure of the originator of the communication. And, in most languages (with the apparent exception of literary German), he must do this with the assumption that the reader makes only one pass at the sentence. Thus, the receiver of the communication must rely heavily upon his temporary memory capacities in order to decode the sentence properly.

One can argue that the skilled reader simply forms a scenario and uses the printed page primarily as a check on his ideas. Thus, he need not see every word, rather only a sufficient number. (See Hochberg and Brooks [1970] for a more complete development of this idea.)

Now what do we know of memory? We know there must be several different kinds. There must be a long-term memory capable of storing information from all sensory modalities, as well as storing the results of the thought processes, material that is entirely self-generated and need not have any sensory representation. It would appear that the very action of each sensory transducer itself provides a brief, transient memory. Thus, there already appears strong evidence for acoustical memories (with time constants on the order of 60 milliseconds), visual memories, and tactile memories. These short-lived memories would appear to be useful in the extraction of physical parameters of incoming signals, and would also appear to be completely automatic in their function, completely unalterable by conscious processing demands. There appears to be short-term memory (STM), a system that seems capable of holding some five to seven items. This memory appears to be a true, working memory. Material can be inserted within it at will, and its contents are readily accessible. (There is no evidence for deliberate erasure, but deliberate lack of rehearsal of particular items can cause their rapid decay.)

Now comes the unknown question. In what format must material in STM be represented? The vast evidence on acoustic confusions indicates that much linguistic material, whether presented auditorily or not, is represented in some format closely related to the articulatory or acoustical representation of language. But clearly we can also retain temporarily, imagine, and rehearse nonauditory images. The feel of motor movements stays with us a while after those movements have been completed; visual images can be retained indefinitely by active "rehearsal" of those images, as well as by deliberate imaging. Posner, Lewis, and Conrad, in their paper, show how useful these images can be in certain experimental tasks. Do these other memories require separate short-term memories, or are they part of the same processing system? The answer is not yet known, but the evidence seems to be piling up that visual memories do not much interfere with acoustical ones. Is this because there are separate memories for each sensory modality, or simply because, within a given single memory, memories from different modalities are dissimilar to one another, and hence interfere with each other but little? Of these various memories we know little, except that they are there and that they appear to be necessary.

The Necessity for Memory

Anyone who seriously studies the steps necessary to understand visual images, written or spoken speech, or the semantic content of sentences soon realizes the enormous complexity of the task. These steps always require many different temporary memory buffers. Yet psychologists, studying the one device known to be capable of doing all these things, seem incredibly naive in their description of the requisite machinery. It would seem quite logical that for each sensory system there be a sensory-oriented storage, and then, after the first stages of the sensory analysis have been performed, another memory to store the results of that analysis, and then eventually a common memory, one much more flexible and versatile in its operations, the one we normally call STM. The main distinctions among these memories would result from the fact that STM is accessible to inputs either from internally generated signals or from sensorily generated signals. It would be capable of maintenance of its items through rehearsal, and it would serve as a working memory in the processing of information. This STM most likely exists for all sensory modalities and for the thought processes as well. Whether this is done through separate STM's or through one versatile one is simply not known.

What Crowder appears to have done for us is to provide evidence for one of these intermediate memories, one that receives automatically the results of acoustical inputs. The evidence he presents suggests that this memory system contains information that has already been analyzed to some extent, for all attributes of sensory signals are not stored equally. But it would not appear to be under conscious control, hence it cannot be the normal STM of which we have talked so much.

Understanding a Message

What does it take to understand a written linguistic message? Clearly, whatever steps of linguistic operations take place at the level of the deep structure or semantic component of the material, the analysis must start with the physical features. Somehow, the physical symbols that make up each printed word must get interpreted into the proper linguistic units. Whatever sense is made out of a language input, that sense must be the same whether the input be heard or read. On this one point, everyone agrees. The meaningful component of language is completely isolated from the physical aspects of the signals that are used to communicate that language. Now, it is clear that the analysis of semantic aspects of language is a complex process. Psychologists have just barely begun the study of semantic memory, and the few psychologically oriented approaches have all been reasonably unsuccessful, despite their enormous complexity (for example, see Collins and Quillian [1972]; Rumelhart, Lindsay et al. [1972]). Only one existing system seems near the target of being able to decipher English sentences [Winograd 1972]. Yet, despite the complexity of semantics, the human decodes linguistic material with great rapidity. The persuasive arguments put forth to support a system of decoding by means of an analysis-by-synthesis require that the meaning of the physical input be determined simultaneously with the decoding of the symbols that comprise that input, for the two aspects of decoding and understanding cannot be separated from one another.

Given the vast complexity of the semantically based component of language, we clearly must have some efficient method of allowing sensory input to get access to the lexical components represented by that input. A number of us in the past have suggested that the sensory input itself helps determine the memory location of the lexical component of that input, at least to a rough approximation [see Hunt 1971; Norman 1968]. Presumably, given this first rough analysis, a process of analysis-by-synthesis works to refine the decoding further, until the result is sufficiently precise to enable the understanding of the input. If this is so, then the lexicon of language is organized, in part, around the sensory features used to communicate the morphemes of language. But which sensory representation? Visual? Auditory?

The normal child learns to understand spoken language before he learns to read. Therefore, given this historical quirk, it is natural to assume that the lexical material is organized around acoustical features of language. This being the case, what would be more natural to assume than the statement that reading takes place by first translating (mentally) the printed word into its spoken sounds, and then letting the acoustical representation be translated exactly the same way as speech that is heard would be translated. This scheme has a certain amount of common sense to it, and is in fact discussed by a number of the papers in this symposium. Although it is a scheme that I myself have viewed with favor in the past, I note several difficulties with it at this time. Aside from statements about the rapidity with which visual material can be read, as well as the evidence about the distinctions between subvocalized "inner speech" used while reading and real speech, it is not clear to me exactly how one encodes printed matter into auditory material without taking note of the meaning of that material. The argument has been given at length in this symposium, so I will not repeat it here (although the reader should be warned that no real resolution of that argument was reached by us).

Pronouncing a word may be a useful way of determining its meaning, especially with novel words, but it would not appear to be necessary. A better argument for the necessity of internally "saying" printed words to oneself would seem to come from the arguments of Conrad and Crowder on the relative efficiency and long life of acoustical short-term memory stores over their visual equivalents. [See also Hochberg and Brooks 1970, and Venezky and Calfee 1970]

Understanding Speech

What is the process for decoding speech? All sensible analyses of process realize that several different stages are necessary. And at each stage, there must be a temporary storage buffer to help out in the decoding process—to give time to detect stress patterns, to give time to reanalyze (back up) when necessary, and in analysis-by-synthesis system (ABS), to give time for iterations.

Let me examine briefly the ABS system, in particular the diagram presented by Cooper as his Figure 5. This diagram is misleading for two reasons. First, it does not sufficiently emphasize the initial analysis of the signal—an analysis that may be sufficiently complete to unambiguously encode some utterances. Another way of putting it is that the first loop in the model need not be a loop: iteration may not be necessary to decode incoming acoustic waveform into some basic features. After all, the cochlea lays out acoustic waveform into a rough frequency space—the frequencies are spread over a spatial layout of some 25,000 neurons—although in the speech region, information is probably conveyed by periodicity of neural firing. In the auditory cortex of the cat there exist frequency glide detectors, on-off, and frequency specific detectors [see Whitfield 1967]. Second, the diagram for the ABS system stops too soon. There must be further stages—at the very least, a place where all the sentence parts can be pieced together.

But aside from my minor surgery, look' at the memory requirements: four memories—three shown explicitly, one assumed.

1. Stage 1 Memory—memory for the acoustic waveform itself.

2. Stage 2 Memory—memory for linguistic features, be they acoustic, articulatory, or whatever.

3. Stage 3 Memory—memory for the decoded waveform.

4. A large capacity, more permanent memory that contains semantic-phonetic–lexical information, and in the words of Phil Gough, is PWSGWTAU, the "Place Where Sentences Go When They Are Understood."

Identifying the Memories

Now, what about these memories?

Stage 1. This would appear to be a sensory waveform, an SIS. We know of one in vision—the VSTM. I tend to believe that this is the memory tapped by Moray and Crowder's 4- and 3-Eared Man experiments. These studies, along with studies on memory for pitch and temporal sequence, imply a tape-recorder memory: just what is needed.

Is such a memory possible? I know of no neurological evidence. But Cooper and I have estimated the capacity of the sensory store must range from some 1,000 to 60,000 bits for one second's worth, depending upon fidelity desired. Even 60,000 bits is not very much, for each of the 25,000 neurons in the basilar membrane need only have a memory store for a few bits.

I realize that this assessment disagrees with that put forth by Crowder. But he has failed to demonstrate that the memory illustrated by his 3-Eared Man (his Figure 3) is the same as PAS. To do this, he needs to repeat the experiment, adding a sound just after the minilist. If it is a tape recorder, any sound will interfere with the memory. If it is PAS, only vowel-like sounds will interfere.

Stage 2. Here I put PAS. All the properties of PAS seem remarkably consistent with properties of selective attention. But look at what is going on in loop 2: a synthesis of the incoming message at a feature level. Suppose only one such "stream of synthesis" can be done at any one time. Look at the properties one would expect of material that undergoes processing in this stage: in brief, the more dissimilar the features to the synthesized loop, the less likely it is to get into or last in that stage. That is sufficient, in my opinion. I won't bore you with predictions, but all one needs is (1) an analysis and a memory for features; (2) an analysis of all speech-like sounds that match the synthesized signal physically; (3) an analysis of all meaningful sounds consistent with the stream being analyzed, even if not physically similar. All the properties of both the attention literature and of PAS drop out.

Stage 3. The normal STM or primary memory so well studied by psychologists, complete with limited capacity and chunking and acoustic confusions. This is the first memory which is conscious, which allows selective rehearsal and conscious examination and manipulation of its contents.

Stage 4. LTM or secondary memory lies beyond the realm of this discussion. This is unfortunate, for herein are many of the important properties of the language analysis system. But we simply do not know enough about this memory to help yet. It is on this topic that I expect the most important developments in the next few years to come.

References

Bryden, M. P., 1971. Attentional strategies and short-term memory in dichotic listening. *Cog. Psych.* 2:99–116.

Collins, A. M., and M. R. Quillian, 1972. How to make a language user. In *Organization and Memory,* E. Tulving and W. Donaldson (eds.), New York: Academic Press.

Corballis, M. C., and L. Luthe, 1971. Two channel visual memory. *Perception and Psychophysics* 9:361–367.

Fillmore, C. J., 1968. The case for case. In *Universals in Linguistic Theory,* E. Bach and R. T. Harms (eds.), New York: Holt, Rinehart and Winston.

———, 1969. Toward a modern theory of case. In *Modern Studies in English,* D. A. Reibel and S. A. Schane (eds.), Englewood Cliffs, N.J.: Prentice-Hall.

Glucksberg, S., and G. N. Cowen, Jr., 1970. Memory for nonattended auditory material. *Cog. Psych.* 1:149–156.

Hochberg, J., and V. Brooks, 1970. Reading as an intentional behavior. In *Theoretical Models and Processes of Reading,* H. Singer and R. B. Ruddell (eds.), Newark, Del: International Reading Association.

Hunt, E., 1971. What kind of computer is man? *Cog. Psych.* 2:57–98.

Norman, D. A., 1968. Toward a theory of memory and attention. *Psych. Rev.* 75:722–536.

———, 1969a. Memory while shadowing. *Quart. J. Exp. Psych.* 21:85–93.

———, 1969b. *Memory and Attention.* New York: Wiley.

Rumelhart, D. E., P. H. Lindsay, and D. A. Norman, 1972. A process model for long-term memory. In *Organization and Memory,* E. Tulving and W. Donaldson (eds.), New York: Academic Press.

Shallice, T., and E. K. Warrington, 1970. Independent functioning of verbal memory stores: A neuropsychological study. *Quart. J. Exp. Psych.* 22:261–273.

Singer, H., and R. B. Ruddell (eds.), 1970. *Theoretical Models and Processes of Reading.* Newark, Del.: International Reading Association.

Treisman, A. M., 1969. Strategies and models of selective attention. *Psych. Rev.* 76:282–299.

Venezky, R. L., and R. C. Calfee, 1970. The reading competency model. In *Theoretical Models and Processes of Reading,* H. Singer and R. B. Ruddell (eds.), Newark, Del.: International Reading Association.

Warrington, E. K., and T. Shallice, 1969. The selective impairment of auditory verbal short-term memory. *Brain* 92:885–896.

Warrington, E. K., and T. Shallice, in preparation. The independence of auditory and visual short-term memory.

Warrington, E. K., and L. Weiskrantz, 1972. An analysis of short-term and long-term memory defects in man. In *Physiological Basis of Memory,* J. A. Deutsch (ed.), New York: Academic Press.

Whitfield, I. C., 1967. *The Auditory Pathway.* London: Arnold.

Winograd, T., 1972. Understanding natural language. *Cog. Psych.* 3:1–191.

General Discussion of Papers by Crowder and Norman

Crowder said that he was in complete agreement with Norman's discussion, except that he would like to believe that the memory in the three-eared man experiment was PAS. He would like to show that the variables that affected the suffix phenomenon also affected the three-eared man's ability to select the required stimulus. An experiment with the three-eared man using stop consonants might help to answer the question. If the two memories are the same, presentation of [b], [d], or [g] at the three ears should show no advantage of partial report over whole report, while if the three-eared man is behaving like a tape recorder, partial report should show some advantage.

Miller said that he was not dismayed by the number of memories or storage buffers hypothesized by students of information processing. A storage buffer is like a mailbox, and he would expect the nervous system to be full of buffers, just as the country is filled with mailboxes.

Halle remarked that PAS had the attributes of a speaker-identification device. This suggestion appealed to Crowder, who recalled Ladefoged and Broadbent's [1957] experiment, which demonstrated that judgments of vowel quality can be biased by the apparent vowel space of the speaker of a sentence preceding the test vowel; and that the effect varies inversely with the duration of the interval between the context sentence and the test vowel.

Liberman said that PAS would be necessary in order to retain over the span of a breath-group the information needed to interpret stress and intonation.

Responding to a question from Conrad, Crowder said that the subject in the suffix experiments did not learn to ignore the suffix: the suffix effect was, if anything, stronger after five days of testing.

Reference
Ladefoged, P., and D. E. Broadbent, 1957. Information conveyed by vowels. *J. Acoust. Soc. Amer.*, 29:98–104.

PART III

Problems Peculiar to Learning to Read

DONALD SHANKWEILER AND ISABELLE Y. LIBERMAN

Misreading: A Search for Causes

Because speech is universal and reading is not, we may suppose that the latter is more difficult and less natural. Indeed, we know that a large part of the early education of the school child must be devoted to instruction in reading and that the instruction often fails, even in the most favorable circumstances. Judging from the long history of debate concerning the proper methods of teaching children to read [Mathews 1966], the problem has always been with us. Nor do we appear to have come closer to a solution: we are still a long way from understanding how children learn to read and what has gone wrong when they fail.

Since the child already speaks and understands his language at the time that reading instruction begins, the problem is to discover the major barriers in learning to perceive language by eye. It is clear that the first requirement for reading is that the child be able to segregate the letter segments and identify them with accuracy and speed. Some children undoubtedly do fail to learn to recognize letters and are unable to pass on to succeeding stages of learning to read; but, as we shall see, there are strong reasons for believing that the principal barriers for most children are not at the point of visual identification of letter shapes. There is no general agreement, however, about the succeeding stages of learning to read, their time course, and the nature of their special difficulties. In order to understand reading and compare it with speech, we need to look closely at the kinds of difficulties the child has when he starts to read, that is, his misreadings, and ask how these differ from errors in repeating speech perceived by ear. In this way, we may begin to grasp why the link between alphabet and speech is difficult.

In the extensive literature about reading since the 1890s there have been sporadic surges of interest in the examination of oral reading errors as a means of studying the process of reading acquisition. The history of this topic has been well summarized by Weber [1968], so need not be repeated here. We ourselves set out in many directions when we began our pursuit of errors and we regard our work as essentially exploratory. If we break new ground, it is not by our interest in error patterns nor even in many of our actual findings, but rather in the questions we are asking about them.

Much of the most recent research on reading errors has examined the child's oral reading of connected text [Goodman 1965, 1968; Schale 1966; Weber 1968; Christenson 1969; Biemiller 1970]. The major emphasis of these studies is therefore on levels beyond the word, though they are concerned to some extent with errors within words. None of these investigations asks what we believe to be a basic question: whether the major barrier to reading acquisition is indeed in reading connected text or whether it may be instead in dealing with words and their components.

We are, in addition, curious to know whether the difficulties in reading are to be found at a visual stage or at a subsequent linguistic stage of the process. This requires us to consider the special case of reversal errors, in which optical considerations are, on the face of it, primary. Our inquiry into linguistic aspects of reading errors then leads us to ask which constituents of words tend to be misread, and whether the same ones tend to be misheard. We examine errors with regard to the position of the constituent segments within the word and the linguistic status of the segments in an attempt to produce a coherent account of the possible causes of the error pattern in reading.

We think that all the questions we have outlined can be approached most profitably by studying children who are a little beyond the earliest stages of reading instruction. For this reason, we have avoided the first grade and focused, in most of our work, on children of the second and third grades of the elementary school. Though some of the children at this level are well on their way to becoming fluent in reading, a considerable proportion are still floundering and thus provide a sizeable body of errors for examination.

The Word as the Locus of Difficulty in Beginning Reading
One often encounters the claim that there are many children who can read individual words well yet do not seem able to comprehend connected text [Anderson and Dearborn 1952; Goodman 1968]. The existence of such children is taken to support the view that methods of instruction that stress spelling-to-sound correspondences and other aspects of decoding are insufficient and may even produce mechanical readers who are expert at decoding but fail to comprehend sentences. It may well be that such children do exist; if so, they merit careful study. Our experience suggests that the problem is rare, and that poor reading of text with little comprehension among beginning readers is usually a consequence of reading words poorly (i.e., with many errors and/or at a slow rate).

Table 1
Correlation of Performance of School Children on Reading Lists* and Paragraph
Fluency as Measured by the Gray Oral Reading Test

Group	n	Grade	List 1	List 2
A	20	2.8	0.72	—†
B	18	3.0	0.77	—†
C	30	3.8	0.53	0.55
D	20	4.8	0.77	—†

* The correlation between the two lists was 0.73.
† No data available.

Table 2
Reading List 1: Containing Reversible Words, Reversible Letters, and Primer Sight
Words

1. of	21. two	41. bat
2. boy	22. war	42. tug
3. now	23. bed	43. form
4. tap	24. felt	44. left
5. dog	25. big	45. bay
6. lap	26. not	46. how
7. tub	27. yam	47. dip
8. day	28. peg	48. no
9. for	29. was	49. pit
10. bad	30. tab	50. cap
11. out	31. won	51. god
12. pat	32. pot	52. top
13. ten	33. net	53. pal
14. gut	34. pin	54. may
15. cab	35. from	55. bet
16. pit	36. ton	56. raw
17. saw	37. but	57. pay
18. get	38. who	58. tar
19. rat	39. nip	59. dab
20. dig	40. on	60. tip

The purpose of our first experiment was to investigate whether the main source of difficulty in beginning reading is at the level of connected text or at the word level. We wished to know how well one can predict a child's degree of fluency in oral reading of paragraph material from his performance (accuracy and reaction time) on selected words presented in lists.

Table 1 shows correlations between a conventional measure of fluency in oral reading, the Gray Oral Reading Test, and oral reading performance on two words lists that we devised. The Gray test consists of paragraphs of graded difficulty that yield a composite score based on time and error from which may be determined the child's reading grade level. Both word lists, which are presented as Tables 2 and 3, contain monosyllabic words. Word List 1 (Table 2) was designed primarily to study the effects of optically based ambiguity on the error pattern in reading. It consists of a number of primer words and a number of reversible words from which other words may be formed by reading from right to left. List 2 (Table 3) contains words representing equal frequencies of many of the phonemes of English and was designed specifically to make the comparison between reading and perceiving speech by ear. Data from both lists were obtained from some subjects; others received one test but not the other. Error analysis of these lists was based on phonetic transcription of the responses, and the error counts take the phoneme as the unit.[1] Our selection of this method of treating that data is explained and the procedures are described in a later section.

In Table 1, then, we see the correlations between the Gray Test and one or both lists for four groups of school children, all of average or above-average intelligence: Group A, 20 second-grade boys (grade 2.8); Group B, 18 third-grade children who comprised the lower third of their school class in reading level (grade 3.0); Group C, an entire class

---

[1] Our method of analysis of errors does not make any hard and fast assumptions about the size of the perceptual unit in reading. Much research on the reading process has been concerned with this problem [Huey 1908; Woodworth 1938; Gough this volume]. Speculations have been based, for the most part, on studies of the fluent adult reader, but these studies have, nevertheless, greatly influenced theories of the acquisition of reading and views on how children should be taught (Fries 1962; Mathews 1966). In our view, this has had unfortunate consequences. Analysis of a well-practiced skill does not automatically reveal the stages of its acquisition, their order and special difficulties. It may be that the skilled reader does not (at all times) proceed letter by letter or even word by word, but at some stage in learning to read, the beginner probably must take account of each individual letter (Hochberg 1970).

Table 3
Reading List 2: Presenting Equal Opportunities for Error on Each Initial Consonant,* Medial Vowel, and Final Consonant*

help	teethe	than	jots	thus
pledge	stoops	dab	shoots	smelt
weave	bilk	choose	with	nudge
lips	hulk	thong	noose	welt
wreath	jog	puts	chin	chops
felt	shook	hood	rob	vim
zest	plume	fun	plot	vet
crisp	thatch	sting	book	zip
touch	zig	knelt	milk	plop
palp	teeth	please	vest	smug
stash	moot	this	give	foot
niece	foot's	that	then	chest
soothe	jeeps	dub	plug	should
ding	leave	vast	knob	clots
that's	van	clash	cook	rasp
mesh	cheese	soot	love	shops
deep	vets	sheath	posh	pulp
badge	loops	stop	lisp	wedge
belk	pooch	cob	nest	hatch
gulp	mash	zen	sulk	says
stilt	scalp	push	zips	watch
zag	thud	cleave	would	kelp
reach	booth	mops	tube	sheathe
stock	wreathe	hasp	chap	bush
thief	gasp	them	put	juice
coop	smoothe	good	rook	thieve
theme	feast	fuzz	loom	chaff
cult	jest	smith	judge	stuff
stood	chief	tots	breathe	seethe
these	god	such	whelp	gin
vat	clang	veldt	smash	zoom
hoof	dune	culp	zing	cliff
clog	wasp	wisp	could	plod
move	heath	guest	mob	rough
puss	tooth	bulk	clasp	nook
doom	lodge	silk	smudge	dodge
talc	jam	moose	kilt	thug
shoes	roof	smut	thing	cling
smooch	gap	soup	fog	news
hook	shove	fez	death	look
took	plebe	bing	goose	

* Consonant clusters are counted as one phoneme.

of 30 third-grade boys and girls (grade 3.8) ; Group D, 20 fourth-grade boys (grade 4.8).[2]

It is seen from Table 1 that for a variety of children in the early grades, there is a moderate-to-high relationship between errors on the word lists and performance on the Gray paragraphs.[3] We would expect to find a degree of correlation between reading words and reading paragraphs (because the former are contained in the latter), but not correlations as high as the ones we did find if it were the case that many children can read words fluently but cannot deal effectively with organized strings of words. These correlations suggest that the child may encounter his major difficulty at the level of the word—his reading of connected text tends to be only as good or as poor as his reading of individual words. Put another way, the problems of the beginning reader appear to have more to do with the synthesis of syllables than with scanning of larger chunks of connected text.

This conclusion is further supported by the results of a direct comparison of rate of scan in good- and poor-reading children by Katz and Wicklund [1971] at the University of Connecticut. Using an adaptation of the reaction-time method of Sternberg [1967], they found that both good and poor readers require 100 msec longer to scan a three-word sentence than a two-word sentence. Although as one would expect, the poor readers were slower in reaction time than the good readers, the difference between good and poor readers remained constant as the length of the sentence was varied. (The comparison has so far been made for sentence lengths up to five words and the same result has been found: D. A. Wicklund, personal communication). This suggests, in agreement with our findings, that good and poor readers among young children differ not in scanning rate or strategy, but in their ability to deal with individual words and syllables.

As a further way of examining the relation between the rate of reading individual words and other aspects of reading performance, we obtained latency measures (reaction times) for the words in List 2 for one group of third graders (Group C, Table 1). The data show a negative correla-

[2] We are indebted to Charles Orlando, Pennsylvania State University, for the data in Groups A and D. These two groups comprised his subjects for a doctoral dissertation written when he was a student at the University of Connecticut (Orlando 1971).

[3] A similarly high degree of relationship between performance on word lists and paragraphs has been an incidental finding in many studies. Jastak [1946] in his manual for the first edition of the Wide Range Achievement Test notes a correlation of 0.81 for his word list and the New Stanford Paragraph Reading Test. Spache [1963] cites a similar result in correlating performance on a word recognition list and paragraphs.

tion of 0.68 between latency of response and accuracy on the word list. We then compared performance on connected text (the Gray paragraphs) and on the words of List 2, and we found that latency measures and error counts showed an equal degree of (negative) correlation with paragraph reading performance. From this, it would appear that the slow rate of reading individual words may contribute as much as inaccuracy to poor performance on paragraphs. A possible explanation may be found in the rapid temporal decay in primary memory: if it takes too long to read a given word, the preceding words will have been forgotten before a phrase or sentence is completed [Gough, this volume].

The Contribution of Visual Factors to the Error Pattern in Beginning Reading: The Problem of Reversals

We have seen that a number of converging results support the belief that the primary locus of difficulty in beginning reading is the word. But within the word, what is the nature of the difficulty? To what extent are the problems visual and to what extent linguistic?

In considering this question, we asked first whether the problem is in the perception of individual letters. There is considerable agreement that after the first grade, even those children who have made little further progress in learning to read do not have significant difficulty in visual identification of individual letters [Vernon 1960; Shankweiler 1964; Doehring 1968].

REVERSALS AND OPTICAL SHAPE PERCEPTION

The occurrence in the alphabet of reversible letters may present special problems, however. The tendency for young children to confuse letters of similar shape that differ in orientation (such as "b, d, p, q") is well known. Gibson and her colleagues [1962, 1965] have isolated a number of component abilities in letter identification and studied their developmental course by the use of letter-like forms that incorporate basic features of the alphabet. They find that children do not readily distinguish pairs of shapes that are 180-degree transformations (i.e., reversals) of each other at age 5 or 6, but by age 7 or 8, orientation has become a distinctive property of the optical character. It is of interest, therefore, to investigate how much reversible letters contribute to the error pattern of 8-year-old children who are having reading difficulties.

Reversal of the direction of letter sequences (e.g., reading "from" for "form") is another phenomenon that is usually considered to be intrinsically related to orientation reversal. Both types of reversals are often thought to be indicative of a disturbance in the visual directional scan of print in children with reading disability (see Benton [1962] for a comprehensive review of the relevant research). One early investigator considered reversal phenomena to be so central to the problems in reading that he used the term "strephosymbolia" to designate specific reading disability [Orton 1925]. We should ask, then, whether reversals of letter orientation and sequence loom large as obstacles to learning to read. Do they covary in their occurrence, and what is the relative significance of the optical and linguistic components of the problem?

In an attempt to study these questions [I. Y. Liberman, Shankweiler et al. 1971] we devised the list (presented in Table 2) of 60 real-word monosyllables including most of the commonly cited reversible words and in addition a selection of words which provide ample opportunity for reversing letter orientation. Each word was printed in manuscript form on a separate $3'' \times 5''$ card. The child's task was to read each word aloud. He was encouraged to sound out the word and to guess if unsure. The responses were recorded by the examiner and also on magnetic tape. They were later analyzed for initial and final consonant errors, vowel errors, and reversals of letter sequence and orientation.

We gave List 1 twice to an entire beginning third-grade class and then selected for intensive study the 18 poorest readers in the class (the lower third), because only among these did reversals occur in significant quantity.

RELATIONSHIPS BETWEEN REVERSALS AND OTHER TYPES OF ERRORS
It was found that, even among these poor readers, reversals accounted for only a small proportion of the total error, though the list was constructed to provide maximum opportunity for reversals to occur. Separating the two types, we found that sequence reversals accounted for 15 percent of the total errors made, and orientation errors only 10 percent, whereas other consonant errors accounted for 32 percent of the total and vowel errors 43 percent. Moreover, individual differences in reversal tendency were large (rates of sequence reversal ranged from 4 to 19 percent; rates for orientation reversal ranged from 3 to 31 percent). Viewed in terms of opportunities for error, orientation errors occurred less frequently than other consonant errors. Test-retest comparisons showed that whereas other reading errors were rather stable, reversals—and particularly orientation reversals—were unstable.

Reversals were not, then, a constant portion of all errors; moreover, only certain poor readers reversed appreciably, and then not consistently. Though in the poor readers we have studied, reversals are apparently not of great importance, it may be that they loom larger in importance in certain children with particularly severe and persisting reading disability. Our present data do not speak to this question. We are beginning to explore other differences between children who do and do not have reversal problems.

ORIENTATION REVERSALS AND REVERSALS OF SEQUENCES:
NO COMMON CAUSE?

Having considered the two types of reversals separately, we find no support for assuming that they have a common cause in children with reading problems. Among the poor third-grade readers, sequence reversal and orientation reversal were found to be wholly uncorrelated with each other, whereas vowel and consonant errors correlated 0.73. A further indication of the lack of equivalence of the two types of reversals is that each correlated quite differently with the other error measures. It is of interest to note that sequence reversals correlated significantly with other consonant errors, with vowel errors, and with performance on the Gray paragraphs, while none of these was correlated with orientation reversals (see I. Liberman, Shankweiler et al. [1971] for a more complete account of these findings).

ORIENTATION ERRORS: VISUAL OR PHONETIC?

In further pursuing the orientation errors, we examined the nature of the substitutions among the reversible letters "b, d, p, g."[4] Tabulation of these showed that the possibility of generating another letter by a ·simple 180-degree transformation is indeed a relevant factor in producing the confusions among these letters. This is, of course, in agreement with the conclusions reached by Gibson and her colleagues [1962].

At the same time, other observations [I. Y. Liberman, Shankweiler et al. 1971] indicate that letter reversals may be a symptom and not a cause of reading difficulty. Two observations suggest this conclusion: first, confusions among reversible letters occurred much less frequently for these same children when the letters were presented singly, even when only briefly exposed in tachistoscopic administration. If visual factors were primary, we would expect that tachistoscopic exposure would

---

[4] The letter g is, of course, a distinctive shape in all type styles, but it was included among the reversible letters because, historically it has been treated as one. It indeed becomes reversible when hand printed with a straight segment below the line. Even in manuscript printing, as was used in preparing the materials for this study, the "tail" of the g is the only distinguishing characteristic. The letter q was not used because it occurs only in a stereotyped spelling pattern (u always following q in English words).

Table 4
Confusions Among Reversible Letters. Percentages Based on Opportunities*

Presented	Obtained				Total Reversals	Other Errors
	b	d	p	q		
b	—	10.2	13.7	0.3	24.2	5.3
d	10.1	—	1.7	0.3	12.1	5.2
p	9.1	0.4	—	0.7	10.2	6.9
g	1.3	1.3	1.3	—	3.9	13.3

* Adapted from I. Y. Liberman, Shankweiler et al., *Cortex*, 1971.

have resulted in more errors, not fewer. Second, the confusions among the letters during word reading were not symmetrical: as can be seen from Table 4, "b" is often confused with "p" as well as with "d," whereas "d" tends to be confused with "b" and almost never with "p."[5]

These findings point to the conclusion that the characteristic of optical reversibility is not a sufficient condition for the errors that are made in reading, at least among children beyond the first grade. Because the letter shapes represent segments that form part of the linguistic code, their perception differs in important ways from the perception of nonlinguistic forms—there is more to the perception of the letters in words than their shape (see Kolers [1970] for a general discussion of this point).

READING REVERSALS AND POORLY ESTABLISHED CEREBRAL DOMINANCE

S. T. Orton [1925, 1937] was one of the first to assume a causal connection between reversal tendency and cerebral ambilaterality as manifested

---

[5] The pattern of confusions among "b, d, p" could nevertheless be explained on a visual basis. It could be argued that the greater error rate on "b" than on "d" or "p" may result from the fact that *b* offers two opportunities to make a single 180-degree transformation, whereas "d" and "p" offer only one. Against this interpretation we can cite further data. We had also presented to the same chilren a list of pronounceable nonsense syllables. Here the distribution of "b" errors was different from that which had been obtained with real words, in that "b–p" confusions occurred only rarely. The children, moreover, tended to err by converting a nonsense syllable into a word, just as in their errors on the real word lists they nearly always produced words. For this reason, a check was made of the number of real words that could be made by reversing "b" in the two lists. This revealed no fewer opportunities to make words by substitution of "p" than by substitution of "d." Indeed, the reverse was the case. Such a finding lends further support to the conclusion that the nature of substitutions even among reversible letters is not an automatic consequence of the property of optical reversibility. (This conclusion was also reached by Kolers and Perkins [1969] from a different analysis of the orientation problem.)

by poorly established motor preferences. There is some clinical evidence that backward readers tend to have weak, mixed, or inconsistent hand preferences or lateral inconsistencies between the preferred hand, foot, and eye [Zangwill 1960]. Although it is doubtful that a strong case can be made for the specific association between cerebral ambilaterality and the tendency to reverse letters and letter sequences [I. Y. Liberman, Shankweiler et al., 1971], the possibility that there is some connection between individual differences in lateralization of function and reading disability is supported by much clinical opinion. This idea has remained controversial because, due to various difficulties, its implications could not be fully explored and tested.

It has only recently become possible to investigate the question experimentally by some means other than the determination of handedness, eyedness, and footedness. Auditory rivalry techniques provide a more satisfactory way than hand preferences of assessing hemispheric dominance for speech [Kimura 1961, 1967].[6] We follow several investigators in the use of these dichotic techniques for assessing individual differences in hemispheric specialization for speech in relation to reading ability [Kimura, personal communication; Sparrow 1968; Zurif and Carson 1970; Bryden 1970]. The findings of these studies as well as our own pilot work have been largely negative. It is fair to say that an association between bilateral organization of speech and poor reading has not been well supported to date.

The relationship we are seeking may well be more complex, however. Orton [1937] stressed that inconsistent lateralization for speech and motor functions is of special significance in diagnosis, and a recent finding of Bryden [1970] is of great interest in this regard. He found that boys with speech and motor functions oppositely lateralized have a significantly higher proportion of poor readers than those who show the typical uncrossed pattern. This suggests that it will be worthwhile to look closely at disparity in lateralization of speech and motor function.

If there is some relation between cerebral dominance and ability to read, we should suppose that it might appear most clearly in measures that take account not only of dominance for speech and motor function,

---

[6] There is reason to believe that handedness can be assessed with greater validity by substituting measures of manual dexterity for the usual questionnaire. The relation between measures of handedness and cerebral lateralization of speech, as determined by an auditory rivalry task [Shankweiler and Studdert-Kennedy 1967], was measured by Charles Orlando in a doctoral dissertation done at the University of Connecticut [1971]. Using multiple measures of manual dexterity to assess handedness, and regarding both handedness and cerebral speech laterality as continuously distributed, Orlando found the predictive value of handedness to be high in eight-year-old and ten-year-old children.

but also of dominance for the perception of written language, and very likely with an emphasis on the relationships between them. It is known [Bryden 1965] that alphabetical material is more often recognized correctly when presented singly to the right visual field and hence to the left cerebral hemisphere. If reliable techniques suitable for use with children can be developed for studying lateralization of component processes in reading, we suspect that much more can be learned about reading acquisition in relation to functional asymmetries of the brain.

Linguistic Aspects of the Error Pattern in Reading and Speech

"In reading research, the deep interest in words as visual displays stands in contrast to the relative neglect of written words as linguistic units represented graphically." [Weber 1968, p. 113]

The findings we have discussed in the preceding section suggest that the chief problems the young child encounters in reading words are beyond the stage of visual identification of letters. It therefore seemed profitable to study the error pattern from a linguistic point of view.

THE ERROR PATTERN IN MISREADING

We examined the error rate in reading in relation to segment position in the word (initial, medial, and final) and in relation to the type of segment (consonant or vowel).

List 2 (Table 3) was designed primarily for that purpose. It consisted of 204 real-word CVC (or CCVC and CVCC) monosyllables chosen to give equal representation to most of the consonants, consonant clusters, and vowels of English. Each of the 25 initial consonants and consonant clusters occurred eight times in the list, and each final consonant or consonant cluster likewise occurred eight times. Each of eight vowels occurred approximately 25 times. This characteristic of equal opportunities for error within each constant and vowel category enables us to assess the child's knowledge of some of the spelling patterns of English.

The manner of presentation was the same as for List 1. The responses were recorded and transcribed twice by a phonetically trained person. The few discrepancies between first and second transcription were easily resolved. Although it was designed for a different purpose, List 1 also gives information about the effect of the segment position within the syllable upon error rate and the relative difficulty of different kinds of segments. We therefore analyzed results from both lists in the same way; and as we shall see, the results are highly comparable. A list of

Table 5
Table of Phoneme Segments Represented in the Words of List 2

Initial Consonant(s)	Vowel	Final Consonant(s)
p	a	lp
t	æ	dʒ
k	i	v
b	I	ps
d	ε	θ
g	ʌ	lt
m	ʊ	st
n	u	sp
w		ts
r		ʃ
l		s
f		ð
θ		ŋ
s		p
ʃ		lk
v		g
ð		tʃ
z		k
t		f
d		m
h		d
pl		z
kl		t
st		m
sm		h

Table 6
Errors in Reading in Relation to Position and Type of Segment. Percentages of Opportunities for Error

Group*	Reading Ability	n	Age Range	Initial Consonant	Final Consonant	All Consonant	Vowel
C_1	Good††	11	9–10	6	12	9	10
C_2	Poor††	11	9–10	8	14	11	16
B	Poor†	18	8–10	8	14	11	27
Clinic	Poor††	10	10–12	17	24	20	31

* The groups indicated by C_1 and C_2 comprise the upper and lower thirds of Group C in Table 1. Group B is the same as so designated in Table 1. The clinic group is not represented in Table 1.
† List 1 (Table 2)
†† List 2 (Table 3)

the phoneme segments represented in the words of List 2 is shown in Table 5.

We have chosen to use phonetic transcription[7] rather than standard orthography in noting down the responses, because we believe that phonetic tabulation and analysis of oral reading errors has powerful advantages that outweigh the traditional problems associated with it. If the major sources of error in reading the words are at some linguistic level, as we have argued, phonetic transcription of the responses should greatly simplify the task of detecting the sources of error and making them explicit. Transcription has the additional value of enabling us to make a direct comparison between errors in reading and in oral repetition.

Table 6 shows errors on the two word lists percentaged against opportunities as measured in four groups of schoolchildren. Group C_1 includes good readers, being the upper third in reading ability of all the third graders in a particular school system; Group C_2 comprises the lower third of the same third-grade population mentioned above; Group B includes the lower third of the entire beginning third grade in another school system; the clinic group contains 10 children, aged between 10 and 12, who had been referred to a reading clinic at the University of Connecticut. In all four groups, the responses given were usually words of English.

Table 6 shows two findings we think are important. First, there is a progression of difficulty with position of the segment in the word; final consonants are more frequently misread than initial ones. Second, more errors are made on vowels than on consonants. The consistency

[7] In making the transcription, the transcriber was operating with reference to the normal allophonic ranges of the phonemic categories in English.

of these findings is impressive because it transcends the particular choice of words and perhaps the level of reading ability.[8]

We will have more to say in a later section about these findings when we consider the differences between reading and speech errors. At this point, we should say that the substantially greater error rate for final consonants than for initial ones is certainly contrary to what would be expected by an analysis of the reading process in terms of sequential probabilities. If the child at the early stages of learning to read were able to utilize the constraints that are built into the language, he would make fewer errors at the end than at the beginning, not more. In fact, what we often see is that the child breaks down after he has gotten the first letter correct and can go no further. We will suggest later why this may happen.

MISHEARING DIFFERS FROM MISREADING

In order to understand the error pattern in reading, it should be instructive to compare it with the pattern of errors generated when isolated monosyllables are presented by ear for oral repetition. We were able to make this comparison by having the same group of children repeat back a word list on one occasion and read it on another day. The 10 children in the clinic group (Table 6) were asked to listen to the words in List 2 before they were asked to read them. The tape-recorded words were presented over earphones with instructions to repeat each word once. The responses were recorded on magnetic tape and transcribed in the same way as the reading responses.

The error pattern for oral repetition shows some striking differences from that in reading. With auditory presentation, errors in oral repetition averaged 7 percent when tabulated by phoneme, as compared with 24 percent in reading, and were about equally distributed between initial and final position, rather than being markedly different. Moreover, contrary to what occurred when the list was read, fewer errors occurred on vowels than on consonants.

The relation between errors of oral repetition and reading is demonstrated in another way in the scatter plot presented as Figure 1. Percent error on initial consonants, final consonants, and vowels in reading is plotted on the abscissa against percent error on these segments in oral repetition on the ordinate. Each consonant point is based on approximately eight occurrences in the list over 10 subjects, giving a total of

[8] For similar findings in other research studies employing quite different reading materials and different levels of proficiency in reading; see for example, Daniels and Diack [1956] and Weber [1970].

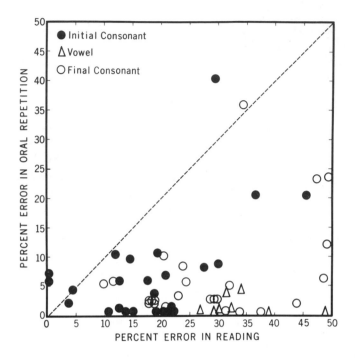

Figure 1. Scatter diagram showing errors on each segment in Word List 2 in relation to opportunities. Percent error in oral repetition is plotted against percent error in reading the same words. Ten subjects.

80. Each vowel point is based on approximately 25 occurrences, giving a total of 250 per point.

It is clear from the figure that the perception of speech by reading has problems which are separate and distinct from the problems of perceiving speech by ear. We cannot predict the error rate for a given phoneme in reading from its error rate in listening. If a phoneme were exactly as difficult to read as to hear, the point would fall on the diagonal line that has been dotted in. Vertical distance from the diagonal to any point below it is a measure of the specific difficulty of reading the phoneme as distinguished from listening to it. Although the reliability of the individual points in the array has not been assessed, the trends are unmistakable. The points are very widely scattered for the consonants. As for the vowels, they are seldom misheard but often misread (suggesting, incidentally, that the high error rate on vowels in reading cannot be an artifact of transcription difficulties).

ACCOUNTING FOR THE DIFFERENCES IN THE ERROR PATTERN
IN READING AND SPEECH

The data presented above show that there are major differences between error patterns in reading and speech. However, they should not be taken to mean that reading and speech are not connected. What they do tell us is that reading presents special problems that reflect the difficulties of the beginning reader in making the link between segments of speech and alphabetic shapes.

WHY THE INITIAL SEGMENT IS MORE OFTEN CORRECT IN READING: We have seen that there is much evidence to indicate that in reading the initial segment of a word is more often correct than succeeding ones, whereas in oral repetition the error rate for initial and final consonants is essentially identical.

One of us [I. Y. Liberman 1971] has suggested a possible explanation for this difference in distribution of errors within the syllable. She pointed out that in reading an alphabetic language like English, the child must be able to segment the words he knows into the phonemic elements that the alphabetic shapes represent. In order to do this, he needs to be consciously aware of the segmentation of the language into units of phonemic size. Seeing the word *cat,* being able to discriminate the individual optical shapes, being able to read the names of the three letters, and even knowing the individual sounds for the three letters, cannot help him in really reading the word (as opposed to memorizing its appearance as a sight word), unless he realizes that the word in his own lexicon has segments. Before he can map the visual message to the word in his vocabulary, he has to be consciously aware that the word *cat* that he knows—an apparently unitary syllable—has three separate segments. His competence in speech production and speech perception is of no direct use to him here, because this competence enables him to achieve the segmentation without ever being consciously aware of it.[9]

Though phonemic segments and their constituent features can be shown to be psychologically and physiologically real in speech perception [A. M. Liberman, Cooper et al. 1967; A. M. Liberman 1968; Mattingly and Liberman 1970] they are, as we have already noted, not necessarily available at a high level of conscious awareness. Indeed, given that the alphabetic method of writing was invented only once, and rather late

---

[9] The idea of "linguistic awareness," as it has been called here, has been a recurrent theme in this conference. See especially the papers included in this volume by Ignatius Mattingly and Harris B. Savin.

in man's linguistic history, we should suspect that the phonologic elements that alphabets represent are not particularly obvious [Huey 1908]. In any event, a child whose chief problem in reading is that he cannot make explicit the phonological structure of his language might be expected to show the pattern of reading errors we found: relatively good success with the initial letters, which requires no further analysis of the syllable and relatively poor performance otherwise.

WHY VOWEL ERRORS ARE MORE FREQUENT IN READING THAN IN SPEECH: Another way that misreading differed from mishearing was with respect to the error rate on vowels, and we must now attempt to account for the diametrically different behavior of the vowels in reading and in oral repetition. (Of course, in the experiments we refer to here, the question is not completely separable from the question of the effect of segment position on error rate, since all vowels were medial.)

In speech, vowels, considered as acoustic signals, are more intense than consonants, and they last longer. Moreover, vowel traces persist in primary memory in auditory form as "echoes." Stop consonants, on the other hand, are decoded almost immediately into an abstract phonetic form, leaving no auditory traces [Fujisaki and Kawashima 1969; Studdert-Kennedy 1970; Crowder, this volume]. At all events, one is not surprised to find that in listening to isolated words, without the benefit of further contextual cues, the consonants are most subject to error. In reading, on the other hand, the vowel is not represented by a stronger signal, vowel graphemes not being larger or having more contrast than consonant ones. Indeed, the vowels tend to suffer a disadvantage because they are usually embedded within the word. They tend, moreover, to have more complex orthographic representation than consonants.[10]

SOURCES OF VOWEL ERROR: ORTHOGRAPHIC RULES OR PHONETIC CONFUSIONS?

The occurrence of substantially more reading errors on vowel segments than on consonant segments has been noted in a number of earlier reports [Venezky 1968; Weber 1970]; and, as we have said, the reason usually given is that vowels are more complexly represented than consonants in English orthography. We now turn to examine the pattern

[10] This generalization applies to English. We do not know how widely it may apply to other languages. We would greatly welcome the appearance of cross-language studies of reading acquisition, which could be of much value in clarifying the relations between reading and linguistic structure. That differences among languages in orthography are related to the incidence of reading failure is often taken for granted, but we are aware of no data that directly bear on this question.

of vowel errors in reading and ask what accounts for their distribution. An explanation in terms of orthography would imply that many vowel errors are traceable to misapplication of rules that involve an indirect relation between letter and sound.[11] Since the complexity of the rules varies for different vowels, it would follow that error rates among them should also vary.

The possibility must be considered, however, that causes other than misapplication of orthographic rules may account for a larger portion of vowel misreadings. First, there could simply be a large element of randomness in the error pattern. Second, the pattern might be nonrandom, but most errors could be phonetically-based rather than rule-based. If reading errors on vowels have a phonetic basis, we should then expect to find the *same* errors occurring in reading as occur in repetition of words presented by ear. The error rate for vowels in oral repetition is much too low in our data to evaluate this possibility, but there are other ways of asking the question, as we will show.

The following analysis illustrates how vowel errors may be analyzed to discover whether, in fact, the error pattern is nonrandom and, if it is, to discover what the major substitutions are. Figure 2 shows a confusion matrix for vowels based on the responses of 11 children at the end of the third grade (Group C_2 in Table 6) who are somewhat retarded in reading. Each row in the matrix refers to a vowel phoneme represented in the words (of List 2) and each column contains entries of the transcriptions of the responses given in oral reading. Thus the rows give the frequency distribution for each vowel percentaged against the number of occurrences, which is approximately 25 per vowel per subject.

It may be seen that the errors are not distributed randomly. (Chi-square computed for the matrix as a whole is 406.2 with $df = 42$; $p < 0.001$). The eight vowels differ greatly in difficulty; error rates ranged from a low of 7 percent for /I/ to a high of 26 percent for /u/. Orthographic factors are the most obvious source of the differences in error rate. In our list /I/ is always represented by the letter i, whereas /u/ is represented by seven letters or digraphs: *u, o, oo, ou, oe, ew, ui*. The correlation (rho) between each vowel's rank difficulty and its number of orthographic representations in List 2 was 0.83. Hence we

---

[11] Some recent investigations of orthography have stressed that English spelling has more rules than is sometimes supposed—that many seeming irregularities are actually instances of rules, and that orthography operates to preserve a simpler relationship between spelling and morphophoneme at the cost of a more complex relation between spelling and sound [Chomsky and Halle 1968; Weir and Venezky 1968].

VOWEL OBTAINED
in Oral Reading

VOWEL PRESENTED in Print	ɑ	æ	i	I	ɛ	ʌ	ʊ	u	OTHER
ɑ	87	2		1		4	1	1	4
æ	4	89		1	2	3			1
i			81	1	13				5
I	1	1		93	1	3			1
ɛ	1	4	5	6	79	2	1		2
ʌ	2			3	2	80	2	4	7
ʊ	1	1				5	90	2	1
u	5	1				8	2	74	10

Figure 2. Matrix of vowel errors in reading Word List 2, transcribed in IPA. Each row gives the distribution of responses as percentages of opportunities for each of the eight vowels represented in the list. Eleven subjects.

may conclude that the error rate on vowels in our list is related to the number of orthographic representations of each vowel.[12]

The data thus support the idea that differences in error rate among vowels reflect differences in their orthographic complexity. Moreover, as we have said, the fact that vowels, in general, map onto sound more complexly than consonants is one reason they tend to be misread more frequently than consonants.[13]

It may be, however, that these orthographic differences among segments are themselves partly rooted in speech. Many data from speech research indicate that vowels are often processed differently from consonants when perceived by ear. A number of experiments have shown that the tendency to categorical perception is greater in the encoded stop consonants than in the unencoded vowels [A. M. Liberman, Cooper et al. 1967; A. M. Liberman 1970]. It may be argued that as a consequence of the continuous nature of their perception, vowels tend to

[12] A matrix of vowel substitutions was made up for the better readers (the upper third) of the class on which Figure 2 is based. Their distribution of errors was remarkably similar.

[13] We did not examine consonant errors from the standpoint of individual variation in their orthographic representation, but it may be appropriate to ask whether the orthography tends to be more complex for consonants in final position than for those in initial position, since it is in the noninitial portion of words that morphophonemic alternation occurs (e.g., *sign–signal*). We doubt, however, that this is a major cause of the greater tendency for final consonants to be misread by beginning readers.

be somewhat indefinite as phonologic entities, as illustrated by the major part they play in variation among dialects and the persistence of allophones within the same geographic locality. By the same reasoning, it could be that the continuous nature of vowel perception is one cause of complex orthography, suggesting that one reason that multiple representations are tolerated may lie very close to speech.

We should also consider the possibility that the error pattern of the vowels reflects not just the complex relation between letter and sound but also confusions that arise as the reader recodes phonetically. There is now a great deal of evidence [Conrad 1964, this volume] that normal readers do, in fact, recode the letters into phonetic units for storage and use in short-term memory. If so, we should expect that vowel errors would represent displacements from the correct vowels to those that are phonetically adjacent and similar, the more so because, as we have just noted, vowel perception is more nearly continuous than categorical. That such displacements did in general occur is indicated in Figure 2 by the fact that the errors tend to lie near the diagonal. More data and, in particular, a more complete selection of items will be required to determine the contribution to vowel errors of orthographic complexity and the confusions of phonetic recoding.

Summary and Conclusions

In an attempt to understand the problems encountered by the beginning reader and children who fail to learn, we have investigated the child's misreadings and how they relate to speech. The first question we asked was whether the major barrier to achieving fluency in reading is at the level of connected text or in dealing with individual words. Having concluded from our own findings and the research of others that the word and its components are of primary importance, we then looked more closely at the error patterns in reading words.

Since reading is the perception of language by eye, it seemed important to ask whether the principal difficulties within the word are to be found at a visual stage of the process or at a subsequent linguistic stage. We considered the special case of reversals of letter sequence and orientation in which the properties of visual confusability are, on the face of it, primary. We found that although optical reversibility contributes to the error rate, for the children we have studied it is of secondary importance to linguistic factors. Our investigation of the reversal tendency then led us to consider whether individual differences in reading ability might reflect differences in the degree and kind of functional asymmetries of the cerebral hemispheres. Although the evidence is at this time not clearly supportive of a relation between cerebral ambilaterality and reading disability, it was suggested that new techniques offer an opportunity to explore this relationship more fully in the future.

When we turned to the linguistic aspects of the error pattern in words, we found, as others have, that medial and final segments in the word are more often misread than initial ones and vowels more often than consonants. We then considered why the error pattern in mishearing differed from misreading in both these respects. In regard to segment position, we concluded that children in the early stages of learning to read tend to get the initial segment correct and fail on subsequent ones because they do not have the conscious awareness of phonemic segmentation needed specifically in reading but not in speaking and listening.

As for vowels in speech, we suggested, first of all, that they may tend to be heard correctly because they are carried by the strongest portion of the acoustic signal. In reading, the situation is different: alphabetic representations of the vowels possess no such special distinctiveness. Moreover, their embedded placement within the syllable and their orthographic complexity combine to create difficulties in reading. Evidence for the importance of orthographic complexity was seen in our data by the fact that the differences among vowels in error rate in reading were predictable from the number of orthographic representations of each vowel. However, we also considered the possibility that phonetic confusions may account for a significant portion of vowel errors, and we suggested how this hypothesis might be tested.

We believe that the comparative study of reading and speech is of great importance for understanding how the problems of perceiving language by eye differ from the problems of perceiving it by ear, and for discovering why learning to read, unlike speaking and listening, is a difficult accomplishment.

References

Anderson, I. H., and W. F. Dearborn, 1952. *The Psychology of Teaching Reading.* New York: Ronald Press.

Benton, A. L., 1962. Dyslexia in relation to form perception and directional sense. In *Reading Disability,* J. Money (ed.), Baltimore: Johns Hopkins Press.

Biemiller, A., 1970. The development of the use of graphic and contextual information as children learn to read. *Reading Res. Quart.,* 6:75–96.

Bryden, M. P., 1965. Tachistoscopic recognition, handedness, and cerebral dominance. *Neuropsychologia,* 3:1–8.

———, 1970. Laterality effects in dichotic listening: Relations with handedness and reading ability in children. *Neuropsychologia,* 8:443–450.

Chomsky, N., and M. Halle, 1968. *The Sound Pattern of English*. New York: Harper and Row.

Christenson, A., 1969. Oral reading errors of intermediate grade children at their independent, instructional, and frustration reading levels. In *Reading and Realism*, J. A. Figurel (ed.), Proceedings of the International Reading Association, 13:674–677.

Conrad, R., 1964. Acoustic confusions in immediate memory. *Brit. J. Psych.* 55:75–83.

Conrad, R. Speech and reading. In this volume.

Crowder, R. Visual and auditory memory. In this volume.

Daniels, J. C., and H. Diack, 1956. *Progress in Reading*. Nottingham: University of Nottingham Institute of Education.

Doehring, D. G., 1968. *Patterns of Impairment in Specific Reading Disability*. Bloomington: Indiana University Press.

Fries, C. C., 1962. *Linguistics and Reading*. New York: Holt, Rinehart and Winston.

Fujisaki, H., and T. Kawashima, 1969. On the modes and mechanisms of speech perception. *Annual Report of the Division of Electrical Engineering*, Engineering Research Institute, University of Tokyo, No. 1.

Gibson, E. J., 1965. Learning to read. *Science*, 148:1066–1072.

Gibson, E. J., J. J. Gibson, A. D. Pick, and R. Osser, 1962. A developmental study of the discrimination of letter-like forms. *J. Comp. Physiol. Psych.* 55:897–906.

Goodman, K. S., 1965. A linguistic study of cues and miscues in reading. *Elementary English,* 42:639–643.

———, 1968. The psycholinguistic nature of the reading process. In *The Psycholinguistic Nature of the Reading Process,* K. S. Goodman (ed.), Detroit: Wayne State University Press.

Gough, P. B. One second of reading. In this volume.

Hochberg, J., 1970. Attention in perception and reading. In *Early Experience and Visual Information Processing in Perceptual and Reading Disorders,* F. A. Young and D. B. Lindsley (eds.), Washington: National Academy of Sciences.

Huey, E. B., 1908. *The Psychology and Pedagogy of Reading*. New York: Macmillan. Reprinted Cambridge: MIT Press, 1968.

Jastak, J., 1946. *Wide Range Achievement Test (Examiner's Manual)*. Wilmington: C. L. Story.

Katz, L., and D. A. Wicklund, 1971. Word scanning rate for good and poor readers. *J. Ed. Psych.* 62:138–140.

Kimura, D., 1967. Functional asymmetry of the brain in dichotic listening. *Cortex,* 3:163–178.

Kimura, D., 1961. Cerebral dominance and the perception of verbal stimuli. *Canad. J. Psych.* 15:166–171.

Kolers, P. A., 1970. Three stages of reading. In *Basic Studies on Reading,* H. Levin (ed.), New York: Harper & Row.

Kolers, P. A., and D. N. Perkins, 1969. Orientation of letters and their speed of recognition. *Perception and Psychophysics* 5:275–280.

Liberman, A. M., 1968. Discussion in *Communicating by Language: The Reading Process,* J. F. Kavanagh (ed.), Bethesda, Md.: National Institute of Child Health and Human Development, pp. 125–128.

————, 1970. The grammars of speech and language. *Cog. Psych.* 1:301–323.

Liberman, A. M., F. S. Cooper, D. Shankweiler, and M. Studdert-Kennedy, 1967. Perception of the speech code. *Psych. Rev.* 74:431–461.

Liberman, I. Y., 1971. Basic research in speech and lateralization of language: Some implications for reading disability. *Bull. Orton Soc.* 21:71–87.

Liberman, I. Y., D. Shankweiler, C. Orlando, K. S. Harris, and F. B. Berti, 1971. Letter confusions and reversals of sequence in the beginning reader: Implications for Orton's theory of developmental dyslexia. *Cortex* 7:127–142.

Mathews, M., 1966. *Teaching to Read Historically Considered.* Chicago: University of Chicago Press.

Mattingly, I. G. Reading, the linguistic process, and linguistic awareness. In this volume.

Mattingly, I. G., and A. M. Liberman, 1970. The speech code and the physiology of language. In *Information Processing in the Nervous System,* K. N. Leibovic (ed.), New York: Springer.

Orlando, C. P., 1971. Relationships between language laterality and handedness in eight and ten year old boys. Unpublished doctoral dissertation, University of Connecticut.

Orton, S. T., 1925. "Word-blindness" in school children. *Arch. Neurol. Psychiat.* 14:581–615.

————, 1937. *Reading, Writing and Speech Problems in Children.* New York: W. W. Norton.

Savin, H. B. What the child knows about speech when he starts to read. In this volume.

Schale, F. C., 1964. Changes in oral reading errors at elementary and secondary levels. Unpublished doctoral dissertation, University of Chicago. Summarized in *Acad. Ther. Quart.* 1966, 1:225–229.

Shankweiler, D., 1964. Developmental dyslexia: A critique and review of recent evidence. *Cortex,* 1:53–62.

Shankweiler, D., and M. Studdert-Kennedy, 1967. Identification of consonants and vowels presented to left and right ears. *Quart. J. Exp. Psych.* 19:59–63.

Spache, G. D., 1963. *Diagnostic Reading Scales (Examiner's Manual).* Monterey: California Test Bureau.

Unpublished doctoral dissertation, University of Florida.
Sparrow, S. S., 1968. Reading disability: A neuropsychological investigation.

Sternberg, S., 1967. Two operations in character recognition: Some evidence from reaction time measures. *Perception and Psychophysics,* 2:45–53.

Studdert-Kennedy, M., in press. The perception of speech. In *Current Trends in Linguistics,* Vol. XII, T. A. Sebeok (ed.), The Hague: Mouton. Also has appeared in *Haskins Laboratories Status Reports on Speech Research,* 23 (1970), pp. 15–48.

Venezky, R. L., 1968. Discussion in *Communicating by Language: The Reading Process,* J. F. Kavanagh (ed.), Bethesda, Md.: National Institute of Child Health and Human Development, p. 206.

Vernon, M. D., 1960. *Backwardness in Reading.* Cambridge: Cambridge University Press.

Weber, R., 1968. The study of oral reading errors: A survey of the literature. *Reading Res. Quart.* 4:96–119.

————, 1970. A linguistic analysis of first-grade reading errors. *Reading Res. Quart.* 5:427–451.

Weir, R. H., and R. L. Venezky, 1968. Spelling-to-sound patterns. In *The Psycholinguistic Nature of the Reading Process,* K. S. Goodman (ed.), Detroit: Wayne State University Press.

Woodworth, R. S., 1938. *Experimental Psychology.* New York: Holt, Chapter 28.

Zangwill, O. L., 1960. *Cerebral Dominance and Its Relation to Psychological Function.* Edinburgh: Oliver & Boyd.

Zurif, E. B., and G. Carson, 1970. Dyslexia in relation to cerebral dominance and temporal analysis. *Neuropsychologia* 8:351–361.

HARRIS B. SAVIN

What the Child Knows about Speech When He Starts to Learn to Read

The Prevailing Theory and Its Account of Failures to Learn to Read
English has a more or less alphabetic writing system. That is to say,
ignoring a large handful of exceptions and anomalies, letters correspond
to phonemes. Practically all discussions of learning to read assume that
the child already perceives speech as a sequence of phonemes and that
the heart of learning to read (at least at the beginning, in the *cat-rat-hat*
stage) is quite simply learning which letters of the alphabet correspond
with which phonemes. If he masters the system of letter-phoneme associations, then the child will know everything he needs to know except
for the treatment of irregular forms.

As this theory would lead one to expect, many children learn to read
quickly and effortlessly. However, and perhaps surprisingly, given the
apparent simplicity of the skill of reading, large numbers of apparently
normal children do not learn to read, or learn only after an inordinate
amount of instruction. From the point of view of the prevailing theory,
there are only a few sorts of difficulties that might explain a seemingly
normal five-year-old's failure to master what is, by hypothesis, only a
handful of rote associations between letters and phonemes: (1) Owing
to some visual anomaly, he has difficulty in recognizing the letters of
the alphabet. (2) For a variety of reasons, he is simply not motivated
to learn to read. It is not intrinsically interesting to him, and his teacher
fails both to make it seem interesting and to persuade him to learn
it anyhow. (3) The child's dialect is so different from that of his teacher
that he cannot make any sense of what she tells him (in her own dialect)
about which letters spell which words. (4) The child's dialect, even
if it is like his teacher's, is so different from standard English that English
orthography simply has no relationship to the way he speaks. (5) The
child has a specific neurological disorder, the only apparent symptom
of which is his failure to learn to read.

As for the last of these five hypotheses, no one thinks it applies to
more than a very small proportion of the children with reading difficulties. We will not discuss it further. The remaining four possibilities
all undoubtedly apply to some children, but there is reason to think
that they also fail to account for large numbers of reading difficulties.

Specifically, in the inner-city schools, where reading difficulties are most prevalent, some of the teachers both speak the children's dialect and understand the children's emotional needs well enough so that the children are obviously devoted to them.[1] Although these characteristics of the teacher are undoubtedly valuable, even such teachers fail to teach many of their pupils to read during the first grade. And the difficulty often arises at the very beginning of reading, when the child is being taught to read such words as *cat, rat, hat, fat, sat, bat, hit, fit, sit,* and *bit.* With respect to such words there simply is no dialect problem in American cities. Different dialects pronounce such words differently, but within each of them, the phoneme-spelling correspondence is exact. Observations such as these, which can be made in any inner-city elementary school, show that hypotheses (2), (3), and (4) cannot account for the majority of reading difficulties in such schools.

The remaining hypothesis—visual anomalies—also accounts for less than is often claimed. The principal evidence that is generally cited is that children fail to remember the names of the letters. In particular, they confuse the names of such letters as "b, d, p, q." Virtually every child who has spent a few months in the first grade but has not learned to read makes such errors in naming letters, but these errors are the effect, not the cause, of illiteracy. The four shapes are extremely similar visually. In all of a child's experience until he learns to read, he has not given different names to the same shape on account of its orientation in space, nor has the mirror image of any shape had a name of its own. An upside-down dog is a dog and, when the child looks in the mirror at the image of a dog, what he sees is as much a dog as the real dog is. Moreover, virtually every child who confuses these letters is able to say which one of "b, b, d" is different from the other two. That is to say, when the test is made truly visual, rather than a test of the memorization of some rather unnatural rote associations, it is not difficult. What is difficult is only remembering to call the same thing by different names depending upon its spatial orientation. Until one understands the significance of the spatial orientation of a letter, such difficulty is hardly remarkable.

To summarize, the prevailing theory of the skill of reading fails to account satisfactorily for the observed pattern of difficulties. This theory fails to identify a component of the skill that is demonstrably lacking in each child who does not learn to read. On the contrary, there are

---

[1] Here and throughout the paper, the source of all factual claims is my own experience in attempting to teach such children to read, augmented by similar experience of colleagues and students.

many illiterate second-graders who have been taught by competent teachers, whose visual abilities are normal, who like school, and whose learning ability is sufficient for them to have mastered the spoken language, not to speak of the rules of various games and the names of more school mates than there are letters of the alphabet.[2] All these auspicious circumstances notwithstanding, they have not learned to read. Evidently, it is worth reexamining the account given at the beginning of this section of the nature of what the child has to learn.

Phonemes and the Perception of Speech

In the preceding section, we have, along with everyone else, made the assumption that a child who perceives speech without difficulty—one who holds up his end of a conversation, carries out spoken instructions, and the like—has perceived the stream of speech as a sequence of phonemes. For example, we have implicitly assumed that the child hears the same segment at the beginning of *cat* and the beginning of *cow*. We have observed that he has no difficulty in seeing the visual identity of the two first letters, and we are concerned to understand why he fails to grasp that the letter *c* is the visual representation of the sound which he hears at the beginning of these two words.

The mere fact that a child understands what is said to him tells us little about what speech segments he perceives. One can represent speech sounds in many different ways: as phoneme sequences, for example, or syllable sequences, or phonetic distinctive-feature matrices. As Mattingly and Klima both observe in their papers in this volume, it is an as yet unresolved empirical question which of the levels of representation of speech children can easily become aware of. Suppose, for the sake of argument, that children up to a certain age segment speech into syllables but are incapable of analyzing syllables into shorter segments. For such children, /kæt/ and /hæt/ would simply be different sounds, as are /kæt/ and /dɔg/. Such a child can be a perfectly competent speaker and listener, but he will obviously be unable to make any sense of an alphabetic writing system.

In the present author's experience everyone who has failed to learn to read even the simplest prose by the end of the first grade has been unable to analyze syllables into phonemes, as shown by the following

---

[2] See Rozin, Poritsky, and Sotsky [1971] for evidence that one group of representative second-grade children with serious reading problems have problems that cannot be explained by any of the hypotheses under discussion here. Specifically, they showed that their children were able to make rapid progress in learning an ideographic writing system for English—one in which each visual symbol stands for a whole word.

observations: They are insensitive to rhyme. (To see that two syllables rhyme, one must notice that they differ only in their prevocalic consonants and are otherwise identical; that is to say, one must analyze syllables into shorter segments.) They show no sign of comprehending such claims as that /kæt/ and /kaʊ/ begin similarly or that /kæt/ ends with the sound of /æt/, even though they have no trouble understanding that /wɪndoʊ/ (*window*) consists of the sounds of /wɪn/ and of /doʊ/, and they are therefore capable in principle of segmenting speech. They are unable to learn Pig Latin, which requires one to modify English by shifting the initial consonant cluster (part of a syllable) of each word to the end of the word and then add the sound /ei/. This disability is especially striking because it is very easy to arouse a six-year-old's interest in the prospect of learning a secret language that most adults do not understand. Children who are able to learn Pig Latin seem invariably to be delighted by it, and those children who cannot learn it obviously do not fail because they are not interested in trying.

Not only do first-grade and second-grade nonreaders show in the foregoing ways that they cannot analyze syllables into phonemes. Virtually every four-year-old has precisely the same limitations. Even the verbally precocious four-year-old children of academic parents, children who will learn to read quickly effortlessly a year or so later, act as if the syllable were an unanalyzable unit. What is unusual about the older nonreaders is simply that they have not yet developed, at age six or seven, an ability that most children of educated parents develop somewhat earlier.

There is also evidence that even for literate adults, the syllable is a far more natural, more easily available perceptual unit than is the phoneme. Savin and Bever [1970], in an experiment that was begun for reasons unrelated to the present discussion, found that undergraduates respond faster when they are told to operate a switch as soon as they hear the word *sit* (for example) than when they are told to react as soon as they hear anything at all beginning with /s/. Whole-syllable targets are responded to more quickly than are single-phoneme targets, whether the phoneme target is a consonant or a vowel and whether the syllables are common words or unfamiliar nonsense syllables. This is true for an initial consonant like /s/, whose acoustic structure is not influenced appreciably by the subsequent context, and true to a still greater extent for initial /b/, which is very much influenced by context. These results show that people do not proceed by perceiving the successive phonemes of speech and grouping the phonemes into syllables, syllables into words, and so on to larger and larger segments of speech.

Rather, they seem to identify phonemes only by analyzing syllables they have already perceived.

A somewhat less recondite observation that also suggests the greater naturalness of the syllable is that adults "sound out" unfamiliar written words syllable by syllable, never phoneme by phoneme, in the fashion of school children who have just begun to master reading. If the adult's first attempt at sounding out syllable by syllable does not satisfy him, he will try again with different syllables, but he does not normally attempt to produce shorter segments than what he momentarily believes to be the syllables of the word.

None of the foregoing observations, whether of children or adults, shows that phonemes play no part in the perception of speech. Speech perception is an extremely complex process and a great deal takes place that the perceiver is never aware of. For reasons discussed by Savin and Bever, it is necessary to assume phonemes somewhere in the theory of language whether or not the speakers of the language are ever aware of them. What is important for the teaching of reading, however, is not whether phonemes play any part at all in speech perception, but whether they play any conscious (or potentially conscious) part—whether, that is to say, the child can be aware of enough of them to make any sense of the things his teacher tells him about the sounds of the letters. There is evidently no point in trying to teach a child who canot make himself aware of phonemes that the letter *s* has the sound /s/. Such conversations are futile, whether or not his perceptual processes involve phonemes at some unconscious level.

"Reading Readiness" and Being Ready to Read

Most school curricular obliquely acknowledge the possibility of perceptual problems like the one we have been discussing in "reading readiness" programs that consist largely of exercises with sets of rhyming words, with alliteration, and with other phonological relationships that are presumably meant to help the child perceive phonemes. But the purpose of these exercises is generally not clearly understood by the teacher, and therefore there is no criterion for deciding when there has been enough of this and for certifying the child as ready for the real business of learning to read. Moreover, the exercises are ineffective enough so that there are some children who have persevered long enough to memorize the members of the "-*at* family" (viz., *cat, hat, rat, sat, fat, bat,* and their ilk) but who seem to have no notion of what the members of that family have in common. They are uncertain, for example, whether *bicycle* is another member of the family. In short, the familiar reading-readiness drills, plausible though they seem as remedies for the problem we are discussing, often fail because the child is not only unready to learn to read but also unready to comprehend the reading-readiness curriculum.

Children who have been both diligent and unsuccessful, by the end of the first grade, may know not only the conventional name of each letter but also what their teacher calls its "sound." The sound of the letter *b*, for example, is /bə/. A child who knows the "sounds" of the letters but cannot read is commonly described as having a difficulty in "blending." When confronted with the written word *bit* he can say /bə ɪ tə/ but he cannot get from this to the pronunciation of the word itself. Linguistically sophisticated people often assume that the real problem here is with the teacher, not the pupil. /bə ɪ tə/, they observe, has three syllables and /bɪt/ only one. Why should the child be expected to know what the rule is for "blending" the three into the one? There is undoubtedly some truth in this, but it fails to explain why it is equally hard to "blend" the sound [s] with the syllable /ɪt/ to produce *sit*. Yet this is quite impossible for many children. In fact, whatever further problems might be introduced by the extra vowels of /bə ɪ tə/, the central problem with blending is that it requires synthesizing syllables out of shorter segments; and, like the analysis of syllables into shorter segments, this synthesis is impossible for many children whether the shorter parts can be pronounced in isolation or not.

Using What the Child Does Know

For the present, there seems to be no plausible answer to the question, Why are some children unable to segment syllables into phonemes? Moreover, there is no training program that is known to help these children. The sort of drill in rhyme, alliteration, and the like that is an important part of many schools' reading-readiness program seems on its face to be an intelligently conceived exercise that ought to develop these perceptual skills, and it may be valuable to some students; but many get nothing from it except a few memorized lists of words: the -*it* family, the -*at* family, and other inscrutable aggregates of words.

Research on the causes and cure of children's inability to segment syllables should be pursued.[3] There is, unfortunately, no good reason

[3] The hypothesis that time invariably brings about a cure ought to be explored. There is surely no point in subjecting large numbers of first-grade teachers and students to great frustration if the unsuccessful pupils would be able to learn to read easily in a year or two. And the harm that is done to the students' motivation and morale by prolonged instruction that he is not yet ready to understand must be immense and, in many cases, long lasting.

to think that answers will be found quickly. Meanwhile, each year the schools attempt to teach a new group of children to read, and a large number of them are given instruction in letter-phoneme correspondences at a time when they cannot hear phonemes. It seems obvious that no good can come of such teaching. The other well-known method of teaching reading—teaching each whole word as a single entity—is currently in rather bad repute, and deservedly so. The number of words one must know is simply too great for this to be feasible method. On a conservative estimate [Seashore and Eckerson 1940], the average college student has some 60,000 words in his active vocabulary, and a vastly greater number that he is able to comprehend when he reads them. It would be inefficient to the point of absurdity to teach all of these tens of thousands of words as though each were an arbitrarily chosen hieroglyph and there were no underlying principle relating the spelling of a word to its sound.

There are, then, persuasive arguments against teaching these children to read either by teaching them the sound of each letter or by teaching whole words. There are, that is to say, persuasive arguments against both of the methods that English-speaking teachers have been alternating between for at least the last 130 years [Fries 1963]. There is, however, a third alternative, which no one seems ever to have considered very seriously but which is well adapted to the known abilities and limitations of most children: teach the spelling of each syllable, without analyzing the spoken syllables into phonemes. For example, one would teach that the letter sequences *doe, dow, dough* all are (sometimes) pronounced as /doʊ/. There will be several thousand such correspondences to be learned, but several thousand syllables is far less formidable than several tens of thousands of words. More to the point, as we have already observed, there is evidence that the proficient reader, by whatever method he was originally taught, reads unfamiliar words syllable by syllable anyhow. That is to say, he has learned for himself the necessary several thousand *syllabic* spelling-sound correspondences rather than settling for the few dozen letter-phoneme correspondences that are all that his schoolteachers meant him to learn.

No one has yet attempted to teach reading in this fashion in any systematic way. I have attempted, in a highly unsystematic way, to teach a handful of syllables to several children, including some who had manfully resisted the Philadelphia public schools' attempts to teach reading letter by letter for as long as two years. The results do not permit any conclusion about how long it would take to truly master reading in this way, but it is clear that all the children made rapid initial progress, and in particular that they were immediately able to recombine the syllables they had learned in a new order and to "sound out" unfamiliar sequences of familiar syllables. There was, that is to say, no counterpart of the problem, very difficult for many children who have learned the sound of each letter, of "blending" the sounds.[4]

References

Fries, C. C., 1963. *Linguistics and Reading.* New York: Holt, Rinehart and Winston.

Rozin, P., S. Poritsky, and R. Sotsky, 1971. American children with reading problems can easily learn to read English represented by Chinese characters. *Science,* 171:1264–1267.

Savin, H. B., and T. G. Bever, 1970. The nonperceptual reality of the phoneme. *J. Verbal Learning and Verbal Behavior* 9:295–302.

Seashore, R., and L. Eckerson, 1940. The measurement of individual differences in general English vocabularies. *J. Ed. Psych.* 40:14–38.

[4] Rozin, Poritsky, and Sotsky [1971] reached a similar conclusion about the ease of initial acquisition of an ideographic writing system.

General Discussion of Papers by Shankweiler and I. Y. Liberman; and Savin

Both Savin's paper and Shankweiler and I. Y. Liberman's paper provoked a good deal of questioning about the nature and cause of the difficulty that poor readers have with phonemic segmentation. Savin's pupils can understand pictures, and they can recognize and name the letters of the alphabet, with the same occasional difficulty with reversible pairs like "p" and "d" and "p" and "q" that Shankweiler and I. Y. Liberman reported. But they cannot segment words into phonemes, and they are not sensitive to rhyme.

O'Neil suggested that even though Savin may have established good rapport with his pupils, the alien school environment was a factor. Savin doubted this, saying that their performance on other intellectual tasks was very good, while, on the other hand, his attempt to teach his pupils Pig Latin, which is very different from what is usually taught in school, had been a failure, and they showed little interest in mastering tongue-twisters like "she sells seashells by the seashore." Also, he had found out which words commonly seen on television they could read and could not read, and there was no more evidence that his pupils made a phonemic analysis of TV words than of the words in school readers.

Gibson suggested that the pupils may originally have been taught to read in a monotonous and unimaginative way, with too much drilling on letter names, and that this may have discouraged their interest in reading. Savin said that of course this was possible, and that his pupils did indeed become bored when asked questions about letters. But his pupils did very well at word games that did not happen to require phonemic segmentation. Moreover, it was hard to see how bad teaching could numb his pupils to rhyme but leave untouched appreciation of other features of verse, in particular, rhythm. Of course, it would have been pointless for the teacher to assume that the pupils could segment words phonemically when in fact they could not do so.

Halle said that while he could believe Savin's account of this group of deprived 7-year-olds, he doubted the claim that normal middle-class children between 2 and 4 had not yet learned to segment phonemically, since they enjoy nursery rhymes. Savin conceded that a few advanced children learned to segment phonemically at a very early age, and then to read, but insisted that normal children of 2 or 3 were not aware of phonemic segments. Nursery songs altered so as to remove the rhymes would remain acceptable as long as the rhythm was preserved. At 4, these children begin to lose this tolerance but will accept, for example, /a/ and /æ/ as rhymes. And by the middle of the first grade, middle-class children have started to read and to sound out words, and therefore they must be segmenting phonemically.

Liberman said that reading teachers often complain about the inability of pupils to "blend": the pupils can identify the individual characters in, for example, *bag*, as *b–a–g*, but when asked to pronounce the word will say /bə æ gə/. The teacher then urges the child to blend, by which she means, say it faster. But the child cannot do this unless he is aware that the spoken word /bæg/, which he already knows, consists of three phonemic segments. Some children have great difficulty in becoming sufficiently conscious of these segments. Even the ability to appreciate rhyme may not mean that the child is sufficiently conscious of phonemic segments to learn to read. Carroll remarked that some recent work by Chall, Roswell et al. [1963] and by Roswell and Chall [1956–1958] indicates that the ability to blend is maturational. Kavanagh noted that the teaching of blending is a major problem in speech therapy. Stevens and Cooper considered inability to blend in speech to be a different problem from lack of awareness of phonemic segmentation. The child who does not blend properly in speech is having trouble with a motor skill, but he might well be a good reader and aware of errors in speech production made by others. Savin's pupils, on the other hand, did not have defective pronunciation, though it was possible, Stevens suggested, that their phonology differed from that of middle-class children.

Gibson pointed out that beginning readers have a very difficult time sorting out spelling patterns and clusters in words without hearing the words. She thought that this skill, like phonemic segmentation, required maturation.

Carroll thought that there might well be wide individual differences even among adults in awareness of phonemic segmentation. He recalled an experiment in which the subject was asked to match sounds presented orally with symbols in phonetically transcribed syllables. Some of his subjects were quite unable to analyze the syllables into segments.

Cooper said that artificially slowed speech makes one very aware of the motor machinery of articulation, and he wondered if such speech might help children like Savin's pupils. Savin said he had not tried this, but that nothing else he had tried had helped noticeably. Kavanagh said he found that adults in a phonetics class who were not able easily to associate sounds and phonemes had been helped by stretched speech and also by immediate feedback.

Miller asked how many children who have reading problems would prove to lack skill in phonemic segmentation. Savin could cite no data, but said that all of the undergraduates he knew who had worked in West Philadelphia, as he had, had reported that their pupils had this same problem.

At Liberman's suggestion, Shankweiler discussed a little further Bryden's [1970] study of "uncrossed" (speech and handedness of the same side) subjects and "crossed" (speech and handedness on opposite sides) subjects. Shankweiler said that Bryden found that among boys 20 percent of good readers, 53 percent of intermediate readers, and 54 percent of poor readers were crossed, while the results for girls were rather less drastic: 33 percent for good readers, 37 percent for intermediate readers, and 43 percent for poor readers.

O'Neil asked that the record show that in Iceland a child starts school at 7 if he has already learned to read at home; otherwise, he must wait a year.

References

Bryden, M. P., 1970. Laterality effects in dichotic listening: Relations with handedness and reading ability in children. *Neuropsychologia* 8:443–450.

Chall, Jeanne S., Florence G. Roswell, and Susan Hahn Blumenthal, 1963. Auditory blending ability: A factor in success in beginning reading. *The Reading Teacher* 16:113–118.

Roswell, Florence G., and Jeanne S. Chall, 1956–1958. *Roswell-Chall Diagnostic Reading Test of Word Analysis Skills. Grades 2–6.* New York: Essay Press.

PHILIP B. GOUGH

One Second of Reading

Suppose the eye of a moderately skilled adult reader (henceforth, the Reader) were to fall on this sentence, and that he were to read it aloud. One second after his initial fixation, only the first word will have been uttered.[1] But during that second, a number of events will have transpired in the mind of the Reader, each the evident result of processes of amazing complexity. If we knew the train of events, we would know what the processes must accomplish and thus something of their nature. If we knew this, we would know what the child must learn to become a Reader.

Accordingly, this paper is concerned with two topics. First, it tries to describe the sequence of events that transpire in one second of reading, in order to suggest the nature of the processes that link them. Second, it attempts to relate this description to some facts about the acquisition of reading. The description of the chain of events is intended to be exhaustive in the conviction that the complexity of the reading process cannot otherwise be fully appreciated. Thus it is detailed by choice, speculative by necessity, and almost certainly flawed. I hope these are virtues, for much of what is written about reading is either too vague to be tested or too banal to bother, and an analysis that can be attacked in detail can yield detailed knowledge. The consideration of research on reading in children, on the other hand, is anything but complete. Quite apart from the familiar methodological shortcomings which abound in this research, most of it is aimed at a level of description too gross to be of any use here. So rather than presenting an unavoidably dreary review of the literature, I have attempted to interpret the acquisition of reading in terms of the present model, and to fit selected experimental results into the resulting framework.

The Reading Process

Reading begins with an eye fixation. The Reader's eyes focus on a point slightly indented from the beginning of the line, and they remain in

---

[1] This estimate is based on my reading, as naturally as possible, 50 sentences drawn from the *Daily Texan* and presented tachistoscopically. The median interval between stimulus and response onset was just over 700 msec, and the average initial word required roughly 300 msec to produce.

that fixation for some 250 msec [Tinker 1958]. Then they will sweep 1–4 degrees of visual angle (say 10–12 letter spaces) to the right, in a saccadic movement consuming 10–23 msec, and a new fixation will begin. Barring regressions, and ignoring return sweeps (which take 40–54 msec), this sequence will be repeated as long as reading continues (up to at least six hours according to Carmichael and Dearborn [1947]). When the initial fixation is achieved, a visual pattern is reflected onto the retina. This sets in motion an intricate sequence of activity in the visual system, culminating in the formation of an icon.

ICONIC REPRESENTATION

The existence of the icon, a relatively direct representation of a visual stimulus that persists for a brief period after the stimulus vanishes, has been amply demonstrated [Sperling 1960, 1963]. I take the icon to be a central event, presumably corresponding to neural activity in the striate cortex [cf. Haber and Standing 1969]. I further assume that the icon is an "unidentified" or "precategorical" visual image, a set of bars, slits, edges, curves, angles, and breaks, perhaps corresponding to the output of simple cells like those identified by Hubel and Wiesel [1962].

Whatever the form of its contents, the iconic buffer has a substantial capacity. Sperling [1963] has shown that it can hold at least 17 of 18 letters presented in three rows of six. In the case of ordinary reading matter, it can be estimated that the useful content of the icon will include everything in an oval roughly two inches wide and an inch high, or about 20 letter-spaces of the line under fixation.[2]

The decay of the icon has been intensively studied [cf. Haber 1968, 1969). It is known to persist for several seconds if the stimulus is followed by darkness, but for less than half a second if in light [Sperling 1963.] It can be erased or masked by a following patterned stimulus [Liss 1968; Spencer 1969].

The *formation* of the icon, on the other hand, has scarcely been studied at all. One reason is that it is excruciatingly difficult to investigate; the question of how long it takes to form an icon is no less than the question of how long it takes us to sense something. Simple threshold data are uninformative, for they only indicate how much (i.e., what duration of) visual energy is necessary to initiate the train of events

[2] I am indebted to Kent Gummerman for this estimate. It is based on "(a) acuity data for viewing in the horizontal meridian [Feinberg 1949], (b) Wertheim's [1894, p. 185] 'iso-acuity' ellipses that show areas of equal acuity in all directions, and (c) the conservative assumption that a letter can be resolved if the thickness of its component lines can be resolved by the eye" (Gummerman, personal communication).

which results in the icon. Masked threshold data tell no more, for they are naturally interpreted as indicating how long one icon exists before it is replaced by another. As far as I can see, the only relevant published data are to be found in studies of visually evoked potentials [e.g., Dustman and Beck 1965]. If a flash of light is presented to the eye, it is reflected in detectable changes in electrical potential at the occipital cortex no less than 50 msec later;[3] Dustman and Beck [1965] have suggested that wave components with mean latencies of 57 and 75 msec are related to awareness of the light. Assuming that patterned visual information is processed no faster than a flash of light, we might infer (acknowledging the length of the leap) that the icon could not be formed in less than 50 msec, and that its full development may require closer to 100 msec.[4]

Given these assumptions, we are led to suppose that the Reader's initial fixation yields an icon containing materials corresponding to the first 15 to 20 letters and spaces of the sentence (e.g., "Suppose the eye of a"). This icon will become fully "legible" in something like 100 msec. It will last until it is replaced by the icon arising from the Reader's second fixation, some 250 msec later.

In the meantime, the lines, curves, and angles of the first icon will be recognized as familiar patterns. I assume they are identified as letters.

LETTER IDENTIFICATION

Letter recognition is very rapid. There is striking evidence that even unrelated letters can be recovered from the icon at rates of 10–20 msec per letter.

One such datum was provided by Sperling [1963], who found that if a random matrix of letters was followed immediately by a patterned mask, the number of letters reported increased linearly with the duration of the matrix, one letter every 10 msec, up to a limit imposed by memory. Since premask stimulus duration is directly related to icon duration, this result presumably reflects the rate of readout of letters from the icon into a more durable register.

Given that simple recognition thresholds have been shown to be lower for words (and even pronounceable nonsense syllables; Gibson, Osser et al. 1963] than for random strings like Sperling's, it would be interesting to see if their letters can be read out even more rapidly. To my knowl-

---

[3] There is an early component of the wave at approximately 43 msec, but Dustman and Beck feel that it is not correlated with stimulus awareness.
[4] Presumably the latency of the icon will vary with the intensity of the stimulus (and perhaps with its complexity).

edge, the relevant experiment has not yet been conducted.[5] But there are data that suggest a comparable rate of letter identification with meaningful materials.

First, Scharf, Zamansky et al. [1966] found the masked recognition threshold (using Sperling's own mask) for familiar five-letter words to be roughly 90 msec (under high luminance). This fact provides little comfort for any assumption that read-out of letters from the icon is more efficient for meaningful or pronounceable materials than for random strings of letters; Sperling's results show that under the same circumstances, four or five unrelated letters can easily be registered.

Second, Michael Stewart, Carlton James, and I [Stewart, James et al. 1969] found that visual recognition latency—the time between presentation of a word and the beginning of its pronunciation—increases steadily with word length in letters, from 615 msec for three-letter words to 693 msec for ten-letter words. The function is negatively accelerated; the increase in latency with length is greater with short words than long. But the data are compatible with the assumption that letters of words are read out of the icon at a rate of 10–20 msec per letter.

Third, W. C. Stewart and I [Gough and Stewart 1970] have measured how long it takes readers to decide that a given string of letters is a word or not. One of the variables we manipulated was word length. We found that four-letter words are acknowledged some 35 msec faster than six-letter words, again consistent with the assumption that each additional letter requires an additional 10–20 msec for readout from the icon.

These data, among others, suggest that letters are recovered from the icon *as* letters, that the evident effects of higher levels of organization (like spelling patterns, pronounceability, and meaningfulness) on word recognition and speed of reading should be assigned to higher, and later, levels of processing. It is worth noting that if this analysis is correct, then it can be, at best, a half-truth to say that we do not read letter by letter.

Suppose that letters identified and read out of the icon at a rate of 10 to 20 msec per letter, starting the moment the icon is formed. Since the icon should endure for some 250 msec, between one and two dozen letters could be identified from it even if readout were strictly serial. With a conservative estimate of three fixations per second, and

[5] Gilbert [1959] came close when he presented linguistic segments (words and phrases) of various lengths for various durations, and examined the amount recovered as a function of length of material and exposure duration. But his materials were presented by film, so that control over stimulus quality and duration was crude, and he presents only a rough general description of his materials.

assuming the average word to contain seven letters, even the lower value of letter transfer (i.e., 12 per fixation) would yield a reading speed in excess of 300 words per minute.

I see no reason, then, to reject the assumption that we do read letter by letter.[6] In fact, the weight of the evidence persuades me that we do so serially, from left to right [cf. White 1969]. Thus I will assume that the letters in the icon emerge serially, one every 10 or 20 msec into some form of character register.

How the letters get here and what form they take once they have arrived are intriguing questions. But more important is what is done with them. Clearly, letters are not the stuff of which sentences are made. They must be associated with meanings; they must be mapped onto entries in the mental lexicon. The specification of the mechanism by which this is accomplished is, as I see it, the fundamental problem of reading.

THE MAPPING PROBLEM

There are two superficially appealing possibilities. First, one might assume that the lexicon is directly accessible from the character register, that the Reader goes "directly" from print to meaning. This possibility is appealing to some theorists [cf. Kolers 1970] at least in part because of the nonalphabetic (i.e., neither phonemic nor syllabic) character of many orthographies. Since readers of such orthographies have to learn thousands of arbitrary associations between printed and spoken words, they could as easily learn direct associations between the orthographic words and their meanings and circumvent the spoken word altogether. And if they can do it, so can we.

We can, indeed, but only at great (and quite unnecessary) expense. Every potential Reader has a lexicon that is accessible through phonological information; he can understand the spoken word. Presumably, then, each of his lexical entries contains a phonological representation, and he has a retrieval mechanism that can address the entry through that representation. If he learns to assign such a representation to the printed word, the mapping problem is solved, and he quickly becomes a Reader. If he does not, he must add an orthographic representation to each of the tens of thousands of lexical entries (to say nothing of constructing a completely new retrieval mechanism to make use of them). The Reader of a nonalphabetic orthography might do this, for his is Hobson's choice. But we have a significant alternative, for while the orthography of

[6] Elsewhere [Gough 1968] I have tried to argue that the traditional arguments against this notion are without foundation.

English is complex and its rules are numerous, no one has seriously proposed that the number of these rules approaches within a factor of 100 the size of our lexicons. If there is any principle of cognitive economy, it surely must demand that we do not acquire tens of thousands of supererogatory associations, and we must not go straight from print to meaning.

The second possibility is, in this respect, appropriate: it is that we go from print to meaning by way of speech. On this view, the Reader applies orthographic rules to the contents of the character register, converting them to speech, and then listens to himself. All the Reader must add to his cognitive equipment are the orthographic rules. Nothing needs to be added to the lexicon; no new retrieval system needs to be constructed.

The advantages of this hypothesis are obvious. It is a venerable one, and it has prompted any number of studies of subvocal activity during reading (cf. Conrad's paper in this volume.) But I find it untenable, for I do not believe that the device it proposes can work fast enough. Recall that M. Stewart, C. T. James, and I [1969] found that production latency for a three-letter word is in excess of 600 msec. A highly motivated and practiced subject can push this down to 500 msec. Subtracting the 32 msec our voice key consumes, the 10 msec or so it requires for a nervous impulse to travel from the midbrain to the larynx [Ohala 1970], and another 5 or 10 for it to get to the midbrain from the motor cortex, one is still left with well over 400 msec for an instruction to speak to be assembled. Even ignoring the additional time required for a circuit through some version (however abstract) of an auditory loop, a Reader would not understand a printed word for better than 400 msec after his eye fell on it.

Clearly, we do not know just how long it takes to understand a word. But what may be relevant evidence was obtained several years ago in a study by Rohrman and myself [Rohrman and Gough 1967]. We asked subjects to decide if pairs of words were synonymous or not, and measured the latencies of their decisions. On some trials, we announced that a pair would be presented in two seconds by saying "set"; on others, the warning signal was one member of the pair to be judged. We found that giving the subject one member in advance reduced his decision latency by roughly 160 msec. If it is assumed that simultaneous presentation of the pair requires a serial search for the two meanings, and that giving one word in advance eliminates only the retrieval of its meaning from the total decision process, then this result indicates that the meaning of a printed word is located in something on the order of 160 msec. (This result is, in light of the present model, fascinating: if the icon of the word was formed in 100 msec, then it suggests that the meaning of a word is located as fast as its letters can be read out of the icon.) This interpretation is clearly open to question, but if the estimate is anywhere near the true value, then the Reader understands a word well before he can begin to utter it, and the speech-loop hypothesis cannot possibly hold.

In light of these considerations, I am led to a third hypothesis, one that claims the advantages of both (and the disadvantages of neither) at the small price of a charge of abstraction. Suppose it is assumed that the Reader maps characters, not onto speech, but rather onto a string of systematic phonemes, in the sense of Chomsky and Halle [1968]. Systematic phonemes are abstract entities that are related to the sounds of the language—the phonetic segments—only by means of a complex system of phonological rules. Thus it is easy to imagine that formation of a string of systematic phonemes would necessarily take place at some temporal distance from (i.e., some time before) the posting of motor commands, and the prohibitive cost of passage through the speech loop would be eliminated. Moreover, since lexical entries must contain, in addition to their semantic and syntactic features, a lexical representation in systematic phonemes, it seems reasonable to assume that the speaker of a language employs, in the comprehension of speech, retrieval mechanisms that access the lexical entries through these lexical representations. If characters are converted into comparable representations, then available retrieval mechanisms could be engaged, and the search for meaning in reading would require no costly new apparatus.

Obviously, this hypothesis is highly speculative, and I can offer no experimental evidence in support of it.[7] But Halle [1969] and N. Chomsky [1970] argue persuasively for a similar view, and I know of nothing to preclude it. More important, it provides the basis for a coherent account of a central problem in the acquisition of reading, as I will attempt to show later.

Thus, I will assume that the contents of the character register are somehow transposed into abstract phonemic representations. If, as Chomsky and Halle argue, the orthography of English directly reflects this level of representation, little processing will be required; otherwise,

[7] Since this paper was delivered, Herbert Rubenstein has reported that subjects take longer to decide that a nonsense word which is homophonic with some English word is *not* a word than to make the same decision about nonsense items which are not homophonic with any English lexical item. This result is, in my view, persuasive evidence for the hypothesis that the printed word is mapped onto a phonemic representation by the Reader.

more complex transformations (e.g., the grapheme-phoneme correspondence rules of Venezky [1970]) will yield a string of systematic
phonemes that can then be used to search the mental lexicon.

LEXICAL SEARCH

Whether the preceding hypothesis is correct remains to be seen. But
whether by this mechanism or by some other, lexical entries are ultimately
reached; the Reader understands the words of the sentence. Too little
is known about word comprehension to suggest how it is accomplished
or even to constrain speculation in any serious way. So I will adopt
what I take to be the simplest assumption: that the words of the sentence
are understood serially, from left to right.

Apparent objections to this hypothesis lie in the prevalence of lexical
ambiguity. First, if words are understood one at a time, then it seems
likely that they will frequently be misunderstood, at least until context
demands and receives assignment of a new reading. Second, it would
seem that prior context would determine the course of lexical search,
a procedure not incorporated in the present model.

The first is no real objection, for words often are misunderstood momentarily, and the presence of lexical ambiguity in a sentence demonstrably increases the difficulty of processing the sentence. For example,
Foss [1970] has found that if subjects are asked to monitor a sentence
for the presence of a given phoneme, their reaction time to the target
is increased if it follows an ambiguous item. As to the second point,
several experiments in our laboratories have failed to find evidence that
the disruptive effect of ambiguity can be eliminated by prior context.
Foss has found the same increase in phoneme monitor latency after
an ambiguous word even when that word is preceded by a context that
completely disambiguates it. In pilot studies, several of my students have
found that it takes longer to decide if a pair of words are related when
one is ambiguous than if it is not, even when the unambiguous word
is presented first (e.g., *prison-cell* takes longer than *prison-jail*). Thus
we have (as yet) found no evidence that disambiguation takes place
until *after* lexical search.

Such evidence suggests that the abstract phonemic representation is
assigned the first lexical entry that can be found. This is consistent
with the results of Rubenstein, Garfield, and Millikan [1970] and W. C.
Stewart and myself [Gough and Stewart 1970], which show that words
are acknowledged to be words more rapidly if they are ambiguous
then if they are not (with form and frequency equated). This result
suggests that the various readings of a polysemous word are stored sepa-

rately in the mental dictionary, rather than under a single heading (as they are in Webster's). Interestingly, Rubenstein, Lewis, and Rubenstein [1971] have found that this result does not hold for systematically ambiguous items (i.e., items like *plow,* in which the ambiguity lies only in grammatical category); consistency demands the assumption that these constitute single entries with alternative syntactic features specified.

Thus, lexical search would appear to be a parallel process, with the race going to the swift. When the first entry is located, its contents are accepted as the reading of the word until it proves incompatible with subsequent data; in the case of a systematically ambiguous word, its grammatical category can remain unspecified until further information is provided. In either event, the contents of the lexical entry yielded by each successive word must be deposited somewhere to be organized into a sentence. Primary memory is a likely spot.

PRIMARY MEMORY

A small-capacity buffer storage system where 4 to 5 verbal items are maintained for a matter of seconds is postulated in many current models of memory [cf. Norman 1970]. An item entering this primary memory (PM) [Waugh and Norman 1965] is generally thought to be subject to any of four fates. If it is ignored, it will simply (and rapidly) decay; on the other hand, it can be renewed through rehearsal. When the PM is full, an item in residence must be displaced if a new item is to enter. Finally, it may be transferred or copied into a more permanent store, the secondary memory.

There is one impediment to the assumption that the PM is the temporary repository for the content of a lexical entry. It is widely assumed that the contents of the PM are primarily acoustic or articulatory or phonemic [e.g., Baddeley 1966; Conrad 1964], largely because it is readily shown that verbal items are easily confused on this basis in short-term memory. I find this argument shaky.

First, confusion based on supraphonological properties of items in short-term memory can be demonstrated quite easily. Cornbleth, Powitzky, and I have found that lists of six nouns are more easily remembered if all are singular or plural than if singulars and plurals are mixed in a list; a variety of controls show that the effect cannot be attributed to confusion at the phonological level. The same appears to be true of verbs and tense, *mutatis mutandis.* If confusion data suggest that phonological information is in the PM, then reasoning from appropriate data leads to the same conclusion regarding syntactic or semantic properties. Second, Craik [1968] has shown that the immediate memory span is virtually identical for words of one to four syllables. This clearly suggests that the capacity of the PM is not defined by acoustic, articulatory, or even phonemic parameters, for all of these surely must vary from one-syllable to four-syllable words.

These data, I think, justify the assumption that the contents of lexical entries, including phonological, syntactic, and semantic information, are deposited in the PM, presumably one entry to a cell. The PM thus would become the working memory for the mechanisms of sentence comprehension.

There are many observations consistent with the assumption that the PM and the comprehension device interact in some such fashion. Three might be noted. First, it is obvious that far more words may be retained in sentences than out of them; sentences are remembered better than lists. In the present model this would be explained by assuming that when words are processed into sentences, the resulting structure is allocated to a further storage system with a much greater capacity. I am inclined to identify it with the secondary memory of the memory theorists, and to propose that items pass into secondary memory only when they are related to one another, or integrated in some fashion akin to comprehension. But that is another matter. For the present purpose, it suffices to assume that when a sentence is understood, it is deposited in the Place Where Sentences Go When They Are Understood (PWSGWTAU).

Second, when the contents of the PM are integrated, the PM can be cleared and new items entered. Support for this notion comes from a series of recent experiments by John Mastenbrook and myself, in which we have found that if a subject is asked to recall a five-word sentence together with five unrelated words, his recall is significantly greater if the sentence is presented before the list than vice versa, independent of recall order. This is easily explained in the present model: if the list is registered first, PM is full when the sentence arrives, and it can be processed only at the cost of some items from the list, whereas if the sentence arrives first, it is quickly understood and the PM is cleared when the list arrives.

Third, the model predicts that any sentence whose initial words exceed the capacity of PM before they can be understood (i.e., before their grammatical relations can be discovered) will prove incomprehensible. This is just the case with sentences self-embedded to a degree of 2 or more.

The evidence, then, supports the assumption that the PM provides a buffer memory for the comprehension device. In my opinion, we have no good idea how that device works; the question is being studied and debated intensively [cf. Gough 1971]. For the present purpose, it suffices to assume that some wondrous mechanism (which we might dub *Merlin*) operating on the information in the PM, tries to discover the deep structure of the fragment, the grammatical relations among its parts. If Merlin succeeds, a semantic interpretation of the fragment is achieved and placed in the ultimate register, the PWSGWTAU. (If Merlin fails, we would assume that the fixation will be maintained to provide further processing time, or that a regressive eye movement would be called for. This is obviously consistent with the well-known facts about eye movements and difficulty of material; cf. Tinker [1958].)

Assuming success, the obtained deep structure provides the basis for the formation of a superficial structure containing the formatives from PM; application of phonological rules to this structure will yield instructions for the pronunciation of the fragment, and the Reader will begin to speak.

At this moment, some 700 msec have passed since the Reader's eye fell on the sentence. By this time, he is probably into his third fixation, perhaps 30 spaces into the sentence. The material from the first fixation is in the ultimate register (the PWSGWTAU); that from the second fixation is crowding into the PM.

I have tried to summarize the history of the 700 msec in Table 1, where the contents of each of the proposed stages of processing are specified at 100-msec intervals. Obviously, most of the entries are little more than plausible guesses. But the table suggests just how much must have happened. Some 20 to 25 letters have been internalized as characters, and converted into abstract phonemes. Perhaps a half dozen lexical entries have been located, and their contents copied into PM. The grammatical relations between some portion of these have been discovered, and the construction of a deep structure has begun. The semantically interpreted items have been inserted into a surface phrase-marker, and that, in turn, has been translated into motor commands.

On the outside, the Reader has rotated his eyes a few millimeters and he has begun to move his mouth. But on the inside, there has been a rapid succession of intricate events. Clearly, this succession could only be the product of a complex information processing system. That which has been proposed herein is outlined in Figure 1. It contains components that are asked to perform amazing feats with amazing rapidity, and precisely in concert. It remains to be seen whether this model bears any resemblance to reality. But it does suggest the complexity of the system that must be assembled in the mind of the child who learns to read.

Table 1
Level of Representation as a Function of Time

Msec	Material under Fixation	Level of Processing: Lines, Curves, Angles	Level of Processing: Letters	Level of Processing: Systematic Phonemes
000	Suppose the eye			
100	" " " "	Suppose the eye	s	
200	" " " "	" " " "	. . . pose th . . .	sŭb = p
300	ose the eye of a mod	ose the eye of a mod	. . . e the e . . .	. . . = pōz#ð . . .
400	" " " "	" " " "	. . . e eye o . . .	. . . z#ðĕ#i . . .
500	of a moderately skil	" " " "	. . . ye of a . . .	. . . i#ŭv#æ . . .
600	" " " "	of a moderately skil	. . . e of a . . .	. .v#æ#m . . .
700	" " " "	" " " "	. . . oderate . . .	. . . #modĕ
800	tely skilled adult r	" " " "	. . . erately . . .	. . . ĕræt# . . .
900	" " " "	tely skilled adult re	. . . led adu . . .	. . . #ly#s . . .
1000	adult reader (hencef	" " " "	. . . d adult . . .	. . . skĭld . . .

Table 1 (Continued)

Msec	Level of Processing: Lexical Entries	Level of Processing: Semantic Representation	Level of Processing: Phonetic Representation	Vocalization
000				
100				
200				
300	$\begin{bmatrix} +V_t \\ +ment \\ \cdot \\ \cdot \\ \cdot \end{bmatrix}$			
400	$\begin{bmatrix} +V_t \\ +ment \\ \cdot \\ \cdot \\ \cdot \end{bmatrix}\begin{bmatrix} +Art \\ +Def \\ \cdot \\ \cdot \\ \cdot \end{bmatrix}$			
500	$\begin{bmatrix} +V_t \\ +ment \\ \cdot \\ \cdot \\ \cdot \end{bmatrix}\begin{bmatrix} +Art \\ +Def \\ \cdot \\ \cdot \\ \cdot \end{bmatrix}\begin{bmatrix} +N_c \\ +Conc \\ \cdot \\ \cdot \\ \cdot \end{bmatrix}$	IMP(_s you will suppose ⁻_s		
600	$\begin{bmatrix} +Art \\ +Def \\ \cdot \\ \cdot \\ \cdot \end{bmatrix}\begin{bmatrix} +N_c \\ +Conc \\ \cdot \\ \cdot \\ \cdot \end{bmatrix}\begin{bmatrix} +Prep \\ +Poss \\ \cdot \\ \cdot \\ \cdot \end{bmatrix}$	... suppose [_s the eye (_s	səpʰōwz	

Table 1 (Continued)

Msec	Level of Processing: Lexical Entries	Level of Processing: Semantic Representation	Level of Processing: Phonetic Representation	Vocalization
700	$\begin{bmatrix} +\text{Prep} & +\text{Art} \\ +\text{Poss} & -\text{Def} \\ \cdot & \cdot \\ \cdot & \cdot \end{bmatrix}$	. . . the eye $(_s X [_s$	ōwzðiyáy	"Su . . ."
800	$\begin{bmatrix} +\text{Prep} & +\text{Art} & +\text{Adj} \\ +\text{Poss} & -\text{Def} & +\text{Deg} \\ \cdot & \cdot & \cdot \\ \cdot & \cdot & \cdot \end{bmatrix}$	. . . eye $(_s X [_s]$ has eye	zðiyáyəv	" . . . ppo . . ."
900	$\begin{bmatrix} +\text{Prep} & +\text{Art} & +\text{Adv} \\ +\text{Poss} & -\text{Def} & +\text{Deg} \\ \cdot & \cdot & \cdot \\ \cdot & \cdot & \cdot \end{bmatrix}$	. . . X $[_s$ X be Y $(_s Y$ mod)	ðiyáyəv	" . . . se . . ."
1000	$\begin{bmatrix} +\text{Art} & +\text{Adv} & +\text{Adj} \\ -\text{Def} & +\text{Deg} & +\text{Anim} \\ \cdot & \cdot & \cdot \\ \cdot & \cdot & \cdot \end{bmatrix}$	. . . X be skilled $(_s \text{skil} \ . . .$	áyəvə	" . . . se . . ."

SUPPOSE THE EYE...   "SUPPOSE..."

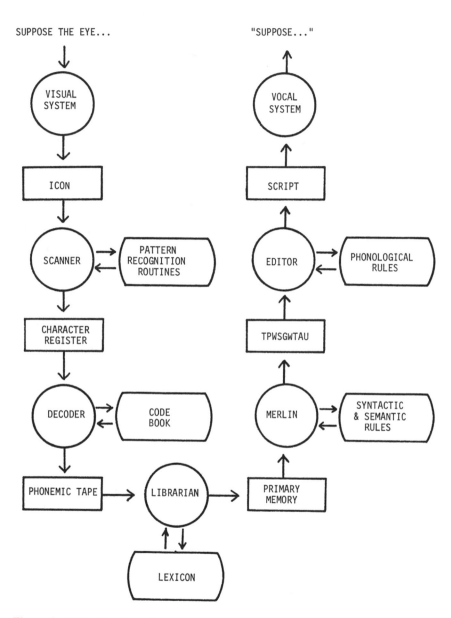

Figure 1. A Model of Reading.

The Acquisition of Reading

The child comes to the task of learning to read with several of the necessary components, or at least with crude versions of them.

Obviously, he comes with a visual system, and it produces an icon. Whether or not the child's visual image is comparable to the adult's is a fascinating question; so far as I know, we know too little of the quantity and quality of the child's icon to say. But there can be little doubt that he has one.

At the other extreme, the child clearly has the capacity to produce and understand sentences. He comes to school equipped with a lexicon, a comprehension device, and a phonological system; in terms of the present model, he incorporates a Librarian, a Merlin, and an Editor. None of these is as elaborate or extensive as they all will be when he reaches adulthood. His lexicon obviously contains fewer entries than it will, and there are indications that the entries it has are not as complete as they will be [cf. McNeill 1970, Chapter 8]. His comprehension device (or at least the grammar it draws upon) is not that of an adult; there are a variety of syntactic structures which he does not yet reliably process [Berko 1958; Chomsky 1969]. His phonological component, at least as it is engaged in speech production, is likely to show considerable deviation from the adult norm.

But at the same time, none of these shortcomings precludes the assembly of (at least) a primitive reading machine, for the child can readily make use of what he has. What is lacking is a character recognition device (the Scanner) and the device which will convert the characters it yields into systematic phonemic representations (the Decoder).

CHARACTER RECOGNITION

There is no doubt that character recognition poses a problem for the child. We know pitifully little about form perception in children [cf. Reese and Lipsitt 1970, Chapter 11]. But it seems clear that letters— "lank, stark, immovable, without form or comeliness, and as to signification, wholly void" [Mann 1841]—are not naturally identified. They can, of course, be discriminated [Caldwell and Hall 1969, 1970], but this is a far cry from the absolute identification demanded by the reading process. For example, while children will make relatively few mistakes in copying a pattern like a letter [Asso and Wyke 1971], indicating that they are quite capable of simultaneous discrimination, they find the same distinction inordinately difficult in a successive discrimination task [Rudel and Teuber 1963].

The difficulties posed for the child by letters that are mirror images of one another (e.g., "b–d, p–q") and, to a lesser extent, by those that are inversions (e.g., "b–p") have long been noted [cf. Monroe 1932]. There have been a number of studies assessing methods of teaching children these distinctions [e.g., Hendrickson and Muehl 1962]. And almost as often, this problem has been taken as a symptom of reading disability [cf. Orton 1937].

In one sense, it must be such a symptom. An inability to reliably identify "b" cannot fail to be a handicap in reading. But as E. Gibson has pointed out, the discrimination our orthography demands of the child runs directly counter to virtually all of his perceptual experience, in which objects differing only in orientation are equivalent. Moreover, Corballis and Beale [1971] have argued persuasively that such equivalence is deeply rooted in the bilateral symmetry of our anatomy. Thus these distinctions must pose a problem for every child, and there is every indication that this is the case.

Aside from orientation, the features that distinguish (or fail to distinguish) one letter from another in the child's icon are little understood. Gibson's studies of letter confusions in early readers and adults [Gibson, Schapiro et al. 1968] have suggested a set of features that may well be those used by the character recognition device. What remains to be disclosed, however, are the features by which the prereader will distinguish the same patterns. This knowledge would indicate which subcomponents of the character recognition device are available in the prereader, and which are not, and we might get some idea of what it takes to assemble the complete device.

It would be comforting to think that character recognition (or better, the lack of it) was the chief impediment to learning to read, for it can be taught (at least with patience). The unwary might be tempted to find support for this in the infamous fact that knowledge of the alphabet is the single best predictor of reading achievement [Bond and Dykstra 1967]. But Samuels [1971] has reported the results of several studies that found no evidence that teaching the alphabet facilitates learning to read.

It remains to be seen, however, if the correlation is entirely spurious. Teaching of the alphabet, the ABC's, dates at least to the time of Socrates [Mathews 1966], and I find it difficult to believe that a tradition that appears to serve no other purpose would survive if it did not serve this one. Whether by means of alphabet books, blocks, or soup, character recognition must be mastered. It is obviously a necessary component of reading; equally obvious, it is not a sufficient one. Given character recognition, the fundamental problem arises, that which is commonly referred to as *decoding*.

DECODING

The Reader converts characters into systematic phonemes; the child must learn to do so. The Reader knows the rules that relate one set of abstract entities to another; the child does not. The Reader is a decoder; the child must become one. The decoding metaphor is familiar, and it would be difficult to argue that it is inappropriate. But if we take seriously the notion that characters are decoded to systematic phonemes, there is an interesting consequence. We can no longer think of the child as a clerk to whom we hand the code, for there is no direct way to display the rules constituting it. We cannot show him that this character goes with that systematic phoneme, for there is no way to isolate a systematic phoneme. We cannot tell him, "This goes with That," for we have no way of representing That.

In short, we cannot teach him the code. This is not to say that he cannot acquire it; every Reader before him has done so. But the child must master the code through a sort of cryptanalysis rather than through memorization. Viewed in this light, what is necessary for the child to learn to read is that he be provided with a set of pairs of messages known to be equivalent, one in ciphertext (writing) and one in plaintext (speech). They must be provided in sufficient quantity to enable him to arrive at a unique solution, and that is all.

A full solution of the code (i.e., one equivalent to that we ascribe to the Reader) can be achieved only if the child correctly identifies the alphabets of the plaintext and of the ciphertext. If we assume that the child has lexical representations in the form of systematic phonemes, the former should pose no special problem. (There is, however, some evidence to suggest that this may be a facile assumption; cf. Savin in this volume. It remains to be seen whether evidence of this sort is indicative of a different sort of phonological organization in the child, or the result of something much more superficial.)

If the child has mastered the character recognition problem as discussed above, then he has isolated the alphabet of the ciphertext, and his problem is reduced to a tractable one: that of searching for correspondences between the message pairs. But if, for some reason, he has not realized the unity of the letters, then he is faced with a cryptanalytic task of demonstrably greater difficulty, that of working out the cipher alphabet and the code simultaneously. In this connection, the

Look-and-Say method obviously comes to mind. In light of the present analysis this method is not totally unreasonable. It provides the essential ingredients for the child's cryptanalysis (i.e., pairs of spoken and written messages). The trouble with it is that it does not appropriately define the problem for the child-cryptanalyst.

The Look-and-Say method confronts the child with a problem of paired-associate (PA) learning. We know that subjects confronted with the PA task will "solve" it as efficiently as they can; they will select some cue, some feature of each stimulus, and associate the defined response with that cue. That cue can be any feature or property of the stimulus item that distinguishes it from the others; in the case of visual material, it might be length, or area, or the presence of a curved line. I know of no reason to suppose that the child is different from the sophomore subject in this respect. Confronted with a word (the Look) to which he must associate a response (the Say), he should be likely to seize upon any feature of the word that differentiates it from the others he must master.

An egregious example of this can be found in a study reported by Coleman (1970) as part of his effort to collect a data base for a technology of reading. One of Coleman's concerns was to rank words that might be used in basic reading programs in order of the ease with which the child could learn to read them. So several hundred words were taught to different children by the look-say method, and the number of errors to criterion was taken as the basic datum. The words *kitten* and *o* were found to be the easiest of all. When it is noted that the words were presented in short lists, and that *kitten* is the only word as long as six letters, it is easy to see why these words were easy (and it is not that they are intrinsically so).

Given the manner in which lists are learned, it seems clear that the Look-and-Say method would not force the child to map characters onto phonemes until simpler strategies will no longer work, and that will not happen until the list reaches a substantial length. At this point, we would expect that some children will tackle the cryptanalysis and learn to read, but we should not be surprised to see others resign in frustration. And that, of course, is what is known to happen with the Look-and-Say method.

It is clearly preferable to confront the child with the mapping problem from the start, and to suggest to him that is solvable. One way is through phonics. In this method (or better, class of methods), the child is explicitly directed to the ciphertext alphabet, and conceivably to the plaintext as well. The method requires that he pair letters (and clusters of letters) with spoken syllables; to the extent that he segments those syllables, such learning might provide material for the necessary cryptanalysis.

It is important to realize, though, that phonics does not teach the mapping required to become a Reader. What the Reader knows is the mapping between characters and systematic phonemes; what the child is taught in phonics is to name a letter (or letter pair) with a syllable that contains the appropriate systematic phoneme. When a child "sounds out" a new word, it is apparent to any auditor that the child is not converting letters into underlying phonemic representations. Rather he is searching for something that he can hear as a word.

In the present analysis, phonics is not a method of teaching the child grapheme-phoneme correspondence rules. The rules he learns are not the rules he must master, but rather heuristics for locating words through the auditory modality. The lexical representations of those words then provide data for the induction of the real character-phoneme rules. Skill in phonics gives the child a means of naming a word *in loco parentis;* it provides him with a valuable means of data collection.

The crucial variable in the cryptanalytic problem is the character of the data: the nature and number of message pairs. Other things equal, the shorter the messages, the fewer the potential solutions; so cryptanalysis is facilitated if the shortest possible messages are provided first. Virtually every method takes advantage of this fact by beginning reading instruction with short words. (It is interesting to note that Jacotot, one of the intellectual ancestors of Gestalt psychology, advocated beginning with a book and gradually working back to the letter, whatever that means; Mathews [1966].) Cryptanalysis is also facilitated if the messages are arranged such that covariation is apparent; if a change in a ciphertext is also accompanied by a change in the corresponding plaintext, the solution is obvious.

From this perspective, the various so-called Linguistic Methods (like those advocated by Bloomfield [1942] and Fries [1963]) appear to be optimal, for they offer the child a sequence of message pairs in which only one element is varied at a time. What is surprising, at least on first inspection, is that this method has not been shown to be superior. Indeed, there is no compelling evidence that any reasonable method of reading instruction yields results different from the others. This is encouraging, in one sense, for it means that children can manage to learn to read under any method, so long as they are provided the appropriate data, and the present hypothesis predicts just that. But it is also frustrating, for differential predictions are the stuff of which theories are made.

The trouble is, of course, that Methods are not methods. That is, a Method describes little more than an orientation on the part of a teacher, and perhaps the use of a particular basal reading series [Chall 1967]. What are desperately needed are experimental studies of reading acquisition in detail, where we know what was presented to the child, when, in what manner, and how often.

There have been very few, and they are not very revealing. The first (that I know of) was conducted by Bishop [1964], using adult subjects. It was intended to compare the transfer effects of word and letter training. One group of subjects was taught to an eight-item paired-associate list, where each stimulus consisted of four Arabic characters (e.g., ن ا ں و) drawn from a set of twelve, and each response was a disyllabic Arabic word (e.g., /faru/. A second group was taught to name each of the twelve characters with its appropriate phoneme (i.e., they were given instruction in Arabic phonics). A third learned an irrelevant task. When all groups were than asked to learn a new eight-item PA list (in which the characters were recombined to form novel words), the phonics group learned it most rapidly. This is scarcely surprising (though it may have been when the study was conducted), for it seems clear that the whole-word group had little reason to detect correspondences, since other strategies requiring no intellectual effort would suffice perfectly well. (In fact, we might have expected to see negative transfer in this group, save for the fact that training and transfer stimuli had no initial characters in common.) What is more interesting is that the word group performed better than the control; some subjects evidently took on the cryptanalysis even though it was not necessary. But these subjects were college students, and it is not obvious that children would go to the same trouble.

A more promising study was conducted with kindergarteners by Jeffrey and Samuels [1967]. They employed an artificial alphabet of six nonsense figures. Three (call them A, B, C), were identified with the consonants /m, s, b/, three (X, Y, Z) with the vowels /e, i, o/. One group of subjects, the Word Group, was taught a four-item PA list: AX–/mo/, BX–/so/, CY–/be/, CZ–/bi/. A Letter Group was taught four isolated correspondences: A–/m/, B–/s/, Y–/e/, and Z–/i/. A control group was taught an unrelated task.

Prior to training, all groups were familiarized with the alphabet, and given practice on "blending" the sounds to be used in the ultimate transfer list, AZ, BZ, BY, and AY. Then each group was given its training. On the transfer list, the phonics group performed significantly better than the others, which did not differ. In this study, the Letter Group was given what amounts to phonics instruction, and the Word Group might be thought of as representing a linguistic method. If this were so, the phonics instruction would seem to be the superior method of (at least) initial instruction. But there is a serious flaw in this analogy, for the Word Group was mistreated.

The Letter Group was exposed to just those four elements that would be involved in the transfer; the Word Group, on the other hand, confronted items composed of six. But more important, the organization of those elements fell short of that which could be expected to yield successful cryptanalysis.

The message pairs which the Word Group was allowed to use may be arranged in a matrix, arrayed by initial and final ciphertext element:

	X	Y	Z
A	/mo/	—	—
B	/so/	—	—
C	—	/be/	/bi/

This display makes clear the structure of the correspondence rules, and it is conceivable that they might be induced by someone who knew that CY can be decomposed to C and Y, and that /be/ consists of /b/ plus /e/. (In fact, the Word Group produced something like eight correct responses—of a possible 80—on the initial transfer trial, so more than one of the 20 must have induced something.) But there is nothing to demand it, for memorizing only four item-item correspondences will solve the problem. In fact, to achieve the solution of the code implicit in this matrix would require the identification of *six* rules. It is surely reasonable for the learner to prefer rote memory in this instance.

Such considerations lead to the hypothesis that the child would most readily learn the true system of correspondences when it provides the simplest solution to the cryptanalytic problem. For example, if, in a design like that of Jeffrey and Samuels, the child had been forced to learn not just four items, but all six lying outside a diagonal of this matrix, then the principled solution would be as simple as the associative one, and we would expect significantly greater transfer to novel items (i.e., the diagonal items).

This analysis suggests that the child's task bears a striking resemblance to those studied in adults under the rubric of miniature linguistic systems. Since the seminal experiments of Esper [1925, 1933] this literature has grown too large to review here (see Smith and Braine, in press). But it provides abundant evidence for the principle proposed here: The greater the advantage afforded by induction of structure (over rote memory), the more frequent the induction. In the present case, we should expect to see that if Jeffrey and Samuels had not only more completely filled the matrix but enlarged it (in either dimension), the Word Method would have yielded dramatically better results [cf. Foss 1968; Palermo and Parrish 1971]. And when one considers that the real task confronting the child involves a matrix in multiple dimensions, the consequences are even more apparent. There have been other studies of teaching methods [e.g., Hartley 1970]—in this experimental sense—but they add little to this picture.

How the child solves the decoding problem is a mystery, but many do. If one does, he should be able to understand and produce any word that conforms to the rules he has mastered. Yet it has long been observed that there are children who can read and pronounce words, children who can decode, but yet do not seem to *read* connected discourse. They "bark at print"; they are "word-callers" or "parrot-readers." Evidently, solving the decoding problem does not automatically make the child a Reader.

THE SPEED PROBLEM

There is a natural interpretation of this problem within the present model. To understand a sentence, it does not suffice to obtain lexical entries, place them in the PM, and pronounce them. If the words of a sentence are to be integrated into a semantic reading, they must be deployed in the PM together.

To be sure, we adults can tolerate substantial delays between words without apparent disruption of comprehension; if the delays are brief enough, as in hesitation pauses, we may not even be aware of them. This is to be expected if the PM is indeed the repository for material waiting to be understood, for it will hold that material for a short while. But Martin [1968] has shown that pauses of as little as two seconds interfere with our ability to perceive sentences in noise, and we have found some evidence in pilot studies that repetition or words within sentences reduces our capacity to remember them.

It seems reasonable to suppose that the child's ability to comprehend sentences is affected in the same way. Furthermore, if—as some evidence suggests [Haith, Morrison et al. 1970]—the child's PM is much smaller than our own, then pauses between words will prove even more disruptive for the child's comprehension. There is an obvious source of pauses in reading sentences: if words are identified slowly, then pauses are inevitable. There is abundant evidence that children do not identify words as rapidly as adults, and that the poor reader does not identify words as rapidly as the good one.

The hypothesis that temporal word spacing will significantly diminish sentence comprehension in the child would be easy to test. But I think that naturalistic observation of children reading aloud suggests that temporal spacing is a ubiquitous problem in early reading. If it takes too long to read a given word, the content of the immediately preceding words will have been lost from the PM, and comprehension will be prevented. If the word in question is read aloud, it will necessarily be read as a citation form, and the child's oral reading will sound like a list just because he is, in fact, reading a list.

To prevent this, the child who would understand must try to read rapidly, and if he cannot quickly identify a word, he must guess. The result will frequently be an oral reading error. These errors have been the subject of considerable study [Weber 1968], and seemingly contradictory conclusions have been drawn from them. On the one hand, it has been argued (e.g., by Goodman [1970] and elsewhere) that reading is normally a kind of guessing game, in which the reader uses the printed word for little more than hints as to whether he is thinking the right thoughts or not. In this view, oral reading errors are nothing but a manifestation of normal function, not a symptom of malfunction, and thus they should not be squelched. On the other hand, it has been argued (by Biemiller [1970]), that at least in the early stages of reading, oral reading errors are an indication that the child is avoiding the decoding problem, and thus a sign that he is unable to identify what lies before him.

From the present point of view, Biemiller is closer to the truth. A guess may be a good thing, for it may preserve the integrity of sentence comprehension. But rather than being a sign of normal reading, it indicates that the child did not decode the word in question rapidly enough to read normally. The good reader need not guess; the bad should not.

In the model I have outlined, the Reader is not a guesser. From the outside, he appears to go from print to meaning as if by magic. But I have contended that this is an illusion, that he really plods through the sentence, letter by letter, word by word. He may not do so; but to show that he does not, his trick will have to be exposed.

References

Asso, D., and M. Wyke, 1971. Discrimination of spatially confusable letters by young children. *J. Exp. Child Psych.* 11:11–20.

Baddeley, A. D., 1966. Short-term memory for word sequences as a function of acoustic, semantic, and formal similarity. *Quart. J. Exp. Psychol.* 18:362–365.

Berko, J., 1958. The child's learning of English morphology. *Word,* 14:150–177.

Biemiller, A., 1970. The development of the use of graphic and contextual information. *Reading Res. Quart.* 6:75–96.

Bishop, C. H., 1964. Transfer effects of word and letter training in reading. *J. Verbal Learning and Verbal Behavior* 3:215–221.

Bloomfield, L., 1942. Linguistics and reading. *Elementary English,* 18:125–130; 183–186.

Bond, G. L., and R. Dykstra, 1967. The cooperative research program in first-grade reading instruction. *Reading Res. Quart.* 2:4, 5–126.

Caldwell, E. D., and V. C. Hall, 1969. The influence of concept training on letter discrimination. *Child Development* 40:63–71.

Caldwell, E. D., and V. C. Hall, 1970. Concept learning in discrimination tasks. *Develop. Psych.* 2:41–48.

Carmichael, L., and W. F. Dearborn, 1947. *Reading and Visual Fatigue.* Boston: Houghton Mifflin.

Chall, J., 1967. *Learning To Read: The Great Debate.* New York: McGraw-Hill.

Chomsky, C., 1969. *The Acquisition of Syntax in Children from 5 to 10.* Cambridge, Mass.: M.I.T. Press.

Chomsky, N., 1970. Phonology and reading. In H. Levin and J. P. Williams (eds.), *Basic Studies on Reading.* New York: Basic Books, pp. 3–18.

Chomsky, N., and M. Halle, 1968. *The Sound pattern of English.* New York: Harper and Row.

Coleman, E. B., 1970. Collecting a data base for a reading technology. *J. Ed. Psych. Monographs* 61:4, Part 2, pp. 1–3.

Conrad, R., 1964. Acoustic confusions in immediate memory. *Brit. J. Psych.* 55:75–84.

Corballis, M. C., and I. L. Beale, 1971. On telling left from right. *Sci. Amer.* 224:96–104.

Craik, F. I. M., 1968. Two components in free recall. *J. Verbal Learning and Verbal Behavior* 7:996–1004.

Dustman, R. E., and E. C. Beck, 1965. Phase of alpha brain waves, reaction time and visually evoked potentials. *Electroenceph. Clin. Neurophysiol.* 18:433–440.

Esper, E. A., 1925. A technique for the experimental investigation of associative interference in artificial linguistic material. *Language Monogr.,* vol. 1.

———, 1933. Studies in linguistic behavior organization: I. Characteristics of unstable verbal reactions. *J. Gen. Psych.* 8:346–379.

Feinberg, R., 1949. A study of some aspects of peripheral visual acuity. *Amer. J. Optometry and Arch. of Amer. Acad. Optometry* 26:49–56, 105–119.

Foss, D. J., 1968. Learning and discovery in the acquisition of structured material. *J. Exp. Psych.* 77:341–344.

————, 1970. Some effects of ambiguity upon sentence comprehension. *J. Verbal Learning and Verbal Behavior* 9:699–706.

Fries, C. C., 1963. *Linguistics and Reading.* New York: Holt, Rinehart, and Winston.

Gibson, E. J., 1965. Learning to read. *Science,* 148:1066–1072.

Gibson, E. J., F. Schapiro, and A. Yonas, 1968. Confusion matrices for graphic patterns obtained with a latency measure. In *The Analysis of Reading Skill: A Program of Basic and Applied Research.* Final report, Project No. 5–1213, Cornell University and U.S.O.E., pp. 76–96.

Gibson, E. J., H. Osser, and A. Pick, 1963. A study in the development of grapheme-phoneme correspondences. *J. Verbal Learning and Verbal Behavior* 2:142–146.

Gilbert, L. C., 1959. Speed of processing visual stimuli and its relation to reading. *J. Ed. Psych.* 55:8–14.

Goodman, K. S., 1970. Reading: A psycholinguistic guessing game. In *Theoretical Models and Processes of Reading,* H. Singer and R. R. Ruddell (eds.), Newark, Del: International Reading Association, pp. 259–272.

Gough, P. B., 1968. We don't read letter-by-letter? Paper presented at a Consortium on Psycholinguistics and Reading, Convention of the International Reading Association, Boston.

————, 1971. (Almost a decade of) experimental psycholinguistics. In *A Survey of Linguistic Sci*ence, W. O. Dingwall (ed.), College Park: Linguistics Program, Univ. of Maryland.

Gough, P. B., and W. C. Stewart, 1970. Word vs. non-word discrimination latency. Paper presented at Midwestern Psychological Association.

Haber, R. N. (ed.), 1968. *Contemporary Theory and Research in Visual Perception.* New York: Holt, Rinehart and Winston.

———— (ed.), 1969. *Information-Processing Approches to Visual Perception.* New York: Holt, Rinehart and Winston.

Haber, R. N., and L. G. Standing, 1969. Direct measures of short-term visual storage. *Quart. J. Exp. Psych.* 21:43–54.

Haith, M. M., F. J. Morrison, K. Sheingold, and P. Mindes, 1970. Short-term memory for visual information in children and adults. *J. Exp. Child Psych.* 9:454–469.

Halle, M., 1969. Some thought on spelling. In *Psycholinguistics and the Teaching of Reading,* K. S. Goodman and J. T. Fleming (eds.), Newark, Del.: International Reading Association.

Hartley, R. N., 1970. Effects of list types and cues on the learning of word lists. *Reading Res. Quart.* 6:97–121.

Hendrickson, L. N., and S. Muehl, 1962. The effect of attention and motor response pretraining on learning to discriminate b and d in kindergarten children. *J. Ed. Psych.* 53:236–241.

Hubel, D. H., and T. N. Wiesel, 1962. Receptive fields, binocular interaction and functional architecture in the cat's visual cortex. *J. Physiol.* 160:106–154.

Jeffrey, W. E., and S. J. Samuels, 1967. Effect of method of reading training on initial learning and transfer. *J. Verb. Learning and Verbal Behavior* 6:354–358.

Kolers, P. A., 1970. Three stages of reading. In *Basic Studies on Reading,* H. Levin and J. P. Williams (eds.), New York: Basic Books, pp. 90–118.

Liss, P., 1968. Does backward masking by visual noise stop stimulus processing? *Perception and Psychophysics* 4:328, 330.

McNeill, D., 1970. *The Acquisition of Language.* New York: Harper and Row.

Mann, 1841; cited by Mathews (1966), p. 77.

Martin, J. G., 1968. Temporal word spacing and the perception of ordinary, anomalous, and scrambled strings. *J. Verbal Learning and Verbal Behavior* 7:1954–157.

Mathews, M. M., 1966. *Teaching to Read: Historically Considered.* Chicago: University of Chicago Press.

Monroe, M., 1932. *Children Who Cannot Read.* Chicago: University of Chicago Press.

Norman, D. A. (ed.), 1970. *Models of Memory.* New York: Academic Press.

Ohala, J., 1970. Aspects of the control and production of speech. UCLA: Working Papers in Phonetics, vol. 15.

Orton, S. T., 1937. *Reading, Writing, and Speech Problems in Children.* New York: W. W. Norton.

Palermo, D. S., and M. Parrish, 1971. Rule acquisition as a function of number and frequency of exemplar presentation. *J. Verbal Learning and Verbal Behavior* 10:44–51.

Reese, H. W., and L. P. Lipsitt, 1970. *Experimental Child Psychology.* New York: Academic Press.

Rohrman, N. L., and P. B. Gough, 1967. Forewarning, meaning, and semantic decision latency. *Psychonomic Sci.* 9:217–218.

Rubenstein, H., L. Garfield, and J. A. Millikan, 1970. Homographic entries in the internal lexicon. *J. Verb. Learning and Verbal Behavior* 5:487–492.

Rubenstein, H., S. S. Lewis, and M. A. Rubenstein, 1971. Homographic entries in the internal lexicon: Effects of systematicity and relative frequency of meanings. *J. Verbal Learning and Verbal Behavior* 10:57–62.

Rudel, R. G., and H.-L. Teuber, 1963. Discrimination of direction of line in children. *J. Comp. Physiol. Psychol.* 56:892–898.

Samuels, S. J., 1971. Letter-name versus letter-sound knowledge in learning to read. *The Reading Teacher,* 24:604–608.

Scharf, B., H. S. Zamansky, and R. F. Brightbill, 1966. Word recognition with masking. *Perception and Psychophysics,* 1:110–112.

Smith, K. H., and M. D. S. Braine, in press. Miniature languages and the problem of language acquisition. In *The Structure and Psychology of Language,* T. G. Bever and W. Weksel (eds.), New York: Holt, Rinehart and Winston.

Spencer, T. J., 1969. Some effects of different masking stimuli in iconic storage. *J. Exp. Psych.* 81:132–140.

Sperling, G., 1960. The information available in brief visual presentations. *Psychol. Monogr.,* 74: No. 11 (whole No. 498).

Sperling, G., 1963. A model for visual memory tasks. *Human Factors,* 5:19–31.

Stewart, M. L., C. T. James, and P. B. Gough, 1969. Word recognition latency as a function of word length. Paper presented at Midwestern Psychological Association,

Tinker, M. A., 1958. Recent studies of eye movements in reading. *Psych. Bull.* 55:215–231.

Venezky, R. L., 1970. *The Structure of English Orthography.* The Hague: Mouton.

Waugh, N. C., and D. A. Norman, 1965. Primary memory. *Psych. Rev.,* 72:89–104.

Weber, R., 1968. The study of oral reading errors: A survey of the literature. *Reading Res. Quart.* 4:96–119.

Wertheim, T., 1894. Ueber die indirekte Sehschärfe. *Z. Psychologie u. Physiologie der Sinnesorgane* 7:172–187.

White, M. J., 1969. Laterality differences in perception: A review. *Psych. Bull.* 72:387–405.

WILLIAM F. BREWER

Is Reading a Letter-by-Letter Process?

A Discussion of Gough's Paper

Gough has given us a most provocative paper. He has attempted to build an explicit model of the reading process and provide a millisecond by millisecond account of what is going on in the mind of the reader. Given our current level of knowledge in this area, this is clearly a courageous thing to do. By proposing an explicit theory of the reading process and taking a firm stand on the fundamental issues in reading research, Gough has performed an extremely valuable service. He states that his model is intended to be an exhaustive description of the reading process, and I intend to take him at his word. In order to explore his model I would like to go through it stage by stage and see how well it accounts for those things we do know about the reading process.

A quick look at the history of theories in this area reveals the ingenious nature of Gough's overall strategy. In the late 1800s it appears that reading was thought to be a serial processing of the letters making up words and then a serial combination of these words into sentences. However, this position was overthrown by a series of studies coming out of Wundt's laboratory soon after the founding of experimental psychology. Perhaps the most influential work opposed to the letter-by-letter theory was a series of studies carried out by James McK. Cattell [1885a, 1885b, 1886a, 1886b]. Cattell rejected the letter-by-letter (serial) theory of word perception in favor of the whole-word (parallel) approach on the basis of the following kinds of evidence: (a) Words in prose passages can be read almost as fast as lists of letters. (b) The immediate visual apprehension span for letters in prose is much greater than for random letters. (c) Latencies to initiate pronunciation of words are shorter than those for letters. (d) Visual recognition thresholds for words are lower than the thresholds for letters.

For the most part, serious research on the reading process stopped with the rise of behaviorism; however, among those few who continued to work in the area, Cattell's arguments were considered to have shown that word perception is parallel, not serial [Woodworth 1938]. In light of this brief history of models of reading Gough's general strategy becomes clear. He has chosen to use the recent work in psycholinguistics and visual information processing to develop a new sophisticated letter-by-letter model of reading. Gough did not take the time to criticize Cattell's position, but I would expect him to make the following types of arguments: (a) The fact that words in prose passages can be read almost as fast as lists of letters does not indicate equal perceptual processing time; higher-order linguistic variables make the response output times of words faster than those of letters. (b) The fact that the immediate visual apprehension span for letters in prose is much greater than that for random letters does not reflect the speed of perceptual processing but simply the fact that the letters processed from a random string are not formed into higher-order units and therefore many are lost in recall. (c) The slower initiation of pronunciation of letters than of words is not due to slower perceptual processing but to a slower response system for letter naming. (d) I am not sure how Gough would handle the effects of linguistic structure on visual recognition thresholds, but probably he would develop some form of response bias explanation. Overall it looks as if Cattell's parallel processing model was resting on a rather weak foundation.

In his new serial processing theory Gough has developed an inflow model with letter-by-letter processing at the lower levels and has rigorously separated this stage from the higher-order linguistic processing. Gough eloquently expressed the motivation behind his approach during a discussion at this conference when he stated that he didn't "see how the syntax can go out and mess around with the print." It is hard not to be in sympathy with this comment, but I have chosen instead to live with the paradox of having higher-order linguistic processes find their way downstream where they should not be. Thus, for the rest of this paper I would like to update Cattell's arguments and help him put down this rejuvenated letter-by-letter model.

Gough's model begins by assuming a regular mechanical left-to-right progression of eye fixations. While we still do not have detailed knowledge about the location of fixations in reading, it seems clear that there are systematic differences in the rate and duration of fixations due to the linguistic characteristics of the material being read [Huey 1908; Hochberg 1970; Mehler, Bever et al. 1967; Woodworth 1938]. Thus, an adequate model of reading will have to include some mechanism to allow an interaction between the higher linguistic processing and the control of eye fixations. It is not clear how Gough's linear inflow model can handle this problem.

The next stage of information processing in the model is the development of an icon in 100 msec that lasts for 250 msec and can hold roughly 20 letter-spaces of material. While none of these time parameters is too well established currently, these estimates are certainly fairly typical of those in the literature.

The next stage is crucial in the development of an updated serial model of the reading process. In order to make a letter-by-letter model function in real time, the rates of letter processing have to be extremely rapid. Gough uses the evidence from Sperling [1963] that icon readout takes place at a constant rate of one letter every 10 msec. There are a large number of problems with this very fast icon readout time. In order to obtain this estimate of readout time, Sperling [1963] assumed that a visual noise field stops the ongoing perceptual processing. It is not at all certain that a visual noise mask does operate this way [Haber 1970b; Kahneman 1968]. If one accepts the use of a visual noise mask, then there is some evidence to support the 10-msec icon readout [Sperling 1963; Scharf, Zamansky et al. 1966].

However, there is also a variety of evidence to suggest that icon readout may not be serial. Sperling [1967] has reported evidence that he interprets as opposing his earlier hypothesis of strict serial readout. Haber [1970a] has obtained evidence for serial processing in word perception with naive subjects, but not with practiced subjects, who show parallel processing in the same task. Eriksen and Spencer [1969] have used sequential presentation of letters at varying rates to test the serial readout hypothesis and have found evidence in favor of parallel processing. Gough reports a study done in his laboratory that shows that the latency to initiate pronunciation of visually presented words is longer for long words than short words. This replicates the results of Cattell [1886b] and Eriksen, Pollack et al. [1970]. Gough uses the evidence from his study to support a serial 10-msec icon readout. However, the experiment by Eriksen et al. included a control condition using stimuli of similar visual complexity which differed in length of verbal response to show that most of the longer latencies must be due to increased time of motor programming, rather than to increased time of visual processing. Overall it appears that the evidence for the crucial 10-msec letter readout component of the model is not very strong.

Because Gough's model does not allow any higher-order processing components to interact with the letter readout level, there should be no difference between words and nonwords in rate of visual processing. However, there are now a large number of studies which show that forced-choice letter recognition is better and letter search times are faster for words than for nonwords [Aderman and Smith 1971; Krueger

1970a,b; Reicher 1969; Smith 1969; Wheeler 1970]. Some of these studies (e.g. Wheeler [1970]) have gone to enormous lengths to show that the effect is due to the word-nonword difference, and not to response bias from some higher level of organization.

There are several additional types of information that I find hard to reconcile with the model. In reading for meaning, typographical errors are frequently not noticed. An early study by Pillsbury [1897] explored the phenomenon in some detail and showed that subjects frequently give a phenomenological report of having seen a word that has not appeared. It is hard to see how Gough's model can deal with this interaction of higher-order levels with the perceptual processing of letters. A similar problem for the model is the subjects' phenomenological report that they can see much more at a given exposure duration if the material is in higher-order units such as words or sentences [Huey 1908; Neisser 1967].

After the letters have been processed they are mapped onto systematic phonemes. As one of several types of processing this may be a reasonable hypothesis. However, Gough's model makes this the exclusive path from the letters to meaning. Thus *any* evidence showing direct processing of words without a phonological transformation is incompatible with the model. Therefore the fact that we can read with understanding homophones such as "chute" and "shoot" cannot be dealt with, since visual information must have been used to retrieve the appropriate meaning. The studies on reading with deaf subjects reported by Gibson, Shurcliff et al. [1970] and by Conrad at this conference also show that reading can take place without a stage of phonological transformation. However, it seems clear that any successful model also needs a system that allows direct translation from the orthography to a phonological level, since adult readers can pronounce words they have never seen before. The arguments that Gough makes in favor of mapping onto the level of systematic phonemes have some merit, but some of the simplicity is lost in those cases where the orthography does not reflect the level of systematic phonemes, since the model will require additional apparatus to handle these instances. Gough's arguments against a mapping from the orthography to speech are not very convincing. If he is willing to use a system as abstract as the level of systematic phonemes in his model, then it seems only fair to allow other theorists a level of speech that is abstract enough to avoid the time parameter difficulties he outlines. In fact Sperling [1967] has proposed a model that maps onto speech, containing a buffer of motor-instruction programs which deal with these time difficulties. In general it looks as if there is enough evidence to reject models that postulate only a letter-to-sound mapping or only a letter-to-meaning mapping, but beyond that there is little constraint about how the systems might function (cf. LaBerge, this volume).

After information has reached the level of systematic phonemes, the meanings of individual words are retrieved word by word, from left to right. The assumption is made that the order of lexical search is not affected by previously processed information. This is a most intriguing assumption. At the level of awareness it is certainly the case that the particular reading given to a word is determined by previous information. For example, take the word *light* in the following two sentences: (a) *The painter said the new paint was lighter, but his assistant still had trouble picking it up.* (b) *The weight lifter said the dumbell was light, but when we came closer we could see that it was actually painted a dark blue.* In the first sentence the first five words give *'lighter'* the reading 'pale' and the remainder of the sentence shifts the reading to 'not heavy'. In the second sentence the initial reading is 'not heavy' and the final reading shifts to 'pale'. Thus, it is clear that at the level of awareness both preceding and following information contribute to the reading given a particular lexical item.

However, the fact that the conscious reading is determined by preceding information does not eliminate the possibility that there is an unconscious lexical search that operates without regard to previous context and then sends one appropriate reading up to the level of awareness. In fact Foss's [1970] finding that response to a probe is slow for a word following an ambiguous word, regardless of the presence or absence of disambiguating context, is consistent with Gough's model. But in general not enough is known about the order of lexical search to constrain model building at this level.

After lexical lookup the information is taken to a buffer that can handle both syntactic and semantic information. It is clear that there has to be a place where the syntactic and semantic relations of the reading matter are worked out, and Gough chooses to identify this with the primary memory box that is part of most current models of memory. One possible problem for the model is the fact that the contents of primary memory are typically available to conscious observation, whereas the intricate syntactic and semantic processing that must go on in sentence understanding appear to be unavailable to conscious observation. But this is another area where there simply is not enough knowledge to put much constraint on alternative models.

The final stage in the model is TPWSGWTAU. This is the place where all sentences go if they have led a good life; if they have not been good they are consigned to a regressive eye-movement.

In summary I think Gough has made a gallant attempt to provide an explicit model of the reading process. However, it is obvious that we have consistently locked horns over the possibility of higher-order processes interacting with lower-order processes. Gough has given new life to the letter-by-letter approach to reading and I have tried to do the same for Cattell's criticisms of such a model. Whatever the merits of Gough's particular model, I think the attempt has been most productive in bringing to the surface some of the fundamental issues in building a psychological model of the reading process.

References

Aderman, D., and E. E. Smith, 1971. Expectancy as a determinant of functional units in perceptual recognition. *Cog. Psych.* 2:117–129.

Cattell, J. McK., 1885a. The inertia of the eye and brain. *Brain,* 8:295–312.

———, 1885b. Ueber die Zeit der Erkennung und Benennung von Schriftzeichen, Bildern und Farben. *Philosophische Studien,* 2:635–650. (Translated as: On the time required for recognizing and naming letters and words, pictures and colors. In A. T. Poffenberger (ed.) *James McKeen Cattell: Man of Science.* Vol. 1. *Psychological Research,* Lancaster, Penn.: Science Press, 1947, pp. 13–23.)

———, 1886a. The time taken up by cerebral operations. III. The perception-time. *Mind* 11:377–392.

———, 1886b. The time taken up by cerebral operations. IV. The will-time. *Mind* 11:524–534.

Eriksen, C. W., M. D. Pollack, and W. E. Montague, 1970. Implicit speech: Mechanism in perceptual encoding? *J. Exp. Psych.* 84:502–507.

Eriksen, C. W., and T. Spencer, 1969. Rate of information processing in visual perception: Some results and methodological considerations. *J. Exp. Psych. Monograph,* 79, No. 2, Part 2.

Foss, D. J., 1970. Understanding comprehending. Paper presented at the meetings of the Midwestern Psychological Association, Cincinnati, Ohio, April 30.

Gibson, E., A. Shurcliff, and A. Yonas, 1970. Utilization of spelling patterns by deaf and hearing subjects. In H. Levin and J. P. Williams (eds.), *Basic Studies on Reading.* New York: Basic Books, pp. 57–73.

Haber, R. N., 1970a. How we remember what we see. *Sci. Amer.* 222:5, 104–112.

———, 1970b. Note on how to choose a visual noise mask. *Psych. Bull.* 74:373–376.

Hochberg, J., 1970. Components of literacy: Speculations and exploratory research. In H. Levin and J. P. Williams (eds.), *Basic Studies on Reading,* New York: Basic Books, pp. 74–89.

Huey, E. B., 1908. *The Psychology and Pedagogy of Reading.* New York: Macmillan. Reprinted: Cambridge, Mass., M.I.T. Press, 1968.

Kahneman, D., 1968. Method, findings, and theory in studies of visual masking. *Psych. Bull.* 70:404–425.

Krueger, L. E., 1970a. Search time in a redundant visual display. *J. Exp. Psych.* 83:391–399.

————, 1970b. Visual comparison in a redundant display. *Cog. Psych.* 1:341–357.

Mehler, J., T. G. Bever, and P. Carey, 1967. What we look at when we read. *Perception and Psychophysics,* 2:213–218.

Neisser, U., 1967. *Cognitive Psychology.* New York: Appleton-Century-Crofts.

Pillsbury, W. B., 1897. A study in apperception. *Amer. J. Psych.* 8:315–393.

Reicher, G. M., 1969. Perceptual recognition as a function of meaningfulness of stimulus material. *J. Exp. Psych.* 81:275–280.

Scharf, B., H. S. Zamansky, and R. F. Brightbill, 1966. Word recognition with masking. *Perception and Psychophysics,* 1:110–112.

Smith, F., 1969. The use of featural dependencies across letters in the visual identification of words. *J. Verbal Learning and Verbal Behavior,* 8:215–218.

Sperling, G., 1963. A model for visual memory tasks. *Human Factors,* 5:19–31.

Sperling, G., 1967. Successive approximations to a model for short term memory. *Acta Psych.* 27:285–292.

Wheeler, D. D., 1970. Processes in word recognition. *Cog. Psych.* 1:59–85.

Woodworth, R. S., 1938. *Experimental Psychology.* New York: Holt.

General Discussion of Papers by Gough and Brewer

Gough made a number of points in response to Brewer's discussion. (1) He conceded that he had neglected to put in his model an arrangement for advance control of eye movement according to the difficulty of the material being read, but pointed out that his model does provide for regression after failure in grammatical processing. (2) By "icon" he did *not* mean "a little picture in the eye" but a little picture in the head, as yet unanalyzed. (3) As for Brewer's objection to left-to-right processing, he did not see that the reader's ability to deal with misspelled words, or words with missing letters, is a real difficulty for his model; such words merely mean that provision for "further inferential processing" is required. In support of the left-to-right model, he referred to one of his own studies, in which reaction time increased the further to the right in the test word a substitution of an asterisk for a letter was made. The special case where the word was intact had the shortest reaction time. Again, when the task was to find a target letter, reaction time increased as the target was shifted from left to right. (This finding contradicts the early studies referred to by Norman, in which no difference was noted between words or fragments of words.) (4) The replication of Sperling's [1960] experiment by Scharf, Zamansky et al. [1966], using Sperling's masks, revealed no difference between the processing of words and individual letters. (5) He did not see any conflict between his position and the conclusion of Eriksen and Spenser [1969] that it is longer before one can begin report of a short word than of a long word. (6) Cattell's [1886] finding that words take less time to process than single letters is not really relevant, but his other finding, that six-letter words take longer to recognize than four-letter words, *is* relevant. There is, in fact, an extensive literature on the processing of visual displays, summed up in White's [1969] review. (7) He conceded that the existence of homophones might require some change in his model. (8) The reading of deaf is not necessarily like the reading of normal persons, and his model does not pretend to explain it. (9) He considered irrelevant Norman's argument that one can go directly from objects to their own representation, and that therefore the same might be true for words. (10) As for the findings of Miller and Isard [1963], he acknowledged that grammatical constraints do operate during reading; the question was at what level. He did not think that they operate in reading very far "downstream." (11) Context does not appear to operate in advance of the linguistic processing of a sentence, as Foss and one of his (Gough's) students have shown. (12) Gough could not imagine a comprehension device without a buffer. (Miller suggested that the buffer be called "context").

Posner referred to an experiment by Eriksen, Pollack et al. [1970] using sequences of numerals as stimuli. Reaction time seemed to be related to the number of syllables in the names of the numerals. Gough said he had experimented with various syllable lengths, both separately and as part of another experiment, and had not discovered any such effects. He had also done experiments with digraphs representing single sounds, like *th*. Here, too, no evidence of effect on reaction time had been noted. Only the number of letters per word affected reaction time. Syllables and digraphs must apparently be dealt with further "upstream."

Lotz noted that competent readers paraphrase when they read aloud. He suggested that this could mean processing by the phonological component, the semantic component, and then the phonological component again. Gough said that the meaning of a sentence was recovered "upstream" from its actual utterance. Lotz also added that the process of writing was closely connected to linguistic processing. Experiments with the subvocal behavior of a subject who is writing would be of great interest.

In response to a question by LaBerge, Gough said that his displays always use lower-case letters. LaBerge pointed out that to use upper-case would force the subject to ignore what he knew about patterns of lower-case letters. Jenkins and Kolers referred to an experiment by Tinker [1963], later replicated by Kolers, in which no change was observed in the rate of reading aloud of texts in which the proportion of upper-case to lower-case letters varied from 0 to 100 percent. But this, Kolers said, does not mean that there was no change in the difficulty of the task, since the subjects may have done more internal processing if this were required to maintain their customary reading rate.

Liberman reminded the group of the linguistic distinction between the phonological level and the phonetic level. The phonetic level describes the behavior of the articulators, but it must also be represented in the central nervous system. Activity at the phonetic level does not necessarily result in any actual or implicit articulation. The fact that one takes pleasure in the phonetic patterns of verse, and that we notice phonetic features of the text, e.g., "the rain in Spain" sentence, suggests (as Mattingly pointed out in his paper) that the phonetic level, as just defined, is engaged during reading, and that Gough could incorporate this in his model without a major revision. Gough was not convinced, and Miller remarked that one does not read verse at 400 words per minute.

Conrad questioned Gough's suggestion that reading by the congenitally deaf may be a different process from ordinary reading. Gough said that his model is an attempt to describe the normal, 400-word-per-minute reader. Lloyd said that by this definition the reading of the deaf is slower and qualitatively poorer than that of normal readers. Liberman said that the difference is more than just a question of speed. The linguistic competence that deaf people acquire by reading is quite different from the linguistic competence of normal persons. Moreover, their writing is generally poor.

Kolers questioned the serial character of Gough's model. Different readers, reading the same text, have different and quite complex eye-movement patterns. There must be some way in which this incoherent input is sorted out. Gough stuck by his model and referred to evidence that readout of connected text under appropriate conditions—threshold with masking—is no better than readout of unrelated letters. There was no influence from the syntactic level.

Brewer said that Pillsbury's [1897] experiment, in which subjects saw words that were not there, was evidence of higher-level processing. Gough thought that Pillsbury's subjects were simply doing something different from ordinary reading. He did not deny that a speaker would reconstruct text if he had to.

Mattingly said that he found the developmental section of Gough's paper, which had not so far been discussed, extremely interesting, and that the notion of the beginning reader as a cryptanalyst is a useful insight in considering what the pupil can do and what the teacher can help him do. Jenkins agreed, remarking that one thing which helps the cryptanalyst is volume: "It may be it is necessary to get, in some sense, the cognitive load up high enough and the volume of input and possibly matches up high enough to give the kid a corpus that is big enough to work on and enough motivation to solve that problem."

Savin questioned the value of the block diagram models with buffers that investigators of information processing produce. What is really important to know is the *form* of the information in the buffer: was it circles and lines, or letters? Information processing experiments are not helpful here.

Jenkins suggested that a reaction time experiment using verbal suffixes of differing length, like *ed* and *ing*, would help to indicate the extent to which processing in reading is serial.

Posner questioned whether reaction time methods are the most appropriate for studying the internal stages of reading. It is not necessarily obvious, as the case of the Eriksen result suggests, what units are being processed. He mentioned the Reicher [1969] and Wheeler [1970] studies in which identification of letters was shown to be 10 percent more accurate in verbal context than in isolation as example of an alternative approach. This experiment, Gough admitted, would create great difficulties for his serial model, but it had not been replicated. But Gibson called attention to a similar experiment by Smith [1969].

Gough said that his model implied that the time for lexical lookup would be highly dependent on word length, but this did not seem to be the case. He referred to an experiment that he and Rohrman had done, which showed that the time required to decide whether two words were synonyms when presented simultaneously differed by 160 msec from the time required when one of the words was presented in advance. This means that the subject is "getting to meaning" as fast as possible, if it is assumed that the icon requires some time to set up and that readout is letter by letter.

Liberman said that he was puzzled by the question of whether syntactic and semantic constraints affect the reading process. They are certainly very important in speech perception. Once the reader has access to the phonology, what happens from then on is the same as what happens with a listener.

References

Cattell, J. McK., 1886. The time taken up by cerebral operations. III. The perception time. *Mind* 11:377–392.

Eriksen, C. W., M. Pollack, and W. Montague, 1970. Implicit speech: Mechanism in perceptual encoding? *J. Exp. psych.* 84:502–507.

Eriksen, C. W., and T. Spenser, 1969. Rate of information processing in visual perception: Some results and methodological considerations. *J. Exp. Psych. Monograph,* 79, No. 2, Part 2.

Miller, G., and S. Isard, 1963. Some perceptual consequences of linguistic rules. *J. Verbal Learning and Verbal Behavior* 2:217–228.

Pillsbury, W. B., 1897. A study in apperception. *Amer. J. Psych.* 8:315–393.

Reicher, G., 1969. Perceptual recognition as a function of meaningfulness of stimulus material. *J. Exp. Psych.* 81:276–280.

Rohrman, N. L., and P. B. Gough, 1967. Forewarning, meaning, and semantic decision latency. *Psychonomic Sci.,* 9:217–218.

Scharf, B., H. S. Zamansky, and R. F. Brightbill, 1966. Word recognition with masking. *Perception and Psychophysics,* 1:110–112.

Smith, I., 1969. The use of featural dependencies across letters in the visual identification of words. *J. Verbal Learning and Verbal Behavior*, 8:215–218.

Sperling, G., 1960. The information available in brief visual presentations. *Psych. Monog.*, 74, No. 11 (whole No. 498).

Tinker, M. A., 1963. *Legibility of Print*. Ames: Iowa State University Press.

Wheeler, D. D., 1970. Processes in word recognition. *Cog. Psych.* 1:59–85.

White, M. J., 1969. Laterality differences in perception: A review. *Psych. Bull.* 72:387–405.

GEORGE A. MILLER

Reflections on the Conference

Let me say immediately that I am not going to attempt to review or evaluate all that has been said here concerning the relations between speech and learning to read. I will select only a few of the ideas that were particularly interesting to me, and try to say why I found them so.

Before I do that, however, I want to take a few minutes of my time to stand back from our topic and to try to see it in perspective. We have, quite properly, been concerned primarily with the internal properties, structural and functional, of speaking and writing; but occasionally we have found it necessary to refer outward to the relation our topic has to broader concerns, and to the reasons, social and personal, why it is currently so important. I shall therefore take these occasional references as a precedent and an excuse for seeking some larger view—in short, a perspective.

The most obvious source of perspective, of course, is history. I find it interesting that writing did not originate as a means for encoding speech. Talking and writing seem to have evolved separately and grown together later. So far as we know, man has always had language, although the details of the evolution of this unique means of communication are lost in the vast distance of time. Writing, however, is a much more recent acquisition, perhaps 6,000 years old, and alphabetic writing— which really brought speech and writing together—is probably less than 3,000 years old. In terms of an evolutionary time scale, therefore, writing the spoken word was invented only a few moments ago.

It has frequently happened that the introduction of writing and the mastery of it by a substantial fraction of a society has immediately preceded profound social and political changes in that society. Indeed, the invention of writing was sufficiently important to justify, for many scholars, the claim that it signaled the birth of civilization. Goody and Watt [1963] have attempted to use ancient Greece as a case history in the study of the consequences of literacy; they make the point that the invention and relatively wide adoption of writing and reading had pervasive effects on Greek culture. Perhaps the most important in our modern view were (1) the rejection of myth and its replacement by history; and (2) the invention of logic as a formal representation of the thought involved in argumentation and rhetoric.

Behind the birth of logic and history there were, no doubt, profound changes of a social and psychological nature. The basic change was that their alphabetic writing objectified language, the product of thought, and gave it a permanence that the spoken word lacked. Writing also objectified and externalized personal memory, and the existence of written records from the past was obviously propaedeutic to historical studies. Thus, one consequence of writing was improved memory, made possible by the physical persistance of the written record.

I believe that the birth of logic, however, requires a more subjective explanation. The written proposition is a tangible representation of an act of thought. It is a physical thing, an object, and it can be reacted to as any other object can. Thus writing made it possible to react to one's own thoughts as if they were objects, so the act of thought became itself a subject for further thought. Thus extended abstraction became possible, and one of the brilliant abstractions recognized by the Greeks concerned the form of valid arguments. And so, out of writing, was logic born.

In my opinion, the more significant of these two intellectual activities was logic, which directly affected the way the mind worked. The development of history was merely a natural response to a larger and more trustworthy data base, made possible by the permanence of the written record. But something more than permanence—something related to the mind's awareness of its operations—was involved in logic.

Let me put it this way. Suppose that, by some anachronistic inversion of events, a phonographic recording device had been invented instead of writing. Suppose further that the Greeks had been clever enough to preserve the spoken word in a permanent and easily accessible form. In short, imagine the permanence had been achieved without the kind of linguistic analysis entailed by alphabetic writing.

Since no one knows what difference this would have made, everyone is free to speculate. My own speculation is that history would have developed in either case, but logic would have been much harder to achieve. Not impossible, I grant, but far more difficult. The analysis of words into sounds, and the analysis of syllogistic arguments into premises and conclusions, are, to my mind, closely akin. Writing makes language self-conscious in a way that recorded echoes probably could not.

In short, therefore, writing not only contributed permanence to the social record, but it also facilitated an awareness of one's own speech that would otherwise have been extremely unlikely. Since the question of linguistic awareness has been a central theme of this conference, I will leave the matter here: not only does writing build on those aspects of language that are accessible to our conscious attention, but writing itself makes accessible aspects of language that are probably beyond the grasp of the illiterate thinker. I shall return to this question of self-awareness later.

Next, however, I want to consider an alternative context for our topic. History gives us one perspective, but the social sciences give us another. Let me try, therefore, to put literacy in a social context. Morris Halle has eloquently reminded us of the social context of our topic, and I know of no way to improve on what he has already said and illustrated in terms of the Cherokee experience. But perhaps even that can be seen in a larger context.

It is a basic fact about the twentieth century that we are moving rapidly into an age when knowledge is becoming increasingly important and valuable. Sociologists and economists have many ways of referring to this transition, but whether one calls it the rise of postindustrial society, or the growth of the knowledge industries, or the birth of an information-based economy, or the latest stage in the Industrial Revolution, the facts are that our population is becoming increasingly urbanized, an increasing fraction of the GNP is devoted to the creation and dissemination of knowledge, and education generally is becoming an indispensible prerequisite to economic survival—education in general, and literacy in particular.

This is not the time and I am not the person to document these generalizations about the Knowledge Revolution, so I must rely on your sense of the century to supply the details. The fact is that our technological progress is creating a socioeconomic system in which the ignorant, illiterate individual is useless and barely tolerated at a level of existence we call "welfare." In order to escape this modern version of purgatory, a person must have enough education to contribute to our technological society. If you have been excluded from access to that education, or have valid reasons for resisting assimilation into the system, your outlook can only be described as bleak.

I will not pursue the reasons why poverty and illiteracy are so inextricably linked in our society. As a political liberal my impulse is to do everything possible—and much more is possible than has been done— to make literacy and assimilation available to everyone who desires them. Those who do not wish to be assimilated, and there are many, may still wish to be literate, and somehow we must learn to accommodate them. But the right to read is not an obligation to read, and those who refuse to read must still be allowed to eat.

My point is simply this. On the one hand, knowledge is becoming increasingly necessary for survival, and literacy is the key tool for the acquisition of that knowledge. On the other hand, the teaching of reading in our public schools—especially in the ghettoes, both urban and rural—is failing badly, and all subsequent education built on reading fails with it. That is the social context in which I must view our present topic, and the reason that our discussion merits all the energy and insight and commitment that the participants have devoted to it.

Professor Halle has said that our scientific analysis of the reading process can deal only with secondary issues, and that the real problem lies beyond our ability to remedy. Perhaps he is right, but I do not believe that that reduces our obligation to do all we can, within the limits of our technical competence, to understand what is going wrong and why. That, then, is the context of special urgency I bring with me. On the one hand, we know that literacy nurtures the growth of knowledge and analytical thinking; and on the other hand, we know that the failure of our efforts to teach reading skills universally is both a cause and a symptom of grave socioeconomic difficulties in our society.

From a distance, therefore, I can only express disappointment that our discussions have contributed so little to these larger questions. In my opinion, the most important issue we raised, chewed on, and returned to repeatedly was the issue Mattingly referred to as "linguistic awareness" and Klima called "accessibility." With respect to the social problems underlying reading difficulties, we had very little to say and even less to contribute. Although we may (or may not) believe that reading materials written in the Black dialect, and teachers willing to respect that dialect, would help to ease the difficulties of millions of children who are handicapped in learning to read a language they do not speak, none of the papers delivered here has attempted to consider the possible effect of dialectal variations on the relation between speaking and learning to read, or to assemble and evaluate the facts relevant to this aspect of the problem. All we have is Savin's observation that one critical source of difficulty is independent of dialect.

Instead, we tended to concentrate on an analysis of the information processing that must occur when a literate Reader casts his eyes over a printed text, and to a lesser extent on the development of those processing skills in a beginning reader who comes to the task with all the linguistic competence that spoken language can instill. Even that is too broad a characterization, for we have repeatedly focused on reading as a process leading to, and evaluated in terms of, comprehension and memory. In short, we have taken a much narrower view of the relation between speech and reading than a disinterested layman might have expected us to.

Lest I sound too censorious, however, let me quickly add that I believe other conferences have done even worse. In October 1968 the Division of Medical Sciences of the National Research Council held a conference whose proceedings have now been published by the National Academy of Sciences under the title *Early Experience and Visual Information Processing in Perceptual and Reading Disorders* [Young and Lindsley 1970]. A very distinguished group of scientists contributed, but the whole enterprise was, in my view, rendered worthless by virtue of a narrow presupposition that reading has something to do with vision, but nothing to do with language. Whatever else one may say about the present conference, at least we recognized that reading skills must derive ultimately from linguistic skills. That in itself represents a giant step forward.

Even so, however, I felt there was too quick a willingness to talk about *the* skill of reading, as if reading were some monolithic, well-defined process used only to suck up sentences, massage them appropriately for comprehension, and deposit the residuum in some capacious receptacle called "long-term memory"; and as if there were only one kind of problem—*the* problem—encountered in learning to read. The word "reading" is ordinarily used to refer to many different and only loosely related perceptual skills—we proofread one way, we memorize another way, and we comprehend still another way; then we go on to read for amusement, or translate from another language, or skim for an overview, or puzzle out a handwritten message, or search for a target, or read aloud to others, or lull ourselves to sleep, or read a label on a bottle in the medicine cabinet, or worship our gods, or sing our verses. Wittgenstein chose the concept of a game to illustrate the diversity of meanings a word can have, but he might have made the point equally well in terms of reading.

In her keynote address Gibson urged us to keep in mind that we read for a purpose, and there are almost as many different ways to read as there are purposes for reading. Moreover, different reading skills may be differently acquired, and may encounter many different forms of disability. By confining ourselves largely to the kind of reading we ourselves do most often and the kind of reading we demand most often of our students, we constantly flirted with the temptation to overgeneralize our results. The proper *caveats* were always issued, of course, but an unwary reader of these proceedings might easily conclude that we did not take them very seriously.

Since we tended to concentrate on that kind of reading, there was an important and recurring theme in the conference having to do with the apparent necessity of going through acoustic, articulatory, phonetic, phonological, or abstract phonological representations of the words one is reading. No doubt most people do go through some or all of these representations when they are reading aloud or reading to understand and remember, and it may be an essential process during the learning period, but Conrad presented clear evidence from his nonarticulatory deaf readers that such imagery is not indispensible. Perhaps a broader conception of what reading can be would have led to even more evidence that it is possible to disconnect the visual from the phonological system. In any event, the case for the *universal* necessity of internal speech representations during reading was not convincing, and we are left rather with the conclusion that such a route into the internal lexicon seems to be the most efficient one, but not the only conceivable one in every situation.

Many of these different forms of internal representation seemed to be intimately linked to a particular method of experimentation, and defined as much in terms of the experimental procedures used as in terms of the language user's normal preferences and aptitudes. Thus, although few of the methods used seemed to have been developed specifically to study the reading process, there was necessarily a considerable amount of discussion devoted to the differences among or convergences between different experimental methods. I am no slavish admirer of parsimony, but I must confess that when every method leads to the postulation of a new wing on the information-processing house, I begin to get a little suspicious.

Years ago the behaviorally inclined psychologists rejected introspection because every experimenter who used it seemed to find whatever process he was looking for. It would be cruelly ironic if our current methods of experimentation were to suffer a similar fate. Such rejections are only temporary, however, as the history of introspection demonstrates.

It was Mattingly, I think, who made the best case for introspection, although he did not call it that. It should be pointed out, I think, that what he called "awareness" and what Klima called "accessibility" are related but not identical concepts. That is to say, I can conceive of some level of linguistic processing being accessible, in the sense that special transformations, like spelling or versification, could take advantage of it, yet it might not be describable at the level of conscious awareness. I say I can conceive of such a situation logically, although I have difficulty in imagining any empirical facts that might settle the issue one way or the other.

If some level of representation more abstract than the final phonetic string is taken as the basis for an orthography, then learning to use the orthography might well make a person aware of that level even though he might not have been aware of it otherwise. Thus, what is accessible and what we can become aware of in using language are not immutable givens, fixed once and for all, but can change with maturation and experience. And I have no difficulty believing that an experienced linguist can be aware of processes that even a literate person does not notice and cannot control voluntarily.

In particular, Savin's fascinating observations seem to mean that a child may use phonemes quite acceptably without being aware of them or having access to them for the purpose of alphabetic writing. But with the proper experience he should be able to become aware of them by additional processing of the syllabic perceptual unit, and so use his new awareness as a basis for reading. The fact that we have no notion how to help the child achieve this level of awareness poses a challenging problem for research.

Most of the component processes that Posner, Conrad, Crowder, and Gough described, however, do not seem to be accessible to consciousness or to voluntary control. Inasmuch as these processes have been inferred from performance data and not from introspection, they represent particularly valuable additions to our knowledge of the system. But, on the other hand, inasmuch as they are not accessible to voluntary control, they cannot provide a basis for our voluntary choices of what to say and how to say it. Their functioning is only indirectly controllable by the language user, and their relevance for linguistic theory—which is, of course, based largely on one kind of introspective data—remains to be determined. This gap is sometimes discussed in terms of a difference between linguistic theories of competence and psychological models of performance, but I think it might better be considered as a gap between two different kinds of data derived from very different methods of observation.

It seems unlikely that a writing system can reflect directly the surface phonetics of speech, for this seems not to be accessible to the language user. Something more abstract is necessary, and Klima gave us several alternative levels of abstractness whose accessibility might be empirically tested. There are advantages in an abstract representation because it can accommodate itself to dialectal variations, it need not change as pronunciation evolves, and it may make the language user appreciate aspects of his language that he would otherwise overlook. But as Lotz pointed out, there are also disadvantages, since it takes longer to learn the more abstract systems, and they may be responsible for more failures to learn. This, too, is an empirical question worth investigating further.

I should confess that I found the detailed analyses and flowcharts that the psychologists used to organize the large and rapidly growing bodies of data about visual and auditory information processing to be impressive, but not wholly convincing. I suspect the data are beginning to overflow even the most elaborate models based on analogies with computers, just as they earlier spilled out of our stochastic processes. Unfortunately, I have no suggestions for a better prototype, so all I can do is express my opinion that we are rapidly approaching a crisis in theorizing which, if not overcome, can lead only to fragmentation and controversy. Our difficulties do not seem to be empirical in nature. Our central problem is that we do not know how to formulate a theory that will integrate the facts we already have. I believe something quite novel is needed, but I have no idea where to find it. However, this is a crisis for human experimental psychology generally, and not something peculiar to our efforts to understand speaking and reading, so I will not pursue it here.

As I listened to all these admirable attempts to organize the experimental data in terms of an information-processing system for spoken and written language, I waited with much interest for the discussion of long-term memory, for that is surely where most of the skills and knowledge that are involved in speaking and learning to read must be lodged. I did not hear much about it, however, perhaps because it was assumed to be well understood, or perhaps because it was thought to play a relatively passive role in processing the linguistic input. Neither reason would be justifiable, of course, so I must be wrong. In any case, I must note that this obviously important psychological component of the system received little attention in our discussions. We left it with a general agreement that long-term memory must be shared by both the speaking and reading systems, and a general agreement that its organization must be inscrutably complicated—neither being a conclusion likely to surprise anybody. Long-term memory thus remains a problem for the long-term future.

In conclusion, and in spite of these largely critical reflections on what has transpired here, I intend to report to my colleagues that this was a successful conference. I consider that judgment to be less a description, however, than a prediction. The obvious interest in reading that has been expressed here by so many distinguished linguists and psychologists, plus the stimulation provided by these three days of intense interaction, seem to me very hopeful signs for the future. My critical reflections are merely intended to spur you on, and to avoid fostering any complacency as to the disparity between what has been accomplished and what remains to be done. I judge the conference to have been successful because I am now far more confident that what needs doing can be done and will be done.

And so I will close by expressing my appreciation to everyone who had a hand in making it possible for us to have this stimulating and, I predict, successful conference.

References

Goody, J., and I. Watt, 1963. The consequences of literacy. *Comp. Stud. in Soc. and Hist.* 5:304–345.

Young, F. A., and D. B. Lindsley, 1970. *Early Experience and Visual Information Processing in Perceptual and Reading Disorders.* Washington, D.C.: National Academy of Sciences.

SUBJECT INDEX

Abbreviations, 117

Abstractions, 4, 6–8, 10

ABX method, 172, 268

Accessibility, linguistic structure, 59–67, 374–379. *See also* Awareness, linguistic

Acoustic cues, 36–43, 50, 135, 137–138; *see also* Cues
and coding of phoentic segments, 47–48
demodulation of, 136
and linguistic awareness, 139
and vowels, 310, 314

Acquisition, reading, 2, 3, 126, 135, 293–294, 331, 346–354; *see also* Reading
and character recognition, 346
and functional asymmetries of brain, 304
and mapping of systematic phonemes, 337

Acuity, auditory, 7, 134
confusability, 178

Adults, 204, 205
and awareness of phonemic segmentation, 328
speech and reading in, 206–217

Alliteration, 323, 324

Allomorphs, 100

Allophones, 313

Alphabets, 57–59, 103–106, 117–118, 120, 122, 217
acoustic, 136
historical evolution of, 373–374
and reading success, 144, 347–348

Altaic peoples, 118

Ambiguity, sentence, 61, 186, 363; *see also* Disambiguation

Ampersand, 87, 118

Amplitude, sound, 49

Analysis-by-synthesis system (ABS), 38–41, 134–139, 143, 155, 284–286
as active model, 203–204
and internal memory system, 166

Aphasia, 169, 224

Appalachia, 153

Arabic, 20

Articulation, 33–35, 40–43, 47, 177, 215, 328; see also Vocalization
and comprehension, 210
cues, 37
and the deaf, 230–231, 233, 242, 249
and difficulty of material, 245
and eye fixations, 210

and phonetic level, 368

and silent reading, 206–209, 216

and STM, 210, 215

suppression of, 211–214

Asahi-Shimbun, Japanese newspaper, 92

Aspiration, 20

Association, word, 6, 179–180

Atlas, 98

Attention, 280
selective, 286
span, 245–247

Awareness, linguistic, 138–141, 157, 321, 376, 378–379
control of, 140–141
and historical evolution of writing, 374–375
individual variation in, 140, 144
and inner speech, 144
and language-based skills, 141–145
and phonemic segments, 309–310, 323, 328, 363

Babbling, 10, 12, 20, 201–202

Bina-View display, 212–213

Blending, 324, 328, 351–352
and maturation, 328

Blindness, 26

Book of Common Prayer, 3

Brain
damage, 169, 204
and hemispheric transfer of information, 173–174, 201–202

Byelorussian, 128

Calligraphy, 85–90

Cantonese, 87

Capitals, 5, 117

Central Asia, 86

Character recognition, 346–348

Cherokee, 152–153, 156, 375

Children, 205
causes of misreading in, 293–314 *passim*
and components of reading, 346
comprehension, 346, 353–354
decoding, 348–353
genesis of speech code, 217–218
and iconic imagery, 346, 347
letter recognition, 346–348
and phonemes, 111–115, 348
primary memory in, 353, 354

Chimpanzees, 4